T0330135

Uncertainty, Expectations, and Financial Instability

Uncertainty, Expectations, and Financial Instability

REVIVING ALLAIS'S LOST THEORY
OF PSYCHOLOGICAL TIME

Eric Barthalon

Columbia University Press   *New York*

Columbia University Press
Publishers Since 1893
New York   Chichester, West Sussex
Copyright © 2014 Columbia University Press
All rights reserved

Library of Congress Cataloging-in-Publication Data
ISBN: 978-0-231-16628-7 (cloth)
ISBN: 978-0-231-53830-5 (ebook)

Library of Congress Control Number: 2014936226

Columbia University Press books are printed on permanent
and durable acid-free paper.
This book is printed on paper with recycled content.

Printed in the United States of America

c 10 9 8 7 6 5 4 3 2 1

COVER DESIGN:
Noah Arlow

References to Internet Web sites (URLs) were accurate at the time of writing.
Neither the author nor Columbia University Press is responsible for URLs that
may have expired or changed since the manuscript was prepared.

To Rozenn

Contents

PART ONE

The Progressive Emergence of Expectations in Economic Theory

CHAPTER ONE
Expectations Before the Rational Expectations Revolution

PART FOUR
The HRL Formulation and Financial Instability

List of Tables

List of Figures

Preface

WHENEVER I read a book or a passage that particularly pleased me, in which a thing was said or an effect rendered with propriety, in which there was either some conspicuous force or some happy distinction in the style, I must sit down at once and set myself to ape that quality. I was unsuccessful, and I knew it; and tried again, and was again unsuccessful and always unsuccessful; but at least in these vain bouts, I got some practice in rhythm, in harmony, in construction and the co-ordination of parts. I have thus played the sedulous ape to Hazlitt, to Lamb, to Wordsworth, to Sir Thomas Browne, to Defoe, to Hawthorne, to Montaigne, to Baudelaire and to Obermann.

. . . That, like it or not, is the way to learn to write; whether I have profited or not, that is the way. It was so Keats learned, and there was never a finer temperament for literature than Keats's; it was so, if we could trace it out, that all men have learned; and that is why a revival of letters is always accompanied or heralded by a cast back to earlier and fresher models. Perhaps I hear some one cry out: But this is not the way to be original! It is not; nor is there any way but to be born so. Nor yet, if you are born original, is there anything in this training that shall clip the wings of your originality.

Robert Louis Stevenson

Never trust the artist. Trust the tale. The proper function of a critic
is to save the tale from the artist who created it.

D. H. Lawrence

That a book having the ambition to build bridges between Allais's
theory of psychological time and behavioral finance—a book furthermore containing many mathematical developments, numbers, and
figures–could start with words borrowed from R. L. Stevenson and
D. H. Lawrence, should surprise more than a few readers. Yet, the
reason for this choice is very simple: these two authors brilliantly express
the motivations that, besides the wish to explain Allais to myself, have
led me to write this book.

Stevenson, first. By tracing any revival of letters back to the discovery
or rediscovery of earlier and fresher models, Stevenson shows a path toward progress that is valid for any intellectual discipline, economics included. The conviction I neither would nor could conceal is that Allais
is a gigantic economist, a true genius, a genuine artist, from whom we
still have a lot to learn. This is true now more than ever, since main-
stream economic theory seems at a loss to explain the economic and
financial crisis that seemingly "started" in 2007, but which had been
in the making for many years.

Then, Lawrence. It is an understatement to say that Allais paid lip
service to the "marketing" of his works: his passion for research has
overwhelmed him time and again. People who knew him well politely
describe him as "not easy to work with." Were the Nobel Foundation
to award a prize for self-promotion, Allais would never make it to the
short list of potential laureates. May this book prompt researchers to
overcome the hurdles, some of them inadvertently erected by Allais
himself, behind which lie, still to be recognized and appreciated, many
theoretical jewels!

Last but not the least, there is no reason to pit mathematics against
letters. Mathematics is nothing but a language that aims at combining conciseness with the utmost lack of ambiguity, two seemingly con-
tradictory requirements. Literature is replete with references, most of
the time implicit, to psychological time, the cornerstone of Allais's
theory of "expectations" under uncertainty. Economics does need
philosophers, novelists, and poets to reveal essential aspects of human

psychology. Guided by their intuition and experience, poets, novelists, and philosophers tend at least to hint at many of the most essential characteristics of human nature and psychology. But economics also needs mathematicians and physicists to rigorously answer the questions raised by people of letters. This is, I believe, what Allais has achieved with his theory of psychological time and memory decay.

Acknowledgments

SOME THIRTY years ago, someone inadvertently triggered the chain of events that has led to this book. Robert Carvallo was his name. Inclined to tolerate trials and errors with benevolence, he has been much more than my first boss. He has been a patient teacher. He had seen me struggling with one of the first HP 12C circulating in Paris as I was trying to calculate the present value of the cash flows expected from an office building that Paribas had bought in downtown Manhattan. This made me apt, according to him, to manage bond portfolios. Without this fresh assignment, I would not have been confronted, early in my professional life, with the issue of expectations formation. I vividly remember how I was wondering in 1983, child of the inflation age that I was, whether it was a good idea to lend money to the French Republic for 7 years at 13.70 percent. Had someone told me then that 22 years later, France would issue a 50-year bond bearing a 4 percent coupon, or that 30 years later we would see negative nominal interest rates on short-dated government bonds, I would have questioned his or her sanity. No wonder that Robert Carvallo used to tell me that nothing is more important in economics and finance than seeking to understand how expectations are formed! To Robert Carvallo's name, I want to associate those of Jean-Paul Villain, who opened Paribas's doors a second time for me in 1992, and of André Lévy-Lang, Dominique Hoenn, and Philippe Dulac. Their decision to appoint me Chief Economist of the Paribas Group in 1996 was bold indeed, since I did not possess any of the usual academic passports one would expect the chief economist of an international banking group to hold. Despite my interest in expectations, I certainly did not expect them to entrust me with such a responsibility. To honor their trust as well as that of the Paribas staff became a duty, which pushed me to broaden and deepen my autodidact's education.

Other persons, many other persons, have helped me, sometimes inadvertently, sometimes not, along this journey. From my days at Paribas, I also remember with some nostalgia my discussions with Olivier de Boysson, Pascal Blanqué, Gavin Francis, Paul Mortimer-Lee, Jean-Luc Proutat, and Philippe Richer. Our freewheeling discussions on many issues, starting with the valuation of long-term bonds, further seeded this book. We had empirically (re)discovered that bond investors in low and stable inflation countries seem to have a longer inflation memory than investors in high and volatile inflation countries. But we lacked the tools and the knowledge to transform this observation into an operational theory. For my days at Allianz, I want to thank wholeheartedly Paul Achleitner, Fethija Alp, Elizabeth Corley, Joachim Faber, Udo Frank, Wolfram Gerdes, Andreas Gruber, Bernd Gutting, Marianne Heidt, Alexander Hirt, Stefan Hofrichter, Alex Langnau, Peter Lockyer, Jacco Maters, Xiaofeng Qi, Markus Riess, Stéphane Szczyglak, Jason Szielinski, Günther Thallinger, Andreas Uterman, and Maximilian Zimmerer. They have often tolerated an employee, a colleague, or a boss, sometimes a friend, who was physically present at his desk, but whose mind was somewhat absent, at least from time to time. It is indeed somewhat difficult to write a book with some academic ambitions when one is immersed in a nonacademic professional life. In the Allianz galaxy, my maverick friend Frank Veneroso deserves a special tribute. Our first conversation, back in 2001, quickly evolved around financial instability, expectations formation, and positive feedback loops. Although my understanding of Allais's theory of psychological time was then still very rudimentary, he immediately grasped its philosophy. His constant questioning has helped me to identify what I did not understand, and sometimes to find answers.

No one can, more than my elder son Pierre, claim credit for this book. Although he was educated as a mining engineer, his interest in finance and economics led him to follow the solo, high-sea navigation on which his father had embarked. Not only did he, like a few other precious friends, urge me to finish this book, but also he offered to convert my Word manuscript into LaTex. Without his work, which went well beyond that of a zealous assistant, and even with Frédéric Samama's valuable introduction, I would never have dared to submit my work to Myles Thompson at Columbia University Press. He and his associate, Bridget Flannery-McCoy, have been instrumental in helping this book to mature. An easy task it was not, to say the least, to find academics willing to spend some of their precious time to review the work of an unknown French practitioner purporting to challenge the rational expectations hypothesis by unearthing a 50-year-old theory conceived by another Frenchman, albeit a more famous one. Bridget did it. I am grateful to my anonymous reviewers for their advice, especially those directing me to a more elaborate discussion of rational learning, prospect theory, and intertemporal choice. Tribute is also due to Ron Harris and Lisa Hamm, respectively project editor and senior designer at Columbia University Press, for being the rigorous and creative architects of the steps that have followed and completed Bridget's work. And, Noah Arlow deserves a very special praise for fathering what is undoubtedly a very brilliant cover: original, suggestive and right to the point. To the team led by Ben Kolstad, the editorial services manager at Cenveo Publisher Services, I want to express not only my gratitude, but also my admiration for the highly professional work they have done to usher this book through the production process: it has been a demanding pleasure to work with them. To Patti Scott, who has meticulously copyedited the manuscript and my occasionally "clunky" English; to Robert Swanson, whose index is a valuable and integral part of this book; to Shashi Kumar and his composition team, who have rigorously gathered together and put in good order the many components of this book; to Pam Andrada, who has read through the page proofs: I wholeheartedly say "well done"! To the members of the Editorial Board of Columbia University Press, I would like to say that I appreciate, beyond what they can imagine, their open-mindedness, their ability to take risks, and their willingness to jump into the unknown. Ironically and at first glance at least, their decision to support my work seems to belie the "expectations" model presented in this book, a model in which the "track record" plays a critical role. With people like them, it is possible to have a dream and to see it come true. And what would life be without dreams?

Jokes about "that book that Daddy will never finish writing" have been the hallmark of many family conversations for more than a decade. Alice and Nicolas, Pierre's sister and brother, and Véronique, their mother, have been very kind and loving to keep on teasing me during all this time. For a father or a husband writing a book is not a very present one, and the time not given when it is due is lost forever. Morgane, Pierre's wife, would probably not disagree with this last statement. I plead guilty. For my defense, I will only say that the world is governed neither by men nor by women, but by ideas. Sometimes, the ideas that rule the world need to be challenged, for they make it not as good as it could be. I have conceived challenging the rational expectations hypothesis as a contribution, intangible as it may seem, to the well-being of my children and the generations that will follow them. Within the narrow circle of close relatives, my mother deserves a special tribute. Thanks to her presence and her example when I was a child or a teenager, she—more than anyone else—taught me to value and to respect effort, work, and rigor. Her scientific education and inclination often led her to wish I had been less attracted by literary disciplines and more by scientific ones. Hopefully, this book contains enough applied mathematics to oblige her, be it belatedly.

As Robert Carvallo and, despite his exceptional longevity, Maurice Allais passed away too early to have a chance to assess my work and to appreciate his influence: I will always miss their assessments. I have not been one of Allais's students. Had he not been awarded the Nobel Prize, I might indeed never have discovered his works. Quite soon after 1988, I gathered that Allais proposed alternative and original solutions to questions I was encountering in my professional life, provided I could rise to the daunting challenge of enhancing my mathematical skills. About 10 years later, when I was editor-in-chief of *Conjoncture*, Paribas' monthly economic bulletin, it happened that I quoted Allais in one of my articles. Somehow, this article landed on his desk. I was more than impressed when my assistant, Patricia Chanoinat, told me on the phone that Professor Allais wanted to talk to me. In the following years, we had a few phone conversations. I met him and his wife Jacqueline only once on April 26, 2002, when they invited me for a lunch at the Racing Club de France. On this occasion, he gave me a set of research materials that have accompanied me ever since, and I informed him about my project to write this book. He encouraged me to do so, curious as he was to see whether his "expectations" theory could be extended to a new field. For many years, I have rightly feared that I would not complete my work soon enough to present it to him. I wish I could have triggered brilliant conversations between Robert Carvallo and Maurice Allais on the themes contained in this book. But my intellectual journey started too late and proceeded too slowly to make it happen. Robert Carvallo had the intuition of hysteresis effects, of the elasticity of time, and of nonlinearities, the three pillars of Allais's HRL formulation. He would have been thrilled to discover a theory that gives a concrete and operational content to such intuitions. And, once convinced of Allais's penetrating originality in this field, he would have embarked on exploring other aspects of Allais's works: his theory of risky choices, his theory of probabilities. Had these conversations been able to take place, this book would be much more advanced than it is. The responsibility for this is mine and mine alone.

Paris–Munich–Kerners, 1998–2014

For the element of time, which is the centre of the chief difficulty of almost every economic problem, is itself absolutely continuous: Nature knows no absolute partition of time into long periods and short; but the two shade into one another by imperceptible gradations, and what is a short period for one problem, is a long period for another.

Alfred Marshall

The subjective cause [of crises] is probably linked to this capacity that men have to forget received impressions. Little by little, new generations, who have not directly suffered the ills produced by the last crisis, come to the management of affairs. A deposit of excitable material re-forms in society.

Vilfredo Pareto

A prominent shortcoming of our structural models is that, for ease in parameter estimation, not only are economic responses presumed fixed through time, but they are generally assumed to be linear.

Alan Greenspan

Unless we know why people expect what they expect, any argument is completely valueless which appeals to [expectations] as *causae efficientes*.

Joseph Schumpeter

The proposition that expectations are volatile and incapable of being rationally calculated is no theory of expectations ... The development of alternative market-specific schemes of expectations formation is, surely, the next logical step in macroeconomic theorising.

Mark Blaug

Introduction

MORE THAN any of the previous crises, through its sheer size, intensity, and costs, the global financial crisis that seemingly started in 2007 has challenged economists and their analytical tools. In a way, it is fair to say that this crisis has been and still is, first and foremost, a crisis in economic theory. Some accepted theories or paradigms, such as rational expectations and efficient markets, seem to have been radically wrong-footed by unnerving facts and pervasive uncertainty.[1]

This is somewhat of a paradox that we should be disappointed by the rational expectations hypothesis (REH), limited as its ambition ever was. Lucas himself, one of its most prominent proponents, wrote that "this REH will not be applicable in situations . . . which Knight called uncertainty . . . in cases of uncertainty, economic reasoning will be of no value."[2]

But, for seeming lack of credible alternatives in a context of uncertainty (see table 1, p. xl), the economic profession as a whole seems reluctant to declare this paradigm obsolete. So strong is the hegemony of rational expectations that there are not many prominent economists who dare to declare the REH a dead end and who call loudly for an alternative theory of expectations formation. Phelps and Frydman are two of them. This is all the more notable that, through his contribution to the debate on the inflation-unemployment trade-off (the so-called Philips curve) in the 1960s, Phelps has been instrumental in pushing expectations to the core of macroeconomic analysis, while Frydman has been an early critic of rational expectations on both epistemological and empirical grounds.

In the introduction to a book, which they have recently co-edited, Phelps and Frydman have defined a research program for an alternative theory of expectations, a theory that would portray expectations as inputs of macroeconomic models instead of being an output of such models, as is the case under the rational expectations hypothesis.[3]

According to Phelps and Frydman, such a theory should acknowledge that

- Neither economists nor market participants have a complete understanding of how the economy works, because the world in which we live is one of uncertainty ("nonroutine change" in Phelps and Frydman's vocabulary).
- Market participants are aware that the decisions made by others do have an impact on aggregate outcomes (interdependence).
- Economic and financial variables tend to switch back and forth between different regimes of low or high volatility (nonstationarity of data and heteroskedasticity[4]).

This alternative theory of expectations should do the following:

- Rest upon clearly specified microeconomic foundations.
- Not allow for systematic forecasting errors (for these would necessarily be arbitraged away).
- Derive expectations from a mathematical formalization.
- Not be mechanical (contrary to the standard adaptive expectations model).
- Be open to and able to deal with "nonroutine change," but its time-varying structure should not be of a Markov-switching type; it should depend on context-dependent regularities.
- Reflect the empirical observation that market participants tend to revise their forecasts in "guardedly moderate ways" (bounded elasticity of expectations).
- Be able to deal with market participants' heterogeneity.
- Be empirically testable.
- Describe the market participants' response to their expectations.
- Offer insights on financial markets and financial instability.

Odd as it may seem, the main claim made in this book is that, already a long time ago, since it was in 1965, Allais has gone a very long way in constructing a theory—his theory of psychological time and of time-varying rate of memory decay—that meets all the requirements of Phelps and Frydman's research program. It goes even beyond, since it very much relies on nonlinear relationships, a requirement enunciated in another book, co-edited this time by Guesnerie.[5]

Economists who are inclined to distance themselves from the REH have always found reasons to do so in financial markets. By their very function, which is to trade claims on future income flows, financial markets are indeed a chosen country for controversies about the nature of expectations. Guesnerie, for example, states that "it is not obvious, to say the least, to explain actual stock markets' fluctuations using dynamic models that adopt some (not too loose) version of the REH." As for Phelps and Frydman, they assert in a much less understated tone that "nowhere have REH's epistemological flaws and empirical disappointments been more apparent than in efforts to model financial market outcomes." In his famous *Manias, Panics and Crashes*, Kindelberger flatly rejects the idea that financial markets are rational and emphasizes the role of mimicking behavior among market participants.

The Kindleberger model of manias, panics, and crashes starts with a positive displacement: something happens—a technological innovation, a change in regulation—that legitimately and rightfully raises profit expectations.[6] As profit expectations rise, so does the demand for credit, which is being accommodated by banks, nonbanks, or both. The early successes draw new participants into the game. As a result, financing structures become increasingly unstable, moving from hedge to Ponzi finance, to borrow Minsky's taxonomy of financing structures.[7] It is hard to conceive such a cumulative process without adaptive expectations playing a significant role, a bigger one at least than rational expectations. Then something else happens, not very well specified to say the least, that causes the tide to reverse and pushes the late entrants into insolvency.

Yet, it is difficult to explain some recent episodes of financial history with the Kindleberger model. There are just too many instances where it is difficult to identify a positive displacement prior to the start of the rise in prices. Similarly, there is no obvious source of credit to explain the continuation of the initial upward move. An interesting counterexample is the US equity market between 1995 and 2000.

With the benefit of hindsight, the rise in real US equity prices from 1982 to the end of 1994 appears to have been a reversion to the secular upward trend. On the basis of cyclically adjusted PEs, this 12-year rally brought valuations back to the record levels of the mid-1960s. Up to that point, it seems inappropriate to speak of a US equity bubble. But from early 1995 onward, things changed dramatically. The upward movement of prices kept on accelerating until April 1999 for the S&P 500 and March 2000 for the NASDAQ. This is when cyclically adjusted valuations entered unchartered territory. If there was a US equity bubble, it was between early 1995 and early 2000. Interestingly, neither the US nor the global money supply heralded the acceleration of the rise in equity prices. At best, it has been coincident. From the end of 1989 to the end of 1994, the annual rate of growth in US M2 and M3 slowed down from 5 percent to virtually zero. As for global money, its growth slowed down from 12 percent to 6.6 percent.[8] Contrary to the US money supply, global money growth did not accelerate between 1994 and 1999. Finally, there was no noticeable change in the growth of nonbank credit in the United States prior to 1994. From all this, it seems difficult to conclude that credit and money started the equity bubble. As for positive displacement, it is only three to four years later that the Internet became an investment theme.

The Japanese equity market provides another interesting counterexample. The switch to bubble mode happened in late 1982 and early 1983, at a time when M2 annual growth was stabilizing between 7 percent and 8 percent, but definitely not accelerating. It is only four to five years later that money growth accelerated and that an alleged Japanese technological leadership became an investment theme.

The laboratory experiments conducted by Vernon L. Smith et al. confirm the shortcomings of the Minsky-Kindleberger model.[9] In these experiments, a group of subjects is invited to trade an asset; contrary to markets for consumer goods, the prospect of resale does exist. An entire experiment consists of a sequence of 15 trading periods lasting altogether approximately 2 hours. In accordance with the REH, each subject is given complete information on the fundamental value of the asset, that is, on the statistical distribution of potential dividends. Furthermore, each subject is regularly reminded of this fundamental value, which converges toward zero as time goes by. Yet, time and again, for different groups of more or less sophisticated traders, bubbles occur in these laboratory markets: one can observe large price deviations from the fundamental value, until the market crashes during the last trading periods. The availability of credit does magnify these bubbles.

In a REH environment, such bubbles and crashes should never oc-cur. Smith explains this paradox by the presence of momentum traders alongside rational value-driven investors. While the latter buy (or sell) when prices fall (or rise) below (or above) fundamental value, momen-tum traders get "into the market when prices are rising because [they] believe that [they'll] be able to sell later at a higher price." A seemingly more accurate definition would be that a momentum trader is someone who gets into the market when prices *have been* rising enough to con-vince him that he'll be able to sell later at a higher price. Clearly keen not to utter the words "adaptive expectations," Smith nevertheless uses this very concept pervasively. Later in this book, it will be shown that, notations aside, Smith's mathematical formulation of the sentiment of momentum traders ("the price trend") is identical to Cagan's formu-lation of adaptive inflation expectations in 1954. Content with this ex-planation of bubble dynamics, Smith nevertheless concedes that "the sparks that ignite [bubbles], and the myopic, self-reinforcing behavioral mechanisms that sustain them, remain unpredictable [or mysteries]."

Time and again, too, Smith's laboratory experiments reveal that "once a group of subjects experiences a bubble and crash over two experiments, and then return for a third experiment, trading departs little from fundamental value." Defeated as it may be in the short run, rationality still seems to prevail in the long term. Or so Smith argues. Let us breathe a sigh of relief! Without strong conviction, Smith alludes to Renshaw's hypothesis that "the severity of price bubbles and crashes in the economy is related to inexperience."[10] As time passes, new in-vestors enter the market, old investors exit, and the proportion of in-vestors remembering the last stock market decline changes. In 1896, Pareto had already formulated the same hypothesis.

Tempting as it is to reject or at least to amend the rational expecta-tions hypothesis, the fact is that both the Minsky-Kindleberger model and Smith's model have some shortcomings, too. Among other things, this book purports to show that the perceived risk of loss, defined as the present value of past drawdowns, may be the "spark" that ignites bubbles when it is low, as well as the safeguard against repeated bubbles when it is high. As a matter of fact, Smith's experiments inadvertently initialize the perceived risk of loss at zero at the beginning of the first sequence of trading sessions.

The first objective of this book is to show that Allais's[11] little-known theory of monetary dynamics contains assumptions and analytical tools that are—*mutatis mutandis*—liable to be easily transposed to financial markets and may contribute to modeling financial behavior. The most seminal of these tools is the hereditary, relativist, and logistic (HRL) formulation of the demand for money. The HRL formulation is indeed a model purporting to describe both how economic agents learn from their experience under the assumption of uncertainty and how they behave on the basis of this knowledge. This formulation contains a theory of psychological time and of time-varying rate of memory decay. Allais firmly believed "expectations" to be rooted in memory. Therefore, he was keen not to use the word "expectations" in his work on monetary dynamics. Yet, there is little doubt that Allais's HRL formulation deals with what Fisher, Wicksell, Knight, Hayek, Keynes, and Hicks progressively identified as the issue of expectations. Milton Friedman made this point rather emphatically:[12]

"This work [the HRL formulation][13] introduces a very basic and important distinction between psychological time and chronological time. It is one of the most important and original paper that has been written for a long time ... for its consideration of the problem of the formation of expectations."

Allais's HRL formulation can be interpreted as a general theory of expectations under uncertainty. It puts numbers on a range of concepts, which play a central role, albeit a purely literary one, in the discussion of endogenous financial instability, along the directions outlined by Irving Fisher, Hyman P. Minsky, and Charles P. Kindleberger.[14]

At the risk of a blatant anachronism, it would unexpectedly highlight the HRL formulation's modernity to introduce it with the terminology that is dear to rational expectations theorists:[15] one can indeed say that the HRL algorithm applies Bayesian inference through a nonlinear filter, the gain of which is time-varying since it is a nonlinear function of the latest estimate of the hidden state variable.[16]

In Cagan's well-known adaptive expectations model, the elasticity of inflation expectations with respect to actual inflation is constant, and so is the elasticity of real money balances with respect to expected inflation.[17] In Allais's HRL formulation, the elasticity of expectations varies dynamically between almost 0, in a deflationary environment, and 1 during hyperinflations. As for the demand for money, it is a monotonic, decreasing, bounded nonlinear function, the elasticity of which with respect to "expected" inflation varies between almost 0, in deflationary conditions, and -1, when hyperinflation is rife.

Another of Allais's seminal contributions is his fundamental equation of monetary dynamics (FEMD). This equation describes how the gap between outstanding and desired money balances influences relative changes in the transactions velocity of money and hence in aggregate nominal spending. The embedding of the HRL formulation into the fundamental equation of monetary dynamics generates different types of equilibrium (stable or unstable) as well as various types of convergence paths toward equilibrium (pseudo-periodic or aperiodic), depending on the values taken by certain parameters. Within this framework, even when the supply of money is constant or hardly grows, it is possible, at least temporarily, to generate convex paths of accelerating growth rates. According to Cagan, while theoretically conceivable, such an outcome has never been observed in the real world. Vernon Smith has observed it in laboratory experiments of asset markets. Furthermore, when the supply of money grows, the HRL model of monetary dynamics can generate paths that mimic Vernon Smith's "echo bubbles."

The second objective of this book is to show that Allais's well-known paradox can be unified with his theory of psychological time and time-varying rate of memory decay into the concept of perceived risk of loss, that is, the present value of the sequence of drawdowns experienced in a given market.[18] In an uncertain world à la Knight, Keynes, and Minsky, the perceived risk of loss is an alternative not only to both rational and standard adaptive expectations models, but also to the variance of returns as a measure of risk.

The third objective of this book is to show that the perceived risk of loss sheds some light on investors' behavior and on the dynamics of financial instability. It suggests in particular that a significant and protracted fall in the perceived risk of loss is a prerequisite for the inflation of major financial bubbles. Kindleberger claimed that some "good" news is the catalyst of a mania. The perceived risk of loss suggests an alternative explanation, namely, the persistent absence of "bad" news in the form of price drawdowns. To that extent, the perceived risk of loss is a concept to consider when discussing moral hazard.

Structure of This Book and Readers' Guidance

This book is divided in four parts. Part I (chapter 1, Expectations Before the Rational Expectations Revolution, and chapter 2, Rational

Expectations) presents what belongs to common knowledge about expectations in economics. Its purpose is to facilitate an assessment of Allais's contribution in this field. Readers who are novice at expectations theory but keenly aware that knowing the history of any discipline is key to understanding its current state of development will find this part more useful than experts in rational expectations.

Part II (chapters 3 to 6) introduces Allais's theory of "expectations" under uncertainty in its original context, namely, macroeconomics and monetary dynamics. If there is one part in this book that even a hurried reader cannot afford to not read, it is this one. This is particularly true of chapter 4 (on the HRL formulation of the demand for money), which is really the heart of this book, since it expounds the theory of psychological time and of the time-varying rate of memory decay. Without knowledge of this chapter, it is not possible to benefit from reading any of the following ones. Readers interested in macroeconomics will find chapters 3 (Macrofoundations of Monetary Dynamics), 5 (The Fundamental Equation of Monetary Dynamics), and 6 (Joint Testing of the HRL Formulation of the Demand for Money and of the Fundamental Equation of Monetary Dynamics) more useful than those exclusively focused on behavioral economics and finance.

Part III (chapters 7 and 8) is essentially an invitation to extend the field of application of the theory of psychological time and memory decay beyond monetary dynamics. Any scholar or practitioner willing to test the HRL formulation in his or her own field of activity must read chapter 7, which illustrates the dynamic properties of the HRL formulation by means of a detailed numerical example based on a recent case of hyperinflation (Zimbabwe between 2000 and 2008). The reader making this effort will spare herself the misunderstandings or misinterpretations that have prevented some in the academic world, even from Chicago, from grasping the HRL formulation, when it was put forward by Allais.

In chapter 8, following Allais, we will extend the field of application of the theory of psychological time and memory decay to nominal interest rates. We will do so by looking at their correlation with the perceived rate of nominal growth in 18 countries, which have experienced over long periods very contrasted economic conditions ranging from deflation to hyperinflation. We will show that the theory of memory decay is also a theory of impatience, albeit not in the way Allais imagined.

This chapter may be of particular interest to readers concerned with intertemporal choice.

Part IV (chapters 9, 10, and 11) applies the HRL formulation to the analysis of financial instability thanks to the perceived returns and risks, which it derives from times series of returns on financial assets.

Chapter 9 presents a few simple models that explain financial behavior by the perceived returns on financial assets and thereby provide evidence of positive feedback from past returns to the demand for risky assets, a frequent conjecture that usually remains formulated in literary terms only. These models bring to light nonlinear relationships between perceived returns and observed investors' behavior.

Chapter 10 highlights the psychological importance of downside risk by presenting Allais's paradox and by contrasting how Allais and prospect theory have interpreted this paradox. Chapter 11 then explains how time can be introduced in the assessment of downside risk, that is, how the Allais paradox and his theory of psychological time can be combined into the perceived risk of loss. It illustrates the relevance of the perceived risk of loss by analyzing the pricing of some financial instruments. It suggests that major bubbles tend to be heralded by a fall in the perceived risk of loss to unprecedented levels. Finally, it discusses potential connections between the perceived risk of loss and moral hazard. These three chapters should interest any reader (scholar, practitioner, policymaker) eager to enhance the tools he or she uses to analyze financial market dynamics and to cope with financial instability.

The conclusion summarizes the key arguments in the form of a comparison of the HRL formulation with the REH.

As just said, the perceived risk of loss unifies two important contributions made by Maurice Allais: first, the well-known paradox that bears his name; second, his still rather confidential hereditary, relativist, and logistic (HRL) theory of economic and financial behavior under uncertainty. That these two contributions were made, respectively, almost 60 and 50 years ago is not a good reason for us to neglect them as outdated or irrelevant—quite the opposite. Often in the history of economic analysis, it has taken quite some time for important contributions to be fully recognized. Cantillon had to wait for Jevons to be recognized as an early master of monetary analysis.[19] Gossen foreshadowed Jevons's, Menger's, and Walras's marginal utility theory by almost three decades.

TABLE 1
Distinction Between Risk and Uncertainty

	Risk	Uncertainty
Definition	Existence and knowledge of a set of stationary frequencies computed by "the" model (the statistical parameters of this set do not change over time and their value is the same, irrespective of the estimation period)	Nonstationary frequencies (Keynes: "by very uncertain, I do not mean very improbable"[21]
Probabilities	Objective (all agents refer to the same set of frequencies)	Subjective (each agent is likely to have its own set of probabilities)
Expectations	Rational (people's expectations are equal to the empirical frequencies)	Adaptive (the learning process takes time and is continuous)

Admittedly, Allais was awarded the Nobel Prize in 1988. Yet, a large part of his works remains relatively unknown, if only because they were first published in French. Almost 30 years have elapsed since Paul Anthony Samuelson commented on Allais in the following terms:[20] "Maurice Allais is a fountain of original and independent discoveries. Had Allais' earliest writings been in English, a generation of economic theory would have taken a different course."

This book will show that Samuelson's statement certainly applies to the Allais theory of psychological time and time-varying rate of memory decay.

Any reader who is kind enough to send me (at *ericbarthalon@gmail. com*) a correction further debugging this book will receive a then-current complete errata sheet and many thanks. It goes without saying that the opinions expressed in this book are mine alone, and do not represent the views of my past employers or those of Allianz SE.

Glossary of Mathematical Symbols in Order of Appearance

Chapter 1

y exponential average

x rate of change (in nominal spending) or rate of inflation or rate of return

k parameter setting the elasticity of an exponential average

Chapter 2

m_n money supply

p_n price level

p_n^e expected value of p_n

y_n volume of output

d_n excess demand/liquidity measured in terms of real money balances

μ demand for real money balances

$\bar{y}$ volume of output when $d_n = 0$

Chapter 3

PUR^j intermediate consumption of goods and services of business j

I^j investment of business j (or of commercial bank k)

W^j wages paid out by business j (or by commercial bank k)

DIV_o^j dividends paid out by business j (or by commercial bank k)

INT_o^j interests paid out by business j (or by commercial bank k)

A_o^j securities amortized (or redeemed) by business j (or by commercial bank k)

SEC_o^j	securities bought by business j (or by commercial bank k)
$d\,M^j$	change in the money balance held by business j
D^j	total applications of funds of business j (excluding $d\,M^j$)
REV^j	sales of goods and services of business j (or of commercial bank k)
DIV_i^j	dividends received by business j (or by commercial bank k)
INT_i^j	interests received by business j (or by commercial bank k)
A_i^j	securities amortized (or redeemed) to business j (or to commercial bank k)
SEC_i^j	securities sold or issued by business j (or by commercial bank k)
$d\,L^j$	new bank loans raised by business j from commercial banks
$d\,L'^j$	new loans raised by business j from the central banks
R^j	total sources of funds of business j (excluding $d\,L^j$ and $d\,L'^j$)
M	broad money supply
M_M	currency
M_S	deposits with commercial banks
M_{hh}	money balances held by households
M_b	money balances held by the business sector (including commercial banks)
INC_{hh}	aggregate income of households
C_{hh}	aggregate consumption of households
SAV_{hh}	aggregate savings of households
CF_b	retained operating earnings of the business sector
D	aggregate nominal spending (cash outlays) of all sectors
R_T	aggregate cash receipts of all sectors
M_T	transaction balances
M_P	precautionary balances
V	transactions velocity of M
t	point on the *physical* (or *calendar*) time scale
V_P	transactions velocity of precautionary balances
V_T	transactions velocity of transaction balances
$f(x)$	demand for money function in Allais's 1953 formulation

$g(x)$ supply of money function in Allais's 1953 formulation

M_D desired money balances

T response period (elementary average planning period for all agents)

f_m lower limit of the demand for money function

f_M upper limit of the demand for money function

g_m lower limit of the supply of money function

g_M upper limit of the supply of money function

D_e aggregate nominal spending in a stationary equilibrium

Chapter 4

r continuous constant periodic rate of decay in an exponential average

V_0 transaction velocity of money in a stationary state

φ_t notional function used to introduce the relationship between the physical and the psychological time scale as well as the variability of the velocity of money and that of the rate of memory decay

T_0 response period in a stationary state

t' a point on the *psychological* time scale

χ continuous rate of memory decay along the physical time scale

χ_0 continuous rate of memory decay along the psychological time scale (or in a stationary state)

Z coefficient of psychological expansion

ϕ_0 scaling parameter (ratio of desired balances to nominal spending when $Z = 0$)

$\Psi(Z)$ relative desired balances, a logistic function of Z

b parameter in the function Ψ, setting its maximum value $\phi_0(Z)$

α parameter in the function Ψ, setting the slope of $\phi_0(Z)$ the asymptotic limit of its elasticity with respect to Z

z dynamic equilibrium rate ("perceived" rate of change)

$\overline{x}$ average rate of growth during a period p

p time-scaling factor used to compute Z in discrete time

Ψ^* estimated value of Ψ

β elasticity of expected inflation with respect to actual price changes in Cagan's 1954 formulation

E expected inflation in Cagan's 1954 formulation

C actual change in prices in Cagan's 1954 formulation

α elasticity of the demand for real balances with respect to expected inflation in Cagan's 1954 formulation

$\overline{\chi}$ elasticity of memorized nominal growth with respect to actual changes in Allais's 1954 formulation

u memorized nominal growth in Allais's 1954 formulation

K elasticity of the demand for desired balances with respect to memorized nominal growth in Allais's 1954 formulation

Z_0 initialization parameter, value of Z for $t = 0$

P a price or a price index

ζ_1 expectations of momentum traders in Smith's formulation

c_1 elasticity of the expectations of momentum traders with respect to price changes in Smith's formulation

q_1 weight given to momentum traders in Smith's formulation

ζ_2 price deviation from fundamental value in Smith's formulation

q_2 weight given to fundamental investors in Smith's formulation

$k(\zeta)$ total investor sentiment function in Smith's formulation

ρ rate of growth in base money

$\gamma(Z)$ base-money multiplier, a logistic function of Z

a' parameter in the function γ, setting its minimum value $(1 - a')$

b' parameter in the function γ, setting its maximum value $(1 + a'b')$

α' parameter in the function γ, setting the slope of the asymptotic limit of its elasticity with respect to Z

B_0 value of base money for $t = 0$

q scaling parameter in the money supply function

Chapter 5

Q volume of transactions

E nonbank credit in Allais's fundamental equation of monetary dynamics

M_{De} demand for money in dynamic equilibrium

M_e supply of money in dynamic equilibrium

x_e rate of growth in nominal spending in dynamic equilibrium

z_e dynamic equilibrium rate
Z_e coefficient of psychological expansion in dynamic equilibrium
V_e transaction velocity of money in dynamic equilibrium
χ_e rate of memory decay in dynamic equilibrium
V_0^* transaction velocity of money in a stationary state
Θ period of endogenous fluctuations in nominal spending

Chapter 6

x^* estimated rate of growth in nominal spending
Z^* estimated coefficient of psychological expansion
K ratio of aggregate nominal spending to national income, ratio of the transaction velocity of money to its income velocity
v income velocity of money

Chapter 7

θ time elapsing between the assessment and the collection of taxes

Chapter 8

i psychological rate of interest
j yield on long-term bonds
i_l pure long-term interest rate
l_j liquidity premium on long-term bonds
λ parameter equal to the ratio of the liquidity premium l_j to the nominal interest j
W an approximation of aggregate nominal spending
j^* estimated yield on long-term bonds with respect to χ
μ ratio of the estimated nominal interest rate j^{**} to z
j^{**} estimated yield on long-term bonds with respect to z
P price of a share
d_0 current dividend
r discount rate of dividends
g^* expected long-term growth rate of dividend
π ex-anti equity risk premium

Chapter 9

O_{MD} outstanding margin debt
M_3 broad money supply
ff federal funds rate

x_{SP} return of the S&P 500 index

x_N return of the NASDAQ index

P rescaled ratio of margin debt to broad money supply O_{MD}/M_3

Chapter 10

x_i an outcome in a risky prospect

p_i the probability of outcome x_i

P a risky prospect consisting of one or several outcomes

V the psychological value of a risky prospect

E the mathematical expectation of a risky prospect

B a neo-Bernoullian index of the psychological value of a risky prospect (ignoring its distribution)

C an individual's capital

u cardinal utility

w decision weights in prospect theory

v the psychological value of an outcome in prospect theory

π the function transforming probabilities into decision weights in prospect theory

μ_l the lth-order moment of a risky prospect

$\bar{s}$ Allais's cardinal utility (or absolute satisfaction) function

U_0 an individual's psychological capital

X the absolute change (gain or loss) in an individual's psychological capital

U_0^* the statistical estimate of an individual's psychological capital

$B_{1/2}$ Bernoulli's index for a constant-probability (1/2), variable-gain prospect

B_{200} Bernoulli's index for a variable-probability, constant-gain (200) prospect

R the psychological value of a risky prospect according to Allais, a function of its moments

Chapter 11

χ_0^i rate of memory decay of age group i in a stationary state

Uncertainty, Expectations, and Financial Instability

PART ONE

The Progressive Emergence of Expectations in Economic Theory

CHAPTER ONE

Expectations Before the Rational Expectations Revolution

HINTS OR even statements about time, uncertainty, and expectations are present in the writings of early economists. In 1755, Cantillon, for example, defined the farmer as "an undertaker who promises to pay to the Landowner ... a fixed sum of money ... without assurance of the profit he will derive from this enterprise."[1]

He reinforced his point by saying that "the price of the Farmer's produce depends naturally upon ... unforeseen circumstances, and consequently he conducts the enterprise of his farm at an uncertainty."

In the same vein, Cantillon defined merchants as "undertakers [who] pay a certain price following that of the place where they purchase it, to resell wholesale or retail at an uncertain price" and stated that competition between them is such that it is impossible for them to ever know "how long their customers will buy of them."

As Cantillon sought to refute the already widely held view according to which low interest rates are the consequence of an abundant supply of money and argued, instead, that what matters is the balance between the supply of and the demand for loanable funds, he explicitly referred to the profit expectations held by the borrowers:[2] "everybody had become an Undertaker in the South Sea scheme and wanted to borrow money to buy Shares, expecting to make an immense profit out of which it would be easy to pay this high rate of Interest rate."[3]

But it is certainly in his chapter on the augmentation and diminution of coins in denomination that Cantillon proved the most farsighted and perceptive as regards the role of expectations in economics. Decided by the Sovereign, changes in the nominal denomination of species were all monetary policy was about in those days and had actually been since

Solon and the Roman Republic. Contracts—like loans—were denominated in money of account, but payments were made in species, which were defined by their weight: for example, in 1714, in France, 1 écu, that is, 1 ounce of silver, was worth 5 Livres Tournois. Resources-strapped states had found very early on that an increase in the nominal value of coins, that is, a devaluation of the money of account (what we would call inflation nowadays), was a way for them to ease their financial strains.

In this fascinating chapter, Cantillon discusses both the short- and long-term effects of decreases and increases in the nominal denomination of coins, depending on whether these changes are made "suddenly without warning" or phased in over a period of time. His discussion implicitly considers there is a diversity of expectations in the marketplace, some undertakers being less "able and accredited" than others.

However perceptive Cantillon's insights may be, they do not constitute per se a conscious theory of time, uncertainty, and expectations. For quite a long time—that is, almost a hundred and fifty years—economists continued to mention expectations in passing, as if they did not fully realize the central role of expectations in dynamic economic analysis, which involves the discussion of how economic adjustments are brought about through time.

Until the formulation of the rational expectations hypothesis between 1960 and 1975, there was no formal academic debate about the nature and role of expectations. As a result, the major contributions of the first half of the twentieth century often give the impression that they were presented without any reference to one another. Despite this apparent lack of structured debate, three trends emerged:

- Some authors—Wicksell, Knight, Keynes, Hayek, Hicks—progressively put expectations at the center of the stage, implicitly considered them to be adaptive, while suggesting at the same time that expectations belonged to the realm of the incalculable, namely, human psychology.
- Other authors—Fisher, Cagan, Allais—dedicated their efforts to quantify the supposedly incalculable by proposing expectations models liable to be confronted with empirical data.
- Inspired by an analysis of the shortcomings and inconsistencies of these efforts, the rational expectations hypothesis proposed that

economic agents form their expectations rationally, that is, by using "the" one and only correct (neoclassical) model of the economy. While this hypothesis has always failed to convince a large body of academics and practitioners, it has become the paradigm in policy-making circles.

1.1   Expectations Are Important, but They Belong to the Realm of the Incalculable

Knut Wicksell, John Maynard Keynes, Frank Knight, and Friedrich Hayek have been the first economists to stress the importance of expectations explicitly, as regards cyclical fluctuations, be it in economic activity or in financial markets.

Wicksell used the word "expectation" as early as 1898, as he made a distinction between "the natural rate of interest on capital" and "the rate of interest on loans":[4]

> For reasons connected with the conception of subjective value, the probability that an entrepreneur will make a profit must always be somewhat greater than the probability that he will make a loss. For otherwise his "moral expectation" would be negative. In many cases, however, the entrepreneurs' gambling spirit will prevent this rule from applying to their behavior.[5]

Wicksell pushed expectations at the forefront of dynamic economic analysis in discussing further the cumulative inflationary (or deflationary) effect of a discrepancy between the market rate of interest and the natural rate of interest.[6] He starts by distinguishing "present prices" and "future prices calculated at present [expected prices]." He also makes a clear distinction between "situations in which a rise in price can be foreseen with more or less certainty" and "the element of speculation which necessarily enters into all business transactions." In that second situation, "the normal assumption is that present prices will remain constant." But according to Wicksell,

> if the market rate [of interest] falls below the marginal productivity of waiting [the natural rate of interest], entrepreneurs, even with current prices as the foundation of their calculation of future prices,

will be able to pay a somewhat higher price. In this way, the present price level will be raised indirectly and therefore the future price level also.[7]

However concise this very last sentence may be, it is an expectation model, albeit a very crude one. In Wicksell's model, expectations are determined by the outcome observed in the previous period, and a change in current prices is assumed to change expected prices in the same direction and in the same proportion.[8] Wicksell's central proposition of cumulative instability is entirely dependent on his assumption that people expect future prices to rise at least as fast as current prices.

Nowadays, Knight is essentially remembered for having forcefully shown that uncertainty is the source of entrepreneurial profit in an economy where entrepreneurs compete for acquiring productive services.[9] In chapter 8 of *Risk, Uncertainty and Profit*, there is, however, much more than this fundamental contribution. This chapter is presented by Knight as an "inquiry into the nature and function of knowledge." In a very Socratic tone, Knight claims that "we must know ourselves as well as the world." Knight reinforces his point with a provocative statement: "In spite of rash statements by over-ardent devotees of the new science of 'behavior,' it is preposterous to suppose that it will ever supersede psychology or the theory of knowledge."

However, says Knight, and this is the whole problem, "the universe may not be ultimately knowable." Yet, we have to act and to make decisions. The question is then: on the basis of which knowledge? Foreshadowing Keynes by a few years, Knight is keen to stress how limited or fragile our knowledge is and how little we know about the way we acquire it:

> At present we are concerned only to emphasize the fact that knowledge is in a sense variable in degree and that the practical problem may relate to the degree of knowledge rather than to its presence or absence in toto ... The essence of the situation is action according to opinion, of greater or less foundation and value, neither entire ignorance nor complete and perfect information, but partial knowledge.

Of course, successful adaptations on our part to a "world of change" require some forward-looking consciousness. But these adjustments take time, and this is precisely where the difficulties lie:

An explanation of the readjustment necessarily runs in terms of stimulus and reaction, in this temporal order. Yet in our own experience we know that we do not react to past stimulus, but to the "image" of a future state of affairs ... However successful mechanistic science may be in explaining the reaction in terms of a past cause, it will still be irresistibly convenient for common sense to think of it as prompted by a future situation present to consciousness. The role of consciousness is to give the organism this "knowledge" of the future.

Needless to say, it is not only convenient, but also reassuring for us, confronted as we are with uncertainty, to think of our response to past stimulus as if it were a forward-looking consciousness. But how does consciousness work? Frustration is palatable in Knight's answer:

The ordinary decisions of life are made on the basis of "estimates" of a crude and superficial character. It is only in very special cases that anything like a mathematical study can be made ... The mental operations by which ordinary practical decisions are made are very obscure, and it is a matter of surprise that neither logicians nor psychologists have shown much interest in them. Perhaps ... it is because there is really very little to say about the subject ... The real logic or psychology of ordinary conduct is rather a neglected branch of inquiry. The processes of intuition or judgment, being unconscious, are inaccessible to study.

Despite this avowed frustration, Knight cannot conceal a clear conviction:

We perceive the world before we react to it, and we react not to what we perceived, but always to what we infer ... The universal form of conscious behavior is thus action designed to change a future situation inferred from a present one ... We know the absent from the present, the future from the now, by assuming that connections or associations among phenomena which have been valid will be so; we judge the future by the past ... Prophecy seems to be a good deal like memory, on which it is based. There is very little that we can tell about the operation of memory, very little "technique" ... In the main, it seems that we "infer" largely from our experience of the past as a whole.

Knight's contention is actually quite strong: if we are to understand how "expectations" are formed and to explain economic behavior, then we have to describe the operations of memory, we have to understand how memory establishes a link between the past and the future, and we have to evaluate the extent to which the past is present in our current decisions. This sounds more as a research program for logicians and psychologists than for economists.

Keynes, too, suggested that expectations are rooted in memory and therefore adaptive, but—like Knight—he did not use this very word. Keynes's insight is focused on uncertainty and the influence of short-period changes on what he called the state of long-term expectations. In a well-known chapter of *The General Theory*, Keynes wrote the following:[10]

> The considerations upon which expectations of prospective yields are based are partly future events which can only be forecasted with more or less confidence.
>
> It would be foolish, in forming our expectations, to attach great weight to matters which are very uncertain (by very "uncertain" I do not mean the same thing as very improbable). It is reasonable, therefore, to be guided to a considerable degree by the facts about which we feel somewhat confident. For this reason the facts of the existing situation enter, in a sense disproportionately, into the formation of our long-term expectations; our usual practice being to take the existing situation and to project it into the future, modified only to the extent that we have more or less definite reasons for expecting a change.
>
> In practice we have tacitly agreed, as a rule, to fall back on what is, in truth, a convention. The essence of this convention lies in assuming that the existing state of affairs will continue indefinitely, except in so far as we have specific reasons to expect a change. This does not mean that we really believe that the existing state of affairs will continue indefinitely. We know from extensive experience that this is most unlikely.
>
> We are assuming, in effect, that the existing market valuation, however arrived at, is uniquely correct in relation to our existing knowledge of the facts which will influence the yield of the investment, and that it will only change in proportion to changes in this knowledge.
>
> For an investor can legitimately encourage himself with the idea that the only risk he runs is that of a genuine change in the news

over the near future, as to the likelihood of which he can attempt to form his own judgement and which is unlikely to be very large. For assuming that the convention holds good, it is only these changes which can affect the value of his investment.

However, most of these persons are, in fact, largely concerned, not with making superior long-term forecasts of the probable yield of an investment over its whole life, but with foreseeing changes in the conventional basis of valuation a short-time ahead of the general public.

Appealing ideas, brilliant exposition, but not very helpful, as Keynes stopped short of defining precisely what he meant by the existing state of affairs and short, too, of proposing any operational model of long-term expectations.[11] Keynes's essential intuition is the inherent instability of "long-term" expectations and their sensitivity to changes in the existing situation. But the concept of elasticity of expectations and its quantification are both absent from Keynes's writings.

Keynes's chapter 12 has become an inevitable and revered reference in any contemporary discussion about the role of expectations in economics. Yet, it is not without criticisms, some of them discretely ironic, that economists concerned with dynamic economic analysis promptly greeted Keynes's "novel" emphasis on expectations. These criticisms are still worth reading, for they highlight the issue of how economic agents learn, an issue that we shall encounter later in this book. In his *Business Cycles*, Schumpeter does not mention Keynes explicitly, but clearly he has Keynes in mind with the following words:[12]

We have admitted any expectations and we have taken them as given. ... We have ourselves to blame if with such tremendous generality we do not get any results. ... We have emptied the schema of everything that matters. In other words, if we discontinue the practice of treating expectations as if they were ultimate data, and treat them as what they are—variable which it is our task to explain—properly linking them with the business situations that give rise to them, we shall succeed in restricting expectations to those which we actually observe and not only reduce their influence to its proper proportions but also understand how the course of events moulds them and at certain times so turns them as to make them work toward equilibrium.

... Another such deus ex machina ... is "anticipation" ... Unless we know why people expect what they expect, any argument is completely valueless which appeals to them as *causae efficientes*. Such appeals enter into the class of pseudo-explanations.

Just one year after the *General Theory*, Haberler had already made the same point, but much more forcefully and directly:[13]

> In recent years, it has become fashionable to lay stress on the element of expectations. It should not, however, be forgotten that even the theories of authors who do not usually refer explicitly to expectations and anticipations can, and should, be interpreted in terms of expectations, as the authors in question [Lindahl, Myrdal, Ohlin, Hicks, Hayek, Morgenstern] are themselves often well aware.
>
> There is ... one feature about Mr. Keynes' system, which has given the impression to many readers that the *General Theory* ... is a dynamic theory—namely, the fact that ... it runs in terms of expectations. [But] if we confine ourselves to saying that it is not actual prices ... but expected prices ... which induce an entrepreneur to produce and to invest, we do not say very much, unless we give some hint as to how these expectations are determined.
>
> A theory which takes expectations as given at any point of time, and does not say anything on how they grow out of past experiences, is of very little value; for such a theory would still be static, and it is almost impossible to determine expectations as such [expectations may almost be called "nonoperational concepts"]. Only if it is possible to give some hypotheses about how expectations are formed on the basis of past experience can a really useful and verifiable theory be evolved. And such a theory is evidently dynamic ... for it links the past with the present. [From a strictly logical point of view, the psychological link between the past and the present consisting of expectations may be dropped and the theory stated in terms of a direct relationship between observable phenomena at different points in time. Psychologically it may, however, be useful to retain the word "expectations," or a similar concept, as a link, because it reminds us of the fact that those dynamic "laws" (relationships) are nothing but hypotheses.]

Not content with this, Haberler rams home his critique of Keynes by quoting Lundberg:[14]

The introduction of expectations can, in a way, be said to mark the stepping-stone to dynamic analysis, because they express the connection linking present plans and activities with future events. However, economists have indulged in too much purely formal exercise with this term ... It is sensible to link actions with expectations, only if the latter can be explained on the basis of past and present economic events. Total lack of correlation here would mean the complete liquidation of economics as a science.

In the year when the *General Theory* was published, 1936, Hayek made a contribution that reads very much as a research program on expectations.[15] If, Hayek said, economic theory is to be valued for its ability to explain the real world rather than for its internal (logical) consistency, then dynamic analysis, that part of economic theory which purports to account for the workings of a monetary economy through time, has no choice but to make explicit assumptions about foresights and anticipations (which are only part of the broader problem of the acquisition of knowledge). The logical conclusions reached in the context of dynamic analysis depend in fact on the assumptions made about foresight and anticipations. These assumptions are the only part of economic theory which can be proven wrong by observed facts: they make economics falsifiable. No one before Hayek had so clearly stated the strategic importance of the theory of expectations.

Hayek goes on by distinguishing two kinds of economic data: objective data, as given ex post to the "observing economist," and subjective data. Economic agents draw their individual plans on the basis of subjective data, that is, what they have in mind. Knight would say that "the essence of the situation [an uncertain one to be sure] is action according to opinion." With this, Hayek defines a dynamic equilibrium as a situation where individual plans are compatible and outcomes (objective data) are in line with expectations (subjective data).

The next decisive step is then to understand the interaction between objective and subjective data, for there is no a priori reason to postulate that they should converge. There are actually two types of change in the objective data: those which are "as expected" (which does not mean the objective data should be constant through time) and those which are unexpected and which cause a change in the subjective data.

For Hayek, it is all too easy to assume that every economic agent knows everything instantly. Experience is the only source of knowledge. There is no such thing as a timeless learning process:

> We must explain by what process people will acquire the necessary knowledge. ... it is these apparently subsidiary hypotheses or assumptions that people do learn from experience, and about how they acquire knowledge, which constitute the empirical content of our propositions about what happens in the real world. ... And these assumptions must necessarily run in terms of assertions about causal connections, about how experience creates knowledge.

This being said, Hayek acknowledges that "we are pretty much in the dark about the nature of the process by which individual knowledge is changed." One very last word on Hayek. All through *Economics and Knowledge*, he emphasizes the need for every agent to form expectations about other people's actions. While Hayek does not explicitly refer to policymakers' actions, nothing in his words precludes from thinking that he also had them in mind. Should we therefore see in Hayek a precursor of the rational expectations hypothesis, which, as we shall soon see, claims that people know the probabilities of the various courses liable to be taken by policymakers and factor in these probable policy responses in their own behavior, thus making policy ineffective? Nothing seems further away from the thinking of Hayek, who never misses an opportunity to remind us that any learning process takes time: "But, as all other people will change their decisions as they gain experience about the external facts and about other people's actions, there is no reason why theses processes of successive changes should ever come to an end."

Without saying it, it is clearly adaptive expectations that Hayek has in mind. Such is also the case of Hicks.

In *Value and Capital*, John Hicks introduced the concept of elasticity of expectations: "I define the elasticity of a particular person's expectations of the price of commodity X as the ratio of the proportional rise in expected future prices of X to the proportional rise in its current price."

Hicks suggested that in most circumstances the elasticity of expectations should be anywhere between 0 and 1, which he regarded as the two "pivotal cases." And he went on to analyze the impact of the elasticity of price expectations on the stability of equilibrium. When expectations are inelastic (elasticity = 0), "all changes in current prices are regarded as being temporary changes, any change in current prices will induce very large substitution effects, . . . subsitution over time will be strongly stabilizing."

When expectations are elastic (elasticity equal to or greater than 1), a rise in prices is interpreted as an "indication that [prices] will go on changing in the same direction," and it does foster excess demand, which in turn feeds back into higher prices; if the rate of interest remains constant, such a system is prone to cumulative instability. However, as Hicks did not formulate any quantitative theory of expectations formation, his perceptive analysis of the implications of various elasticities of price expectations did not lend itself to some form of confrontation with observed data.

In particular, Hicks does not seem to have contemplated the possibility that price expectations for a given commodity might be rather inelastic at some times and very elastic at other times. As a consequence, he did not give any hint as to what might cause the elasticity of expectations to be variable over time. But the mere introduction of the concept of elasticity of expectations was nevertheless a great step forward, for it clearly showed that different regimes of expectations were theoretically possible. This is clearly revealed by the following sentence:

> The elasticity of expectations will be greater than unity, if a change in current prices makes people feel that they can recognize a trend, so that they try to extrapolate; it will be negative if they make the opposite kind of guess, interpreting the change as the culminating point of a fluctuation.

The different regimes of expectations are not given their current names—adaptive, extrapolative, or rational—but the idea is clearly present.

1.2   Early Attempts to Quantify Expectations

The distinctive feature of the approach presented by Fisher as early as 1896 is its focus on empirical data, that is, the observed relationship between price movements and interest rate fluctuations.[16] From this empirical starting point, Fisher was led to introduce key concepts:

- The distinction between foreseen and unforeseen changes in the value of money.
- The distinction between imperfection of forecast, which causes wealth transfer between creditors and debtors, on one hand and, on the other hand, inequality of foresight, which causes cyclical fluctuations.[17]

Fisher's crucial empirical observation is twofold. First, it takes time for interest rates to adjust to price movements. Second, this adjustment is generally inadequate (partial). According to Fisher, the "borrowing class" (or the "managers of capital") tends to have better foresights than lenders. This is so because these managers are in a position where they are the first to know of pressures on prices. Hence, they have an advantage over lenders when it comes to assessing the return on capital employed. In short, rising prices tend to inflate profits. Thanks to these elevated profits, entrepreneurs can afford to pay higher interest rates. But, as the "ignorant lenders" do not demand an immediate upward adjustment in interest rates, the borrowing class is enticed to develop expectations of even higher profits and to increase the volume of investment.

Translated into the current terminology of economics, Fisher's insights are surprisingly modern. What Fisher described as early as 1896 is a model of cyclical fluctuations in which a cumulative process depends upon

- The heterogeneity of agents.
- Information asymmetry.
- A blend of adaptive and nonadaptive expectations.

More than thirty years later, in *The Theory of Interest*, Irving Fisher came back on the same issue, but with additional insights.[18] As in his earlier work, Fisher's starting point is an empirical observation: the "delayed, but accumulated, adjustment" of interest rates to prices. Fisher did not deny that economic agents are making their best efforts to "look ahead" as he studied the relation between prices and interest rates, but he also recognized that

if perfect foresight existed, continuously rising prices would be associated not with a continuously rising rate of interest but with a continuing high rate of interest ... , and a constant price level would be associated with a constant rate of interest—assuming in each case, that other influences than price change remained the same.

If this perfect foresight correctly described reality, nominal interest rates should be more volatile than actually observed, with "real interest ... comparatively steady." This is exactly the reverse of what we can actually see.

This latter observation led Fisher to successfully test the assumption that the influence of past price changes is distributed in time, "as, in fact, must evidently be true of any influence." In other words, "the assumption that a change in prices occurring during one year exhausts its influence upon interest rates in the same year or in another single year is shown to be quite wrong."

Fisher added the following crucial remarks: "when we make the much more reasonable supposition that price changes ... manifest their influence with diminishing intensity, over long periods which vary in length with the conditions, we find a very significant relationship, especially ... when prices were subject to violent fluctuations."

Nobody before Fisher had ever formulated this assumption of the diminishing intensity of the influence of the past in current affairs. Nobody before Fisher had suggested that the speed of this diffusion process could vary through time, and be context-dependent. Finding the law of diminishing intensity of the influence of the past was to become the focus of much of subsequent research.

Fisher used a very crude method to distribute the effect of past inflation rates over time: instead of using constant weights—as would have been the case with a geometric average of past inflation rates computed over a certain arbitrary number of years—he assigned to each of them coefficients that decline linearly with the lag of actual inflation (i.e., a weighted average of current and past values with weights that decline linearly with time into the past until the weight reaches zero).

Cagan and Allais refined this lag distribution in 1953–54.[19] Although they worked independently of each other, used different notations, and gave different interpretations of their respective work, they both used the same mathematical formulation, namely, exponential averages, to model inflation expectations.[20] In an exponential average, the weighting coefficients decline exponentially at a constant rate with the lag of past inflation rates.

There are different ways of defining the *exponential average y* of a variable *x*. The simplest one is the following recurrence relationship in discrete time:

$$y_n = y_{n-1} + k(x_n - y_{n-1}) \qquad \text{with} \qquad 0 < k < 1 \qquad (1.1)$$

which, after rearranging the terms in the right member, is equivalent to

$$y_n = kx_n + (1 - k)y_{n-1} \qquad (1.2)$$

By recurrence, and with $y_0 = kx_0$, one can easily demonstrate that relationship 1.2 is equivalent to

$$y_n = k[x_n + (1 - k)x_{n-1} + (1 - k)^2 x_{n-2} + \cdots + (1 - k)^n x_0] \quad (1.3)$$

or, in a more concise form,

$$y_n = k \sum_{i=0}^{n} (1 - k)^i x_{n-i} \qquad (1.4)$$

The sequence of exponentially declining coefficients $1, 1-k, (1-k)^2, (1-k)^3, \ldots, (1-k)^n$ in relationship 1.3 is a geometric sequence having $1 - k$ as common ratio and $1/k$ for sum when $n \to +\infty$, since $0 < 1 - k < 1$. Hence, the weighted sum of coefficients

$$\frac{k + (1 - k) + (1 - k)^2 + \cdots + (1 - k)^n}{1/k}$$
$$= k[k + (1 - k) + (1 - k)^2 + \cdots + (1 - k)^n] \qquad (1.5)$$

is equal to 1, which justifies calling *y* an average.

As exponential averages foreshadowed Allais's HRL formulation, chapters 2 and 4 of this book will deal with them in great detail. Therefore, at this stage, there is no need to describe this mathematical tool further.

Adaptive expectations came under fire not so much because they failed to deliver good econometric results, but rather because they appeared logically flawed.

CHAPTER TWO

Rational Expectations Are Endogenous to and Abide by "the" Model

THE *rational expectations hypothesis* (REH) is a much more ambitious, comprehensive, and complex theory than any of the expectations theories that we have just reviewed. It is a pillar of the neo-Walrasian approach to general equilibrium, a mathematically demanding theory purporting to show how the interaction between rational agents engaged in constrained maximization of consumption, production, profits, etc., over time, generates a unique and stable intertemporal equilibrium. The explicit consideration of time in this general equilibrium approach calls either for future markets in all goods or, failing such markets, for an expectations theory of future prices, so as to account for the influence of these expected prices on current transactions.

2.1   Overview

Like many other revolutions, the REH started as a criticism and a rejection of the preexisting order, namely, adaptive expectations and economic models in which expectations are assumed to be exogenous, that is, independent of the forecasts made by the model of interest. John Muth is the economist who launched this revolution in 1960. But this revolution went much further than a mere rejection of adaptive expectations.

The first positive proposition made by the REH is that, for a model to be logical and therefore valid, expectations have to be endogenous; that is, they must coincide with the forecasts made by this model. Muth asserted that this identity between the model's forecasts and agents' expectations defines rational expectations. This first positive proposition implies the second one, according to which all economic agents use *the* same model of the economy. Almost simultaneously, Fama formulated the *efficient market hypothesis*, which develops very much the same line of argument in the context of financial markets.

Last but not the least, if all agents use the same correct model of the economy, it follows—as argued by Lucas—that they know how to forecast and how to adjust to the consequences of the decisions made by monetary and fiscal authorities. Therefore, concludes the REH, monetary policy and fiscal policy are ineffective or neutral, and policymakers should not even seek to steer real macroeconomic variables such as growth and employment. Markets can be trusted to do this in the most effective way.

In particular, policymakers should not fear triggering a contraction in private demand when they fight inflation by curbing money creation or when, to rebalance public finances, they cut public expenditures and raise taxes. In the first case, economic agents will recognize that money is neutral; in the second one, according to the Ricardian equivalence, they will reduce their current savings, as they figure out that they will pay less tax in the future. In this view of the world, there cannot be any endogenous cyclical fluctuations. Whichever fluctuations there may exist, according to the real business cycle theory, should be explained in terms of exogenous random shocks, that is, unexpected shocks. Let us elaborate on these different points.

2.2   Muth's Critique of Exponential Averages

The central insight of the REH is that economic agents should form their expectations by making the most efficient use of all available information. Even if this information were limited to the past values of the data they need to forecast, the least they can do is to learn from their forecasting errors. There should be no exploitable pattern in their forecasting errors, which should be randomly distributed. If, for example, monthly inflation rates are in a constantly rising trend, an exponential average of past inflation rates is bound to be "behind the curve" of observed inflation. This systematic error is information that the public can exploit to improve its understanding of the dynamics of inflation.

Despite this potential weakness, exponential averages had, in the 1950s, become a widely used and rather successful forecasting technique. This led Muth to search for the conditions under which an exponential average produces unbiased and minimum mean square error forecasts of a variable, assumed to be a linear combination of independent random shocks.[1] (see proof C.1, p. 277.)

To put it differently, Muth has demonstrated that exponential smoothing is an optimal filtering method, if the variable of interest follows a random walk. By looking at exponential smoothing as a linear regression, one can shed further light on Muth's insight. It is easy to demonstrate that the function[2]

$$f(a) = \sum_{i=0}^{n-1}(1 - k)^i(x_{n-i} - a)^2 \qquad \text{with} \qquad 0 < k < 1 \qquad (2.1)$$

is minimized for

$$a = \frac{k}{1 - (1 - k)^n} \sum_{i=0}^{n-1}(1 - k)^i x_{n-i} \qquad (2.2)$$

and that

$$\lim_{n \to +\infty} a = k \sum_{i=0}^{n-1}(1 - k)^i x_{n-i} \qquad (2.3)$$

which is the very definition of y_n (see relationship 1.4 and proof C.2 p. 280).

The function $f(a)$ formulates a weighted linear regression of the time series x_n on a constant a, with the weighting coefficients declining exponentially with respect to the age i of each observation (since $0 < k < 1$). This approach clearly shows that exponential smoothing is appropriate only when one can fit the time series x_n by a horizontal line in the neighborhood of n. If the times series exhibit a trend, be it rising or declining, or fluctuations, exponential smoothing should not be used. In other words, exponential smoothing is not an appropriate tool to deal with the accelerating rates of change that characterize hyperinflation (or financial bubbles).[3]

Finally, one can also interpret an exponential average as a filter, which maintains the filtering error $x_n - y_n$ in a constant ratio to the forecasting error $x_n - y_{n-1}$, irrespective of the latter's magnitude. From relationship 1.1, we get indeed

$$\frac{x_n - y_n}{x_n - y_{n-1}} = 1 - k \qquad \text{with} \qquad 0 < k < 1 \qquad (2.4)$$

For $k \approx 0$, the filtering error is close to the forecasting error. For $k \approx 1$, the filtering error is small, since $y_n \approx x_n$. This relationship illustrates the trade-off presented by exponential averages. If $k \approx 1$, the filtering error is small, but the smoothing effect is negligible. This is what is needed in the presence of very volatile time series and regime changes. Conversely, if $k \approx 0$, the smoothing effect is strong, but the filtering error is large. This is what is needed for well-behaved time series, without regime changes. For lack of flexibility, an exponential average is not fit to deal with a time series, the volatility of which is variable over time. In any case, the filtering and the forecasting errors are of the same sign, be it positive or negative.

In retrospect, Muth's discussion of exponential averages clearly opened the way to the REH because, for the first time, it asserted that the mathematical expectation of a variable x is the benchmark against which the forecasting performance of its exponential average y should be measured.

By showing that the use of exponential averages should be restricted to certain cases, Muth had struck his first blow against adaptive expectations.

Since he posited that the mathematical expectation of a variable is the benchmark against which the performance of a specific forecasting method, that is, exponential average, should be measured, it was natural and logical on the part of Muth to push his argument further. He did so by stating that the probability distribution indicated by "the relevant economic theory" is what rational economic agents take as their expectation of the variable of interest.

2.3   Model Consistent Expectations

In general, the variable of interest is not autonomous with respect to other variables; it does not have a life of its own, and available information is not limited to its past values. Time series are also available for other variables that may influence the variable of interest or that may be influenced by it. For example, intuition tells us that there must be some interaction between inflation, on one side, and wages, commodities prices, taxes, interest rates, the money supply, exchanges rates, and so on, on the other side. Building an economic model consists in quantifying these interactions. The REH argues that it is not logical to build a model in which expectations are assumed to be exogenous, that is, formed as if this very model did not exist or remained unknown to economic agents. For example, in a model where inflation results from money growth, it is not logical to assume that inflation expectations are a mere exponential average of past inflation rates. Two of Muth's followers, Sargent and Wallace, express this idea very well:[4]

> The usual method of modeling expectations involves supposing that they are formed by extrapolating past values of the variable being predicted, a scheme that usually, though not always, assumes that the people whose expectations count are ignorant of the economic forces governing the variable they are trying to predict.

But it was Muth who first struck this second blow to adaptive expectations. As a matter of fact, the idea of rational expectations was suggested to Muth by the two following observations he made about the expectations data collected through surveys:[5]

> 1. Averages of expectations in an industry are more accurate than naive models and as accurate as elaborate equation systems, although there are considerable cross-sectional differences of opinion.
> 2. Expectations generally underestimate the extent of changes that actually take place.

Muth explained these observations by suggesting that

> expectations, since they are informed predictions of future events, are essentially the same as the predictions of the relevant economic theory. At the risk of confusing this purely descriptive hypothesis with a pronouncement as to what firms ought to do, we call such expectations "rational." It is sometimes argued that the assumption of rationality in economics leads to theories inconsistent with, or inadequate

to explain, observed phenomena, especially changes over time. Our hypothesis is based on exactly the opposite point of view: that dynamic economic models do not assume enough rationality.

The hypothesis can be rephrased a little more precisely as follows: that expectations of firms (or, more generally, the "subjective" probability distribution of outcomes) tend to be distributed, for the same information set, about the prediction of the theory (or the "objective" probability distribution of outcomes).

The hypothesis asserts that ... the way expectations are formed depends specifically on the structure of the relevant system describing the economy.

If the prediction of the theory were substantially better than the expectations of the firms, then there would be opportunities for the "insider" to profit from the knowledge.

Translated in mathematical terms, this show of modesty on the part of economists says that the expected value x_n^e of a variable x at n consists of its probability distribution, conditional on the information provided by the "relevant economic theory" at time $n - 1$:

$$x_n^e = \varphi(I_{n-1}) \tag{2.5}$$

Strictly speaking, the expectation x_n^e should be represented by the probability distribution predicted by the relevant economic theory. In practice, for the sake of computational convenience, most of the time it is represented by a single quantity, that is, the mathematical expectation of this probability distribution

$$x_n^e = E(x_n/I_{n-1}) \tag{2.6}$$

Being thus defined as the mathematical expectation of all potential outcomes, this rational expectation will naturally tend to "underestimate the extent of changes that actually take place."

Having thus defined rational expectations, Muth continues with a series of very important statements that further part ways with Keynes's "vision" of financial markets as a beauty contest where herding and destabilizing speculation are rife:

Allowing for cross-sectional differences in expectations is a simple matter, because their aggregate effect is negligible as long as the deviation from the rational forecast for an individual firm is not strongly correlated with those of the others. Modifications are necessary only if the correlation of the errors is large and depends systematically on the other explanatory variables ... Whether such biases in expectations are empirically important remains to be seen.

If price expectations are in fact rational, we can make some statements about the economic effects of commodity speculation ... Speculation reduces the variance of prices by spreading the effect of a disturbance over several time periods.

Muth claimed that his hypothesis does a better job than alternative theories at explaining relevant data. What he did was to compare the empirical implications of the REH with those of the cobweb "theorem," which purports to describe the formation of prices in agricultural markets, under the assumption that farmers do not learn from experience and form very naive—extrapolative or adaptive—expectations.

Nevertheless, Muth's REH had very little influence on the development of economic theory during the 1960s. Muth's attempt to turn the existing order—Keynesianism as it happens—upside down was probably too much to swallow by the high priests of the day. Furthermore, the agricultural markets in which the REH was tested were probably seen as too incidental to deserve a lot of attention.

2.4   REH and Macroeconomics

It was Lucas who brought the REH to the forefront of macroeconomic theory, with two seminal articles published, respectively, in 1972 and 1976. In the first one, Lucas used rational expectations to explain why there should be no trade-off in the long run between higher inflation and lower unemployment, contrary to what the Philips curve suggested, at least in the short run.[6] The insight of this paper is that policymakers cannot hope to fool all people all the time: workers should not be expected to persistently mistake a rise in nominal wages for a rise in real wages. Therefore, monetary policy is neutral. In the second paper, the famous Lucas's critique, he used rational expectations again, but this time to explain why most econometric models fail tests for structural changes.[7] According to Lucas's critique, this is so because the coefficients of such models incorporate the expectations that people rationally form, not only about policy instruments, but also about exogenous variables:[8]

> If expectations are rational and properly take into account the way policy instruments and other exogenous variables evolve, the coefficients ... of the model will change whenever the processes governing those policy instruments and exogenous variables change.

In other words, these coefficients are not policy-invariant. They change whenever the rules of the game change.

As a transition to a critical discussion of the REH, let us quote Arrow's own presentation of its main insights.

Although Arrow, as we shall soon see, has strong arguments against the REH, he gives a fair presentation of its structure:[9]

> The new theoretical paradigm of rational expectations holds that each individual forms expectations of the future on the basis of a correct model of the economy, in fact, the same model that the econometrician is using ... Since the world is uncertain,[10] the expectations take the form of probability distributions, and each agent's expectations are conditional on the information available to him or her ... Each agent has to have a model of the entire economy to preserve rationality. The cost of knowledge ... has disappeared; each agent is engaged in very extensive information gathering and data processing.
>
> Rational expectations theory is a stochastic form of perfect foresight.

A simple model, borrowed from E. Malinvaud, will help to illustrate how a model with endogenous expectations is constructed.[11] This model purports to describe the relationships among excess demand, prices, and output (see proof C.3, p. 280).

While the REH has reached a prominent position in contemporary economic thought, it has never succeeded to silence the many economists who challenge it. The critiques of the REH fall into three categories. A first group of critiques points to the mathematical or computational difficulties present in RE models. A second group of critiques goes one step further by questioning the key assumptions underpinning these models. Last but not the least, the compatibility of RE models with empirical data remains an open question.

2.5   Mathematical Difficulty #1: Modeling RE with Risk

Let us start with the first mathematical difficulty. While Muth originally defined rational expectations in terms of probability distributions, in most RE models, it is the mathematical expectation of a given variable that represents a rational expectation. In other words, a single number, a weighted average, is thus substituted for a set of numbers. The reason for this substitution is obvious: it is much easier to handle a single number than a set of numbers, even when they are distributed according to a certain statistical law.

As pointed out by Malinvaud, a purist might feel uneasy with such substitution for it involves neglecting risk in general and the tails of distributions in particular, while empirical research suggests that decision-makers deemed "rational" tend to minimize the cost of being wrong by avoiding strategies entailing low-probability, but potentially catastrophic, outcomes. We shall come back to this point in chapter 10, when we discuss the Allais paradox.

The alternative consisting of dealing with probability distributions requires computational abilities that dwarf even advanced statistical software, such as Eviews. Here is what the Version 6 users' manual said in 2007, repeating what the Version 5 manual had said a few years earlier:

> If we assume that there is no uncertainty[12] in the model, imposing model consistent expectations simply involves replacing any expectations that appear in the model with the future values predicted by the model ... A deterministic simulation of the model can then be run using Eviews ability to solve models with equations which contain future values of the endogenous variables. When we add uncertainty[13] to the model ... the expectations of agents should be calculated based on the entire distribution of stochastic outcomes predicted by the model ... At present, Eviews does not have built in functionality for automatically carrying out this procedure. Because of this, Eviews will not perform stochastic simulations if your model contains

equations involving future values of endogenous variables. We hope to add this functionality to future revisions of Eviews.

2.6   Mathematical Difficulty #2: Nonlinearity

Let us now turn to the second mathematical difficulty. In Malinvaud's example and in much, if not most, of the literature on REH, the relationships considered are linear in their variables. This revealed preference for linear relationships is not an accident. Rather, as Lucas and Sargent put it, it is "a matter of convenience, not of principle."[14] The convenience in question is computational; it has to do with the "computer bill," not with mathematical theory (see proof C.4, p. 283).

Lucas and Sargent argue that, theoretically, we know how to deal with nonlinear forms via expensive recursive methods: the problem is only one of the cost of the computing power required to do this exercise. Nevertheless, their statement that "it is an open question whether for explaining the central features of the business cycle there will be a big reward to fitting nonlinear models" seems to owe more to a desire for analytical tractability and economical computing than to genuine economic conjectures and research, as chapters 3 to 6 of this book will show.

Whether a rational expectations model is linear or not is neither a pure question of computer bill, nor a mere challenge to its ability to accurately represent the real world. It is first and foremost an issue of relevance and utility. Dynamic linear models tend indeed to generate multiple equilibria. That a problem may admit several solutions is not an unknown situation: many well-known equations have several solutions depending on the values of their parameters. The problem with dynamic linear rational expectations models is rather that they admit, as stated by Guesnerie, an "embarrassing number of solutions."[15] By this, Guesnerie actually means a potentially infinite number of solutions, including bubble equilibria or sunspot equilibria, which are the expression or the fruit of self-fulfilling expectations that may or may not have anything to do with reality. If, for example, economic agents come to believe that an exogenous factor, say sunspots, has an impact on stock market returns and if, furthermore, they have good reasons to believe that they widely share this view, then, this expectation will fulfill itself, not directly of course, but indirectly by affecting investors' behavior.

The next round of critiques of the REH challenges the assumptions that it makes about the modeling ability of economic agents. Many economists consider these assumptions to be either nonrealistic or illogical.

2.7   Model Discovery in Uncertainty and Risk

Even if one is willing to accept the existence of *the* relevant model, there remains an important question as regards the learning process whereby this model has been discovered and estimated. The point has been made that the REH would need to specify the learning process whereby empirical frequencies are discovered and modeled into objective probabilities. How long does it take to discover them? As we have seen earlier, Hayek would answer that it can only be a never-ending process. Others think that it should in any case take a lot of time. According to Modigliani,[16] "Benjamin M. Friedman has called attention to the omission from REH of an explicit learning model, and has suggested that, as a result, it can only be interpreted as a description not of short-run but of long-run equilibrium."[17]

From this point of view, in the REH as in many other fields of economics, time is in fact absent.

The weight of Benjamin M. Friedman's remark is indirectly increased by Lucas himself, who adds a very important disclaimer to his advocacy of the REH by saying that it cannot be valid when people are faced with uncertainty as defined by Knight. Right at the beginning of this book, we emphasized that the REH has a limited ambition, since it cannot deal with Knightian uncertainty. Let us again quote Lucas to clarify the relationship among the REH, uncertainty, and risk.[18] "In order that the latter assumption [REH] have an operational meaning, the analysis will be restricted to the situation in which the relevant distributions have settled down to stationary values and can thus be 'known' by traders."

Leaving uncertainty aside and content with assuming risk, Lucas and Sargent answer Benjamin M. Friedman's argument that one should assume economic agents to be Bayesian learners when they are confronted with stochastic outcomes, such as the daily, weekly, monthly returns on a given security or asset class. Aware as agents should be of the variability of the observed mean and variance of returns from one set of observations to the next, they should, for lack of sufficient data, take with a pinch of salt whichever beliefs their experience may lead them to hold about the true, but unknown (or yet to be discovered) values of these two parameters. They should be open to revising their prior beliefs (not to say their expectations) in a systematic and rigorous way whenever fresh data become available. In other words, they should practice Bayesian inference (see table 2.1).

Bayesian learning uses Bayes's theorem, which says[19]

$$P(H \mid E) = \frac{P(E \mid H) \times P(H)}{P(E)} \qquad (2.7)$$

where H is a hypothesis (e.g., the distribution of monthly returns is normal with parameters μ and σ) and E is any particular event or fresh evidence (such as the average $\overline{X}$ of a new set or sample of monthly returns).

- $P(H)$, the prior probability, is the *ex ante* probability of H (i.e., before E is observed).
- $P(H \mid E)$, the posterior probability, is the *ex post* probability of H (i.e., after E is observed).
- $P(E \mid H)$, the likelihood, is the probability of observing E if H holds.
- $P(E)$, the marginal likelihood or model evidence, is the same for all possible hypotheses (i.e., it is independent of any hypothesis).[20]

Nothing in relationship 2.7 prevents $P(H)$ from being a subjective probability (a "guesstimate"), even though there is not always an obvious prior distribution to take. In the real world, the lack of data often leaves no choice, but subjectivity.

Hence, the beauty of Bayes's theorem is that it "enables us to pass from a particular experience to a general statement."[21] Bayes's inference can, of course, be used recursively, each and every time new

TABLE 2.1
Bayesian Learning Process

	Belief/events/proposition	Probabilities/degree of belief
Initial belief	Prior (H)	$P(H)$
New evidence	Particular evidence (E)	$P(E)$
Updated belief	Posterior ($H \mid E$)	$P(H \mid E) = \frac{P(E \mid H)}{P(E)} P(H)$

observations become available:

$$P(H_n \mid E_n) = \frac{P(E_n \mid H_{n-1}) \times P(H_{n-1})}{P(E_n)} \qquad (2.8)$$

In this relationship, $P(H_0)$ can be interpreted as an initialization parameter.

For all its apparent conciseness, Bayesian inference is not that easy to implement.[22] To compute the posterior probability, one needs to compute the marginal likelihood (or model evidence). This can be discouragingly complex if the hypothesis H pertains to many parameters. For in this case, the term $P(E)$ takes the form of a complex multiple integral. Yet, too many multidimensional distributions cannot be expressed in analytic terms. Modern technology makes it possible to make these computations, but the "computer bill" is not negligible.

On the other hand, for simpler models such as the normal distribution, which is used pervasively in finance despite the fact that empirical distributions have fat tails, Bayesian inference does not add a lot, if at all, to the simpler frequentist approach. The results of both approaches converge.

When H is the assumption that the empirical distribution of a stochastic variable can be modeled with a normal distribution, the purpose of Bayesian inference is indeed to revise the prior estimates of its unknown mean μ and standard deviation σ.[23] With μ_{n-1} being the prior estimate of μ, N_{n-1} the number of observations used to make this prior estimate, and $\overline{X}_n$ the mean return observed on a new sample of N_n observations, the posterior estimate of μ is

$$\mu_n = \frac{N_{n-1}\mu_{n-1} + N_n \overline{X}_n}{N_{n-1} + N_n} \qquad (2.9)$$

which is nothing else but the definition of a cumulative sequential average.

One can easily rearrange relationship 2.9 to write[24]

$$\mu_n = \mu_{n-1} + \frac{N_n}{N_{n-1} + N_n}(\overline{X}_n - \mu_{n-1}) \qquad (2.10)$$

The similarity between relationships 2.10 and 1.1 is striking, when one substitutes y for μ, k for $N_n/(N_{n-1}+N_n)$, and x for $\overline{X}_n$. In the case of a random variable assumed to be normally distributed, all that Bayesian inference does is to substitute the variable term $N_n/(N_{n-1} + N_n)$ for the constant k. In other words, the elasticity of expectations becomes time-varying, which is a step forward. However, as the total number of observations grows, it converges towards 0, since

$$\lim_{N_{n-1} \to +\infty} \frac{N_n}{N_{n-1} + N_n} = 0 \qquad (2.11)$$

which is at least two steps backward.

If, in the case of a normally distributed variable, Bayesian inference seems to be an unduly long roundabout to reintroduce a muted form of adaptive expectations by the backdoor, so be it! This is not to mention the fact that the underlying assumption that underpins Bayesian learning is that there exists a true, stationary distribution, which only quietly awaits to be discovered by perceptive economic agents. Yet, in our world, uncertainty is arguably the rule, and risk the exception. Or to borrow Knight's words; "It is a world of change in which we live, and a world of uncertainty."

Moreover, while it does take time to learn through Bayesian inference, that is, the time needed to collect new evidence, a close examination of relationship 2.10 shows that time is in fact absent from it. The sequential order of both the N_{n-1} prior observations and the N_n new observations is simply irrelevant. Both samples can be reshuffled in any arbitrary order without having any impact on the value of the posterior mean μ_n. Everything happens as if all observations were given simultaneously to the observing agent. This crucial observation remains valid even in more sophisticated forms of Bayesian inference, such as recursive least squares learning, which theorists present as the ultimate form of rational learning.

2.8   Rational Learning, Recursive Ordinary Least Squares, and 1990s Adaptive Expectations

Thanks to its parsimony, the normal distribution is useful to highlight the basic mechanisms involved in Bayesian inference. That said, Bayesian inference encompasses much more than the mere updating of the normal distribution's parameters. Under the umbrella of Bayesian inference, one finds more or less complex algorithms that process new information and update preexisting knowledge in a systematic way.

This generic concept underpins the idea of rational learning, which is meant to complete the REH by providing an explicit model of how agents learn from available data.

Under the rational learning assumption, economic agents use an ordinary linear regression model to form their expectations. In other words, they all use the same linear combination of $m - 1$ explanatory variables (m with the constant) to predict the variable of interest. The vector β consisting of the m coefficients of this linear combination is estimated through ordinary least squares (OLS). If needed, please see proof C.5, p. 285, for a remainder of the formulation and proof of this classic estimation problem, the well-known solution of which is

$$\beta_{n-1} = (X_{n-1}^T X_{n-1})^{-1} X_{n-1}^T Y_{n-1} \qquad (2.12)$$

Of course, the coefficients estimated at a given point $n - 1$ in time depend on the observations Y_{n-1} and X_{n-1} available up to this time. Ex ante, one can never rule out that new observations would yield different estimates of the regression coefficients. In fact, parameter drift is the rule rather than the exception. This is where rational learning and recursive OLS linear regression step in by assuming that economic agents update their estimates of the regression coefficients whenever a new data point becomes available.

This exercise leads to the following recursive relationship between successive estimates of the regression coefficients

$$\beta_n = \beta_{n-1} + K_n(y_n - x_n\beta_{n-1}) \qquad \text{see C.5, p. 285} \qquad (2.13)$$

in which

$$x_n = \begin{pmatrix} x_{1n} & x_{2n} & \cdots & \cdots & x_{(m-1)n} & 1 \end{pmatrix} \qquad (2.14)$$

and

$$K_n = \frac{(X_{n-1}^T X_{n-1})^{-1} x_n^T}{1 + x_n(X_{n-1}^T X_{n-1})^{-1} x_n^T} \qquad (2.15)$$

The term K_n is called the *gain*. Of course, to compute β_n, according to relationship 2.12, one could directly compute $(X_n^T X_n)^{-1} X_n^T Y_n$. However, such a computation would require handling all the data in the sample (the n observations) at each new step, that is, increasingly large matrices. In contrast, only the last observations are needed to compute 2.15 and 2.13, assuming that $(X_{n-1}^T X_{n-1})^{-1}$ has been previously computed. Since X_{n-1} and X_{n-1}^T are, respectively, $(n-1) \times m$ and $m \times (n-1)$ matrices, $(X_n^T X_n)^{-1}$ is an $m \times m$ matrix; hence, its size is independent of the number of observations. As for x_n and x_n^T, they are, respectively, $1 \times m$ and $m \times 1$ vectors. It follows that $x_n (X_n^T X_{n-1})^{-1} x_n^T$ is a scalar and K_n an $m \times 1$ vector.

Besides being more economical to compute, relationship 2.13 also highlights the role played by new information in the updating process of the prior knowledge represented by the vector β_{n-1}. The term $y_n - x_n \beta_{n-1}$, which is a 1×1 vector, represents indeed the forecasting error observed in n, since y_n is the actual outcome and $x_n \beta_{n-1}$ the forecast made under the assumption that the coefficients estimated in $n-1$ are still valid in n. In other words, the posterior knowledge is equal to the prior one plus a fraction of the forecasting error. One can demonstrate that recursive OLS linear regression is a restricted form of the Kalman filter.[25] It is interesting to compare relationships 2.13 and 1.1 while bearing in mind the equivalence between notations displayed in table 2.2.

The two relationships have very similar structures, the main difference being that with recursive OLS linear regression, the gain is not constant, but time-varying. This being said, time remains in fact absent from this updating process. As long as y_i and x_i remain on the same line, the lines of the vector Y_{n-1} and of the matrix X_{n-1} (the observations available up to $n-1$) can be reshuffled in any arbitrary vertical order without having any impact on β_{n-1} (the coefficients estimated in $n-1$). To put it differently, economic agents are implicitly assumed to process and to give the same weight to all available data, even those

TABLE 2.2
Equivalence Table

	Exponential average	Recursive OLS linear regression
Prior	y_{n-1}	β_{n-1}
Forecast	y_{n-1}	$x_n \beta_{n-1}$
Fresh information	x_n	y_n, x_n
Forecasting error	$x_n - y_n$	$y_n - x_n \beta_{n-1}$
Gain	k	K_n
Posterior	y_n	β_n

collected long before the beginning of their lifetime. One can easily question the plausibility of this rather strong assumption.

It is to address this criticism that scholars have suggested to embed forgetting[26] in recursive OLS linear regression.[27] This they achieve by introducing an exponential weighting in the function to be minimized (the loss function). Instead of minimizing the sum of the squared residuals, the problem becomes one of minimizing their exponentially weighted sum, which gives greater weight to the more recent residuals.

$$S_{n-1}^k = \sum_{i=0}^{n}(1-k)^i \epsilon_{n-i}^2 = \epsilon_n^2 + (1-k)\epsilon_{n-1}^2 + \cdots + (1-k)^{n-1}\epsilon_1^2$$

$$(2.16)$$

with $0 < k < 1$.

One can easily prove that this formulation leads to substituting exponential averages, variances, and covariances for arithmetic ones in the formulation of the coefficients $(c_1, c_2, \ldots, c_m)$, the same arbitrarily chosen forgetting factor being applied to the dependent variable and all the independent variables (see proof C.6, p. 289). Once again, it looks somewhat as if adaptive expectations were stealthily reintroduced by the backdoor, a fact at least partially acknowledged by Sargent, who calls recursive OLS linear regression with forgetting "1990s adaptive expectations."

2.9   One Model?

The starting point of the REH is hardly controversial: everybody agrees that economic agents do—or at least should do—their best to exploit all available information. But, its final destination and conclusions are not immune from many relevant critiques, even if—or maybe because—the Royal Swedish Academy of Sciences awarded the Nobel Prize in Economic Sciences in 1995 to Lucas "for having developed and applied the hypothesis of rational expectations, and thereby having transformed macroeconomic analysis and deepened our understanding of economic policy."[28]

Interestingly, in its citation, the Royal Swedish Academy seemed to be willing to defuse a potential critique by watering down the REH with the following comment: "The REH does not imply that all agents have the same information, or that all agents know the 'true' economic model."

It seems hard to reconcile this comment with the various texts we have quoted above. In fact, nothing seems further away from the truth. If John Kay is to be believed, here is how Sargent—another REH theorist and 2011 Nobel laureate—replied, when asked if differences among people's models mattered: "The fact is you simply cannot talk about their differences within the typical rational expectations model. There is a communism of models. All agents within the model, the econometricians and God share the same model."[29]

Notwithstanding Muth's claim that the REH is not normative, but simply descriptive, Sargent's words have a definite normative, not to say totalitarian, tone. What initially looked as a show of modesty on the part of economists turns out to be a show of false modesty. The assumption that all agents use the same model is the easiest to criticize, for it immediately begs the following question: Which model? As one would "expect," the answer is, of course, the model constructed by the advocates of the REH according to "the relevant economic theory," to quote Muth once again. Sadly, there is no such thing as the relevant economic theory. Instead, there is a persistent conflict between different theories. Although it was written almost seventy years ago, Rist's brilliant chapter *Le conflit des théories des crises* is still an interesting read, if only because it is humble.[30] Even then, exogenous explanations of cyclical fluctuations—not yet called real business cycle theories—conflicted with endogenous explanations, which in turn disagreed about the causes of business cycles.

The simple model that we borrowed from Malinvaud contains a number of more or less explicit assumptions that are easy to challenge. For example, is the money supply really exogenous? Is the concept of real money balances the appropriate one to measure the demand for money? Why ignore potential changes in the velocity of money? Why assume that the relevant relationships are linear in their variables? And so on.

Much closer to us, the European sovereign debt crisis provides an interesting example of conflicting models of debt dynamics: while the public debt-to-GDP ratio is at the center of politicians and policymakers' analysis and communication, the cross-country structure of sovereign spreads indicates that market participants focus much more on public debt–to–tax revenues ratios. This is not a minor difference: in the first model, governments are implicitly assumed to own national income (probably because they can tax it); in the second one, their financial position is assessed through the lens of corporate finance!

2.10   How Complex a Model?

The existence of a model that agents use to form expectations seems to be more of an academic ideal than an accurate description of the real world. Malinvaud notes that, simple—if not simplistic—as it may seem, the model that he gives as an example is nevertheless representative of the models used by RE theorists. Indeed, the model discussed by Sargent and Wallace in *Rational Expectations and the Theory of Economic Policy* is hardly more elaborate than Malinvaud's example.[31] By their own admission, even the most prominent economists struggle with the mathematics of the more complex models. The extent to which central banks are incorporating RE in their own models seems at best incomplete, if not tentative: it is often limited to assuming that economic agents' inflation expectations are equal to the central banks' inflation targets. Yes, of course! But who would expect a central bank to construct a model assuming that its policy is not credible?

In terms of operational models, the REH has promised much more than it has actually delivered. This notwithstanding, it has remained the ruling paradigm, at least until the outbreak of the subprime crisis in 2007, for this crisis has challenged the belief that markets are rational and cannot deviate much and for long from fundamental value. As Edmund Phelps put it,[32] "The lesson the crisis teaches, though it is not yet grasped, is that there is no magic in the market: the expectations underlying asset prices cannot be 'rational' relative to some known and agreed model since there is no such model."

2.11   Internal Contradiction

Ironically, the REH would be less vulnerable if it allowed for competition between different models. For, as highlighted by Arrow, if all agents use the same model, an insurmountable internal contradiction presents itself, particularly in the case of financial markets:[33]

But if all individuals are alike, why do they not make the same choice? ... In macroeconomic models involving durable assets, especially securities, the assumption of homogeneous agents implies that there will never be any trading, though there will changes in prices.

This dilemma is intrinsinc. If agents are all alike, there is really no room for trade.... But if agents are different in unspecifiable ways, then ... very few, if any, inferences can be made ... identical individuals do not trade. Models of the securities markets based on homogeneity of individuals would imply zero trade.

If not all economic agents are alike, various modes of expectations formation can and must coexist, thus creating a set of permanently heterogeneous expectations. Within these various modes of expectations formation, one is likely to be dominant, one is likely to shape the so-called consensus and to drive the behavior of a majority of agents, if not in terms of headcount at least in terms of income or wealth. Whether this dominant mode of expectations formation is rational is not a theoretical question to be answered a priori on the basis of logical consistency. It is an empirical question that can only be addressed through the test of compatibility with data.

2.12   Rational Adaptive Expectations

We can nevertheless infer that rational expectations are unlikely to be the dominant form of expectations. With Lucas's insistence that there is no room for rational expectations in an uncertain world, we have already encountered one strong reason for their scope to be limited. With Sargent and Wallace's case that if inflation happens to feed back into money creation, it can be rational to form adaptive inflation expectations, we encounter a second reason to further limit the scope for rational expectations.[34] Keen as they clearly are to, so to say, take over adaptive expectations by proving that it can be rational to form such expectations in the presence of interdependent variables, Sargent and Wallace give in fact, albeit inadvertently, a very strong reason to extend the scope for adaptive expectations in a kind of reverse takeover. For interdependence between variables (such as money and inflation), on the one hand, and endogenous money creation, on the other, is not—contrary to what they conjecture with a lot of restraint—an exceptional situation only encountered during periods of hyperinflation, but rather what economics is all about.[35]

2.12.1　*Falsifiability and Compatibility with Data*

That, considering the pervasiveness of uncertainty and interdependence in economics, it seems "rational" to limit the scope for rational expectations exempts neither the advocates nor the critics of the REH from the test of compatibility with data. Sadly, this is easier said than done.

For endogenous expectations raise some serious methodological difficulties, when it comes to testing the relevance of RE models: indeed, can the REH be falsified? Since rational expectations cannot be observed directly (for they have an impact on the forecasted variables and are supposed to be formed in exactly the same way as variables are determined in an economic model of the economy), "how do we ever discover," asks Blaug, "whether the REH theory is true or not?"[36]

According to Blaug, the REH is a proposition, which cannot be proved wrong; hence, it is not a scientific proposition.

This difficulty probably contributes to fostering the impression that, on rational expectations as on many other issues, economists can only agree to disagree over issues of empirical methodology. Acrimonious disagreements persist about the extent to which this theory is compatible with available data. Screpanti and Zamagni blame the new classical economics for its "ability to ignore constant attacks from empirical research."[37] The advocates of the REH claim, of course, that its degree of compatibility with data is high. Its critics, be they Keynesian or not, retort that they are not convinced, on the ground that RE theorists indulge in excessive calibration of parameters.

One of the features of RE models is indeed their lack of parsimony. They tend to contain many parameters, for example, to account for the lagged effects of a given variable on another one. This great number of parameters facilitates getting fits that are statistically good but neither easy to interpret nor economically meaningful. With many parameters to calibrate, goes the criticism, it is almost impossible not to fit the data. This calibration problem is exacerbated when Bayesian learning leads, as new data become available, to an almost continuous revision of the estimated values of the parameters.

This being said, many tests of the policy neutrality hypothesis, one of the main implications of the REH, have been carried out by RE theorists, largely with negative results, according to Blaug, Malinvaud, and Woodford, to name but a few.[38] However, Blaug qualifies this empirical refutation by stressing the fact that these tests may not be conclusive, for it is impossible to isolate the rational expectations hypothesis from joint assumptions.[39] In the absence of absolutely unambiguous empirical conclusions, it is quite legitimate to consider that the problem of expectations remains unsolved and to look for alternative theories, as suggested by Woodford:[40] "The macroeconomics of the future ... will have to go beyond conventional late-twentieth-century methodology ... by making the formation and revision of expectations an object of analysis in its own right."

2.12.2   *Policy Implications*

That the issue of expectations remains unsettled is further evidenced by the fact that some of the REH's policy implications, such as the alleged possibility to fight inflation without causing a slowdown in the economy, have not been verified, at least in the United States and in the United Kingdom in the early 1980s. In the same vein, almost three years into the European sovereign debt crisis, one can doubt that economic agents are rational enough to let themselves be guided by the Ricardian equivalence, according to which since fiscal austerity now implies less taxes in the future, they should save less now, thus offsetting the deflationary impact of fiscal austerity. If anything, the exact opposite seems to be happening. The way episodes of hyperinflation have come to a sudden end in Germany, Austria, Hungary, and Poland in 1923–24, following changes in fiscal and monetary policy, is often presented as proof that credible policy announcements can "break" allegedly rational inflation expectations and instantly create a new set of rational expectations. The same historical facts can nevertheless be explained within an adaptive expectations framework: one just needs to assume that toward the end of a hyperinflation episode, as we shall see in chapters 4 and 7 of this book, the elasticity of expectations with respect to observed inflation is close to 1, so that the slightest slowdown in actual inflation, induced by some effective and persistent change in fiscal and monetary policy, is powerful enough to turn the tide and to trigger a fall in inflation expectations.

2.12.3   Conclusion

What, in the end, should we make of the REH? Its limited methodological relevance when it comes to modeling observed economic behavior is probably the most important point to bear in mind. Its relevance is limited:

- First, by the pervasive presence of uncertainty in our world.
- Second, by its reluctance to consider nonlinear relationships between economic variables.
- Third, by the fact that it is "rational" to form adaptive expectations when economic variables are interdependent, which is generally the case.

What about the policy relevance of the REH? It seems somewhat immoderate to claim, as Lucas did in his Nobel lecture, that[41] "the main finding that emerged from the research of the 1970's is that anticipated changes in money growth have very different effects from unanticipated changes."

Even though generals are known to have a propensity to prepare for the latest war they have fought, the idea that any strategy becomes ineffective as soon as the enemy can easily anticipate it has been at the core of military thinking for centuries. Actually, even early economists, such as Cantillon in 1755, were conscious of the fact that the effectiveness of monetary policy—the increase or decrease in the denomination of coins as it happened—depended on whether such decisions were officially announced or implemented without warning. To reach, on one hand, the conclusion that a deflationary policy ordering the lowering of the écu from 5 to 4 livres over a period of 20 months (i.e., a monthly depreciation of 1.11 percent), as a Royal Arrêt did in France in 1714, will prompt borrowers to make haste to pay back their debts and lenders to offer loans on generous terms, or to reach, on the other hand, the conclusion that such behaviors will fail to materialize if the diminution of coins is "made suddenly, without warning," one does not need to assume that all agents are forming rational expectations in all circumstances.

Somehow, the REH has never managed to convince those economists having a first-hand experience of financial markets. The

REH's failure to convince practitioners is well illustrated, for example, by Roger Bootle's following comments:[42]

> The financial world has not yet adjusted to the current reality of low inflation, let alone to the possibility of falling prices. . . . This is because it does not expect the currently low rates of inflation to continue.
>
> Indeed, the very word "expectation," which is so common in markets as well as in academic and policy circles, fails to capture the state of mind of investors. They do not really "expect" anything. Rather, they operate with a normal presumption and then add something for protection against an outbreak from normality.
>
> Why are financial markets so slow to recognize the collapse of inflation which is now so evident to many business people and consumers? The short answer is because in trying to look forwards, they always start by looking back.
>
> After 15 years working in the financial markets, I have come to believe that there is something strange about the way financial markets form their expectations.
>
> Market practitioners are trapped by the impossibility of knowing the future. Financial institutions frequently invest in financial instruments with a life of 20 to 30 years. Yet how can anyone begin to know what the world will be like in 20 years' time . . . ?
>
> Market practitioners deal with this problem in two related ways. First, they assume that although the instrument itself is long lived, they can dispose of it when they wish by selling it to someone else.
>
> Secondly, they try to assess the future by looking at the past. What the market appears to do is to go back perhaps 15–25 years, to form a basic assumption about the norm, and then they modify it by giving special weight to very recent experience and current levels. Why 15–25 years? There is no logical reason, but the explanation may be because this corresponds to the working lives of the senior people and the living memory of just about everyone in the markets. This history forms the markets' expectational hinterland.
>
> When you put these two methods of dealing with uncertainty together, they begin to make more sense. If the owner of an asset expects to sell it at some point in the immediate future, it is not of key relevance how the market will perform over 20 years. What he or she needs is some assurance that it will trade well in the immediate

future, in relation to what was paid for it, even though at that point in the immediate future, the far future which is relevant to the asset over the whole of its life will be just as uncertain as it is now.

Each investor can do this by adopting conventional assumptions about valuation. ... This is essentially the view propounded by the great economist John Maynard Keynes. ... But this view of market behavior has the same penetrating relevance today as it did then.

"Expectations" which are formed in this way may be believed, but they do not have to be. They are used in the formation of market prices because they are useful. What makes them useful is that others use them. They can be thought of, if you like, rather as a form of currency.

But when expectations are formed in this "conventional" way, they are difficult to dislodge. The mere passage of time may eat away at them as the convention comes to seem more and more incongruous when set against current reality. But this can be a very long process.

It isn't only the markets, which are affected by conventional expectations. The monetary authorities are also drawn in, for they set interest rates at levels which seem appropriate given the level of inflation expectations in the market.

Be that as it may, as the REH established its rule on the academic world in the 1960s, attempts to describe expectations within an adaptive framework became a nonstarter for anyone with ambitions for a successful academic carrier. The REH managed to be influential enough to eclipse a major contribution made in 1965 by Maurice Allais. That Allais's contribution has been overshadowed is clearly illustrated by the fact that the economists who should have shown greatest interest in Allais's works—such as critics of the REH and advocates of "bounded rationality"—do not seem to be aware of them, as shown by Simon's following comment, a comment made in 1997:[43]

To a certain extent, but not within the formal theory, macroeconomics ... today does incorporate executives' expectations about the future. But it has little to say about how such expectations are formed except when it claims, implausibly, that entrepreneurs carry around in their heads neoclassical models of the economic system, and thereby form their expectations "rationally."

PART TWO

Allais's Theory of "Expectations" Under Uncertainty

THE HRL FORMULATION we are going to present in part II of this book, and to transpose in Part III to financial behavior, is originally one element of Allais's theory of monetary dynamics. To fully appreciate what the HRL formulation is liable to bring to the modeling of financial behavior, it is necessary to give an overview of Allais's theory of monetary dynamics. This is not a minor challenge since it implies summarizing 50 years of research and a 1300-page book in a few pages.[1] Since this exercise is meant to be an overview, it will be limited to presenting Allais's assumptions and conclusions; the sometimes long proofs leading from the former to the latter are given at the end of this book (in any case, all these proofs are gathered in *Fondements de la dynamique monétaire*). Nevertheless, in a few instances (e.g., formulation of elasticities), this book presents brief original demonstrations in its main text to facilitate the understanding of some aspects of Allais's theory of monetary dynamics.

In the course of this exercise, we are going to meet Cagan's work on hyperinflation.[2] Allais and Cagan worked independently of each other. But, at the same point in time (1953–54), it happened that their respective research efforts converged. Both used the same mathematical formulation, namely, exponential averages, to model the argument of their respective demand for money functions. But they later parted ways, as Allais was led to his HRL formulation thanks to his analysis of the shortcomings of simple exponential averages.

As Cagan's work is a reference in the English-speaking world and as Allais's HRL formulation can be considered to be an enhancement of their mid-1950s common approach, it will be useful, too, to compare the HRL formulation with Cagan's formulation.[3] When inflation becomes high relative to real growth, Allais's model becomes indeed a hyperinflation model liable to be directly compared with Cagan's model.

Allais's seminal economic experience was the Great Depression, which he witnessed as a student during an internship in the United States in 1932–33, when he was aged 21. He was so shocked by what he then saw—"large quantities of unemployed resources when so many human wants were left unsatisfied"—that he set for himself the objective of understanding the mechanisms at work in such circumstances.

This objective led Allais to construct step by step a set of analytical tools, which constitute a very original, structured, and comprehensive contribution to dynamic monetary macroeconomics, a construction that is not Keynesian, monetarist, or neoclassical. The HRL formulation of the demand for money is only one of these tools, albeit probably the most important one. Allais's contributions to monetary macroeconomics can be classified in six blocks, three of them being logically independent of the HRL formulation of the demand for money:

- The establishment—through the aggregation of the cash flow statements of individual businesses—of the accounting identities linking, in static terms, nominal macroeconomic variables, including transactions on securities, bank credit, and money (chapter 3).
- The endogenous generation of cyclical fluctuations in aggregate nominal spending by a stylized model in which the driving factor is the gap between the supply of and the demand for money, both of them being nonlinear, bounded, but analytically not specified functions, the former increasing, the latter decreasing with respect to nominal growth (chapter 3).
- The HRL formulation of the demand for money, according to which the ratio of desired money-to-aggregate nominal spending is a logistic decreasing function of the present value of past growth rates in nominal spending (chapter 4).
- The fundamental equation of monetary dynamics(FEMD), which introduces the gap between desired and effective money balances in the differential expression of the Newcomb-Fisher equation of exchanges and shows this gap to be the factor explaining the variability of money velocity (chapter 5).

- The HRL formulation of monetary dynamics, which analyzes the various theoretical types of endogenous fluctuations in aggregate nominal spending that the fundamental equation of monetary dynamics can generate, when the demand for and the supply of money are assumed to obey the HRL formulation (chapter 5).
- The simultaneous testing of the compatibility of both the HRL formulation of the demand for money and the fundamental equation of monetary dynamics with empirical data (chapter 6).

CHAPTER THREE

Macrofoundations of Monetary Dynamics

IT IS MOST MEANINGFUL that Allais's first foray in monetary macroeconomics[1] consisted in laying its foundations on a set of comprehensive accounting identities that link exchanges of goods and services, securities transactions, and, last but not least, bank credit (and therefore money creation).[2] How he did that is even more telling. In contrast to Kalecki and Keynes, Allais's methodology is a "bottom-up" one, in which macroaggregates are derived from the summation of microdata, namely, of what corporate finance knows as the cash flow statement (or the statement of sources and applications of funds) of a given business. His methodology is also a gradual one: it starts with the deceptively simple case of a two-sector (businesses and households) closed economy, but it can be easily broadened to encompass a government sector and the rest of the world.[3]

3.1 Static Analysis: Comprehensive Macroeconomic Identities

Innocuous as it may seem, this accounting framework lends itself to rigorously clarifying controversial issues such as the relationship between investment and saving, forced investment as well as the crucial difference between savings and hoarding. All that is needed is a few clear assumptions, definitions, and elementary algebra.

Allais starts with the following assumptions:

- There are only two sectors in the economy: the business sector and the households sector (there is no government, nor any foreign sector).

- The business sector consists of n industrial and commercial businesses, p commercial banks, and one central bank.
- Total business sales are the sum of final consumption, intermediate consumption, and business investment.
- Households are assumed not to carry any investment activity (or, to put it differently, households' investment–like residential investment–is aggregated with business investment).
- All transactions are paid in cash: there is no such thing as trade credit.
- The money supply M is equal to the total assets of the banking sector: it is equal to the loans made by commercial banks L and by the central bank L'; it consists of currency M_M (money issued by the central bank) and bank deposits M_S; it is held by households M_{hh} or businesses M_b.

From the assumptions pertaining to bank credit and money, it follows that

$$M = L + L' = M_M + M_S = M_b + M_{hh} \qquad (3.1)$$

For each individual industrial and commercial business j, for any time period T between t and $t + T$, the aggregate application of funds must be equal to the aggregate source of funds, as shown in table 3.1.

TABLE 3.1
Cashflow Statement of Business j

Applications of funds	Source of funds
Purchases of goods and services PUR^j	Sales of goods and services REV^j
Investments I^j	
Wages W^j	
Dividend paid out DIV$_o^j$	Dividend received DIV$_i^j$
Interest paid out INT$_o^j$	Interest received INT$_i^j$
Securities amortization A_o^j	Securities amortized A_i^j
Securities bought SEC$_o^j$	Securities sold SEC$_i^j$
Change in cash balances dM^j	New loans from commercial banks dL^j
	New loans from the central bank dL'^j
Total applications of funds $D^j + dM^j$	Total source of funds $R^j + dL^j + dL'^j$

The budget constraint is expressed as follows:

$$\text{REV}^j + \text{DIV}_i^j + \text{INT}_i^j + A_i^j + \text{SEC}_i^j + dL^j + dL'^j$$
$$= \text{PUR}^j + I^j + W^j + \text{DIV}_o^j + \text{INT}_o^j + A_o^j + \text{SEC}_o^j + dM^j \quad (3.2)$$

Let us now turn to the cash flow statement of a commercial bank. Like any other business, a commercial bank pays wages, buys goods for intermediate consumption, invests, receives and pays interest and dividends, etc. Therefore, for the most part, the cash flow statement of a commercial bank presents itself as that of an industrial or commercial business. The one and only, but notable, difference is the position of loans and deposits. It is symmetrical to the position they have in the cash flow statement of a nonbank business. For banks, deposits are a source of funds and loans are an application of funds.

For each bank, we have

$$dL^k = dM_S^k \quad (3.3)$$

and for all banks

$$\sum_{k=1}^{p} dL^k = \sum_{j=1}^{n} dL^j = dL = dM_S \quad (3.4)$$

The same holds true for the central bank. The currency it issues is a source of funds, while the loans it makes are an application of funds.

$$\sum_{j=1}^{n} dL'^j = dL' = dM_M \quad (3.5)$$

Now, if we sum all the loans made by the p commercial banks and the central bank, we measure a quantity that is exactly equal to the money issued by the banking system, be it in the form of deposits or currency.

$$dL + dL' = dM = dM_M + dM_S \quad (3.6)$$

For any item on the cash flow statement of the business sector we can easily compute aggregate quantities; for example, total wages W_b are obtained by summing the wages paid out by the n businesses and the $p + 1$ banks:

$$W_b = \sum_{j=1}^{n} W^j + \sum_{k=1}^{p+1} W^k \quad (3.7)$$

We can easily repeat this exercise for each source and application of funds, as shown in table 3.2. However, for the banking system, the same quantity dM is bound to appear twice, once as an application of funds as $dL + dL'$ and another time as a source of funds as $dM_M + dM_S$. Its presence on both sides of the aggregate cash-flow statement of the banking system does not bring any information as regards the transactions conducted by the business sector as a whole. Therefore, it should be neglected. The only information we need as regards loans and deposits relates to the business sector excluding banks.

For the business sector as a whole, the budget constraint will therefore be formulated as follows:

$$\mathrm{REV}_b + \mathrm{DIV}_{i(b)} + \mathrm{INT}_{i(b)} + A_{i(b)} + \mathrm{SEC}_{i(b)} + dL_b + dL'_b$$
$$= \mathrm{PUR}_b + I_b + W_b + \mathrm{DIV}_{o(b)} + \mathrm{INT}_{o(b)} + A_{o(b)}$$
$$+ \mathrm{SEC}_{o(b)} + dM_b \tag{3.8}$$

This accounting identity expresses the budget constraint of the business sector (including the banking sector) in a closed monetary economy with no government.

The aggregate income of households INC_{hh} is the sum of wages and net capital income:

$$\mathrm{INC}_{hh} = W_b + (\mathrm{INT}_{o(b)} - \mathrm{INT}_{i(b)}) + (\mathrm{DIV}_{o(b)} - \mathrm{DIV}_{i(b)}) \tag{3.9}$$

TABLE 3.2
Cashflow Statement of the Business Sector in a Closed Economy with No Government

Applications of funds	Source of funds
Purchases of goods and services PUR_b	Sales of goods and services REV_b
Investments I_b	
Wages W_b	
Dividend paid out $\mathrm{DIV}_{o(b)}$	Dividend received $\mathrm{DIV}_{i(b)}$
Interest paid out $\mathrm{INT}_{o(b)}$	Interest received $\mathrm{INT}_{i(b)}$
Securities amortization $A_{o(b)}$	Securities amortized $A_{i(b)}$
Securities bought $\mathrm{SEC}_{o(b)}$	Securities sold $\mathrm{SEC}_{i(b)}$
Change in cash balances dM_b	New loans from commercial banks dL_b
	New loans from the central bank dL'_b
Total applications of funds $D_b + dM_b$	Total source of funds $R_b + dL_b + dL'_b$

The aggregate consumption of households C_{hh} is equal to the difference between total business sales on one hand and intermediate consumption and business investment on the other hand.

$$C_{hh} = \mathrm{REV}_b - \mathrm{PUR}_b - I_b \tag{3.10}$$

Household savings are equal to the difference between household income and household consumption:

$$\mathrm{SAV}_{hh} = \mathrm{INC}_{hh} - C_{hh} \tag{3.11}$$

To see how households allocate their aggregate savings, we just need to bear in mind that the sum of loans granted by commercial banks L_b and by the central banks L'_b is equal to the money supply M, which is in turn equal to the sum of the money balances held by the business sector M_b and by households M_{hh}.

$$L_b + L'_b = M = M_b + M_{hh} \tag{3.12}$$

From relationship 3.12, it immediately follows that we have

$$dL_b + dL'_b = dM = dM_b + dM_{hh} \tag{3.13}$$

and

$$dM_{hh} = dL_b + dL'_b - dM_b \tag{3.14}$$

Finally, the net sales of securities by the corporate sector are equal to the net purchases of securities by households.

$$\mathrm{SEC}_b = (A_{i(b)} - A_{o(b)}) + (\mathrm{SEC}_{i(b)} - \mathrm{SEC}_{o(b)}) = \mathrm{SEC}_{hh} \tag{3.15}$$

Now, if we rearrange the various terms in identity 3.8 by placing all those related to exchanges of goods and services to the left and all the others to the right, we get

$$[W_b + (\mathrm{INT}_{o(b)} - \mathrm{INT}_{i(b)}) + (\mathrm{DIV}_{o(b)} - \mathrm{DIV}_{i(b)})] - [\mathrm{REV}_b - \mathrm{PUR}_b - I_b]$$
$$= [(A_{i(b)} - A_{o(b)}) + (\mathrm{SEC}_{i(b)} - \mathrm{SEC}_{o(b)})] + dL_b + dL'_b - dM_b \tag{3.16}$$

By substituting identities 3.11, 3.14, and 3.15 in 3.16, we get

$$\mathrm{SAV}_{hh} = \mathrm{SEC}_b + dM_{hh} \tag{3.17}$$

an identity that shows that households savings are allocated between net investment in securities and increases (or decreases) in money balances. Admittedly, this is a rather intuitive identity, but it will lead us to interesting observations as regards the financing of business investment.

To this end, let us first define businesses' retained operating earnings (i.e., business savings) as follows:

$$CF_b = REV_b - PUR_b - W_b - (INT_{o(b)} - INT_{i(b)})$$
$$- (DIV_{o(b)} - DIV_{i(b)}) \tag{3.18}$$

Once again, we can rearrange the various terms in identity 3.8, this time by placing I_b alone on the left side and all the other terms on the right side, so that

$$I_b = [REV_b - PUR_b - W_b - (INT_{o(b)} - INT_{i(b)}) - (DIV_{o(b)} - DIV_{i(b)})]$$
$$+ [(A_{i(b)} - A_{o(b)}) + (SEC_{i(b)} - SEC_{o(b)}) + (dL_b + dL'_b - dM_b)] \tag{3.19}$$

By substituting identities 3.17 and 3.18 in 3.19, we get

$$I_b = CF_b + SAV_{hh} \tag{3.20}$$

an identity that shows that business investment is financed not only by household savings, but also by business savings—an element which the Keynesian relationship $I = S$ seemingly overlooks.

Keynes notwithstanding, as business investment is partly financed by business savings, the coordination between investment plans and savings plans is not the central issue it would be, were savings and investment decisions made by two totally distinct groups of economic agents.[4]

Identity 3.20 also sheds light on the Austrian monetary overinvestment theory. The thrust of this theory is that when bank credit is available under too-generous terms, it is liable to generate imbalances in both the size and the composition of the stock of productive capital.

The Austrian monetary theory of overinvestment considers a fiat monetary system. In such a system, the expansion of bank credit is potentially unfettered, even at full employment. The provision of credit by banks—on top of the loanable funds generated by savings—pushes interest rates below their equilibrium level, that is, below the level that would prevail if the supply of loanable funds were limited to voluntary savings. As interest rates are too low, some otherwise nonprofitable investment projects become profitable. Thanks to the credit they get from banks, entrepreneurs bid resources away from the consumer.

The Austrian theory of monetary overinvestment has been criticized by Keynesian economists as "contentious, complex and cast almost entirely in non operational terms."[5] In their mind, this applies in particular to the concept of "forced" investment and "forced" savings. But this is not quite true. For there is an easy and accurate way to measure the volume of forced investment and savings. Identity 3.20 can be reformulated as

$$I_b = \mathrm{CF}_b + \mathrm{SEC}_b + dM_{hh} \tag{3.21}$$

or, using relationship 3.14,

$$I_b = \mathrm{CF}_b + \mathrm{SEC}_b + (dL_b + dL'_b - dM_b) \tag{3.22}$$

which means that aggregate business investment is financed by three means:

- Retained corporate earnings.
- Funds raised through the sales of securities to households.
- The difference between new bank loans raised and new deposits held by the corporate sector.

There is a fundamental difference between the first two items—retained business earnings and funds raised through the sales of securities—and the third one. While the first two result from a voluntary transfer of pre-existing purchasing power from consumption to investment through savings, the third one is a net addition of fresh purchasing power created out of thin air by bank credit.

From identity 3.14, we know that the difference between the new bank loans raised and the new deposits held by the corporate sector is equal to the net increase in the deposits held by households. Alongside the funds invested in securities, these new cash balances are part of household savings. But in the absence of bank credit, they would not exist. Hence their name of "forced savings." The share of investment that is financed by them is called "forced investment."

The most interesting and somewhat counterintuitive insight of this analysis is that bank credit is a source of savings, as it inflates business spending and hence at least to a certain extent households' income. In other words, an alleged savings glut should in fact be traced back to a surfeit of bank credit.

The cash flow statement of the business sector can be summarized as follows:

$$D_b + dM_b = R_b + dL_b + dL'_b \tag{3.23}$$

Under our assumptions, the cash flow statement of the household sector is

$$D_{hh} + dM_{hh} = R_{hh} \tag{3.24}$$

Therefore, the cash flow statement of the whole economy is

$$D_b + D_{hh} + dM_b + dM_{hh} = R_b + R_{hh} + dL_b + dL'_b \tag{3.25}$$

Since

$$dM_b + dM_{hh} = dM = dL_b + dL'_b \tag{3.26}$$

we have

$$D_b + D_{hh} = R_b + R_{hh} \tag{3.27}$$

or

$$D = R_T \tag{3.28}$$

an identity that simply means that someone's disbursements are necessarily someone else's receipts. Intuitive as it is, this identity is rigorously demonstrated within Allais's macroaccounting framework.

Let us now turn to the hoarding issue. Like many of his predecessors, Keynes included, Allais finds two reasons to hold money balances:

- The first one is to bridge the time elapsing between outlays and receipts.
- The second one is to speculate on price differences through time and, above all, to hedge oneself against the risk of a fall in receipts (i.e., to hold a reserve for future contingencies).

To the first motive correspond transactions balances M_T and to the second one precautionary balances M_P. Therefore, the money supply can be split into two components

$$M = M_T + M_P \tag{3.29}$$

and we have

$$dM = dM_T + dM_P \qquad (3.30)$$

Identity 3.30 shows that hoarding, $dM_P > 0$, an increase in precautionary balances, or dishoarding, $dM_P < 0$, a decrease in precautionary balances can happen irrespective of the sign of dM. As a matter of fact, hoarding or dishoarding can occur even when the money supply is constant. It is totally distinct from the term dM_b in relationship 3.23 and dM_{bb} in relationship 3.24.

Neither Allais's accounting framework nor available statistical data make it possible to directly observe hoarding or dishoarding.[6] But Allais's framework lends itself to illustrating and analyzing the effects of hoarding (respectively dishoarding) on aggregate nominal spending D and on money velocity V.

The starting point is Newcomb-Fisher's equation of exchanges

$$M(t)V(t) = D(t) \qquad (3.31)$$

Let us assume that the money supply is constant:

$$\frac{dM}{dt} = 0 \qquad (3.32)$$

Then, from 3.30, we get

$$\frac{dM_T}{dt} = -\frac{dM_P}{dt} \qquad (3.33)$$

In other words, dishoarding, $dM_P < 0$, implies an increase in transaction balances, $dM_T > 0$. What is the impact of this increase in transaction balances on nominal spending D? To answer this question, we must introduce a distinction between the velocity of transaction balances V_T and the velocity of precautionary balances V_P.

Since precautionary balances are hoarded, their velocity V_P is equal to 0:

$$V_P = 0 \qquad (3.34)$$

Therefore, relationship 3.31 can be reformulated as

$$M_T(t)V_T(t) = D(t) \qquad (3.35)$$

Now, in the following period when dishoarding occurs, under the assumption that V_T remains constant, aggregate nominal spending is

$$D(t+dt) = \left[M_T(t) + \frac{dM_T}{dt}\right] V_T(t) = M_T(t)\,V_T(t) + \frac{dM_T}{dt}\,V_T(t)$$

(3.36)

or using 3.35,

$$D(t+dt) = D(t) + \frac{dM_T}{dt}\,V_T(t) \qquad (3.37)$$

Since $\frac{dM_T}{dt} > 0$, we have

$$D(t+dt) > D(t) \qquad (3.38)$$

One can see that an increase in transaction balances triggered by the dishoarding of precautionary balances causes aggregate nominal spending to rise, even if the supply of money is constant.

As for money velocity, since $M(t+dt) = M(t)$, we have

$$V(t+dt) = \frac{D(t) + \frac{dM_T}{dt}\,V_T(t)}{M(t)} = V(t) + \frac{1}{M}\frac{dM_T}{dt}\,V_T(t) \qquad (3.39)$$

Since $\frac{dM_T}{dt} > 0$, we have

$$V(t+dt) > V(t) \qquad (3.40)$$

An increase in transaction balances triggered by the dishoarding of precautionary balances causes money velocity to rise, once again even if the supply of money is constant.

This analysis shows that the velocity of transaction balances magnifies the impact of dishoarding on aggregate nominal spending: the net addition to nominal spending is indeed $\frac{dM_T}{dt}\,V_T(t)$, and not just $\frac{dM_T}{dt}$. This injection of fresh purchasing power is liable to increase demand on any market; absent additional information (e.g., on relative prices), there is no reason to believe that one specific market is the first natural destination of dishoarded balances. According to the Cantillon effect, dishoarding brings about successive but not necessarily even increases in investment, savings, employment, and consumption. Conversely, hoarding causes nominal spending and money velocity to fall. Hoarding is liable to impact investment as well as consumption. This brings us to the distinction between hoarding and savings. The question is whether hoarding is a form of savings.

Keynesian economists consider hoarding to be part of savings, as shown by Mark Blaug in the following comment:[7]

> When J. S. Mill defined savings as income not consumed by the person who saves it and hoarding as income not consumed at all, we can only infer that intended savings in the modern sense is equivalent to classical savings plus hoarding, because the excess of intended savings over intended investment in modern analysis produces the same economic effects as an increase of hoarding in classical economics.

Allais's accounting framework illustrates that there is indeed a fundamental difference between forgoing consumption to finance purchases of investment goods, be it directly or through investment in shares and bonds, on one hand, and cutting on all kinds of expenditures to hoard cash balances. In both cases, according to popular parlance, "money" is "set aside." But in the first case its allocation to investment reflects confidence in the future, while in the second one it expresses fear of it. Mixing up savings and hoarding, as Keynes did, illustrates the drawback of defining saving negatively as nonconsumption.[8]

With that, enough has been said to suggest that Allais's macroeconomics parts way with Keynesianism by rejecting an alleged imbalance between intended investment and intended savings as the cause of cyclical fluctuations in real income. Allais's focus is on nominal spending, the fluctuations of which he explains by monetary factors.

3.2 Generation of Endogenous Fluctuations in Nominal Spending Within a Nonlinear Framework

Fruitful as it is to prove or to refute certain relationships, a set of accounting identities between macroaggregates is nothing but an exercise in static analysis. It does identify necessary relationships between certain aggregates during a certain period of time. But it cannot explain their fluctuations through time.

With the three papers he presented between 1953[9] and 1955,[10] Allais moved logically in the realm of dynamic analysis, building upon the insights provided by his static analysis. These three papers—the

Innsbruck, Uppsala, and Paris papers—read very much like a research program and contain the seeds of all of Allais's theoretical contributions in the field of monetary dynamics during the following 50 years.

The common thrust of these three papers is as follows:

- First, to represent both the supply of and the demand for money with two monotonic bounded nonlinear functions, respectively, g and f, the former increasing, the latter decreasing with respect to economic agents' confidence.[11]
- Second, to explain fluctuations in aggregate nominal spending D by the difference $M - M_D$ between effective and desired money balances, that is, by hoarding and dishoarding.
- Third, to show that under these assumptions and even if the analytic form of the two functions f and g remains to be specified, the interaction between the monetary imbalance $M - M_D$ and nominal growth generates endogenous cycles akin to relaxation processes in physics, that is, cycles featuring delayed regulation.

In the context of this book, a review of the Innsbruck paper will suffice to drive home Allais's key insights.

With the Great Depression obviously in mind, Allais set himself the task of explaining situations in which prices and volumes fall or rise simultaneously, causing large fluctuations in aggregate nominal spending. He leaves aside other fluctuations in which prices and volumes in some sectors of the economy move in opposite directions. Classical economists were mainly concerned with fluctuations in prices; to this, Keynes substituted a concern for fluctuations in real income. With his focus on aggregate nominal spending, Allais's research agenda differs from both the classical and the Keynesian ones.

Having defined the ultimate objective of his research, Allais further defines intermediate ones. He does so by stating that a theory of fluctuations in aggregate nominal spending must be able to explain:

- Their persistence.
- The existence of an unstable equilibrium in the form of a limit cycle.
- Finally, the endogenous process, which generates these fluctuations (the difficulty being to explain the transition from growth to contraction).

Considering the Newcomb-Fisher equation of exchanges

$$D = MV \tag{3.41}$$

Allais observes that fluctuations in D can happen only if M or V fluctuates. In other words, two monetary factors—changes in the liquidity preference (the inverse of money velocity) and endogenous fluctuations in the money supply (changes in the multiplier of the monetary base)—are the sine qua non causes of fluctuations in aggregate nominal spending. Failing these two factors, aggregate nominal spending cannot fluctuate. Other factors may, of course, amplify the effects of these two monetary factors: for example, overinvestment in a certain sector may cause nonperforming bank loans to increase and prevent banks from further expanding their balance sheets.

More formally, with M being the money balances held by the public and M_D the balances they desire to hold, the difference $M - M_D = \frac{dM_T}{dt}$ represents hoarding or dishoarding during a certain period $T = dt$, assumed to be constant for the time being. As the aggregate spending of economic agents (households and businesses) during a certain period is equal to their receipts in the preceding period plus dishoarding (or minus hoarding), we have

$$TD(t+T) = TR_T(t) + M(t) - M_D(t) \tag{3.42}$$

where $D(t+T)$ and $R(t)$ represent the average expenditures and receipts, respectively, by unit of time during the period T. This period represents the average time lag between receipts and expenditures, that is, the time economic agents need to adjust their money balances. Following Allais, we shall call T the response period.

Now, since according to relationship 3.28, $D = R_T$, relationship 3.42 is equivalent to

$$D(t+T) - D(t) = \frac{1}{T}[M(t) - M_D(t)] \tag{3.43}$$

This equation is the fundamental equation, that, according to Allais in 1953, describes monetary dynamics. As an aside, let us note that relationships 3.42 and 3.43 both neglect new loans dM as a source of purchasing power available in period T. Let us also note that relationship 3.43 bears a strong resemblance to relationship 3.37, a relationship not given by Allais, but demonstrated in this book under the assumption of a constant money supply. Considered together, relations 3.43 and

3.37 suggest an equivalence between money velocity and the inverse of the response period, a proposition that Allais demonstrated in 1968. From the point of view of the genesis of theoretical propositions, it is fascinating and enlightening to observe that it took a mind as alert and creative as Allais's almost 15 years to identify this essential equivalence and to incorporate money creation in relationship 3.43.

Be that as it may, in 1953, Allais made some already significant steps forward by assuming that M and M_D are two monotonic bounded non-linear functions of x, the rate of growth in aggregate nominal spending:

$$x = \frac{1}{D}\frac{dD}{dt} \tag{3.44}$$

Allais did not even bother to specify the analytic expressions of these two functions. He simply assumed that the demand for money is commensurate with aggregate nominal spending

$$M_D = f(x)D \tag{3.45}$$

his Marshallian $k = f(x)$, so to say, being a monotonic, *decreasing,* bounded, non-linear function:

$$f'(x) < 0 \tag{3.46}$$

$$f_m < f(x) < f_M \tag{3.47}$$

$$\lim_{x \to -\infty} f'(x) = \lim_{x \to +\infty} f'(x) = 0 \tag{3.48}$$

As for the money supply, Allais assumed it to be a monotonic, *increasing,* bounded, and nonlinear function

$$M = g(x) \tag{3.49}$$

$$g'(x) > 0 \tag{3.50}$$

$$g_m < g(x) < g_M \tag{3.51}$$

$$\lim_{x \to -\infty} g'(x) = \lim_{x \to +\infty} g'(x) = 0 \tag{3.52}$$

That f should be decreasing and g increasing with respect to x is easy to justify by the observation that experience influences the behavior of economic agents. When the economy is perceived to be "doing well," that is, when aggregate nominal spending (and income) *has been* increasing $(x > 0)$, confidence tends to increase: banks are willing to lend, their clients are willing to borrow, and economic agents as a whole are more and more inclined to dishoard precautionary balances. The opposite happens when aggregate nominal spending has been contracting and confidence falls.

But why should the money supply function be bounded? Because, for a given level of base money, commercial banks are normally keen to maximize their revenues, subject to a liquidity constraint. It is not in their interest to hold idle cash balances and to leave some lending capacity unused: therefore, the base money multiplier has a lower bound. On the opposite side, when confidence is high, banks are normally careful not to overextend their balance sheets for fear of becoming too illiquid. Hence, there is an upper limit to the base money multiplier.

And why should the demand for money be bounded? Practical operational considerations justify the lower limit. Even in the extreme circumstances of hyperinflation, one needs some money balances to accomplish the elementary transactions required for day-to-day survival. At the other end of the spectrum, when confidence is very low, the desire to hoard precautionary balances cannot be unlimited. First, the ratio of capital (including money) to income is known to have an upper limit. Therefore, the ratio of money balances to income must have an upper limit, too. Secondly, while selling assets is the only way to raise cash in a contraction, the prices at which assets can be exchanged for money necessarily contain the potential selling pressure.

Under these assumptions, we can now describe the endogenous process whereby cyclical fluctuations are generated from any initial point. From relationships 3.43, 3.45, and 3.49 we get

$$M - M_D = g(x) - f(x)D \tag{3.53}$$

and

$$D(t+T) - D(t) = \frac{1}{T}\{g[x(t)] - D(t)f[x(t)]\} \tag{3.54}$$

with

$$x(t) = \frac{D(t) - D(t-T)}{TD(t-T)} \tag{3.55}$$

In a depression, relative desired money balances are close to their maximum, $f \approx f_M$, while the money supply is close to its minimum,

$g \approx g_m$. Any increase in nominal spending causes relative desired balances to fall and the money supply to increase:

$$x > 0 \Rightarrow df < 0, \qquad dg > 0 \tag{3.56}$$

As a result, the difference between effective and desired balances increases, which in turn causes aggregate spending to increase further at an accelerating rate. This self-reinforcing process exhausts itself when relative desired balances approach their minimum

$$f \rightarrow f_m \tag{3.57}$$

and the money supply tends toward its maximum

$$g \rightarrow g_M \tag{3.58}$$

The switch from expansion to contraction happens when $M - M_D$ falls below 0, which is bound to happen for the following reason. As the expansion continues, we have indeed

$$g - fD \rightarrow g_M - f_m D \tag{3.59}$$

where g_M and f_m are constant. As long as $g_M - f_m D > 0$, D keeps on growing, which implies that $g_M - f_m D$ keeps on decreasing until it falls below 0. When this happens, aggregate nominal spending starts to contract and the two functions f and g turn back: f increases again, while g decreases.

It is very easy to illustrate this endogenous cyclical process with a simple numerical example. In discrete time, relationship 3.54 becomes

$$D_{n+1} - D_n = \frac{1}{T}[g(x_n) - D_n f(x_n)] \tag{3.60}$$

with

$$x_n = \frac{D_n - D_{n-1}}{TD_{n-1}} \tag{3.61}$$

The hyperbolic tangent function is a monotonic, bounded, and nonlinear function, which can be used to represent relative desired balances[12]

$$f(x) = \tanh(-x) + 2 \Rightarrow f(0) = 2 \tag{3.62}$$

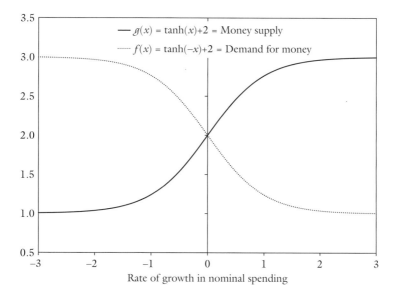

Figure 3.1 Stylized nonlinear model of monetary dynamics.

and the supply of money

$$g(x) = \tanh x + 2 \Rightarrow g(0) = 2 \qquad (3.63)$$

as shown in figure 3.1.

From 3.53, 3.62, and 3.63, it follows that, in stationary equilibrium, we have

$$D_e = \frac{g(0)}{f(0)} = 1 \qquad (3.64)$$

To run a simulation, one simply needs to initialize the recurrence equation 3.60, for example, with $D_1 = 1.02$ and $x_1 = 5\%$. The resulting paths depend on the value of T. For $T = 1.42$, a limit cycle exists, the period of which is 7.10 (see figure 3.2). For $T = 1.50$, one observes an aperiodic convergence toward a stable equilibrium, the pseudo-period being 7.50 (see figure 3.3).

As we have just seen, according to Allais's nonlinear model of cyclical fluctuations in nominal spending, their fundamental cause is the imbalance between effective and desired money balances. How can such a situation occur and how do economic agents cope with it? Leaving hyperinflation episodes aside for the moment, Allais assumes the supply of

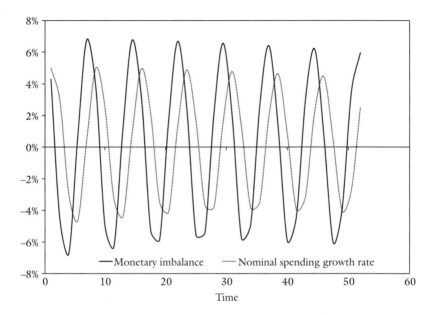

Figure 3.2 Endogenous fluctuations: example of a limit cycle.

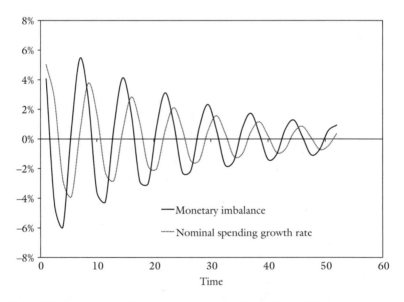

Figure 3.3 Endogenous fluctuations: example of a stable equilibrium.

money to be endogenous to the private sector, springing as it does from both the banks' willingness to lend and their clients' willingness to borrow. Yet, since the agents borrowing from the banks are not—at least to a large extent—the same as the ones holding deposits with these banks, it is to be expected that effective money balances do not match desired balances. Since effective balances can only change hands but cannot be reduced or increased by those holding them, it is through an adjustment of desired balances that the monetary imbalance is worked out.

If, for example, effective balances exceed desired balances, then economic agents will be in a dishoarding mode, that is, they will reduce precautionary balances so as to increase transactions balances. As a result, while aggregate nominal spending D will increase, *relative* desired balances—the function f—will decrease (the preference for liquidity will decrease or money velocity will increase). With a delay and up to a certain point, the increase in nominal spending will offset the decrease in the preference for liquidity, causing desired balances to increase in absolute terms and to converge toward effective balances. As we have seen earlier, this adjustment process will be all the more powerful as the system is further away from stationary equilibrium, that is, the closer the relative desired balances will be to their minimum f_m.

This is how desired balances are adjusted with respect to effective balances. To put it differently, while effective and desired balances are two clearly distinct quantities, they cannot part ways too much, and we have

$$M_D \approx M \qquad (3.65)$$

As we shall see in the rest of this book, the conjecture that effective balances, which are directly observable, are always very close in relative terms to desired balances, which are not directly observable, plays a crucial role in Allais's theory of monetary dynamics, especially in its application to empirical data.

To close this summary of Allais's Innsbruck paper, let us stress again that it already contains all the seeds that make Allais's contributions so original:

- The focus on fluctuations in aggregate nominal spending.
- The fundamental role played by the gap between effective and desired money balances, the difference between these two quantities being nevertheless small in relative terms.

- The existence of a response period during which economic agents seek to hoard or dishoard money balances.
- The endogenous nature of the money supply in normal circumstances.
- The instability of the money supply.
- The instability of the preference for liquidity (the variability of the velocity of money).
- The influence of past developments on economic agents' confidence.
- The bounded nonlinear response of economic agents with respect to their assessment of growth prospects.

As we shall see in the next three chapters, Allais's works in the field of monetary dynamics during the following fifty years have essentially aimed at elaborating on these fundamental principles and at confronting them with empirical data. Since Allais had reached this point in his research and given that desired balances are not directly observable, it was logical on his part to now concentrate his efforts on the formulation of the demand for money. This led him to his most seminal contribution: the HRL formulation of the demand for money, to which we now turn our attention.

CHAPTER FOUR

Microfoundations of Monetary Dynamics: The HRL Formulation of the Demand for Money

ALLAIS PRESENTED THE HRL formulation of the demand for money in 1965.[1] As said in the Introduction, although this HRL formulation can be interpreted as a general theory of expectations under uncertainty, Allais always refrained from calling it a theory of expectations, concerned as he was to stress that our "expectations" are in fact rooted in memory. Therefore, to be consistent with Allais's thinking, we must agree on the following semantic convention. We shall refer to the variables produced by the HRL formulation as being perceived as opposed to being "expected." We shall talk of perceived inflation (or return) instead of expected inflation (or return). When we nevertheless use the words "expectations" or "expected," it will always be within."

The HRL formulation assumes relative desired money balances to be a monotonic, decreasing, nonlinear, bounded (logistic) function of the present value of past growth rates in nominal spending (i.e., past inflation rates during hyperinflation episodes). Like Cagan, Allais had started to work on hyperinflation in the 1950s. Unlike Cagan, who built his model on inflation expectations, Allais assumed that the demand for money was a function of nominal growth "expectations."[2] Like Cagan, he assumed that "expectations" were formed adaptively and could be represented by an exponential average of the sequence of historic rates of nominal growth.[3]

But there are two equivalent ways to define an exponential average and two different ways to interpret it. As seen in chapter 1, p. 16 and with $e^{-r} = 1 - k$, the exponential average can be defined:

- Either in a cumulative way

$$y_n = \frac{\sum_{i=0}^{n} x_i e^{-(n-i)r}}{\sum_{i=0}^{n} e^{-(n-i)r}} \tag{4.1a}$$

$$= \frac{x_n + x_{n-1}e^{-1r} + \cdots + x_1 e^{-(n-1)r} + x_0 e^{-nr}}{1 + e^{-1r} + \cdots + e^{-(n-1)r} + e^{-nr}} \tag{4.1b}$$

- Or as a recursive difference[4]

$$y_n - y_{n-1} = (1 - e^{-r})(x_n - y_{n-1}) \approx r(x_n - y_{n-1}) \quad \text{for} \quad r \approx 0 \tag{4.2}$$

These two relationships can be written in discrete time, as we just did, or in continuous time.

$$y(t) = \frac{\int_{-\infty}^{t} x_\tau e^{-(t-\tau)r} d\tau}{\int_{-\infty}^{t} e^{-(t-\tau)r} d\tau} \tag{4.3}$$

$$\frac{dy}{dt} = (1 - e^{-r})(x - y) \approx r(x - y) \quad \text{for} \quad r \approx 0 \tag{4.4}$$

While the differential definition says, as suggested by Cagan, that "expectations" are formed through an error correction mechanism, the cumulative one states that expectations are the present value of past observations, as suggested by Allais. In both cases, the difficulty is to estimate the parameter r, which sets the elasticity of expectations with respect to x (figure 4.1).

Like Cagan, Allais observed that exponential averages were good at fitting empirical data on average over whole samples, but were struggling with the different phases of inflationary processes. "Expectations" tended to be too elastic during the initial phase when inflation was still low. They were just elastic enough when inflation rates were close to the sample arithmetic average. They tended to be not elastic enough when inflation accelerated and morphed into hyperinflation. Both Cagan and Allais also observed that the higher the arithmetic average rate of inflation on a given sample, the higher the elasticity of "expectations" required to fit the data. This is where Allais decisively

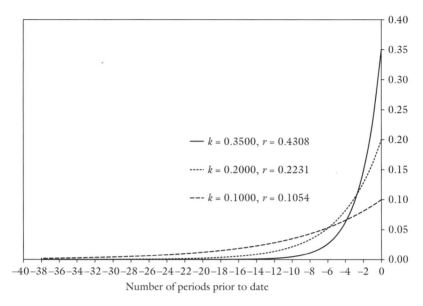

Figure 4.1 Exponential average–spot weightings.

parted way with Cagan by modeling this observed variability of the elasticity of "expectations." He did so by formulating three psychological assumptions.

4.1   The Hereditary Assumption

First, he kept the assumption that "expectations" are hereditary by nature. Like in any other adaptive "expectations" model, in Allais's HRL model, our "expectations" are what we remember from experience. They are our collective memory of the past. It is the present value of the past, the present value of the sequence of historic rates of changes, that drives our present behavior. Minsky would say, "yesterday, today and tomorrow exist."[5] And we forget the past as we discount the future: the more distant in the past is an observation, the less weight we give to it.

4.2   The Relativist Assumption

With the second assumption, the relativist assumption, comes the first creative twist in Allais's HRL model in comparison with a classic adaptive "expectations" model à la Cagan. This assumption is that there exists a psychological time scale. This psychological time scale is assumed to be the fundamental "beat" through which we perceive our environment.

That a theory of the demand for money could contain a theory of time is at first glance disconcerting and not very intuitive. Yet, it is quite logical as soon as one remembers that a theory of the demand for money seeks to explain the variability of money velocity. What is indeed money velocity? It is what mathematicians and physicists call a frequency: it measures how often money changes hands during a certain period of calendar time, for example, 16 times a year. However, one can also describe the same phenomenon by saying that money changes hands every 3.25 weeks or that it takes 3.25 weeks to complete a full cycle of payments in the economy.

To any frequency f corresponds a period T, defined by

$$T = \frac{1}{f} \Leftrightarrow fT = 1 \tag{4.5}$$

Therefore, to any velocity of money V corresponds a period T such that

$$T = \frac{1}{V} \tag{4.6}$$

This period T measures the calendar time it takes for money to change hands. It measures the length of the average elementary planning period in an economy, the period that matters to economic agents. To say that V varies over calendar time is equivalent to saying that T, too, is variable over calendar time. Let us assume there exists a function φ_t of some "expectational" variable, modeling how V varies, and let us further assume $\varphi_t(0) = 1$ when agents "expect" a stationary state. If such a function exists, it will also explain how T varies through calendar time. If, for example, we have

$$V_t = V_0 \varphi_t \tag{4.7}$$

where V_0 represents money velocity in a stationary state, then we will have

$$T_t = \frac{1}{V_t} = \frac{1}{V_0 \varphi_t} = \frac{T_0}{\varphi_t} \tag{4.8}$$

where T_0 is a constant that represents the elementary planning period in a stationary state, the fundamental beat of the economy. From relationship 4.8, we have either

$$T_t = \frac{1}{\varphi_t} T_0 \qquad (4.9)$$

or

$$T_0 = \varphi_t T_t \qquad (4.10)$$

In both cases, we have a correspondence between two time scales t and t', since we can write

$$dt = T_t \qquad (4.11)$$

and

$$dt' = T_0 \qquad (4.12)$$

We know from experience that money velocity increases as inflation accelerates. Hence, φ_t must increase as inflation accelerates. From 4.5, 4.6, and 4.8, we have

$$dt = \frac{1}{\varphi_t} dt' \qquad (4.13)$$

Since dt' is a constant, relationship 4.13 means that the effective planning horizon shrinks when inflation accelerates. We can express this by saying:

- Either that the planning horizon falls to a certain number of calendar days, weeks, or months.
- Or that it falls to a certain fraction of the fundamental beat of the economy, defined as the length of the planning horizon in a stationary state.

While the first formulation refers to the calendar (or physical) time scale, the second one refers to what Allais calls the psychological time scale. According to the HRL formulation, the existence of these two time scales explains how we remember and how we forget the past. The following quote from Albert Einstein sheds some light on the psychological phenomenon, which is at the heart of Allais's theory:[6] "An hour[7] talking with a pretty girl sitting on a park bench passes like a minute,[8] but a minute[9] sitting on a hot stove seems like an hour."[10,11]

Let us call χ_0 the rate of memory decay along the psychological time scale and $\chi(t)$ the rate of memory decay along the calendar time scale. Einstein's statement can be written as follows:

$$e^{-\chi(t)\,dt} = e^{-\chi_0 dt'} \Leftrightarrow \chi(t)\,dt = \chi_0\,dt' \qquad (4.14)$$

Since $dt = dt'/\varphi_t$, relationship 4.14 is equivalent to

$$\chi_t = \chi_0 \varphi_t \qquad (4.15)$$

As money velocity increases (and the planning horizon shrinks), the rate of memory decay increases, so that economic agents forget the past faster than in a stationary state. The important thing to observe is that it has to be the same function φ_t that converts calendar time into psychological time, that links memory along the calendar time scale with memory along the psychological time scale, and that represents the variability of money velocity.

According to the HRL formulation, while our memory has a constant reach along the psychological time scale, it is neither long, nor short relative to the physical time scale. Actually, it can be both long and short at the same time or through time; it all depends on what we are experiencing. If inflation (or the price of some asset) tends to move up rapidly, if physical time is "full," it is compressed along the psychological time scale, we forget the past quickly, and we have a short and elastic memory of this price movement. Conversely, if, simultaneously, inflation in another country (or the price of some other asset) falls persistently, if physical time is "empty," it is expanded along the psychological time scale, we have a long and inelastic memory of this other price movement.

4.3   The Logistic Assumption

With the third assumption comes the second creative twist in Allais's HRL formulation. This third assumption, the logistic assumption, is that our *relative* demand for money balances is a monotonic, decreasing, nonlinear, bounded function with respect to the present value of the past. There are lower and upper thresholds beyond which we do not respond to changes in our "expectations," and between these lower and upper limits, we don't move in a linear way.

Allais assumes *absolute* desired money balances to be proportional to nominal spending. But his Marshallian k, which he calls *relative* desired balances, is not constant; it is time-varying.

$$M_D(t) = k(t)D(t) \tag{4.16}$$

It is a decreasing function of the variable $Z(t)$, the coefficient of psychological expansion, that is, the present value, at time t, of the sequence of past nominal growth rates $x(\tau)$ in aggregate nominal spending.

$$Z(t) = \int_{-\infty}^{t} x(\tau) e^{-\int_{\tau}^{t} \chi(u)\,du}\,d\tau \tag{4.17}$$

with $\chi(u)$ being a time-varying rate of memory decay.

With θ being time, we have the following elementary dimensions:

$$[\chi(u)] = \theta^{-1} \tag{4.18}$$

$$[du] = [d\tau] = \theta \tag{4.19}$$

$$[x(\tau)] = \frac{[d\ln P]}{[d\tau]} = \theta^{-1} \tag{4.20}$$

Hence,

$$[\chi(u)\,du] = \theta^{-1}\theta = 1 \tag{4.21}$$

and

$$[e^{-\int_{\tau}^{t} \chi(u)du}] = 1 \tag{4.22}$$

Similarly,

$$[x(\tau)\,d\tau] = \theta^{-1}\theta = 1 \tag{4.23}$$

Hence,

$$[Z] = 1 \tag{4.24}$$

Z is a dimensionless number. It does not have any unit.

As we shall see throughout this book, the variable Z plays the central role in Allais's theory of monetary dynamics. Yet, on first encounter with its definition, its meaning is not easy to grasp, especially if one is not used to the conciseness of continuous notations and integral signs. Therefore, it might be helpful to write relationship 4.17 in discrete time (see proof C.7, p. 292).

Allais assumes that *relative* desired money balances decrease with respect to the coefficient of psychological expansion

$$k(t) = \phi_0 \Psi(Z(t)) \tag{4.25}$$

with ϕ_0 being the value of $k(t)$ when $Z = 0$, to which is assumed to correspond $\Psi(Z = 0) = 1$.

From 4.16 and 4.25, we have

$$\frac{D}{M_D} = \frac{1}{\phi_0 \Psi(Z)} \tag{4.26}$$

Since $M \approx M_D$, relationship 4.26 implies

$$V \approx \frac{1}{\phi_0 \Psi(Z)} \tag{4.27}$$

By comparing relationship 4.27 with relationship 4.7, we infer that the function φ is the inverse of the function Ψ:

$$\varphi_t = \frac{1}{\Psi(Z)} \tag{4.28}$$

From now on, following Allais, we shall only refer to the function $\Psi(Z)$. Allais defines this function by specifying the desired properties of its first derivative. The relative variation in desired money balances is assumed to be proportional to the change in the coefficient of psychological expansion and of opposite sign

$$\frac{1}{\Psi} \frac{d\Psi}{dt} = -q \frac{dZ}{dt} \tag{4.29}$$

with the coefficient q being in turn proportional to the initial position of Ψ relative to its maximum $1 + b$.

$$q = \alpha \left(1 - \frac{\Psi}{1 + b} \right) \tag{4.30}$$

From relationships 4.29 and 4.30, we get

$$\frac{1}{\Psi}\frac{d\Psi}{dt} = -\alpha\left(1 - \frac{\Psi}{1+b}\right)\frac{dZ}{dt} \qquad (4.31)$$

from which, by integration, we get in turn

$$\Psi(Z) = \frac{1+b}{1+be^{\alpha Z}} \qquad \text{see proof C.8, p. 294} \qquad (4.32)$$

Allais's demand for money function is a logistic function: it is bounded by two horizontal and parallel asymptotes, 0 for the lower bound and $1 + b$ for the upper limit, and it is nonlinear. All this boils down to saying that *relative* desired balances can neither grow to infinity nor fall to zero. Figure 4.2 shows the shape of the bounded nonlinear response assumed in Allais's HRL model. This is what one may want to call the second-hour problem: even with the same pretty girl sitting next to you, the second hour may not provide as much fun as the first hour.

According to the rules of differentiation under the integral sign, relationship 4.17 implies the following differential one:[12]

$$\frac{dZ}{dt} = x - \chi Z \qquad \text{see proof C.9, p. 295} \qquad (4.33)$$

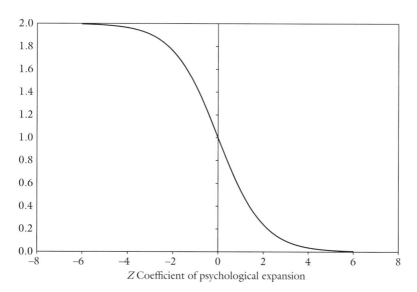

Figure 4.2 Function $\Psi(Z)$: Psychological transformation of calendar time and/or relative desired balances.

From the previous relationship, it immediately follows that the dynamic equilibrium rate z such that $dZ/dt = 0$ is given by

$$x = \chi Z = z \qquad \text{see proof C.10, p. 296} \qquad (4.34)$$

Now, since we have $z = \chi Z$, it follows that $[z] = [\chi][Z] = \theta^{-1}$; hence, z is a rate of change by unit of time.

This dynamic equilibrium rate z plays the same role as y in a classic exponential average.

From relationships 4.15 and 4.28, the time-varying rate of memory decay is defined by the relationship

$$\chi(t) = \frac{\chi_0}{\Psi(Z(t))} \qquad (4.35)$$

where χ_0 is a constant representing the rate of memory decay in psychological time and Ψ the nonlinear bounded function describing the relationship between the psychological and the physical time scale. In Allais's works on money demand, the estimated value of χ_0 is the one that minimizes the squared difference between estimated and observed money data. After analyzing many different cases, through time and space, Allais concluded that

$$\chi_0 \approx 4.8\% \text{ a year} \qquad (4.36)$$

Our own work confirms Allais's finding. In proof C.11, p. 297, the reader will find the long demonstration, which discretizes relationship 4.33 using relationship 4.31, thus making it possible to compute Z and z by recurrence, using relationships 4.37 to 4.44.

$$\overline{x_n} = \frac{\ln(D_n/D_{n-1})}{p} \qquad (4.37)$$

where p is a time-scaling factor used to express returns at the desired rate (daily, weekly, monthly, quarterly, annually) and D a time series of nominal spending, an inflation index (or the price of a financial asset).

$$k'_n = \overline{x_n} - \frac{\chi_0}{\Psi^*_{n-1}} Z_{n-1} = \overline{x_n} - z_{n-1} \qquad (4.38)$$

In Cagan's framework, this term would designate the "unexpected outcome" or the "forecasting error."

$$k_n = \frac{\chi_0}{\Psi^*_{n-1}}\left[1 + \alpha Z_{n-1}\left(1 - \frac{\Psi^*_{n-1}}{1+b}\right)\right] \tag{4.39}$$

$$Z_n = Z_{n-1} + \frac{k'_n}{k_n}(1 - e^{-p k_n}) \tag{4.40}$$

$$\Psi^*_n = \frac{1+b}{1 + be^{\alpha Z_n}} \tag{4.41}$$

$$\chi_n = \frac{\chi_0}{\Psi^*_n} \tag{4.42}$$

$$z_n = \chi_n Z_n \tag{4.43}$$

$$g_n = e^{z_n} - 1 \tag{4.44}$$

Figure 4.3 shows the shape of the function Ψ with respect to g instead of Z.

Using relationship 4.41, relationship 4.39 can be written as

$$k_n = \frac{\chi_0}{1+b}(1 + be^{\alpha Z_{n-1}} + \alpha b Z_{n-1}e^{\alpha Z_{n-1}}) \tag{4.45}$$

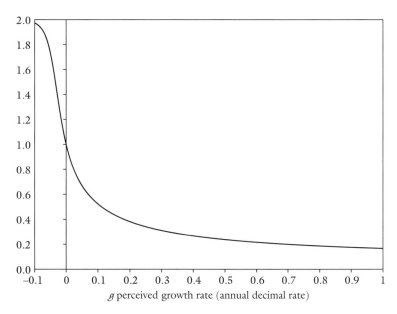

Figure 4.3 Function $\Psi(Z)$, for $\alpha = b = 1$, relative desired balances and/or psychological transformation of calendar time.

We shall encounter this expression when we discuss elasticities in the HRL formulation.

One can also write this relationship as

$$k_n = \chi_{n-1} + \frac{\chi_0 \alpha b Z_{n-1} e^{\alpha Z_{n-1}}}{1 + b} \tag{4.46}$$

Since $\chi'(Z) = d\chi/dZ = \chi_0 \alpha b e^{\alpha Z}/(1 + b)$, one can finally write

$$k_n = \chi_{n-1} + Z_{n-1}\chi'_{n-1} \tag{4.47}$$

This algorithm is very simple to implement. The only potential difficulty is to ensure that p and χ_0 are time-consistent. If p is set to express the relative changes at a monthly rate, then χ_0 must also be expressed as a monthly rate, and so will z. Table 4.1 shows the various time-consistent (χ_0, p) couples that are available, depending on the frequency of data.

From relationship 4.40, we obtain the following recursive relationship between z_n and z_{n-1}:

$$z_n = z_{n-1} + \chi_n \frac{1 - e^{-pk_n}}{k_n}(\overline{x}_n - z_{n-1}) + Z_{n-1}(\chi_n - \chi_{n-1}) \tag{4.48}$$

which allows us to establish the following relationship between the filtering and forecasting errors:

$$\overline{x}_n - z_n = \left\{ 1 - \left[\chi_n \frac{1 - e^{-pk_n}}{k_n} + Z_{n-1}\frac{(\chi_n - \chi_{n-1})}{(\overline{x}_n - z_{n-1})} \right] \right\}(\overline{x}_n - z_{n-1}) \tag{4.49}$$

We have found the analytical form of the function $\Psi(Z)$ by integrating relationship 4.31, which specified an assumed property of its

TABLE 4.1
Various Time-Scaling Alternatives

p values	Daily data	Weekly data	Monthly data	Quarterly data	Annual data
$\chi_0 = 0.4\%/\text{month}$	$1/30.44 = 0.03$	$7/30.44 = 0.23$	1	3	12
$\chi_0 = 1.2\%/\text{quarter}$	$1/91.31 = 0.01$	$7/91.31 = 0.08$	$1/3$	1	4
$\chi_0 = 4.8\%/\text{year}$	$1/365.25 = 0.003$	$7/365.25 = 0.01$	$1/12$	$1/4$	1

first derivative. In doing so, we have taken the point of view of desired relative balances. We could have reached the same result by taking the alternative route of the rate of memory decay, a perhaps more intuitive route thanks to its more obvious connection with the flow of time.

From relationship 4.35, we get

$$\frac{1}{\Psi}\frac{d\Psi}{dt} = -\frac{1}{\chi}\frac{d\chi}{dt} \tag{4.50}$$

By substituting, according to relationships 4.35 and 4.50, all the terms in χ for their equivalents in Ψ in relationship 4.31, we get, after simplifying and rearranging,

$$\frac{d\chi}{dt} = \alpha\left(\chi - \frac{\chi_0}{1+b}\right)\frac{dZ}{dt} \tag{4.51}$$

or

$$\frac{d\chi}{dZ} = \alpha\left(\chi - \frac{\chi_0}{1+b}\right) \tag{4.52}$$

in which $\chi_0/(1+b) = \lim_{Z\to-\infty}\chi(Z)$. In other words, the derivative of the rate of memory decay with respect to the coefficient of psychological expansion is proportional to the difference between the rate of memory decay and its minimum.[13] One can easily verify that integration of relationship 4.52 yields

$$\chi(Z) = \chi_0\frac{1+be^{\alpha Z}}{1+b} \tag{4.53}$$

4.4   Elasticities in the HRL Formulation

In Cagan's formulation, both the elasticity β of expected inflation E with respect to actual price changes C and the elasticity α of the demand for real balances with respect to expected inflation E are explicitly identified and constant.

As already said, Allais's initial formulation is not interpreted in terms of "expectations" but in terms of memory, and it uses different notations. Yet, its structure is very much the same as Cagan's (see table 4.2).

TABLE 4.2

Comparison of Allais Versus Cagan

	Allais (1954)	Cagan (1954)
Nominal growth rate/ inflation rate	$x = \frac{d \ln D}{dt}$	$C = \frac{d \ln P}{dt}$
Argument of demand for money function	u	E
Determination of argument of demand for money function	$\frac{du}{dt} = \overline{\chi}(x - u)$	$\frac{dE}{dt} = \beta(C - E)$
Rate of memory decay/ elasticity of expectations	$\overline{\chi}$	β
Demand for money function[14]	$\frac{M}{D} \approx \phi_0(1 - Ku)$	$\frac{M}{P} = e^{-\alpha E - \gamma}$
Elasticity of demand for money function	$\frac{-Ku}{1 - Ku}$	$-\alpha E$
Demand for money function in a stationary state	ϕ_0	$e^{-\gamma}$

Therefore, even if Allais uses neither the word "expectations" nor the word "elasticity," it is quite straightforward to find in Allais's initial formulation the constant parameters equivalent to Cagan's elasticities. Allais's constant rate of memory decay $\overline{\chi}$ is equivalent to Cagan's β. For small values of Cagan's E (i.e., Allais's u), Cagan's α is equivalent to Allais's K.

Since Allais's HRL formulation is derived from Allais's initial formulation in terms of exponential average, one is naturally curious to analyze the properties of the former in terms of elasticity. Yet, disconcerting as it may seem—the concept of elasticity remains essentially absent from Allais's own comments on the HRL formulation. This apparent absence has certainly contributed to the serious mistakes made by Darby when he tried to analyze the elasticity of the HRL formulation.

The question is indeed somewhat complex, given the dynamic interdependences built in the HRL formulation. The argument of the demand for money function Ψ is no longer u, an exponential *average*, but a *sum*, Z, the so-called coefficient of psychological expansion, the determination of which depends upon a time-varying rate of memory decay χ, which is itself a function of Z, since $\chi(Z) = \chi_0/\Psi(Z)$. As for the demand for money function Ψ, it is nonlinear with respect to Z:

$$\Psi(Z) = \frac{1+b}{1+be^{\alpha Z}} \qquad (4.54)$$

To finish, the variable equivalent in the HRL formulation to u (or Cagan's E) is

$$z(Z) = \chi(Z)Z = \frac{\chi_0(1+be^{\alpha Z})Z}{1+b} \qquad (4.55)$$

The elasticities of $\Psi(Z)$, $\chi(Z)$, and $z(Z)$ with respect to Z are easy to compute:

$$e(\Psi(Z); Z) = Z\frac{\Psi'(Z)}{\Psi(Z)} = \frac{-\alpha Z be^{\alpha Z}}{1+be^{\alpha Z}} \qquad (4.56a)$$

$$e(\chi(Z); Z) = Z\frac{\chi'(Z)}{\chi(Z)} = \frac{\alpha Z be^{\alpha Z}}{1+be^{\alpha Z}} \qquad (4.56b)$$

$$e(z(Z); Z) = Z\frac{z'(Z)}{z(Z)} = \frac{1+be^{\alpha Z}+\alpha Z be^{\alpha Z}}{1+be^{\alpha Z}} \qquad (4.56c)$$

From these three relationships, it immediately follows that

$$\lim_{Z\to+\infty} e(\Psi(Z); Z) = -\alpha Z \qquad (4.57a)$$

$$\lim_{Z\to+\infty} e(\chi(Z); Z) = \alpha Z \qquad (4.57b)$$

$$\lim_{Z\to+\infty} e(z(Z); Z) = 1+\alpha Z \qquad (4.57c)$$

Let us now turn to the elasticity of Z with respect to x. From relationships 4.33 and 4.34, we can write

$$\frac{dZ}{dt} = x - \chi Z \qquad (4.58)$$

$$\Leftrightarrow \frac{dZ}{Z\,dt} = \frac{x-z}{Z} \qquad (4.59)$$

$$\Leftrightarrow \frac{dZ}{Z\,dt} = \frac{x-z}{z/\chi} \qquad (4.60)$$

$$\Leftrightarrow \frac{\frac{dZ}{Z}}{\frac{x-z}{z}} = \chi\,dt \qquad (4.61)$$

Hence

$$e(Z(x); x) = \chi \, dt \qquad (4.62)$$

Having established that the elasticity of Z with respect to x is $\chi \, dt$, we can finally find the analytical formulation of the elasticity of z with respect to x.

Since, according to relationship 4.55,

$$z = \chi Z = \chi_0 \frac{1 + b e^{\alpha Z}}{1 + b} Z \qquad (4.63)$$

z is indeed a function of Z, which in turn depends on x, and we can write

$$z = z(Z(x)) \qquad (4.64)$$

It is easy to prove that for any differentiable functions f and g

$$e(g[f(x)]; x) = e(g[f(x)]; f(x)) \times e(f(x); x) \qquad (4.65)$$

Hence,

$$e(z[Z(x)]; x) = e(z(Z); Z) \times e(Z(x); x) \qquad (4.66)$$

Since

$$e(z(Z); Z) = Z \frac{z'(Z)}{z(Z)} = Z \frac{\chi + Z \, d\chi / dZ}{\chi Z} = \frac{\chi + Z \, d\chi / dZ}{\chi} \qquad (4.67)$$

and given relationship 4.62, we finally get

$$e(z[Z(x)]; x) = (\chi + Z \, d\chi / dZ) \, dt \qquad (4.68)$$

By transposing these proofs from continuous to discrete time, relationship 4.62 becomes

$$e(Z(\overline{x}_n), \overline{x}_n) = \frac{\frac{(\overline{x}_n - z_{n-1})(1 - e^{-pk_n})}{k_n Z_{n-1}}}{\frac{\overline{x}_n - z_{n-1}}{\chi_{n-1} Z_{n-1}}} = \frac{(1 - e^{-pk_n}) \chi_{n-1}}{k_n} \qquad (4.69)$$

with $\qquad \chi_{n-1} = \dfrac{\chi_0 (1 + b e^{\alpha Z_{n-1}})}{1 + b} \qquad (4.70a)$

and $\qquad k_n = \dfrac{\chi_0 (1 + b e^{\alpha Z_{n-1}} + \alpha b Z_{n-1} e^{\alpha Z_{n-1}})}{1 + b} \qquad (4.70b)$

which is equivalent to

$$e(Z(\overline{x}_n), \overline{x}_n) = \frac{(1 - e^{-pk_n})(1 + be^{\alpha Z_{n-1}})}{1 + be^{\alpha Z_{n-1}} + \alpha b Z_{n-1} e^{\alpha Z_{n-1}}} \qquad (4.71)$$

and by multiplying relationship 4.56c by relationship 4.71, relationship 4.68 becomes

$$e(z[Z(\overline{x}_n)]; \overline{x}_n) = 1 - e^{-pk_n} \qquad (4.72)$$

One can easily check that relationships 4.62 and 4.68 are the respective limits of relationships 4.69 and 4.72 when $p \to 0$, that is, when $p = dt$. For example,

$$\lim_{p \to 0} \frac{(1 - e^{-pk_n})\chi_{n-1}}{k_n} = \frac{1 - (1 - pk_n)}{k_n}\chi_{n-1} = p\chi_{n-1} \approx \chi \, dt \quad (4.73)$$

The limits of relationships 4.69 and 4.72 when $Z_{n-1} \to \pm\infty$ are displayed in table 4.3.

In section 2.2, we have observed that, due to their constant elasticity, standard exponential averages present a permanent dilemma to their users: to smooth or not to smooth the data? To track or not to track the most recent data points? The trade-off between minimizing the filtering errors, which implies a volatile filter ($k \approx 1$), and minimizing the filter's volatility, which implies large filtering errors ($k \approx 0$), is made particularly hard to find by the fact that, under uncertainty, the future volatility of data is not only unknown but also likely to vary over time. Volatile conditions require an alert filter, while more stable ones call for a sticky one. Bearing this dilemma in mind, a key benefit offered by the HRL formulation is that the elasticity of "expectations" with respect to realized outcomes varies dynamically and continuously between almost

TABLE 4.3
Limit Elasticities with Respect to x

	$e(Z; x)$	$e(z; x)$
Continuous time	$\chi \, dt$	$(\chi + Z d\chi/dZ) \, dt$
Discrete time	$\frac{(1 - e^{-pk_n})\chi_{n-1}}{k_n}$	$1 - e^{-pk_n}$
$\lim Z_{n-1} \to -\infty$	$p\chi_0/(1 + b) \approx 0$	$p\chi_0/(1 + b) \approx 0$
$\lim Z_{n-1} \to +\infty$	0	1

0 and 1, and this in a less constrained way than in a Markov switching model.

Since Z is actually a function of x, we have the following identities

$$\Psi(Z) = \Psi[Z(x)] \tag{4.74a}$$

$$\chi(Z) = \chi[Z(x)] \tag{4.74b}$$

Therefore, using relationship 4.65 again, we obtain

$$e(\Psi[Z(x)]; x) = e(\Psi(Z); Z) \times e(Z(x); x) \tag{4.75a}$$

$$= \frac{-\alpha b Z e^{\alpha Z}(1 - e^{-pk})}{1 + b e^{\alpha Z} + \alpha b Z e^{\alpha Z}} \tag{4.75b}$$

$$e(\chi[Z(x)]; x) = e(\chi(Z); Z) \times e(Z(x); x) \tag{4.75c}$$

$$= \frac{\alpha b Z e^{\alpha Z}(1 - e^{-pk})}{1 + b e^{\alpha Z} + \alpha b Z e^{\alpha Z}} \tag{4.75d}$$

When $Z \to +\infty$, which implies $z \to +\infty$, the elasticities with respect to x have the following limits

$$\lim_{Z \to +\infty} e(\Psi[Z(x)]; x) = -1 \tag{4.76a}$$

$$\lim_{Z \to +\infty} e(\chi[Z(x)]; x) = 1 \tag{4.76b}$$

Cagan would interpret these results by saying that in Allais's HRL formulation, when inflation tends toward infinity, the elasticity of "expected" inflation with respect to actual inflation tends toward 1, while the elasticity of the demand for money with respect to "expected" inflation tends toward minus 1.

From relationship 4.72, we have

$$\lim_{Z \to +\infty} e(z[Z(x)]; x) = 1 \leftrightarrow \lim_{z \to +\infty} \frac{\frac{dz}{z}}{\frac{x-z}{z}} = 1 \tag{4.77a}$$

$$\leftrightarrow dz \approx x - z \tag{4.77b}$$

$$\leftrightarrow z + dz \approx x \tag{4.77c}$$

In other words, when the perceived rate of inflation z tends to infinity and its elasticity tends toward 1, the perceived rate of inflation converges toward the instantaneous rate of inflation, as we shall verify later in chapter 7, when studying a case of hyperinflation.

The convergence of the perceived return toward the spot return when the present value of past returns tends toward infinity implies that the HRL formulation minimizes the squared difference between the perceived and the spot returns when these variables become very large.

$$\lim_{Z \to +\infty} dz = x - z \Rightarrow z + dz \to x \Rightarrow z_n \to x_n \Rightarrow (z_n - x_n)^2 \approx 0$$

$$(4.78)$$

This observation shows that the HRL formulation can be interpreted as a filtering algorithm minimizing the difference between spot returns and their smoothed values in extreme conditions.

Figures 4.4 and 4.5 show the behavior of the different elasticities discussed above. Table 4.4 summarizes their analytic expressions and limits.

To demonstrate his asymptotic postulate according to which $\alpha = 1$, Allais follows a rather tortuous and somewhat confusing road along the psychological time scale.[15] (See proof C.12, p. 302, for an alternative demonstration, which places itself along the calendar time scale and is therefore more intuitive.)

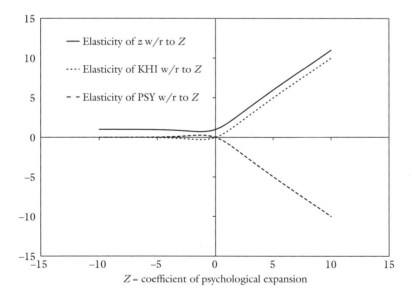

Figure 4.4   HRL formulation elasticities.

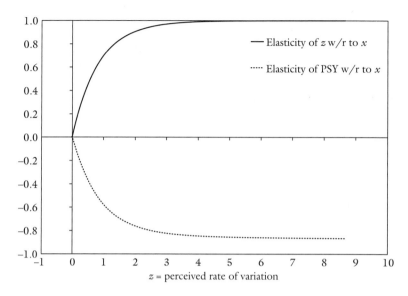

Figure 4.5 HRL formulation elasticities.

The postulate of psychological symmetry according to which $b = 1$ is easier to demonstrate. It follows from the assumption that the response of economic agents to a fall in Z of a given magnitude has the same intensity as the response to a rise in Z of the same magnitude. More formally, this means that the first derivative of $\Psi(Z)$ must be an even function.

Since we have

$$\Psi(Z) = \frac{1+b}{1+be^{\alpha Z}} \Rightarrow \Psi'(Z) = \frac{-(1+b)\alpha be^{\alpha Z}}{(1+be^{\alpha Z})^2} \qquad (4.79)$$

with $\alpha = 1$ and $b \neq -1$

$$\Psi'(Z) = \Psi'(-Z) \Rightarrow b = 1 \qquad (4.80)$$

which implies

$$\Psi'(0) = -\frac{1}{2} \qquad (4.81)$$

In our own work, we have been unable to improve our adjustments by having $\alpha \neq 1$ or $b \neq 1$. In other words, we have not changed any of the structural parameters χ_0, α, and b used by Allais.[16] Under these

TABLE 4.4
Elasticities in the HRL Formulation

Elasticity	Functional expression	Limit for $Z \to -\infty$	Limit for $Z \to +\infty$	Limit of relative variations for $Z \to +\infty$
$e(Z;x)$	$\dfrac{(1-e^{-pk})(1+be^{\alpha Z})}{1+be^{\alpha Z}+\alpha Zbe^{\alpha Z}}$	$px_0/(1+b)$	0	0
$e(\Psi;Z)$	$-\alpha Z\left(1-\dfrac{\Psi}{1+b}\right)=-\alpha Z\dfrac{be^{\alpha Z}}{1+be^{\alpha Z}}$	0	$-\alpha Z \to -\infty$	$-\alpha\,dZ$
$e(X;Z)$	$\alpha Z\left(1-\dfrac{\Psi}{1+b}\right)=\alpha Z\dfrac{be^{\alpha Z}}{1+be^{\alpha Z}}$	0	$\alpha Z \to +\infty$	$\alpha\,dZ$
$e(z;Z)=$ $e(X;Z)+e(Z;Z)$	$\dfrac{1+be^{\alpha Z}+\alpha Zbe^{\alpha Z}}{1+be^{\alpha Z}}$	1	$1+\alpha Z \to +\infty$	$-\alpha\,dZ$
$e(z;x)=$ $e(z;Z)e(Z;x)$	$1-e^{-pk}$	$px_0/(1+b)$	1	$dz=x-z$
$e(\Psi;x)=$ $e(\Psi;Z)e(Z;x)$	$\dfrac{-\alpha Zbe^{\alpha Z}(1-e^{-pk})}{1+be^{\alpha Z}+\alpha Zbe^{\alpha Z}}$	0	-1	$\dfrac{d\Psi}{\Psi}=-\dfrac{dx}{z}$
$e(X;x)=$ $e(X;Z)e(Z;x)$	$\dfrac{+\alpha Zbe^{\alpha Z}(1-e^{-pk})}{1+be^{\alpha Z}+\alpha Zbe^{\alpha Z}}$	0	1	$\dfrac{dX}{X}=\dfrac{dx}{z}$

assumptions, $\Psi(0) = 1$ and $\chi(0) = \chi_0 = 4.80$ percent, which means that, in a steady state, the HRL formulation implies that we forget the past at a decimal rate of nearly 5 percent a year (4.92 percent to be accurate). To put things differently, in a steady state, memory goes back a little more than 20 years ($1/0.0492 = 20.33$).

Table 4.5 translates in Wall Street's parlance the meaning of the psychological coefficients α and b.

In light of the preceding developments, table 4.6 summarizes our comparison of Cagan's formulation with Allais's HRL formulation.

As in classic exponential averages, the value Z_0 is an initialization parameter. Its influence vanishes over time. This is the only parameter that is truly "discretionary" and case-specific.

As an aside, it is very easy to demonstrate that Smith's formulation of the sentiment of momentum traders is nothing but Cagan's formulation of inflation expectations, with different notations (see proof C.13, p. 304)[17].

Our final words of presentation of the HRL formulation will mention that Allais proposed an HRL formulation of the supply of money in 1970. In this formulation, base money is assumed to grow at a constant rate ρ, and the base money multiplier γ is supposed to be a monotonic, increasing, bounded, nonlinear function with respect to Z.

$$\gamma(Z) = 1 - a' + a' \frac{1 + b'}{1 + b'e^{-\alpha' Z}} \qquad (4.82)$$

$$M(t) = qB_0 e^{\rho t}\gamma(Z(t)) \qquad (4.83)$$

Contrary to the demand for money, the supply of money is a directly observable variable. Therefore, its HRL formulation is of lesser empirical interest than that of the demand for money. Allais's next contribution to monetary dynamics, the fundamental equation of monetary dynamics (chapter 5), will soon illustrate this point.

From a theoretical point of view, however, the HRL formulation of the supply of money is important in at least two respects. First, as we shall see in section 5.2, it is an essential building block of the HRL formulation of endogenous cyclical fluctuations in nominal spending. Second, as we shall see in chapter 9, it provides a template for modeling the demand for risky assets, because this demand is—to a certain extent—the mirror image of the supply of money.

TABLE 4.5
Psychological Meaning of the Coefficients α and b

	$b < 1$	$b = 1$	$b > 1$
$\alpha < 1$	Propensity to downplay a negative coefficient of psychological expansion but low responsiveness to changing conditions: **the die-hard bull**	No bias in one direction or another but slow responsiveness to changing conditions: **the would-be trader (the long-term institutional investor)**	Propensity to be impressed by a negative coefficient of psychological expansion and low responsiveness to changing conditions: **the die-hard bear**
$\alpha = 1$	Propensity to downplay a negative coefficient of psychological expansion but normal responsiveness to changing conditions: **the constructive bull**	The perfectly unbiased observer: **central bankers?**	Propensity to be impressed by a negative coefficient of psychological expansion and normal responsiveness to changing conditions: **the constructive bear**
$\alpha > 1$	Propensity to downplay a negative coefficient of psychological expansion and high responsiveness to changing conditions: **the unfettered bull**	No bias in one direction or another but high responsiveness to changing conditions: **the perfect trader**	Propensity to be impressed by a negative coefficient of psychological expansion and high responsiveness to changing conditions: **the unfettered bear**

TABLE 4.6
Comparison of Cagan and Allais HRL Formulations

	Cagan (1954)	Allais (1965)
Cases studied	Hyperinflation only	Normal situations, hyperinflation, deflation
Desired money balances	Equal to outstanding balances	Different from but close to outstanding balances
Input data	Inflations rates	Nominal growth rates
Argument of demand for money function	Simple exponential average of past inflation rates (constant decay factor)	Dynamic exponential average of past nominal growth rates (time-varying decay factor)
Interpretation	Forecasting error correction, constant elasticity of expectations	Memory decay, time-varying elasticity of memory between 0 and 1
Form of demand for money function	Linear, constant elasticity with respect to expectations	Nonlinear and bounded (logistic) time-varying elasticity with respect to expectations between 0 and −1
Intrinsic parameters	0	3
Psychological constants	No single formulation	Single formulation
Case-specific parameters (incl. initialization parameter)	4	2
Output	Estimates of real money balances (money balances–price level ratio)	Estimates of relative desired money balances (money balances–nominal spending ratio)
Performance	Good for the intermediate phase of hyperinflation Bad for the early and final phases	Good for all phases of all cases studied, including hyperinflation

The economic agents who borrow funds from banks play indeed an instrumental role as regards the supply of money: without their willingness to borrow, banks cannot make loans and, since loans make deposits, money cannot be created. But these borrowers do not borrow funds from banks to hold them as deposits. They borrow funds from banks to get rid of them by purchasing goods, services, and financial assets. The motives for borrowing funds must therefore be closely connected with the motives for buying these goods, services, and financial assets. In other words, the shape of the demand for risky assets function must be similar to that of the supply of money function: monotonic, increasing, bounded, and nonlinear.

To provisionally conclude the HRL formulation of the supply of money, let us mention its implications in terms of elasticity. The elasticity of the supply of money with respect to the present value of past rates of nominal growth is

$$e(\gamma(Z); Z) = \frac{\alpha' a' b' Z (1 + b') e^{-\alpha' Z}}{[(1 - a')(1 + b' e^{-\alpha' Z}) + a'(1 + b')](1 + b' e^{-\alpha' Z})}$$
(4.84)

With respect to the perceived rate of nominal growth, the elasticity of the supply of money is

$$e(\gamma(Z(x)); x) = e(\gamma(Z); Z) \times e(Z(x); x)$$
(4.85)

$$e(\gamma(Z); x) =$$

$$\frac{\alpha' a' b' Z (1 + b') e^{-\alpha' Z}}{[(1 - a')(1 + b' e^{-\alpha' Z}) + a'(1 + b')](1 + b' e^{-\alpha' Z})} \frac{(1 - e^{-pk})(1 + b e^{\alpha Z})}{1 + b e^{\alpha Z} + \alpha b Z e^{\alpha Z}}$$
(4.86)

Therefore, we have the following limit elasticities:

$$\lim_{Z \to -\infty} e(\gamma(Z); Z) = \lim_{Z \to +\infty} e(\gamma(Z); Z) = 0$$
(4.87a)

$$\lim_{x \to -\infty} e(\gamma(Z(x)); x) = \lim_{x \to +\infty} e(\gamma(Z(x)); x) = 0$$
(4.87b)

The elasticity of the demand for money with respect to the perceived rate of nominal growth tends toward -1 when the latter tends toward positive infinity; it is noteworthy that, in the same circumstance, the elasticity of the supply of money tends toward 0.

4.5   The Perceived Flow of Calendar Time

That calendar time seems to flow slowly in certain conditions, but rapidly in others is a personal experience, which probably all human beings share. By way of a conclusion to this chapter, it is high time to analyze how the HRL formulation quantifies this universal experience. If m is a calendar minute and m' a psychological minute, Einstein's quip that "an hour talking with a pretty girl sitting on a park bench passes like a minute" can be translated as follows

$$60m = 1m'$$
(4.88)

which is equivalent to

$$\frac{m'}{m} = 60 \tag{4.89}$$

Therefore, the ratio m/m' measures the speed at which calendar time is perceived to flow relative to the psychological time scale: 60 in Einstein's example.

Now, from relationships 4.13 and 4.28, it follows that

$$dt = \Psi(Z)\, dt' \tag{4.90}$$

which is in turn equivalent to

$$\frac{dt'}{dt} = \frac{1}{\Psi(Z)} = \frac{1 + be^{\alpha Z}}{1 + b} \tag{4.91}$$

Relationship 4.91 shows that, according to the HRL formulation, it is the function $1/\Psi(Z)$ which measures the speed at which calendar time is perceived to flow relative to the psychological time scale. At the risk of anticipating chapter 7, column (6) of Table 7.1 on p. 133 shows that in July 2008, toward the end of the Zimbabwean hyperinflation, the function $\Psi(Z)$ was very close to its lower bound, since we had

$$\Psi(Z) = 0.0066 \tag{4.92}$$

which meant that calendar time was then perceived to flow 151.57 ($= 1/0.0066$) times faster than normal and that Einstein must have had a very pretty girl in mind when he coined his quip.

Just as we have written $\chi(t)\, dt = \chi_0 dt'$ in relationship 4.14, we can write

$$x(t)\, dt = x'(t')\, dt' \tag{4.93}$$

where x' is the psychological rate of change, that is, the non-observable rate of change which—measured along the psychological time scale—corresponds to the observed calendar rate of change x.

According to relationships 4.93 and 4.90, we get

$$x' = x\Psi(Z) \tag{4.94}$$

Georges Prat, one of Allais's students, has reported, but not explained, the interesting observation according to which the variable x' exhibits

TABLE 4.7
Calendar and Psychological Rates of
Change: Comparative Distributions

Monthly log rates	$x\,(\%)$	$x'\,(\%)$
Minimum	0.00	0.00
Maximum	329.59	3.54
Average	24.23	1.33
Standard-deviation	44.34	0.64
$\sqrt[3]{\mu_3}$	71.97	0.47
$\sqrt[4]{\mu_4}$	99.06	0.84

the valuable property of being stationary, even during hyperinflation episodes.[18] At the risk once again of anticipating on chapter 7, table 4.7 illustrates Prat's observation in the case of the monthly inflation rates experienced in Zimbabwe between 2000 and 2008 (115 observations). We add to Prat's analysis the consideration of the nth root of nth order moment for $n = 3$ and $n = 4$ (see section 10.2.2 p. 213 for a definition of moments). One can easily further verify that the variable x' is normally distributed, which is not the case of variable x.

The low variability of x' springs from its limit-elasticity with respect to x when Z tends towards infinity.

Since, according to 4.94,

$$x'(x) = x\Psi(Z(x)), \qquad (4.95)$$

the rules that we have encountered in section 4.4 p. 79 as regards the elasticity of a product of functions and the elasticity of a composite function allow us to write

$$e(x'(x); x_0) = e(x; x_0) + e(\Psi(Z); Z) \times e(Z(x); x_0) \qquad (4.96)$$

from which, according to relationships 4.75a and 4.75b, we obtain

$$e(x'(x); x_0) = 1 - \frac{\alpha Z b e^{\alpha Z}(1 - e^{-pk})}{1 + b e^{\alpha Z} + \alpha Z b e^{\alpha Z}} \qquad (4.97)$$

As, according to relationship 4.76b

$$\lim_{Z \to +\infty} \frac{\alpha Z b e^{\alpha Z}\left(1 - e^{-pk}\right)}{1 + b e^{\alpha Z} + \alpha Z b e^{\alpha Z}} = 1 \qquad (4.98)$$

it follows that

$$\lim_{Z \to +\infty} e(x'(x); x_0) = 0 \qquad (4.99)$$

In other words, in comparison to the variable x, which measures speed in calendar time, the variable x', which measures speed in psychological time, is quasi-constant. Odd as it may seem, this psychological transformation of calendar speed bears a striking resemblance to the process whereby honeybees seem to regulate their flight: with respect to the nearest obstacle, they keep their angular velocity constant.[19]

The Fundamental Equation of Monetary Dynamics

IN SECTION 3.2, we have observed that money creation was absent from relationship 3.43, which shows the impact of hoarding (respectively dishoarding) on the fluctuations in aggregate nominal spending. The fundamental equation of monetary dynamics, which Allais presented in 1968, not only corrects this omission, but it also explains the fluctuations in money velocity.[1]

The major contribution of the fundamental equation of monetary dynamics is indeed to introduce the relative difference between effective and desired money in the differential expression of the Newcomb-Fisher equation of exchange, thereby showing that this is the factor that causes money velocity to fluctuate. Alongside the relative change in the money supply (and nonbank credit), this factor causes fluctuations in nominal spending.

5.1   Beyond the Equation of Exchange: The Fundamental Equation of Monetary Dynamics

In its simplest form, the quantity theory of money is a relationship between four macroeconomic variables:

- The volume level of transactions Q.[2]
- The price level of transactions P.
- The quantity of money M held by economic agents.

- Last, but not the least, the *transactions* velocity of money V, which measures how frequently money changes hands per unit of time.

$$MV = PQ = D \qquad (5.1)$$

In its standard form, the equation of exchange is at best a means of measuring the transactions velocity of money ex post, by writing:[3]

$$V = \frac{D}{M} \qquad (5.2)$$

and, at worst, nothing more than a tautology.

This becomes particularly clear by looking at the differential expression of the Newcomb-Fisher equation of exchange:

$$\frac{1}{D}\frac{dD}{dt} = \frac{1}{V}\frac{dV}{dt} + \frac{1}{M}\frac{dM}{dt} \qquad (5.3)$$

This relationship means that the rate of change in aggregate nominal spending is equal to the sum of the rates of change in the transactions velocity of money and the quantity of money in circulation. Failing a model explaining and forecasting changes in the transactions velocity of money, the quantity theory of money ends up in a dead end.

Allais's fundamental equation of monetary dynamics takes monetary theory out of this deadlock. It does so by using two important insights presented in chapter 3:

- First, the distinction between M, the quantity of money that economic agents effectively hold, and M_D, the quantity of money that economic agents desire to hold.
- Second, the fact that M and M_D remain close to each other over time ($M \approx M_D$).

What is most important to note is that although Allais's fundamental equation of monetary dynamics calls for a model estimating M_D, the desired level of cash balances, this equation is actually independent of any particular formulation of the demand for money, including Allais's own formulation, the HRL formulation. It is theoretically possible to reject Allais's HRL formulation of the demand for money, and yet to adopt his fundamental equation of monetary dynamics.

To demonstrate this equation, Allais starts with a question, notionally asked at time t, as shown in figure 5.1, which marks both the end

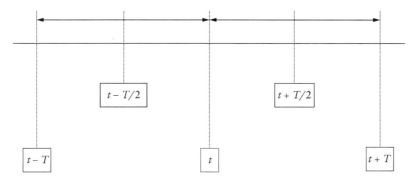

Figure 5.1   Elementary periods of reference.

and the beginning of two consecutive periods of undefined duration T:
which sources of purchasing power can economic agents use to finance
their spending over the following period?

There are three sources of purchasing power that economic agents
can tap:[4]

- The fresh cash balances that they have accumulated prior to time t
  through the sales of goods, services, and securities.
- The new loans they obtain from banks after time t.
- Last, but not least, the cash balances they are willing to dishoard,
  that is, the excess of cash balances effectively held over desired balances at time t.

Let $R_T(\tau)$ be the instantaneous level of cash inflows generated by
the sale of goods, services, and securities. Strictly speaking, the receipts
during period T are measured by the following integral:

$$\int_{t-T}^{t} R_T(\tau)\, d\tau \tag{5.4}$$

But we know that there is a point τ^* somewhere between $t - T$ and t,
such that

$$\int_{t-T}^{t} R_T(\tau)\, d\tau = R_T(\tau^*)T \tag{5.5}$$

Therefore, and for the sake of simplicity, the aggregate cash *inflows* in
period T preceding time t are $R_T(t - T/2)T$. Similarly, the aggregate
cash outflows in period T following time t are $D(t + T/2)T$. Since

bank loans make bank deposits, the net increase in bank loans is $M(t + T/2) - M(t - T/2)$.

Last but not the least, the change in transaction balances (hoarding or dishoarding) equals $M(t) - M_D(t)$.

Adding these three elements together, we can write the following relationship, which answers the question initially asked:

$$TD\left(t + \frac{T}{2}\right) = TR_T\left(t - \frac{T}{2}\right) + [M(t) - M_D(t)]$$
$$+ \left[M\left(t + \frac{T}{2}\right) - M\left(t - \frac{T}{2}\right)\right] \qquad (5.6)$$

Now, as we have seen in section 3.1, p. 47, since someone's payments are necessarily someone else's receipts, we have

$$D(t) = R_T(t) \qquad (5.7)$$

Substituting D for R_T in relationship 5.6, we get

$$T\left[D\left(t + \frac{T}{2}\right) - D\left(t - \frac{T}{2}\right)\right] = [M(t) - M_D(t)]$$
$$+ \left[M\left(t + \frac{T}{2}\right) - M\left(t - \frac{T}{2}\right)\right]$$
$$\qquad (5.8)$$

Since, for any differentiable function f, we have

$$f(x) - f(x_0) \approx (x - x_0) f'(x_0) \qquad (5.9)$$

we can write

$$D\left(t + \frac{T}{2}\right) - D\left(t - \frac{T}{2}\right) \approx T\frac{dD}{dt} \qquad (5.10)$$

and

$$M\left(t + \frac{T}{2}\right) - M\left(t - \frac{T}{2}\right) \approx T\frac{dM}{dt} \qquad (5.11)$$

Therefore, relationship 5.8 can be reformulated as follows:

$$T^2\frac{dD}{dt} = M - M_D + T\frac{dM}{dt} \qquad (5.12)$$

Since $V/D = 1/M$, relationship 5.12 is equivalent to

$$T^2 \frac{V}{D}\frac{dD}{dt} = \frac{M - M_D}{M} + T\frac{1}{M}\frac{dM}{dt} \tag{5.13}$$

and

$$\frac{1}{D}\frac{dD}{dt} = \frac{1}{VT^2}\frac{M - M_D}{M} + \frac{1}{VT}\frac{1}{M}\frac{dM}{dt} \tag{5.14}$$

In dynamic *equilibrium*, effective and desired balances are equal, $M = M_D$, which implies that the velocity of money is constant. Therefore, in dynamic *equilibrium*, relationship 5.3 becomes

$$\frac{1}{D}\frac{dD}{dt} = \frac{1}{M}\frac{dM}{dt} \tag{5.15}$$

while relationship 5.14 becomes

$$\frac{1}{D}\frac{dD}{dt} = \frac{1}{VT}\frac{1}{M}\frac{dM}{dt} \tag{5.16}$$

Hence, in dynamic *equilibrium*

$$VT = 1 \Leftrightarrow T = \frac{1}{V} \tag{5.17}$$

By formally demonstrating that the response period T is the inverse of the transactions velocity of money V in dynamic equilibrium, Allais achieved a major analytical step forward, as we shall see in the rest of this book. Using this equivalence, relationship 5.14 becomes

$$\frac{1}{D}\frac{dD}{dt} = V\frac{M - M_D}{M} + \frac{1}{M}\frac{dM}{dt} \tag{5.18}$$

But, in dynamic *equilibrium*, this relationship is of limited interest, since $M - M_D = 0$. What can we say about dynamic *disequilibrium*, that is, when $M \approx M_D$?

Let us first write the following relationship:

$$VT^2 = VT^2 - T + T = T(VT - 1) + T \tag{5.19}$$

Using relationship 5.19, we can write relationship 5.13 as follows:

$$(VT - 1)T\frac{1}{D}\frac{dD}{dt} + T\frac{1}{D}\frac{dD}{dt} = \frac{M - M_D}{M} + T\frac{1}{M}\frac{dM}{dt} \tag{5.20}$$

In dynamic *disequilibrium*, since $M \approx M_D$, we have

$$VT - 1 \approx 0 \tag{5.21}$$

The product $(VT - 1)\frac{1}{D}\frac{dD}{dt}$ is of second order. Therefore, it can be neglected and relationship 5.20 can be written as

$$T\frac{1}{D}\frac{dD}{dt} \approx \frac{M - M_D}{M} + T\frac{1}{M}\frac{dM}{dt} \tag{5.22}$$

which is equivalent to

$$\frac{1}{D}\frac{dD}{dt} \approx V\frac{M - M_D}{M} + \frac{1}{M}\frac{dM}{dt} \tag{5.23}$$

The relationship 5.18 that we had demonstrated in dynamic equilibrium also holds in dynamic disequilibrium. Allais calls it the *fundamental equation of monetary dynamics* (FEMD). This FEMD can be extended to include nonbank credit E.

$$\frac{1}{D}\frac{dD}{dt} \approx V\frac{M - M_D}{M} + \frac{1}{M}\frac{dM}{dt} + \frac{E}{M}\frac{1}{E}\frac{dE}{dt} \tag{5.24}$$

The fundamental equation of monetary dynamics most clearly identifies the two elementary factors that determine growth in nominal spending during a given period:

- The relative difference between effective and desired cash balances at the beginning of the period multiplied by the transactions velocity of money at the same point in time.
- The rate of growth in the quantity of money during the period.

In its most general formulation, the fundamental equation of monetary dynamics identifies an additional source of finance: The rate of growth in nonbank credit during the period multiplied by the ratio of nonbank credit to bank credit at the beginning of the period.

The FEMD demonstrates what Allais had long suspected, namely, that the response period is variable over time. This springs from the fact that the velocity of money is itself variable over time. Allais's response period T is reminiscent of Hicks's planning interval, which he decided to call a "week" to distinguish it from Marshall's "day."[5] Hick's "week" is not a calendar week. It is an elementary period of time, short enough for prices to be constant. Hicks assumes that all planning decisions are made on Mondays, the planning dates, and executed during the remainder of the week. In Allais's work, the planning date is t.

There is, however, a major difference between Hicks's week and Allais's response period. While Hicks does consider the possibility of "making plans at irregular intervals," the variability of the planning interval does not play a central role in his analytical framework, as he more or less explicitly assumes such interval to be constant over time.[6] On the contrary, Allais's fundamental equation of monetary dynamics demonstrates that the response period is variable over time.

5.2   The HRL Formulation of Monetary Dynamics

5.2.1   *The Model*

The HRL model of endogenous cyclical fluctuations brings together all the various elements presented up until now, namely, the HRL formulation of the demand for money, the HRL formulation of the supply of money, and the fundamental equation of monetary dynamics.

From the latter, we have

$$x = \frac{1}{D}\frac{dD}{dt} = V\frac{M - M_D}{M} + \frac{1}{M}\frac{dM}{dt} \tag{5.25}$$

with $D = MV$ and $T = 1/V$. From 5.3 and 5.25, it follows that relationship 5.25 is equivalent to

$$T\frac{1}{V}\frac{dV}{dt} = 1 - \frac{M_D}{M} \tag{5.26}$$

According to the HRL formulation, both the demand for and the supply of money are functions of Z, the coefficient of psychological expansion (i.e., the present value of the sequence of past growth rates in nominal spending).

$$M_D = \phi_0^* D \Psi(Z) \tag{5.27a}$$

$$M = q B_0 e^{\rho t} \gamma(Z) \tag{5.27b}$$

Finally, from the HRL formulation, we also have

$$\frac{dZ}{dt} = x - \chi Z \qquad (5.28)$$

Therefore, we have a set of relationships in which x depends upon Z and dZ depends on x and Z. What does this interdependence imply? Does it generate an equilibrium? If so, is this equilibrium stable? And how is this equilibrium reached through time?

To answer these questions, Allais starts by defining a dynamic monetary equilibrium. In such a situation, first, the demand for money and the supply of money are and remain equal:

$$M_{De}(t) = M_e(t) \qquad (5.29)$$

Second, in a dynamic monetary equilibrium, nominal spending grows at a constant rate x_e and "expectations" are stable, which means that Z_e—and therefore z_e—is constant. In other words, the rate of growth in nominal spending must be equal to the dynamic equilibrium growth rate associated to Z_e.

$$x_e = \frac{\chi_0^* Z_e}{\Psi(Z_e)} = z_e \qquad (5.30)$$

These premises imply that nominal spending, the demand for money, and the supply of money all grow at the same constant rate ρ as the monetary base.

$$x_e = \frac{1}{D}\frac{dD}{dt} = \frac{1}{M_D}\frac{dM_D}{dt} = \frac{1}{M}\frac{dM}{dt} = \rho \qquad (5.31)$$

They also imply that, in equilibrium, the transactions velocity of money is constant.

Allais demonstrated in great and subtle details (see proof C.14, p. 306) how these premises allow to merge relationships 5.26 and 5.28 in one single second-order linear differential equation, the coefficients of which only depend on ρ and V_0^*, once the structural parameters α, b, a', b', and χ_0^* are set.[7]

$$\frac{1 - K_e'}{V_e}\frac{d^2 g(t)}{dt^2} + \left[1 - K_e' - K_e + \left(\frac{x_e + K_e \rho}{V_e}\right)\right]\frac{dg(t)}{dt}$$

$$+ (x_e + K_e \rho)g(t) = 0 \qquad (5.32)$$

with

$$g(t) = Z(t) - Z_e \tag{5.33a}$$

$$K_e' = \frac{\gamma'(Z_e)}{\gamma(Z_e)} \tag{5.33b}$$

$$K_e = \frac{-\Psi'(Z_e)}{\Psi(Z_e)} \tag{5.33c}$$

$$V_e = \frac{V_0^*}{\Psi(Z_e)} \tag{5.33d}$$

$$\chi_e = \frac{\chi_0^*}{\Psi(Z_e)} \tag{5.33e}$$

It is interesting to observe that up to the term Z_e, the terms K_e' and K_e represent the respective elasticities of the supply of money and of the demand for money with respect to Z for $Z = Z_e$.

An identical equation exists for $f(t) = V(t)/V_e - 1$:

$$\frac{1 - K_e'}{V_e} \frac{d^2 f(t)}{dt^2} + \left[1 - K_e' - K_e + \left(\frac{\chi_e + K_e \rho}{V_e} \right) \right] \frac{df(t)}{dt}$$

$$+ (\chi_e + K_e \rho) f(t) = 0 \tag{5.34}$$

This second-order linear differential equation is of the well-known following type:[8]

$$A y^{(2)} + B y^{(1)} + C y = 0 \tag{5.35}$$

Depending on the values taken by the coefficients A, B, and C, this equation can generate stable or unstable equilibrium, reached in either case through a periodic or pseudo-periodic convergence (see figures 5.2 and 5.3). When the equilibrium is unstable and the convergence pseudo-periodic, the endogenous fluctuations tend toward a limit cycle, that is, persist over time with a certain period and amplitude, instead of being dampened or explosive, as is systematically the case with Samuelson's oscillator. The speed of convergence toward equilibrium increases as the value taken by $-B/2A$ decreases. In the pseudo-periodic case, the period of the fluctuations is

$$\Theta = \frac{4\pi A}{\sqrt{4 AC - B^2}} \tag{5.36}$$

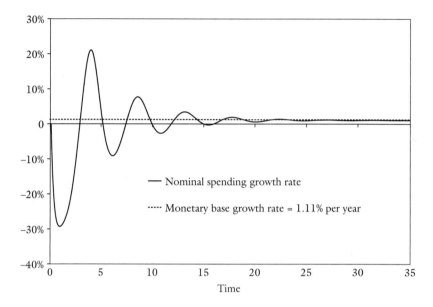

Figure 5.2 Stable equilibrium with pseudo-periodic convergence.

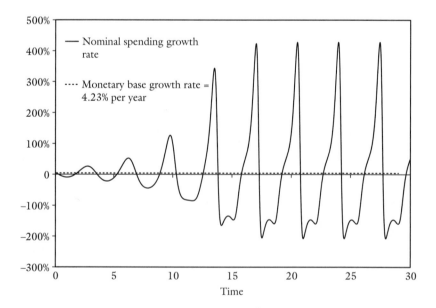

Figure 5.3 Unstable equilibrium with limit cycle.

For the purpose of computing endogenous cyclical fluctuations, relationships 5.26 and 5.28 can be written in the following discrete form (see proof C.15, p. 322):

$$\ln \frac{V_{n+1}}{V_0^*} = \ln \frac{V_n}{V_0^*} + 1 - \frac{V_n \Psi(Z_n)}{V_0^*} \tag{5.37}$$

$$Z_{n+1} = Z_n + \frac{1 - \frac{V_n \Psi(Z_n)}{V_0^*} - T_0^* \chi_0^* Z_n + \rho T_0^* \Psi(Z_n)}{1 - \frac{\gamma'(Z_n)}{\gamma(Z_n)}} \tag{5.38}$$

By adding the successive response periods, we get the successive positions on the calendar time scale.

$$t_n = \sum_1^n T_n = \sum_1^n T_0^* \Psi(Z_n) \tag{5.39}$$

To sum it up, the HRL model of monetary dynamics generates endogenous fluctuations, which belong to one of four types:

- The equilibrium can be stable at the rate of growth in base money or unstable around this level.
- The convergence process can be pseudo-periodic or aperiodic.

The shape of these endogenous fluctuations depends on the nine parameters defining the HRL model of monetary dynamics:

- the six structural parameters α, b, a', b', χ_0^*, and V_0^*.
- the two initialization parameters Z_1 and V_1.
- the assumed rate of growth in the monetary base ρ.

Everything else being equal, how do changes in the values taken by any of these parameters impact the shape of the endogenous fluctuations generated by the HRL model of monetary dynamics? How do they impact their amplitude, their speed of convergence toward equilibrium, if any, and finally their period, if any? Actually, there is no need to test all nine parameters to answer these questions. From the HRL formulation of the demand for money, we know that we can work with the following assumption:

$$\alpha = b = 1 \tag{5.40}$$

From the HRL formulation of the supply of money, we know that we have $0.8 \le b' \le 1.2$ and $1/3 \le a' \le 2/3$. For the sake of simplicity, we shall use the following central values:

$$b' = 1 \qquad a' = 0.5 \qquad\qquad (5.41)$$

As for the other parameters, we shall use the following default values:

$$\chi_0^* = 4.80\% \qquad\qquad (5.42a)$$
$$V_0^* = 16(T_0^* = 1/16) \qquad\qquad (5.42b)$$
$$Z_1 = 68\%(V_1 = 23.79) \qquad\qquad (5.42c)$$
$$\rho = 5\% \qquad\qquad (5.42d)$$

The quantities χ_0^*, V_0^*, and ρ are expressed at annual rate.

Under these assumptions, we have the following equilibrium values:

$$Z_e = 69.42\% \qquad\qquad (5.43a)$$
$$z_e = 5\% \qquad\qquad (5.43b)$$
$$V_e = 24.02 \qquad\qquad (5.43c)$$

In each of our simulations, we shall systematically compare two cases:

- The case in which the supply of money is endogenous, that is, when the multiplier of the monetary base is $\gamma(z)$.
- The case in which the supply of money is exogenous, that is, when the multiplier of the monetary base is constant, in which case the rate of growth in the money supply is assumed to be constant and equal to the rate of growth of the money base ρ.

To simplify the presentation of our observations, let us say that in our series of simulations, we have not encountered any case of unstable equilibrium associated with a limit cycle. When the supply of money is exogenous, the convergence process is always aperiodic. In contrast, when the supply of money is endogenous, the convergence process is most of the time, but not always, pseudo-periodic.

It is quite remarkable that the convergence process is always more rapid and the fluctuations always less pronounced when the supply of money is assumed to be exogenous instead of endogenous. In other words, according to the HRL formulation, fractional reserve banking is bound to be a source of inherent and undue macroeconomic instability even when it does not end up in bank runs. As one would expect following this observation, Allais was a very vocal advocate of full-reserve banking.

5.2.2   *Sensitivity with Respect to the Rate of Growth in Base Money ρ*

The tested values range from -5 to $+20$ percent. The amplitude of fluctuations (defined as the difference between the highest and the lowest rates of growth in nominal spending) increases as ρ increases above or decreases below 5 percent. This phenomenon is more pronounced when the supply of money is endogenous. Still in this case, the convergence speed increases as ρ increases above or decreases below 0 percent. When the supply of money is exogenous, the convergence speed remains virtually stable and always higher than in the case when it is endogenous. The period of fluctuations tends to fall as ρ increases.

5.2.3   *Sensitivity with Respect to the Rate of Memory Decay in Stationary State χ_0^**

Allais's as well as our own adjustments suggest that $\chi_0^* = 4.8$ percent, but it is quite conceivable that institutional or demographic changes alter this parameter so as to induce a structural shortening (or lengthening) of the duration of collective memory (section 11.4 will elaborate further on this point). The tested values range from 1 percent to 20 percent. The amplitude of fluctuations increases as χ_0^* decreases below or increases above 5 percent. This phenomenon is more pronounced when the supply of money is endogenous. When the supply of money is exogenous, the convergence speed is unaffected. When it is endogenous, the convergence speed falls continuously as the rate of memory decay increases. The period of fluctuations also falls in response to a rising rate of memory decay.

5.2.4   *Sensitivity with Respect to the Transactions Velocity of Money in Stationary State*

Allais's as well as our own adjustments suggest that $V_0^* = 16$. As with the rate of memory decay, one cannot rule out structural changes bringing about an increase (or decrease) of V_0^*. The tested values range from 5 to 32. When the supply of money is endogenous, the amplitude of fluctuations barely increases as V_0^* rises. When it is exogenous, the amplitude remains virtually constant. The speed of convergence increases with V_0^*. This phenomenon is more pronounced when the money supply is exogenous. The period of fluctuation is virtually stable when V_0^* remains between 5 and 20, but increases sharply beyond this threshold.

5.2.5   Sensitivity with Respect to Initial Condition Z_1 (or V_1)

Under the assumption that $V_1 = V_0^*/\Psi(Z_1)$, the value taken by Z_1 sets the initial elasticity of the model. The tested values range from -100 percent to $+200$ percent for Z_1 (i.e., from 10.94 to 67.11 for V_1). The amplitude of fluctuations increases as V_1 increases above or decreases below 24.11 ($Z_1 = 70$ percent), the tested value that is the closest to the equilibrium one. When the money supply is endogenous, this phenomenon is more pronounced, especially for the lower values of V_1. Changes in initial conditions affect neither the speed of convergence, nor the period of fluctuations.

5.2.6   Sensitivity with Respect to the Initial Gap Between Outstanding and Desired Money Balances (Misalignment Between V_1 and Z_1)

In section 5.2.5, we assumed $V_1 = V_0^*/\Psi(Z_1)$. Let Z_1 now be a constant, and let us have V_1 vary between 5 and 32, so that $V_1 \neq V_0^*/\Psi(Z_1)$. Under this assumption, since we have $\frac{V_1}{V_0^*}\Psi(Z_1) = \frac{M_{D_1}}{M_1}$, the quantity $\frac{V_1}{V_0^*}\Psi(Z_1)$ measures the initial gap between outstanding and desired money balances. The amplitude of fluctuations increases as V_1 rises above or falls below 24 (i.e., as the initial monetary gap is inflationary or deflationary). Neither the speed of convergence nor the period of fluctuations is affected by changes in V_1.

To sum it up, according to the HRL formulation of monetary dynamics, but in plain English, the road to large and brief but persistent fluctuations in nominal spending is drawn by a regime of endogenous money, an initial imbalance between outstanding and desired money balances, a proactive central bank, and, last but not least, bulled-up private agents (bankers, borrowers, and depositors) having a short memory. If this rings a bell, so be it!

Even when the money supply is assumed to be exogenous ($a' = b' = \alpha' = 0$) and constant ($\rho = 0$), all other parameters being set at their default values, the HRL formulation of monetary dynamics lends itself to the generation of sequences of positive growth rates in nominal spending. These sequences are cases of aperiodic convergence toward a stable equilibrium. Their occurrence is dependent on the initial conditions Z_1 and V_1. Let us first assume that there is no disequilibrium in the economy and that Z_1 is negative. Numerical simulations show that the more negative the value of Z_1 is, the more positive are the growth rates in the associated sequence.

This is quite understandable. The fact that Z_1 is negative means that prior to this time the economy has reached an equilibrium in response to a contraction in the money supply. Now, the assumption that the money supply no longer shrinks but remains constant means that nominal spending has to reach a new equilibrium consistent with a zero growth rate. The transition between the old equilibrium and the new one implies positive growth rates in nominal spending.

This phenomenon is more pronounced if it is further assumed that the economy has to deal with an initial inflationary gap, that is, a situation in which outstanding money balances exceed desired balances. Then, not only does nominal spending need to catch up with a higher rate of money growth, but also it must accommodate excess cash balances through an increase in the velocity of money. In this case, the sequence of rates of growth in nominal spending will gradually decline from a level all the more elevated as the initial inflationary gap is high.

When the money supply is assumed to be endogenous ($a' = 0.5$, $b' = 1$, $\alpha'a' = 1$) and growing ($\rho > 0$), all other parameters being set at their default values, the HRL formulation of monetary dynamics also lends itself to the generation of what Vernon Smith would probably call "echo bubbles," that is, patterns in which a first cycle of boom and bust is followed by a second one of smaller amplitude. These sequences are examples of pseudo-periodic convergence toward a stable equilibrium. During the boom phase of the cycle, the growth rate of nominal spending is accelerating. For example, for $\rho = 55$ percent, $Z_1 = 68$ percent $\Leftrightarrow z_1 = 4.85$ percent and $V_1 = 23.73$, the first cycle

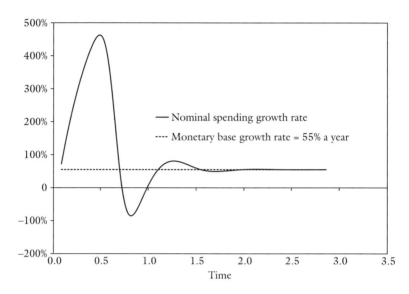

Figure 5.4 Echo bubble.

starts with an annualized instantaneous growth rate of 71.77 percent and peaks half a year later at 462.91 percent. The second cycle peaks at 80.91 percent (see figure 5.4).

However, the growth rate of the monetary base does not need to be elevated for accelerating growth rates to occur. Once again, and for the same reasons as in the previous case, this phenomenon is more pronounced if the economy is initially in an inflationary disequilibrium. For example, for $\rho = 1$ percent, $Z_1 = -60$ percent $\Leftrightarrow z_1 = -2.23$ percent and $V_1 = 12.30$ (instead of 12.39, i.e., an initial inflationary gap of 0.73 percent), the resulting sequence starts with an annualized instantaneous growth rate of 21.89 percent and peaks almost two years later at 68.08 percent (see figure 5.5).

5.3   Superimposition of Exogenous "Random" Shocks

To close this presentation of the HRL formulation of monetary dynamics, let us briefly mention that, as Allais did, one can easily introduce an exogenous factor in the model discussed above.[9] One simply needs to assume that the coefficient of psychological expansion Z is the present

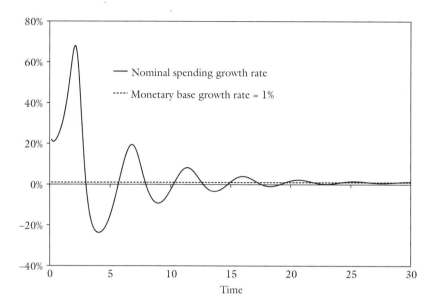

Figure 5.5 Exponential path with near-zero money growth.

value not just of the sequence of nominal growth rates

$$x(t) = \frac{1}{D}\frac{dD}{dt} \tag{5.44}$$

but also of the sum of this variable and an exogenous factor $X(t)$

$$x(t) + X(t) \tag{5.45}$$

which gives

$$Z(t) = \int_{-\infty}^{t} [x(\tau) + X(\tau)]e^{-\int_{\tau}^{t} \chi(u)du}\, d\tau \tag{5.46}$$

and

$$\frac{dZ}{dt} = x + X - \chi Z \tag{5.47}$$

To mimic "randomness" by application of Allais's T-theorem on the normal distribution of the values generated, under very general conditions, by almost-periodic functions, the term $X(t)$ could be taken to be such an almost-periodic function, that is, a linear combination of periodic functions, the frequencies of which are irrational and therefore incommensurable[10]

$$X(t) = \sum_{i=1}^{l} a_i \cos(2\pi f_i(t - t_i)) \qquad a_i > 0 \qquad \text{and} \qquad f_i = \frac{1}{T_i}$$

$$(5.48)$$

It is easier, however, to start investigating the interaction between endogenous forces and exogenous factors, by assuming a simpler form for the latter:

$$X(t) = a \cos \frac{2\pi t}{\theta} \tag{5.49}$$

Simulations made by Allais on this basis lead to the following observations:

- The influence of the exogenous factor $X(t)$ tends to override that of endogenous fluctuations.
- When, failing an exogenous disturbance, there is convergence toward a stable equilibrium and no limit cycle, the overlay of an exogenous periodicity with a given period θ gives rise to a limit cycle having this very period.
- When, failing an exogenous disturbance, there is an unstable equilibrium and a limit cycle, the overlay of an exogenous periodicity causes the period of the limit cycle to become that of the exogenous disturbance.

We leave it to further research to investigate the impact of an exogenous factor having an almost-periodic structure.

CHAPTER SIX

Joint Testing of the HRL Formulation of the Demand for Money and of the Fundamental Equation of Monetary Dynamics

AS WE HAVE PRESENTED Allais's fundamental equation of monetary dynamics (FEMD) in chapter 5, we have insisted on the fact that this equation is logically independent of Allais's HRL formulation of the demand for money. Any formulation of the demand for money is indeed liable to be compatible with the fundamental equation of monetary dynamics.

Nevertheless, the HRL formulation of the demand for money and the fundamental equation of monetary dynamics complement each other and are in practice interdependent. Through the coefficient of psychological expansion Z, the HRL formulation of the demand for money establishes a link between the sequence of rates of growth in nominal spending and relative desired balances $\Psi(Z)$, while the fundamental equation of monetary dynamics shows how the gap between effective and desired balances determines growth in nominal spending. Yet, appealing as these complementarity and interdependence may be from a theoretical point of view, they remain to be confronted with empirical data. Needless to say, a joint test of the HRL formulation of the demand for money and of the fundamental equation of monetary dynamics is more difficult to pass than two independent tests.

6.1   Early Tests of the HRL Formulation of the Demand for Money

Contrary to many an economist, Allais has always been very keen to test whether his theoretical propositions were compatible with empirical data. As we have seen in chapter 4 when we compared Cagan's formulation with Allais's early formulation of the demand for money, it is this very confrontation with empirical data that led Allais to the presentation of the HRL formulation in 1965. To test the HRL formulation, Allais computed adjustments between estimates of desired money balances and the money supply in 9 different countries and 15 different periods.

The principle underpinning these adjustments is derived from the assumption that desired and effective balances have to remain close to each other

$$M_D \approx M \tag{6.1}$$

and consists in finding whether there exist values for the parameters ϕ_0 and Z_0 such that the sum of the squared differences between desired and effective balances

$$e^2 = \sum [\ln(M/M_D)]^2 \tag{6.2}$$

can be minimized at a very low level, with the other parameters taking the following values:

$$\alpha = b = 1 \qquad \chi_0 = 0.40\% \text{ per month} \tag{6.3}$$

The interpretation of these adjustments gave rise to a controversy between Allais and Friedman's praetorian guard. For the sake of brevity, we refer our reader to Part VI of *Fondements de la dynamique monétaire* for a review of the arguments exchanged by the two sides *in English*. Besides what the reader has already encountered in previous paragraphs, there is nothing this book can add to this controversy.

6.2   Joint Testing of the HRL Formulation of the Demand for Money and the Fundamental Equation of Monetary Dynamics

6.2.1   *Problem*

In contrast, this book is the right place to elaborate on Allais's last contribution to the theory of monetary dynamics, namely, a *simultaneous* test of the HRL formulation of the demand for money and of the fundamental equation of monetary dynamics. It is only in 2000–at the age of 89 and 32 years after the presentation of the fundamental equation–that Allais found a way to conduct such a test, the principle and the results of which he presented *in French* in 2001 in appendix B to *Fondements de la dynamique monétaire*. The problem Allais had eventually solved can be formulated as follows: under the twofold assumption that the HRL formulation of the demand for money and the fundamental equation of monetary dynamics are valid, is there a way to compute estimates of empirical rates of growth in nominal spending and how close are these estimates to empirical data? The difficulty lies in computing estimates of the relative desired balances $\Psi(Z)$ without using the observed rates of growth x as inputs. Here is how Allais solved this problem.

6.2.2   *Solution*

On one hand, the HRL formulation of the demand for money states what the demand for money should be, given the sequence of historic growth rates of nominal spending. Here, the causality runs from nominal growth to the demand for money.

$$x_0, x_1, \ldots, x \to Z \to \Psi(Z) \to M_D \tag{6.4}$$

with

$$M_D = \phi_0^* D \Psi(Z) \tag{6.5}$$

and

$$\frac{dZ}{dt} = x - \chi Z \tag{6.6}$$

On the other hand, the fundamental equation of monetary dynamics states what the rate of growth in nominal spending should be, given the growth in money supply, the transactions velocity of money and, last but not least, the difference between effective and desired money balances.

$$x = \frac{1}{D}\frac{dD}{dt} = V\frac{M - M_D}{M} + \frac{1}{M}\frac{dM}{dt} \tag{6.7}$$

In the fundamental equation of monetary dynamics, the causality runs in the opposite direction, from monetary imbalances to nominal growth (see figure 6.1).

If the fundamental equation of monetary dynamics is to be used to produce estimates of the observed nominal growth rates consistent with the HRL formulation of the demand for money, $\Psi(Z)$ has to be estimated indirectly, without any reference to the observed rates of growth, contrary to what we did when we studied the endogenous generation of cyclical fluctuations in section 5.2.

Neither the philosophy nor the technicalities of Allais's appendix B are easy to understand, at least on the first reading. But the effort is worth making, as appendix B is the point of convergence of 50 years of research in the field of monetary dynamics.

The philosophy of Allais's simultaneous test is as follows:

- First, estimate $\Psi(Z)$ not directly from the observed growth rates, but indirectly from the observed velocity of money.
- Second, use this estimate of $\Psi(Z)$ to estimate Z.

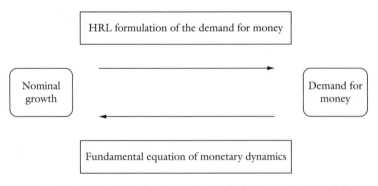

Figure 6.1 Interdependence of the HRL formulation of the demand for money and of the fundamental equation of monetary dynamics.

- Third, derive an estimate x^* of x from dZ.
- Finally, compare these estimates x^* with the actual sequence of observed growth rates x.

Each of these successive estimations is made in such a way that it be consistent with both the fundamental equation of monetary dynamics and the HRL formulation of the demand for money.

These two independent theoretical propositions share one common assumption, namely, that desired and effective balances, albeit distinct, are two quantities that remain close to each other:

$$M_D \approx M \qquad (6.8)$$

Therefore, as we have seen in chapter 4 with relationship 4.27, we have

$$V \approx \frac{1}{\phi_0^* \Psi(Z)} \qquad (6.9)$$

and

$$VT \approx 1 \Leftrightarrow T \approx \frac{1}{V} \qquad (6.10)$$

On one hand, if the fundamental equation of monetary dynamics is valid, we know from relationship 5.26 that

$$T \frac{1}{V} \frac{dV}{dt} = 1 - \frac{M_D}{M} \qquad (6.11)$$

On the other hand, if the HRL formulation of the demand for money is valid, both T and M_D/M are linked to $\Psi(Z)$. Since $T \approx 1/V$, relationship 6.9 yields

$$T \approx \phi_0^* \Psi(Z^*) \qquad (6.12)$$

where Z^* and ϕ_0^* are estimates of, respectively, Z and ϕ_0.

As for M_D/M, we have

$$\frac{M_D}{M} = \frac{\phi_0^* D \Psi(Z)}{M} = \phi_0^* V \Psi(Z) \qquad (6.13)$$

From relationships 4.8 and 4.27, we also know that:

$$T = T_0^* \Psi(Z^*) \qquad (6.14)$$

From relationships 6.12 and 6.14, it follows that

$$T_0^* = \phi_0^* \tag{6.15}$$

Using relationships 6.12 to 6.15, relationship 6.11 can be written as follows:

$$T_0^* \Psi(Z^*) \frac{1}{V} \frac{dV}{dt} = 1 - T_0^* V \Psi(Z^*) \tag{6.16}$$

Relationship 6.16 opens up the possibility of expressing Z^* directly as a function of V and $\frac{1}{V}\frac{dV}{dt}$, which are empirical data, without any reference to the sequence of historic growth rates x. Since the growth rate of nominal spending x^* can in turn be estimated as a function of Z^* by using relationship 6.6, relationship 6.16 actually opens up in turn the possibility of estimating the growth rate of nominal spending x^* directly from the times series of the observed transactions velocity of money, with

$$x^* = \frac{dZ^*}{dt} + \frac{\chi_0^*}{\Psi(Z^*)} Z^* \tag{6.17}$$

If both the fundamental equation of monetary dynamics and the HRL formulation of the demand for money are valid, there must exist a value of T_0^* such that the sum of the squared differences between the estimated values x^* derived from relationships 6.16 and 6.17 and the actual values x is minimized at a low level.

From relationship 6.16, for $\alpha = b = 1$, we get:

$$Z^* = \ln\left(2T_0^* \left(\frac{1}{V} \frac{dV}{dt} + V \right) - 1 \right) \tag{6.18}$$

To simplify the next steps, let us define F as follows:

$$F = \frac{1}{V} \frac{dV}{dt} + V \tag{6.19}$$

Then, relationship 6.18 becomes

$$Z^* = \ln(2T_0^* F - 1) \tag{6.20}$$

and we also have

$$1 + e^{Z^*} = 2T_0^* F \tag{6.21}$$

Since

$$\chi(Z^*) = \frac{\chi_0^*}{\Psi(Z^*)} = \frac{\chi_0^*(1 + e^{Z^*})}{2} \qquad (6.22)$$

we have

$$\chi(Z^*) = \chi_0^* T_0^* F \qquad (6.23)$$

From relationship 6.17, we get

$$x^* = \frac{dZ^*}{dt} + T_0^* \chi_0^* F \ln(2T_0^* F - 1) \qquad (6.24)$$

If both the fundamental equation of monetary dynamics and the HRL formulation of the demand for money are valid, there must exist a value of the parameter T_0^* such that the estimated values x^* of x derived from relationship 6.24 are very close to the observed rates of growth x.

Let us define

$$e = x - x^* \qquad (6.25)$$

In the end, the simultaneous test of the HRL formulation of the demand for money and of the fundamental equation of monetary dynamics consists in finding whether there exists a value of T_0^* that minimizes the average squared estimation error.

Now that we have specified a theoretical framework to simultaneously test the HRL formulation of the demand for money and the fundamental equation of monetary dynamics, we can confront the estimates it yields with empirical data. However, the nature of standard empirical data can give rise to two implementation problems:

- As the contemporary set of times series contains neither the aggregate value of nominal transactions D, nor the transactions velocity of money V, we have to derive them from the national income R and the income velocity of money v, under the admittedly questionable assumption that the ratio between nominal transactions and national income is constant:

$$D = KR \Leftrightarrow V = Kv \qquad (6.26)$$

- Furthermore, we have to consider the case where R and v are available not in current money terms, but in the form of an index number. For the sake of brevity, we shall not elaborate on this case.

6.3 Allais's Test on the US Economy from 1918 to 1941: An Alternative Interpretation of the Great Depression

It cannot be by accident that Allais chose the US economy between 1918 and 1941 as the data set on which to simultaneously test the fundamental equation of monetary dynamics and the HRL formulation of the demand for money. For the Great Depression is the traumatic personal experience that caused Allais to become an economist. Like Ulysses after his long odyssey, Allais had to come back to where his own scientific adventure had started, almost 70 years earlier.

The data used by Allais are annual index data.[1] They are given on page 1192 of *Fondements de la dynamique monétaire*. They were initially presented on page 59 of *The empirical approaches of the hereditary and relativistic theory of the demand for money: Results, interpretation and rejoinders*, Economia della Scelte Pubbliche, Journal of Public Finance and Public Choice, 1986, pp. 3–83. A comment on page 431 of *Fondements de la dynamique monétaire* suggests that these data are "those of Milton Friedman." Nevertheless, Allais does not say which of Milton Friedman's works is their source.

The results of Allais's adjustments are presented at 5-year intervals in Table III on page 1268 of *Fondements*. For the year 1933, this table contains a misprint as regards the index of nominal income: instead of 1.720, one should read 1.113, as on page 1192 (after 1.172 in 1932). This misprint has, however, no consequence at all on the results presented in this table. Table 6.1 of this book presents at a 1-year interval the correct input data as well as the results of our own computations. As for the parameters, we have used the same values as Allais:

$$\alpha = 1 \qquad (6.27a)$$

$$b = 1 \qquad (6.27b)$$

$$\chi_0 = 4.80\% \text{ per year} \qquad (6.27c)$$

$$p = 1 \qquad (6.27d)$$

$$K = 30 \qquad (6.27e)$$

$$\phi_0^{**} = 1.85 \qquad (6.27f)$$

As for the average estimation error, we have $e = 0.45$ percent. The (x^*, x) joint adjustment is more accurate than the (M_D, M) adjustment of the HRL formulation on a stand-alone basis, which has an average estimation error of 2.83 percent.

TABLE 6.1
Great Depression Joint Adjustment

	R	M	v	$\frac{d\ln v}{dt}$ (%)	$\frac{d\ln v}{dt}/K$ (%)	F	Z^* (%)	$\frac{dZ^*}{dt}$ (%)	x^* (%)	x (%)
1918	1.720	1.569	1.096	na	na	1.0973	111.84	na	na	na
1919	2.012	1.777	1.132	3.23	0.11	1.1291	115.61	3.77	14.67	15.68
1920	2.050	1.990	1.030	−9.45	−0.31	1.0221	102.30	−13.31	−1.72	1.87
1921	1.525	1.887	0.808	−24.27	−0.81	0.8118	69.50	−32.81	−23.52	−29.58
1922	1.755	1.947	0.901	10.92	0.36	0.9035	85.14	15.64	20.65	14.05
1923	2.050	2.134	0.961	6.37	0.21	0.9591	93.56	8.41	15.25	15.54
1924	2.038	2.222	0.917	−4.63	−0.15	0.9166	87.19	−6.37	1.60	−0.59
1925	2.174	2.412	0.901	−1.74	−0.06	0.9011	84.76	−2.43	4.66	6.46
1926	2.259	2.525	0.895	−0.74	−0.02	0.8933	83.51	−1.24	5.54	3.84
1927	2.239	2.608	0.859	−4.12	−0.14	0.8582	77.72	−5.80	0.83	−0.89
1928	2.321	2.730	0.850	−0.97	−0.03	0.8518	76.62	−1.09	4.83	3.60
1929	2.457	2.754	0.892	4.82	0.16	0.8875	82.59	5.97	11.76	5.69
1930	2.109	2.715	0.777	−13.85	−0.46	0.7697	61.40	−21.19	−14.68	−15.27
1931	1.656	2.640	0.627	−21.38	−0.71	0.6208	26.01	−35.39	−31.19	−24.18
1932	1.172	2.267	0.517	−19.34	−0.64	0.5181	−8.66	−34.67	−33.24	−34.57
1933	1.113	2.081	0.535	3.40	0.11	0.5384	−0.79	7.87	7.47	−5.17
1934	1.366	2.295	0.595	10.69	0.36	0.5977	19.18	19.98	19.94	20.48
1935	1.597	2.490	0.641	7.47	0.25	0.6424	31.99	12.80	13.82	15.62
1936	1.819	2.748	0.662	3.16	0.11	0.6649	37.85	5.87	7.69	13.02
1937	2.069	2.859	0.724	8.92	0.30	0.7212	51.18	13.33	15.56	12.88
1938	1.895	2.824	0.671	−7.55	−0.25	0.6710	39.38	−11.80	−8.52	−8.78
1939	2.038	3.042	0.670	−0.16	−0.01	0.6706	39.30	−0.08	2.26	7.28
1940	2.286	3.342	0.684	2.08	0.07	0.6887	43.72	4.42	6.76	11.48
1941	2.918	3.702	0.788	14.18	0.47	na	na	na	na	24.41

Most importantly, the joint adjustment tells a much more credible story about the gap between effective and desired money balances during the interwar period. In 1920, which was marked by recession and deflation, according to the joint adjustment, the liquidity gap was negative, while it is estimated to be positive by the HRL adjustment. Between 1921 and 1928, the boom years, the joint adjustment suggests the liquidity gap was close to 0; the HRL adjustment has it constantly negative. Both adjustments show a negative liquidity gap in 1929, but the joint adjustment has it until 1931, while the HRL adjustment has it positive as early as 1930. Finally, according to the joint adjustment, the liquidity gap remained inflationary from 1932 to 1936, while it is estimated to be deflationary by the HRL adjustment.

This pattern suggests that the liquidity gap, as measured through the joint adjustment, has been a reliable leading indicator of fluctuations in nominal spending during the interwar period. It also suggests an alternative to the standard monetarist interpretation of the Great Depression.[2]

According to the interpretation advocated by Friedman, the Great Depression was caused by a contraction in the money supply, a contraction that started in 1929. The weak point in this interpretation is the recovery. Friedman and Schumpeter both think it started in the second half of 1932; the NBER cycle trough date is March 1933. Both dates in any case precede the pickup in the money supply, which only started in 1934. If the monetarist explanation were relevant, the recovery should not have started before the money supply picked up. And yet, it definitely did.

Allais's framework explains this paradox. Yes, money supply was still contracting in 1932 and 1933. But so, too, was the demand for money, as a result of the contraction in nominal activity, even after allowing for a rise in the preference for liquidity (or a fall in the velocity of money). Since the demand for money was contracting faster than effective balances, there came a point in 1932 when the liquidity gap, which had been deflationary since 1929, became positive. As a result, instead of falling further, money velocity picked up and its increase was more than enough to offset the continued contraction in the money supply. Thus were planted the seeds of the subsequent recovery.

This book presents three new joint tests of the fundamental equation of monetary dynamics and of the HRL formulation of the demand

TABLE 6.2
Joint Tests of the HRL Formulation of the Demand for Money
and of the Fundamental Equation of Monetary Dynamics on
Four Data Sets

	United States	Japan	EMU	Global
Frequency	Annual	Quarterly	Quarterly	Quarterly
Beginning	1918	1955	1970	1987
End	1941	Q4 2006	Q4 2006	Q4 2006
ϕ_0^*	1.774	1.702	4.728	2.370
$e(M_D, M)$	2.83%	5.72%	5.86%	3.19%
K	30	15	11	20
ϕ_0^{**}	1.85	6.60	4.74	10.20
$e(x^*, x)$	4.49%	1.22%	0.91%	0.77%
$e(M_D^*, M)$	0.45%	0.34%	0.21%	0.19%

for money on more contemporary data sets, all ending in 2006 (table 6.2):

- Japan since 1955.
- The member countries of the European Monetary Union (EMU) since 1970.
- The global economy since 1987.

In the first two cases, we have used Datastream time series. In the latter case, we have first constructed Fisher's indices of the global nominal GDP and of the global money stock. These indices aggregate data from the main developed as well as emerging economies.

Figures 6.2 and 6.3 illustrate two outputs from the joint adjustment of Japanese data. Figure 6.2 is a scatterplot that shows the empirical relationship between the estimated gap between desired and effective money balances, on the horizontal axis, and, on the vertical one, the relative change in money velocity observed during the subsequent quarter. According to relationships 6.3 to 6.6, the estimated gap between desired and effective money balances is

$$1 - \phi_0^* V \Psi(Z) \qquad (6.28)$$

As for figure 6.3, it compares the estimated quarterly rate of nominal growth x^* with the observed one x.

The quality of our three new adjustments is comparable to that of Allais's original one. Furthermore, the values of the parameters are

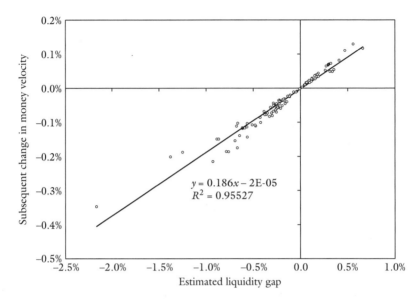

Figure 6.2 Japan 1955–2006, joint test of the HRL formulation and the FEMD.

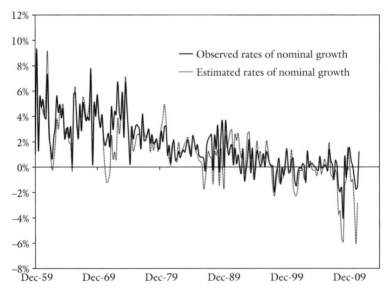

Figure 6.3 Japan 1955–2006, joint test of the HRL formulation and the FEMD.

also of the same order of magnitude. We therefore submit that the three new tests presented in this book confirm Allais's original test—subject to one important caveat: in all three cases, from 2004 onward, the estimated and actual rates of nominal growth increasingly diverged, as actual growth turned out to be much stronger than estimated growth. This divergence lasted until 2007, when actual growth collapsed and caught up with estimated growth, at a much lower level.

The coincidence is striking: the joint test systematically underestimated nominal growth just as the so-called shadow banking system flourished; actual growth caught up with the model's estimate in the wake of the subprime crisis as nonbank credit was suddenly unwound. This coincidence suggests that Allais's framework is indeed relevant if and when nonbank credit can be neglected. Where the threshold lies that makes this assumption acceptable or not is of course debatable.

From 1984 to 2003, the annual flow of credit provided by the US shadow banking system grew from 0 to about 2 percent of GDP without showing any of the cyclical fluctuations seen in bank credit. Toward the end of this period the flow of nonbank credit was still one-half of the bank credit flow (or one-third of the aggregate credit flow). Things changed drastically from 2003 onward when the flow of nonbank credit started to catch up with the flow of bank credit. By 2007, the former had become as large as the latter. These observations may suggest that nonbank credit can be neglected as long as it contributes to less than one-third of aggregate new credit. If that is the case, Allais's framework would be valid in quite a broad set of empirical conditions. Furthermore, the regulatory response to the subprime crisis may now more effectively curb the role and the growth of the shadow banking system relative to the banking system.

6.4 Bridges Between Allais's Monetary Dynamics and Behavioral Finance

Chapters 3 to 6 of this book might have looked disproportionately, if not excessively, long. However, Allais's contributions to monetary dynamics are so original, diverse, and comprehensive and yet so little known that they do not lend themselves to a brief summary. Hopefully, these four chapters will have convinced our reader that Allais's contributions are worth exploring further.

By way of a conclusion to the second part of this book, it may be useful to summarize the insights and assumptions that behavioral finance could or should borrow from Allais's monetary dynamics in order to test them in its own field:

- Investors' return expectations are rooted in their memory of past price movements.
- Perceived returns, their so-called expectations, are in fact the present value of the sequences of past returns.
- The collective rate of memory decay varies through time in response to changing market conditions: the duration of investors' memory shortens as a bull market accelerates and conversely lengthens as prices fall persistently, and so does their planning period.
- In other words, the elasticity of "expectations" with respect to actual market movements varies through time, from almost 0 in a major bear market to 1 in an hyperbull market.
- Investors' behavior, that is, their demand for risky assets or their desired portfolio, is increasing, bounded, and nonlinear with respect to their perceived returns.
- The elasticity of investors' behavior with respect to the present value of past returns varies between $\alpha' p \chi_0 Z/(1 + b)$ and 0.
- The adjustment process whereby the desired portfolio converges toward the effective portfolio generates endogenous aperiodic or pseudo-periodic cyclical fluctuations.
- The resulting equilibrium may be stable or unstable.

For policymakers, the main takeaway may be that deflationary "expectations" are sticky, while "inflationary" ones are volatile.

Allais uses the word "hereditary" to indicate the presence of the lagged values of the first-order relative difference of a given variable in an equation modeling the perceived rate of change in this variable, this perceived rate of change being in turn the argument of a logistic behavioral function. As we have seen, the same word could have been used by Cagan to describe his formulation of inflation expectations.

The use of lagged values of a variable, of the residuals of a model, or of a set of variables underpins state-of-the-art statistical techniques such as autoregressive integrated moving average (ARIMA), general autoregressive conditional heteroskedasticity (GARCH), vector autoregression (VAR), and Granger causality tests.[3] This is because all of these state-of-the-art specifications acknowledge the existence of serial correlation in many empirical time series and the need to account for the persistence of the effects of a given variable on itself as well as on others in most dynamic processes.

The fact that both the HRL formulation and these specifications use lagged values of given variables begs the following question: what are the similarities and the differences between these specifications, on one hand, and the HRL formulation, on the other hand? The one and only similarity has already been mentioned: it is the presence of lagged values of a certain variable. The differences are the following:

- In all these specifications, the length of the lag is assumed to be constant through time, while, owing to its relativist structure, the HRL formulation assumes the lag to be time-varying.[4]
- In all these specifications, the length of the lag (or the order of the autoregression) and the shapes of lag distributions (the coefficients of the lagged values) have to be optimized on a case-by-case basis by the analyst, using ordinary least squares regression or more complex algorithms, while in the HRL formulation, both the length of the lag and the shapes of lag distributions seem to obey an invariant law, the law of memory decay, with parameters known ex ante ($\chi_0 = 0.40$ percent, $\alpha = b = 1$).
- Finally, the HRL formulation assumes the behavior of economic agents to be logistic (nonlinear) with respect to the perceived rate of change of any variable, while most, if not all these specifications, seem to assume linear relationships.

An analyst accustomed to using ARIMA, GARCH, VAR, and Granger causality techniques should find it rather natural to test the flexibility embedded in the HRL formulation through the relativist assumption.

PART THREE

Transposing the HRL Formulation to Financial Markets: Preliminary Steps

Allais's HRL Formulation: Illustration of Its Dynamic Properties by an Example of Hyperinflation (Zimbabwe 2000–2008)

THREE FUNDAMENTAL NOTIONS underpin Allais's HRL formulation: memory, psychological time, and satiety.[1] Every one of us has at least an intuition of these three concepts. Their expression in mathematical terms is what makes the HRL formulation difficult to command. In their comments on the HRL formulation, Cagan, Darby, and Scadding all invoked Milton Friedman's authority.[2]

Yet, there is little doubt that Cagan, Darby, and Scadding did not fully understand how the HRL formulation really works.

Allais replied to their comments in great detail, but his answers remained mostly theoretical. This is not to say that Allais did not accept the challenge of empirical data—quite the opposite. In his original work of 1965, he had presented nine examples of estimation of the demand for money, with a high degree of accuracy. But the intermediate process consisting in computing the value of Z step by step, month after month, was not shown at all.[3]

Had Allais provided a numerical example showing how to compute relationships 4.38 to 4.44 through time, and had Cagan, Darby, or Scadding tried to replicate these computations on their own, it is quite probable that their controversy would have been more fruitful and that the dynamic properties of the HRL formulation would have been better understood. To be fair, what is now easy to do in an Excel spreadsheet was certainly costly and time-consuming to perform some 45 years ago.[4]

Therefore, we kindly invite the reader to compute on her or his own the values shown in table 7.1. There is no better way to understand the HRL formulation than to use it in a hyperinflation context. This is why the example analyzed in table 7.1 is the hyperinflation observed in Zimbabwe between 2000 and 2008. Over that period, the price level was multiplied by 1.2226×10^{12}, with a clear acceleration from mid-2005 onward. In July 2008 alone, prices increased by 2600 percent (i.e., a multiplication by 27).

For lack of space, table 7.1 only shows the sequence from December 2006 onward. The value of Z at this date, namely, 351.11 percent, can be considered as an initialization parameter, albeit it is the result of the computations pertaining to the 7 preceding years. As for the intrinsic psychological parameters, we have used $\alpha = b = 1$ and $\chi_0 = 0.40$ percent a month.

7.1   Dynamic Equilibrium Simulation: $x_n = z_{n-1}$

The perceived rate of inflation, expressed as an annual continuous rate, is shown in column 12. One can easily check that the perceived rate of inflation (expressed as a monthly log rate) shown in column 13 for July 2008, that is, 346.24 percent, is the dynamic equilibrium rate by plugging it in as the monthly inflation log rate from August 2008 onward. Since, under this assumption, $x_n = z_{n-1}$, the "forecasting error" $k'_n = x_n - z_{n-1} = 0$ and all other values remain constant ad infinitum:

$$k_{n+1} \quad = \quad k_n \quad = 405.73\% \qquad (7.1a)$$
$$Z_n \quad = Z_{n-1} \quad = 571.095\% \qquad (7.1b)$$
$$\Psi_n \quad = \Psi_{n-1} \quad = 0.66\% \qquad (7.1c)$$
$$\chi_n \quad = \chi_{n-1} \quad = 727.54\% \qquad (7.1d)$$
$$z_n \quad = z_{n-1} \quad = 346.24\% \qquad (7.1e)$$

7.2   Dynamic Disequilibrium Simulation: $x_n \neq z_{n-1}$

Now, let us examine what happens in the general case when $x_n \neq z_{n-1}$, and let us start from March 2008. In that month, prices increased by 133.84 percent in log terms.

$$x_{2008/03} = 133.84\% \qquad (7.2)$$

TABLE 7.1
Zimbabwe Hyperinflation Example

	(1) x	(2) k'	(3) k	(4) $1 - e^{-pk}$	(5) Z	(6) Ψ	(7) $\frac{d\Psi}{dt}$	(8) V	(9) $\frac{dV}{dt}$	(10) χ	(11) $\chi/12$	(12) z	(13) $z/12$	(14) Monthly decay factor	(15) Cumulative decay factor	(16) Memory duration
31-dec-06	30.9%	9%	27.6%	24.1%	351.1%	5.8%	-7.6%	17.24	7.9%	82.8%	6.9%	290.6%	24.2%	93.3%	2.7%	18.76
31-jan-07	37.5	13.2	30.4	26.2	362.5	5.2	-11.1	19.27	11.7	92.5	7.7	335.3	27.9	92.6	2.9	17.75
28-feb-07	32.1	4.1	34.9	29.5	366.0	5.0	-3.4	19.93	3.5	95.7	8.0	350.2	29.2	92.3	3.1	17.13
31-mar-07	40.9	11.7	36.4	30.5	375.8	4.6	-9.6	21.94	10.1	105.3	8.8	395.8	33.0	91.6	3.4	16.18
30-apr-07	69.7	36.7	41.0	33.6	405.9	3.4	-29.5	29.47	34.3	141.5	11.8	574.3	47.9	88.9	3.8	14.25
31-may-07	44.1	-3.8	58.8	44.5	403.1	3.5	2.8	28.65	-2.8	137.5	11.5	554.4	46.2	89.2	4.3	13.60
30-jun-07	62.2	16.0	56.9	43.4	415.3	3.1	-12.0	32.30	12.7	155.0	12.9	643.8	53.7	87.9	4.9	12.45
31-jul-07	27.5	-26.2	65.7	48.2	396.1	3.7	18.8	26.75	-17.2	128.4	10.7	508.6	42.4	89.9	5.4	12.53
31-aug-07	11.2	-31.2	52.3	40.7	371.8	4.7	23.8	21.09	-21.2	101.2	8.4	376.3	31.4	91.9	5.9	13.14
30-sep-07	32.7	1.3	39.0	32.3	372.9	4.7	-1.1	21.31	1.1	102.3	8.5	381.4	31.8	91.8	6.4	12.94
31-oct-07	85.7	53.9	39.6	32.7	417.4	3.0	-43.7	32.99	54.8	158.3	13.2	660.9	55.1	87.6	7.3	11.12
30-nov-07	83.9	28.8	67.4	49.1	438.4	2.5	-20.7	40.57	23.0	194.7	16.2	853.6	71.1	85.0	8.6	9.83
31-dec-07	122.4	51.3	86.5	57.9	472.7	1.8	-34.0	56.97	40.4	273.4	22.8	1292.5	107.7	79.6	10.8	8.04
31-jan-08	79.2	-28.5	129.6	72.6	456.7	2.1	15.8	48.63	-14.6	233.4	19.5	1066.1	88.8	82.3	13.2	7.52
29-feb-08	81.5	-7.4	107.4	65.8	452.2	2.2	4.5	46.51	-4.4	223.2	18.6	1009.4	84.1	83.0	15.9	7.05
31-mar-08	133.8	49.7	101.8	63.9	483.4	1.6	-30.9	63.35	36.2	304.1	25.3	1469.8	122.5	77.6	20.4	5.90
30-apr-08	114.0	-8.5	146.9	77.0	478.9	1.7	4.4	60.60	-4.3	290.9	24.2	1393.1	116.1	78.5	26.0	5.35
31-may-08	167.4	51.3	139.4	75.2	506.6	1.3	-27.5	79.77	31.6	382.9	31.9	1939.8	161.6	72.7	35.8	4.36
31-jun-08	224.0	62.4	192.5	85.4	534.3	1.0	-27.5	105.03	31.7	504.1	42.0	2693.5	224.5	65.7	54.5	3.28
31-jul-08	329.6	105.1	265.4	93.0	571.1	0.7	-36.7	151.57	44.3	727.5	60.6	4154.9	346.2	54.5	100.0	2.09
31-aug-08	na	na	405.7	98.3	na	na	na	na	na	na	na	na	na	na	na	na

As the perceived rate of inflation was 84.12 percent at the end of February, we have

$$z_{2008/02} = 84.12\% \tag{7.3}$$

Therefore, at the end of March, the "forecasting error" was

$$k'_{2008/03} = x_{2008/03} - z_{2008/02} = 133.84\% - 84.12\% = 49.72\% \tag{7.4}$$

This "surprise," whereby inflation turned out to be higher at the end of March 2008 than "expected" at its beginning, triggers a chain reaction in which

- The elasticity of "expectations" $1 - e^{-pk_{n+1}}$ rises from 63.87 percent to 76.97 percent per month.
- The coefficient of psychological expansion Z increases from 452.19 percent to 483.38 percent.
- Relative desired balances Ψ fall from 2.15 percent to 1.58 percent.
- The rate of decay of memory χ rises from 18.60 percent to 25.43 percent per month.
- The perceived rate of inflation z increases from 84.12 percent to 122.48 percent per month.

Up to the constant ϕ_0, relative desired balances are an estimate of real desired balances.

$$M_D = \phi_0 \Psi(Z) P \Leftrightarrow \phi_0 \Psi(Z) = \frac{M_D}{P} \approx \frac{1}{V} = T \tag{7.5}$$

Therefore, a fall of relative desired balances from 2.15 percent to 1.58 percent implies a 26.58 percent contraction in relative desired real balances, *irrespective of the change in the money supply during that month.* Since, up to the constant ϕ_0, money velocity is close to the inverse of relative desired balances, it can also be said that, as a result of higher than "expected" inflation, the velocity of money increases by 36.21 percent from 46.51 to 63.35. Finally, as a result of higher than "expected" inflation, the planning horizon shrinks.

The next month, April 2008, provides an example in the other direction, namely, lower than "expected" inflation. We let the reader verify that all the consequences of this outcome are the opposite of those we have just analyzed.

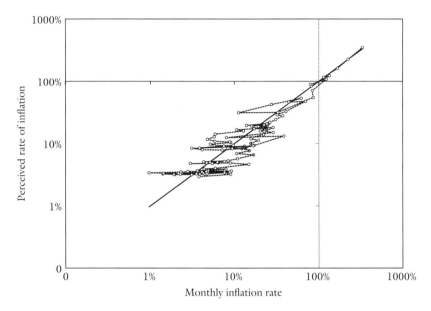

Figure 7.1 Zimbabwe: asymptotic convergence of the perceived rate of inflation toward the instantaneous rate of inflation.

7.3 Asymptotic Convergence of z_n Toward x_n

As shown in figure 7.1, as hyperinflation kept on accelerating from May to July 2008, the perceived rate of inflation converged asymptotically toward the instantaneous rate of inflation. This asymptotic convergence happens because the rate of memory decay grows exponentially (column 10 or 11) and the elasticity of the perceived rate of inflation z with respect to the instantaneous rate of inflation x converges toward unity (column 4). If, for example, we assume the August 2008 rate of inflation to be very close to the perceived rate of inflation in July 2008

$$x_{2008/08} = z_{2008/07} + 1\% = 347.24\% \qquad (7.6)$$

we observe that the perceived rate of inflation in August 2008 will be very close to the hypothetical August 2008 rate of inflation

$$z_{2008/08} = 347.23\% \approx x_{2008/08} \qquad (7.7)$$

To put things in different words, this convergence of the perceived rate of inflation toward the instantaneous rate of inflation happens because the relevant past shrinks to almost nothing. This is illustrated by the lag structure as of July 2008, as shown in columns (14) and (15).

- The July 2008 rate of inflation (329.59 percent), information that has not started to age, is given a weight of 1.
- The June 2008 rate of inflation (224.00 percent), 1-month-old information, is given a weight of $0.5454 = 1 \times 0.5454$.
- The May 2008 rate of inflation (167.41 percent), 2-month-old information, is given a weight of $0.3583 = 1 \times 0.5454 \times 0.6570$.
- The April 2008 rate of inflation (113.96 percent), 3-month-old information, is given a weight of $0.2604 = 1 \times 0.5454 \times 0.6570 \times 0.7268$.
- And so on.

7.4   The Duration of Memory

The most recent data points, which are also the largest in absolute size, are given the greatest weight. As we move backward along the calendar time scale, it is natural to assign to each point in time a weight equal to the present value of the corresponding information and to sum the resulting weighted maturities.

$$\theta = (0 \times 100\% \times 329.59\%) + (1 \times 54.54\% \times 224\%)$$
$$+ (2 \times 35.83\% \times 167.41\%) + (3 \times 26.04\% \times 113.96\%) + \cdots$$
$$(7.8)$$

It is also natural to normalize the weighting coefficients by their sum, which is, by definition, equal to Z, the coefficient of psychological expansion.

$$Z = (100\% \times 329.59\%) + (54.54\% \times 224\%)$$
$$+ (35.83\% \times 167.41\%) + (26.04\% \times 113.96\%) + \cdots \qquad (7.9)$$

Hence, we have

$$\frac{\theta}{Z} = \frac{(0 \times 100\% \times 329.59\%) + \cdots + (3 \times 26.04\% \times 113.96\%) + \cdots}{(100\% \times 329.59\%) + \cdots + (26.04\% \times 113.96\%) + \cdots}$$
$$(7.10)$$

A bond analyst will recognize in relationship 7.10 the definition of duration. Exactly as we can compute the duration of a string of future values discounted at a constant rate, we can compute the duration of a string of past values discounted at a time-varying rate. In the case of Zimbabwe, this exercise leads to the conclusion that in July 2008, the duration of the memory of inflation was 2.0875 months (or 63.5 days), down from nearly a year, 9 to 10 months earlier. It makes intuitive sense that the memory should be so short, when prices are multiplied by 27 in a month, after having been multiplied by 9.39 in the previous month. Just try to divide the price index at the end of this 2-month period 35,000,520,626,246.50 by 253.64 = 27 × 9.39, without a computer! If it takes you only an hour, your purchasing power has depreciated by 0.45 percent in the meantime!

7.5   The Perceived Rate of Inflation and the Distribution of Forecasting Errors

The critics of the REH have mainly aimed at the extreme economic modeling abilities it assumes and demands on the part of economic agents. This being said, not everything in the REH should be dismissed as being wishful nonthinking. Such is the case of the idea that for an "expectations" theory to be valid, it must generate a certain type of forecasting errors:

- Their average must be equal to zero.
- They must not exhibit any discernible and therefore exploitable pattern.

In short, the forecasting errors must be randomly distributed. Were it not the case, it would imply that economic agents would be given an opportunity to exploit some valuable information. Hence, the standard requirement to accept (or reject) an "expectations" theory is that the forecasting errors it generates be normally distributed.

Does the HRL formulation pass the test of normally distributed errors? As said earlier in this book, Allais never missed an opportunity to stress that his HRL formulation is not an expectations theory proper, but a theory of memory decay. To make his point, he explicitly considered the case of a regularly increasing rate of inflation and clearly stated that in this particular case, his perceived rate of inflation would always lag behind actual inflation.[5] The case of a regularly accelerating rate of inflation is, however, a very particular one, rarely, if ever, encountered in the real world. For example, it has never happened during the 1999 to 2008 inflationary episode in Zimbabwe. A world of regularly increasing rates of inflation would be a world of risk, not a world of uncertainty.

Bearing in mind that the HRL formulation would fail to deal with a regularly increasing rate of inflation, how does it perform in the real world? For example, are its forecasting errors normally distributed in the case of the Zimbabwean inflation between 1999 and 2008? Let us remember that the forecasting error is the difference between the inflation rate observed in a given period $\overline{x_n}$ and the perceived rate of inflation at the end of the preceding period z_{n-1}.

From relationship 4.38, we know that the forecasting error is

$$k'_n = \overline{x_n} - z_{n-1} = \overline{x_n} - \frac{\chi_0}{\Psi^*_{n-1}} Z_{n-1} \qquad (7.11)$$

Table 7.2 shows key statistical parameters for the times series of monthly actual inflation rates and monthly forecasting errors.

To study the distribution of the forecasting errors, we have performed a Henri adjustment (known in the English-speaking literature as a QQ-plot), whereby empirical quantiles are compared with theoretical quantiles, the latter forming a straight line (Henri's line).[6] The two extreme quantiles (respectively, $k'_n \leq -5.00$ percent and $k'_n \geq 11.00$ percent) contain 15 observations each. The intermediate quantiles are defined by a 0.50 percent step from -5.00 percent to 11.00 percent. Thus altogether 33 points represent the empirical distribution of forecasting errors.

TABLE 7.2
Key Statistical Parameters of the Distribution of Monthly Inflation Rates and Forecasting Errors— Zimbabwe 2000–2008

Log rates	$\overline{x_n}(\%)$	$k'_n(\%)$
Minimum	0.00	−31.22
Maximum	329.59	105.14
Average	24.23	4.79
Standard deviation	44.34	16.61

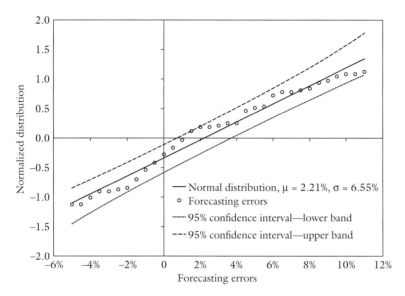

Figure 7.2 Zimbabwe: perceived rate of inflation and distribution of forecasting errors.

The normal distribution that best fits (R-SQ = 97.54 percent) this empirical distribution has the following parameters:

$$\mu = 2.21\% \qquad (7.12a)$$
$$\sigma = 6.55\% \qquad (7.12b)$$

Figure 7.2 shows that the empirical distribution falls within the lower and upper bounds defining the 95 percent confidence interval around the normal distribution. From this, we can conclude that the forecasting errors generated by the HRL formulation in the case of the Zimbabwean inflation are normally distributed. The average forecasting error is admittedly different from zero, but is small in comparison with the average monthly rate of inflation (24.23 percent).

All in all, it seems reasonable to conclude that the HRL formulation meets (or is at least very close to meeting) the requirements enunciated by the REH as regards the distribution of forecasting errors. However, this Zimbabwean example is arguably limited in terms of both duration and nature as it only covers 115 months of accelerating inflation.

Argentina, Brazil, Chile, and Mexico provide us with more challenging time series of monthly inflation rates and forecasting errors. The

TABLE 7.3
Normality Test on Inflation Forecasting Errors

	Argentina	Brazil	Chile	Mexico
Datastream	AGCONPRCF	BRCONPRCF	CLCONPRCF	MXCONPRCF
Months	322	277	360	396
Beginning	March 1980	December 1983	January 1977	January 1974
End	December 2006	December 2006	December 2006	December 2006
Minimum	−46.73%	−38.94%	−3.88%	−5.97%
Maximum	67.40%	17.38%	6.17%	8.50%
Skewedness	1.4537	−2.0499	1.8965	1.3567
Kurtosis	23.9555	11.3889	12.8519	5.8733
R-SQ	95.09%	96.26%	98.15%	95.68%
Average	−0.54%	−0.38%	−0.58%	−0.04%
Std-deviation[7]	4.39%	4.38%	0.87%	1.43%
R-SQ	94.12%	95.73%	74.25%	95.75%
Std-deviation[7]	4.44%	4.43%	1.16%	1.43%
Normality	No	No	No	No
Leptokurtosis	Yes	Yes	Yes	Yes

Datastream times series start between January 1974 and December 1983. They cover at least one full cycle of accelerating/decelerating inflation. Table 7.3 summarizes the results of the normality tests performed on these time series up to the end of 2006. In all cases, the average forecasting errors are close to zero, so close to zero that in three cases out of four—Argentina, Brazil, and Mexico—the quality of the adjustment is not materially altered if the constant is forced to zero, that is, if the average forecasting error is assumed to be equal to zero (in one case, the quality of the adjustment improves a little bit).

But the distributions are not normal: like the distributions of the actual inflation rates, they all have fat tails. In the current state of our knowledge, this is a situation that we do not know how to exploit.

To summarize these observations, we submit that the HRL formulation should be at least given the benefit of the doubt as regards its ability to generate randomly distributed forecasting errors of average value equal to zero. Or, to put it differently, the burden of the proof seems to lie on the proposition that the HRL formulation does not generate randomly distributed forecasting errors of average value equal to zero.

As a transition to the next part of this book, we have also performed a normality test on the forecasting errors generated by the HRL

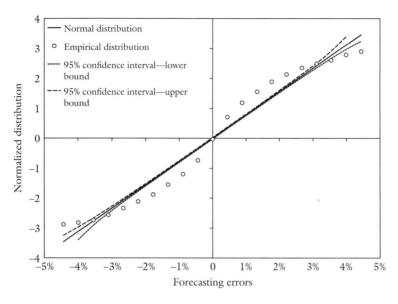

Figure 7.3 S&P 500 daily returns: distribution of forecasting errors.

formulation when it is applied to the daily return on the S&P 500 equity index. Here, we have a time series made of 10,507 observations. The forecasting errors range from −9.48 percent to +10.24 percent. The directly computed average and standard deviation of the forecasting errors are, respectively, 0.01 percent and 0.94 percent. The normal distribution that best fits (R-SQ = 96.68 percent) the empirical distribution is defined by $\mu = 0.01$ percent and $\sigma = 1.28$ percent. Here again, the constant can be forced to zero ($\mu = 0$) without losing any accuracy. Here again, the distribution of the forecasting errors is not normal: like the distribution of the daily returns, it has fat tails (figure 7.3). If anything, this additional example further supports the claim made in the preceding paragraph.

7.6   Money Creation during Hyperinflation

As an aside, let us note that Allais—like Cagan—considers the money supply to be exogenous to the private sector during hyperinflation episodes. Under such circumstances, because of the time needed to collect taxes, a time lag that drastically erodes their value, the public deficit ends up being entirely funded by the central bank and the income from money creation that is appropriated by the government is equal to a constant share of national income. Here is how Allais demonstrates and verifies this analysis.

Let α be the ratio of public expenditures to national income, θ the time needed to collect taxes, and $R(t)$ the national income by time unit. The public deficit in period T is

$$\Delta = \alpha T [R(t) - R(t - \theta)] \tag{7.13}$$

As this deficit is entirely funded by the central bank, we have

$$M_M(t) - M_M(t - T) = \alpha T [R(t) - R(t - \theta)] \tag{7.14}$$

Since we assume hyperinflation, the taxes computed at time $t - \theta$ but collected at time t are negligible with respect to public expenditures at time t. Therefore, we have

$$R(t) >> R(t - \theta) \Rightarrow M_M(t) - M_M(t - T) \approx \alpha T R(t) \tag{7.15}$$

In other words, the absolute increase in the money supply is equal to a constant share α of nominal national income. Relationship 7.15 is equivalent to

$$\ln(M_M(t) - M_M(t - T)) \approx \ln R(t) + \ln \alpha T \tag{7.16}$$

Let us have

$$y = \ln(M_M(t) - M_M(t - T)) \tag{7.17a}$$
$$x = \ln P(t) \tag{7.17b}$$

For this theory of money creation during hyperinflation to be compatible with empirical data, we should find

$$c_1 \approx 1 \tag{7.18}$$

when we seek to adjust empirical data through linear regression:

$$y = c_1 x + c_0 \tag{7.19}$$

Allais finds $c_1 = 0.98$ in the case of the German hyperinflation. Table 7.4 shows the values we have found for Zimbabwe between 1999 and 2008.

TABLE 7.4
Estimates of the Inflation Tax

	c_1	c_0	R^2 (%)	$\alpha = \exp(c_0)/T$ (%)
$T = 3$	1.1142	−0.4531	99.0049	21.19
$T = 6$	1.0816	0.3575	99.2934	21.83
$T = 12$	1.0539	0.9629	99.4535	21.83

The values taken by c_1 are close to 1. The estimated value of α is close to one-fifth of nominal national income. Allais's thorough analysis of money creation during episodes of hyperinflation contrasts with Sargent and Wallace's prudent conjecture of a possible feedback from inflation into money.[8]

7.7   Some Historical Puzzles in Macroeconomic Behavior

The main aim of this chapter was to illustrate how Allais's HRL formulation operates during hyperinflation. This makes it the right place to show too how this formulation sheds light on what Kindleberger calls "some historical puzzles in macro-economic behavior."[9] Two of these puzzles are related to the French and German experiences with paper money and hyperinflation during the early years of, respectively, the French Revolution (1790–1795) and the Weimar Republic (1919–1923). How come, wonders Kindleberger, these two experiences have left a seemingly indelible footprint in the collective memory of the French and the German people for at least half a century? Doesn't this footprint "controvert the simple hypothesis that collective memory in economic questions fades monotonically with the passage of time"? In the same vein, Kindleberger notes that the British experience with unemployment in the interwar period has had a long-lasting influence on the macroeconomic policy mix in Great Britain. In all three cases, "once bitten, twice shy" seems to have been the motto.

To make things even more puzzling, Kindleberger quotes two other historical events, which on the contrary seem to have faded away from collective memory too early. First, he argues that the deflationary consequences of the return of the British pound to gold convertibility in 1819, after the Napoleonic wars, should have enlightened British policymakers, after World War I, when they sought to reestablish gold convertibility, at the prewar parity. Finally, Kindleberger suggests that the recurrence of financial crises almost every 10 years over many centuries is proof of a definite collective ability to forget. Why, then, has collective memory been long in the former circumstances and short in the latter ones?

With respect to the HRL formulation, the lasting presence of hyperinflation in collective memory is at first glance quite paradoxical. Haven't we just seen that, as far as the holding of money balances is concerned, the duration of memory shrinks to virtually nothing during hyperinflation episodes? Doesn't it follow that hyperinflation should be forgotten in all respects as soon as it is over? No, it does not. The HRL formulation actually implies exactly the opposite. Here is why.

Hyperinflation is usually presented as an exponential rise in the prices of goods and services. However, the general price level is nothing but the inverse of the real value of money. If the price P of a basket of goods and services is 10 USD, one can always invert this relationship and say that 1 USD (that is, one unit of currency) buys one-tenth of this basket. In other words, the real value $\overline{m}$ of one unit of currency is equal to $1/P$

$$\overline{m} = \frac{1}{P} \tag{7.20}$$

which implies

$$\ln \overline{m} = -\ln P \tag{7.21}$$

and

$$\frac{d \ln \overline{m}}{dt} = -\frac{d \ln P}{dt} \tag{7.22}$$

Therefore, hyperinflation can also be presented as an almost sudden and in any case total and irreversible depreciation of money, that is, a brutal, total, and irreversible failure of money to fulfill its store-of-value function.[10] What comes after hyperinflation is at best moderate inflation or mild deflation, but certainly not any restoration of the purchasing power of money to its pre-hyperinflation level. Whatever holders of money balances have lost through hyperinflation is lost forever.

If $x = d \ln P/dt$ is the rate of change in prices, it follows that $-x = -d \ln P/dt$ is the rate of depreciation of money. Let us now see how the

HRL algorithm responds to a long sequence of ever more negative rates of depreciation, as Zimbabwe experienced between January 1999 and July 2008, with a clear acceleration after 2005 (as a reminder, inflation multiplied prices by 1.22×10^{12} during this whole period). To compute the coefficient Z and the perceived rate of depreciation of money z between January 1999 and July 2008, we first need to estimate the initialization parameter Z_0 as of the end of 1998. An IMF annual time series that starts in 1964 suggests taking $Z_0 = -299.88$ percent. A sequence of increasingly negative rates of depreciation of money has the following consequences:

- The coefficient of psychological expansion Z and the perceived rate of depreciation of money both fall since $-x < z < 0 \Rightarrow dz/dt < 0$.
- The function $\Psi(Z)$ increases, since $\Psi(Z) = (1 + b)/(1 + be^{\alpha Z})$.
- The rate of memory decay $\chi(Z)$ decreases, since $\chi(Z) = \chi_0/\Psi(Z)$.

Ultimately, Z and z will become more and more negative, $\Psi(Z)$ will tend toward 2, $\chi(Z)$ toward 2.40 percent a year, and their elasticities with respect to Z will both tend toward 0 (see table 4.4, p. 87). In other words, the rate of memory decay with respect to the depreciation of money will become not only fairly small (2.40 percent a year) but also quite inelastic. Under the assumption $Z_0 = -299.88$ percent, the HRL formulation yields the following values as of July 2008:

$$Z = -2{,}904\% \tag{7.23a}$$
$$\Psi(Z) = 2 \tag{7.23b}$$
$$\chi(Z) = 2.40\% \tag{7.23c}$$
$$z = -69.70\% \tag{7.23d}$$
$$e(\Psi; Z) = e(\chi; Z) = 0 \tag{7.23e}$$
$$e(z; x) = 0.20\% \tag{7.23f}$$

Please note that a perceived (continuous annual) rate of depreciation of money of -69.70 percent is almost equivalent to a perceived halving of the value of money every year, as $e^{-0.6970} = 0.4981$. At this pace, money needs only 4 years to lose almost 95 percent of its purchasing power.

Actually, inflation did not stop in Zimbabwe in July 2008. But our time series stops at this point in time, probably because inflation then became too difficult to measure. As a consequence, there are no inflation data available for the second half of 2008. Despite this lack of data, it seems reasonable to assume that Z and z almost certainly fell to even lower levels in the final months of 2008. According to Hanke and Krus, who use an implied exchange rate to measure inflation, it actually peaked in November and the highest daily inflation rate was 98%, which means that price doubled every 24.7 hours (or equivalently that money lost 2.8% of its value per hour).[11] In any case, the time elapsed since the end of 2008, when a new time series starts, is too short to observe the long-term behavior of the perceived rate of money depreciation after inflation has slowed down. To do this, we need to turn to a country that has experienced hyperinflation in a more distant past. Brazil provides us with an example of hyperinflation between 1986 and 1994, followed by moderate inflation rates to the present day.

In Brazil, hyperinflation has been less pronounced than in Germany 70 years earlier. It has multiplied prices by 3.08×10^8 only. The perceived rate of money depreciation reached it lowest point in July 1994 at -57.67 percent. Yet, at this time, the rate of memory decay had already reached its lower limit of 2.40 percent a year. Figure 7.4 shows how slowly such a trauma has been fading away from collective memory during the last 20 years. That the rate of memory decay associated with the depreciation of money is both small and inelastic toward the end of hyperinflation explains why the memory of hyperinflation is so persistent. Furthermore, bear in mind that prices were only multiplied by 3.08×10^8 in Brazil versus 5.8×10^{11} in Germany: between November 1918 and November 1923, the German people suffered a much more brutal trauma than the Brazilian people over a slightly longer period of time. Therefore, the recovery from the German trauma starts from a lower point and has to take more time.

Our discussion of hyperinflation highlights the relativist nature of collective memory. It can be both long and short at the same time, depending on the point of view relevant to economic agents. There is no inconsistency in having a short memory of inflation when managing money balances and a very long memory of the depreciation of money when expressing policy preferences as, for example, inflation aversion. Surviving hyperinflation by being more or less alert at disposing of one's money balances does not imply it is so negligible an outcome that one could and should forget it quickly; it is not

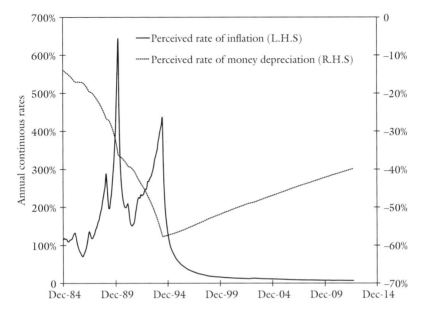

Figure 7.4 Brazil: perceived rates of inflation and money depreciation.

incompatible with saying, "Never again" as the German people still do. To the extent that British unemployment in the interwar period was both widespread and persistent, one can also interpret it as a total and irreversible loss of income for a large part of the population. Therefore, following the same line of reasoning as with the depreciation of money, widespread and persistent unemployment qualifies as an "unforgettable trauma."

Whether a loss is total and irreversible or partial and recovered is, according to the HRL formulation, what makes it hard or easy to forget. Painful as they may have been, the crises considered by Kindleberger in his last two puzzles have not been as traumatic as the German hyperinflation. British capitalists and workers did suffer during the 7 years from 1815 and 1822, but they were not ruined and they were much better off almost a century later, when World War I broke out. The same holds true of the serial economic and financial crises experienced during the nineteenth century in different countries. In chapter 11, when we introduce the concept of the perceived risk of loss, we will elaborate further on how collective memory deals with partial and recovered losses.

7.8   Summary

Hyperinflation is to the Allais HRL formulation what caricature is to reality. It sheds light on its most original characteristics:

- In an uncertain world, our so-called inflation "expectations" are ultimately what we remember from past inflation, what we remember from the sequence of monthly inflation rates.
- How much we remember from past inflation depends on how inflation has behaved: the duration of our memory gets shorter and shorter as inflation accelerates, and it becomes very short during hyperinflation episodes; conversely, it gets longer and longer when inflation decelerates, and it becomes very long during deflation phases (the elasticity of time and of our inflation "expectations" is high when inflation is high and low when inflation is low).
- The higher our inflation "expectations," the lower our demand for money; but this relationship is bounded and nonlinear, which means that the elasticity of the demand for money with respect to inflation "expectations" is not constant.

In standard economic parlance, the HRL formulation is a "dynamic adaptive expectations" theory with the following characteristics (figures 7.5, 7.6, 7.7, and 7.8):

- Path dependence.
- Variable distributed lag.
- Time-varying elasticity of expectations with respect to "unexpected outcome," in a range from virtually 0 to 1.
- Monotonic, decreasing, nonlinear, and bounded demand for money function, the elasticity of which with respect to "expectations" varies between 0 and −1.

Table 7.5 illustrates the dynamic properties of the HRL formulation. It considers various scenarios in which the initial perceived return is zero and the monthly return is constant—from 5 percent to 130 percent. It shows how many months it takes for the perceived return to reach the annualized constant value of the monthly return.

Arguably, Allais did not have financial markets in mind when he conceived his HRL formulation of the demand for money. But any

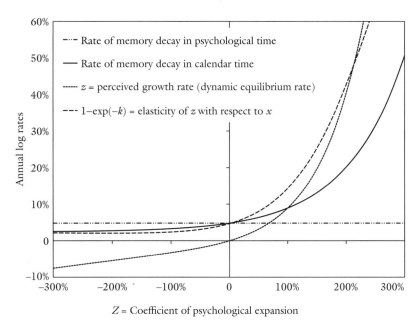

Figure 7.5 Rate of memory decay, perceived growth rate (dynamic equilibrium rate), and elasticity as functions of z.

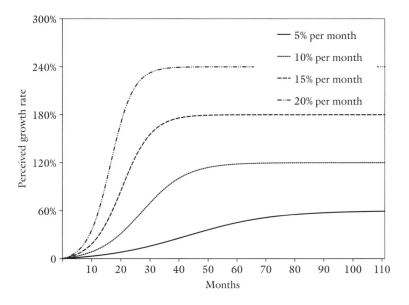

Figure 7.6 Time needed to converge toward the average annualized rate.

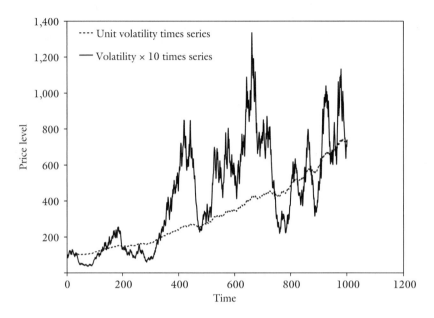

Figure 7.7 Two artificial time series differing only by their volatility.

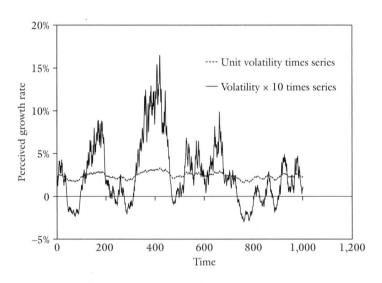

Figure 7.8 Sensitivity of the perceived rate of growth to the volatility of inputs.

TABLE 7.5
Dynamic Properties of HRL Formulation

x (monthly log rate)	5%	10%	13%	15%	20%	60%	130%
Z_0	0	0	0	0	0	0	0
z (annual log rate)	60%	120%	156%	180%	240%	720%	1,560%
k	6.72%	12.98%	16.70%	19.16%	25.28%	73.29%	155.64%
n (months)	184	105	94	76	60	24	12

financial markets practitioner will probably agree that Allais's psychological assumptions are indeed very general and describe behavior he or she has observed on trading floors, in investment committees, or during pitches to clients, at least from time to time. Therefore, our own assumption is that if Allais's insights are valid in their own field, namely, monetary dynamics, they should be helpful in other areas, first and foremost in financial markets. All one needs to do, at least as a first step, is to apply Allais's HRL algorithm to sequences of daily, weekly, monthly returns on specific securities or assets classes and test whether the perceived returns thus computed can be used as explanatory variables in modeling investors' behavior.

If we simply substitute returns on financial assets for inflation (or rates of growth in nominal spending) on the one hand and the demand for risky assets for the supply of money on the other, the HRL formulation gives us a model liable to explain how expectations are formed in traded asset markets and how market participants respond to changes in their expectations. The key assumptions of this model are that both the elasticity of "expected" returns with respect to past returns and the elasticity of behavior with respect to "expected" returns are path-dependent and time-varying, respectively, between 0 and 1 and $\alpha' \chi_0 Z/(1 + b)$ and 0. This is a model many prominent academics or policymakers have been calling for.

It is, for example, a missed opportunity that Allais's HRL formulation meets, to name just him, Shiller's intuitions, without the latter being seemingly aware of this convergence:[12]

- As the coefficient of psychological expansion is the present value of all past observations, investors do indeed respond "not so much to a sudden price increase as to a pattern of consistency in price increases."[13]

- Investors do "look back over many days, weeks or months of price changes" but the length of that reference period varies, because neither the rate of decay of memory nor the duration of memory is constant.
- The speculative bubble does not "grow forever" because, first, it requires to be fed with ever-larger price increases and, second, investors' demand for securities is not a linear but a logistic function of the perceived return, which ends up being inelastic as the perceived return reaches certain thresholds.

The potential relevance of the HRL formulation vis-à-vis the financial instability hypothesis is threefold:

- First, it explicitly incorporates a feedback loop allowing for positive and self-reinforcing price movements.
- Second, it suggests that exuberant "expectations" are inherently unstable and volatile, while bearish "expectations" are stable and sticky.
- Third, it explains why bubbles inevitably burst, when the upper bound of the response function is reached and the potential for positive feedback is exhausted.

CHAPTER EIGHT

The HRL Formulation and Nominal Interest Rates

ALLAIS'S THEORY of psychological time and memory decay plays a central role in his formulation of the demand for money. However, this theory purports to describe the operation of memory in general, not just in the context of monetary dynamics. It is, in fact, independent of monetary dynamics. It can be interpreted as a general theory of "expectations" under uncertainty. Can it, therefore, explain other phenomena?

With his theory of the psychological rate of interest, Allais suggests that the theory of psychological time and memory decay is indeed liable to shed light on the determination of nominal interest rates.

Allais conjectured that the rate i at which we discount the future and the rate χ at which we forget the past should be identical, thereby constructing what he called the theory of the psychological rate of interest.[1] To test the compatibility of this theory with empirical data, Allais selected the yield on British Consols during the nineteenth century. To a modern mind, this choice may seem strange, if not irrelevant. Yet, it has a simple scientific motivation. As Allais tested his HRL formulation of the demand for money in different countries having experienced hyperinflation in the twentieth century, he hypothesized that the values found to be optimal for the three psychological parameters ($\alpha = b = 1$ and $\chi_0 = 4.8$ percent a year) were constant through time and space. He now wanted to test this assumption further, this time in a totally different context: the British nineteenth century, which has seen an alternation of long cycles of inflation-free prosperity and deflation.

This chapter starts with a presentation of Allais's theory of the psychological rate of interest and a discussion of its application to the yield on British Consols during the nineteenth century. We will then test whether the same model can be applied during the last 50 years or so to the nominal yields on long-term bonds issued by governments in a diversified set of 18 countries. Like Allais, we will conclude that the theory of the psychological rate of interest is, in its original formulation at least, not compatible with a broader set of empirical data.[2] Allais' psychological rate of interest has too much inertia, especially when nominal growth is volatile.

A closer inspection of the data leads, however, to unearth an empirical relationship that Allais did not contemplate or see: the rather stable link, through time and space, not between the long-term bond yield j and the rate of memory decay χ, but between the long-term bond yield and the perceived rate of growth $z = \chi Z$ of nominal GDP. After noting that such a model has less explanatory power as regards short-term interest rates, we shall give a theoretical interpretation of this reformulation of Allais's theory of the psychological rate of interest.

8.1   The Postulate of Psychological Symmetry Between Memory Decay and Future Discounting

Allais's first contributions to the theory of interest predate his theory of the psychological rate of interest by almost 30 years.[3] One of these contributions is that there exists a pure rate of interest, which Allais defines as the cost of using (or renting) a capital (or a sum of money), excluding risks and management costs. This rate of interest can also be interpreted as an exchange premium measuring the preference for present goods (or money balances) over future ones. It varies of course with the maturity of the loan.

Allais uses this classic, but often implicit, notion of pure rate of interest to account for the diversity of interest rates observed in credit markets. The interest rate on a given loan is indeed the sum of at least three components:

- A pure rate of interest.
- A risk premium.
- A management fee.

Unfortunately, remarked Allais, the pure rate of interest is not directly observable. Therefore, it does not lend itself to empirical applications. In 1947, Allais suggested however that the interest rate on loans free of default risk and involving very low management costs could be taken as a proxy for the pure rate of interest.

Allais's theory of the psychological rate of interest purports to estimate the pure rate of interest by means of the theory of psychological time and memory decay. To this end, it distinguishes three different rates of interest:

- The rate of interest j observed in credit markets on long-term risk-free bonds.
- The corresponding pure rate of interest i_j.
- The psychological rate of interest i used by economic agents to discount the future.

To any risk-free market rate of interest j corresponds a pure rate of interest i_j such that

$$i_j = j + l_j \qquad (8.1)$$

where l_j is a positive liquidity premium, which implies $j < i_j$. The negotiability of fixed-income securities at low transaction costs in liquid markets is the main reason why the interest rates observed in financial markets on risk-free claims must be lower than the pure rates of interest i_j. Once issued, interest-bearing financial instruments are indeed negotiable in secondary markets. Since fixed-income securities can thus be exchanged for money, they offer a liquidity advantage for which investors must pay a premium in the form of higher prices. Market interest rates must therefore be lower than the pure interest rate i_j, this difference being the liquidity premium l_j.

Allais then assumes that the pure rate of interest i_j and the psychological rate of interest i are in general not equal, but that the operation of the economy tends to equalize the former with the latter, so that we have

$$i_j = i + \epsilon \qquad (8.2)$$

where ϵ can be considered as a random variable of relatively small size and zero mean. Hence, from relationships 8.1 and 8.2, we have

$$i = j + l_j - \epsilon \qquad (8.3)$$

Allais's next assumption is that the liquidity premium l_j should be proportional to j. Under this assumption, we have

$$i = (1 + \lambda)j - \epsilon \quad \text{with} \quad \lambda > 0 \tag{8.4}$$

Then comes Allais's most original assumption: the postulate of psychological symmetry between forgetting and discounting. Since we forget the past at a certain rate χ, variable over time, we should be discounting the future at the same rate. According to this postulate, the psychological rate of interest i at which we discount the future should be equal to the rate of memory decay χ at which we forget the past:

$$i = \chi \tag{8.5}$$

So much for the theory. Does it pass the test of empirical data? Two time series are needed for that matter: a times series of bond yield j and a time series W representing nominal economic activity, from which the values of i are computed, under the assumptions $\alpha = b = 1$, $\chi_0 = 4.80$ percent per year, subject to an initialization parameter Z_0.

$$i = \frac{\chi_0}{\Psi(Z)} \tag{8.6}$$

The psychological rate of interest i being thus estimated, setting up a value for λ, the parameter measuring the liquidity premium, yields an estimate j^* of the bond yield

$$j^* = \frac{i}{1 + \lambda} \tag{8.7}$$

If the theory of the psychological rate of interest holds, there exists a value of λ minimizing e^2, the sum of the squared *relative* differences between j and j^*, at a low level

$$e^2 = \sum_{n=1}^{p} \left(\ln \frac{j_n}{j_n^*} \right)^2 \tag{8.8}$$

which is equivalent to

$$e^2 = \sum_{n=1}^{p} [\ln j_n - \ln i_n + \ln(1 + \lambda)]^2 \tag{8.9}$$

Once Z_0 is given, all the i_n follow, and e^2 only depends on λ. Hence, equation 8.9 can be written as follows:

$$e^2 = \sum_{n=1}^{p} [f(\lambda)]^2 \tag{8.10}$$

To minimize e^2, we need to find the value of λ, such that

$$\frac{de^2}{d\lambda} = 2\sum_{n=1}^{p} f(\lambda)f'(\lambda) = 0 \tag{8.11}$$

which is equivalent to

$$\lambda = \exp \overline{\ln \frac{i_n}{j_n}} - 1 \tag{8.12}$$

To any value of Z_0 corresponds a specific value of λ, and the minimization exercise boils down to finding, by iteration, the value of Z_0 that minimizes e^2.

In a standard univariate linear regression, the function to be minimized is

$$e^2 = \sum_{n=1}^{p} (y_n - y_n^*)^2 = \sum_{n=1}^{p} (y_n - c_1 x_n - c_0)^2 \tag{8.13}$$

Here, the function to be minimized is

$$e^2 = \sum_{n=1}^{p} [\ln j_n - \ln i_n + \ln(1 + \lambda)]^2 \tag{8.14}$$

The formulations 8.13 and 8.14 are equivalent with the following notations:

$$y_n = \ln j_n \qquad c_1 = 1 \qquad x_n = \ln i_n \qquad c_0 = -\ln(1 + \lambda) \tag{8.15}$$

Allais's adjustment is therefore equivalent to a linear regression of $\ln j$ on $\ln i$, with the coefficient c_1 being forced to 1.

8.2   Yield on British Consols Between 1815 and 1913

The annual data used by Allais in the case of the yield on British Consols can be found in his 1972 article. The time series representing nominal activity is defined as the product of an industrial production index and a price index. Allais found that the average relative estimation error e is minimized at 8.50 percent for $Z_0 = 120$ percent and $\lambda = 0.90$ (our own calculation suggests that $Z = 119$ percent and $\lambda = 0.91$ minimize e at the slightly lower level of 8.46 percent).

As the average yield on British Consols has been 3.23 percent between 1815 and 1913, an average relative estimation error of 8.50 percent means that yields are estimated with a 27-basis-point average absolute error (8.50 percent $\times$ 3.23 percent $=$ 0.27 percent). Allais also observed that if the psychological rate of interest is lagged by 2 years, the adjustment is better as the average relative estimation error falls to 7.36 percent.

A number of questions arise at this stage. Why should $Z_0 = 120$ percent? Has such a value any economic meaning? Does it make sense? To answer these questions, the perceived rate of nominal growth is more enlightening than the coefficient of psychological expansion. To $Z_0 = 120$ percent corresponds $z_0 = 12.44$ percent. An annual continuous rate of 12.44 percent is equivalent to a decimal rate of 13.25 percent. In other words, by setting $Z_0 = 120$ percent, Allais assumed that investors who bought British Consols in 1815, based on their experience at that time, perceived nominal growth to be close to 13 percent.

Such an assumption seems a little bit excessive, even in the historic context of the Napoleonic Wars. Admittedly, in 1815, Napoleon had just been finally defeated, after a long struggle, which had caused Britain to suspend the gold convertibility of its currency since 1797. During nearly two decades, Britain had financed an important war effort, by issuing paper money. In the market, gold was trading at a 20 percent to 25 percent premium over its mint parity. Ricardo was engaged in the bullion controversy. The recent history was that of a time of inflation, especially between 1794 and 1812 (3.8 percent on average, according to a recent study).[4] Therefore, people must have "expected" abnormally high nominal growth—but not as high as 13.25 percent a year, which—given what we know of price movements during the Napoleonic Wars—would imply very high rates of real growth. Based on the data presented by O'Donoghue et al., the perceived rate of inflation was not higher than 1 percent to 2 percent in 1815, that is, significantly below 13.25 percent. It is doubtful that the difference between these two numbers can be accounted for by real growth. It is more likely that Allais's initialization parameter is just too high to be realistic.

Furthermore, the case of British Consols from 1815 to 1913 is arguably a special one for at least four reasons:

- This period has been described as the "100-year peace." A lack of major conflict has spared Britain the usual inflationary consequences of war, such as the ones experienced during the twentieth century.[5]
- During the entire period, there was no such thing as monetary policy (at least in the modern sense of the term) as Britain led the entire world into the gold standard.
- Under the Gladstone doctrine, there was no such thing either as fiscal policy.
- As a result, for most of the period, nominal growth and nominal interest rates have been much lower and much less volatile than in the twentieth century.

Therefore, the single case studied by Allais may not be representative enough to forcefully support his theory of the psychological rate of interest. Can this theory explain nominal interest rates in more than one country and over the last four or five decades, in a set of much more diverse economic conditions, including higher and more volatile rates of interest?

8.3   US AAA Corporate Bond Yields Since 1951

In March 1951, the Federal Reserve System adopted the "bills-only rule" whereby it stopped buying U.S Treasury notes and bonds in the open market at fixed prices, as it had since March 1942. From that date onward, US bond yields can be considered to be "free" market rates. Since there exists a quarterly time series of US nominal GDP that starts in 1945, we can initialize the computation of Z seven years before the start of the estimation period, thus limiting the influence of this initialization parameter.[6]

The undisputable fact is that the psychological rate of interest i computed from the sequence of quarterly nominal GDP growth rates is not compatible with US AAA corporate bond yields since 1952. It has too much inertia, too little volatility relative to that of nominal bond yields. While the secular trend in bond yields is linked with the psychological rate of interest, their cyclical fluctuations are not. Examples in other countries suggest the same observation.

There are two ways of illustrating the incompatibility of the theory of the psychological rate of interest, as stated by Allais, with US data in the post-WWII era.

The first one is a figure plotting the AAA corporate bond yield, the rate of memory decay, and finally the perceived rate of nominal growth. Figure 8.1 shows the obvious superiority of the perceived rate of nominal growth over the rate of memory decay when it comes to accounting for nominal interest rates.

Interestingly, a brutal use of linear regression would fail to make any distinction between these two variables. Let us assume we want to estimate the two following relationships:

$$j^* = c_1 \chi + c_0 \qquad (8.16a)$$
$$j^* = c_1 z + c_0 \qquad (8.16b)$$

Linear regression yields the results shown in table 8.1.

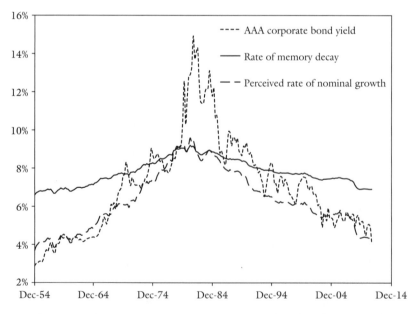

Figure 8.1 US AAA corporate bond yields and the HRL formulation.

TABLE 8.1

Nominal Interest Rate Linear Regressions on χ and z

	Regression on χ	Regression on z
R-SQ	87.24%	87.31%
e	0.96%	0.96%
c_1	3.4640	1.5341
T-stat (c_1)	36.32	36.44
c_0	−0.1994	−0.0266
T-stat (c_0)	26.51	9.47

At best, one could remark that the value of the constant c_0 is less odd in the regression on z (−2.66 percent) than in the regression on χ (−19.94 percent). In any case, despite the high R-SQ, one would struggle to explain the order of magnitude of the coefficients c_1. Yet, with T-stats ranging from 9.47 to 36.44, all these coefficients would be deemed to be highly statistically significant—proof, if need be, that econometrics without economics can be quite misleading, if not dangerous.

This leads us to the second way of illustrating the superiority, as an explanatory variable, of the perceived rate of nominal growth over the rate of memory decay.

Let us now assume we want to estimate the two relationships

$$j^* = c_1 \chi \tag{8.17a}$$
$$j^* = c_1 z \tag{8.17b}$$

where the constant c_0 is forced to 0. Linear regression yields the results shown in Table 8.2: by and large, the perceived rate of nominal growth z is a better explanatory variable of nominal interest rates than the rate of memory decay χ.

These empirical observations contradict Allais's postulate of psychological symmetry. Logical and seductive as it may be, this postulate does not fit with observed data. From this, one might conclude that the theory of psychological time and memory decay has nothing relevant to say about the determination of nominal interest rates. This would be a conclusion drawn with haste. The rejection of Allais's postulate of psychological symmetry indeed needs to be supplemented by one empirical observation of great importance, which Allais has not noticed:

TABLE 8.2
Nominal Interest Rate Linear Regressions on χ
and z, with $c_0 = 0$

	Regression on χ	Regression on z
R-SQ	40.78%	81.41%
e	2.07%	1.16%
c_1	0.9467	1.1475
T-stat(c_1)	50.33	92.17

the close link between nominal interest rates j and the perceived rate of nominal growth $z = \chi Z$. This empirical observation suggests the reformulation of the theory of the psychological rate of interest that follows.

8.4   Nominal Interest Rates and the Perceived Rate of Nominal Growth: Empirical Observations

The relationship between nominal interest rates j and the perceived rate of nominal growth z holds in 18 different countries (large and small, creditors and debtors, . . .), which we have studied for their quite different economic environments (accelerating inflation, disinflation, near deflation, slow growth, high growth):

- 14 developed countries.
- 4 Latin American countries, which have been prone to hyperinfla-tion in the past.

As a result of this diversity, the nominal interest rates on which the HRL formulation sheds some light range from 0.50 to 725 percent. Depending on the availability of data, the estimation periods range from 11 to 50 years. In all cases, they end at the end of 2006. All 18 models share the same very simple structure, in which the bond yield in a given country is estimated as the product of a country-specific constant μ and the "perceived rate of nominal growth" z in this country.

$$j^{**} = \mu z \quad \text{with} \quad \mu > 0 \tag{8.18}$$

The reason for writing $j^{**} = \mu z$ instead of $j^{**} = z/(1 + \lambda)$ will appear in section 8.7, when we search for the theoretical foundations of the correlation between j^{**} and z. In any case, we just near to bear in mind that

$$\mu = \frac{1}{1 + \lambda} \tag{8.19}$$

The coefficient μ is found by minimizing the sum of the squared relative differences

$$e^2 = \sum_{n=1}^{p} \left(\ln \frac{\dot{j}_n}{j_n^{**}} \right)^2 \tag{8.20}$$

which is equivalent to

$$\mu = \exp \left(\overline{\ln \frac{\dot{j}_n}{z_n}} \right) \tag{8.21}$$

By transposing relationships 8.13, 8.14, and 8.15, we get

$$y_n = \ln \dot{j}_n \qquad c_1 = 1 \qquad x_n = \ln z_n \qquad c_0 = \ln \mu \tag{8.22}$$

This new adjustment is therefore equivalent to a linear regression of $\ln j$ on $\ln z$, with the coefficient c_1 being forced to 1.

All 18 different models use the same values for the three structural psychological parameters ($\alpha = 1$, $b = 1$, $\chi_0 = 4.80$ percent). Appendix B (p. 275) gives the details of the 18 adjustments. Several facts stand out:

- Given the parsimony of this model (only one explanatory variable in each country), the R-SQ are high (minimum $= 66.57$ percent, maximum $= 89.54$ percent, average $= 79.2$ percent).
- The average relative estimation error is reasonably small (18 percent on average).
- In two-thirds of the cases, the coefficients μ have a high degree of statistical significance.
- Except for two cases, the coefficients μ are remarkably close to 1 (average $= 0.92$).
- In a few instances, the perceived rate of nominal growth leads nominal interest rates by a few quarters.

It is interesting to look at the following alternative formulation, in which a constant term η is introduced:

$$j^{**} = \mu z + \eta \qquad (8.23)$$

For the longest time series, it barely improves the quality of the adjustment, but the values of μ become much more dispersed, and the T-stat of η is generally low. For shorter-time series (the last 20 years or less), the R-SQ increases a lot, but the constant η takes large negative values, which implies that nominal interest rates could be negative, even if the perceived rate of nominal growth were positive!

Granger causality tests are absolutely unambiguous: the causality is a one-way causality running from perceived nominal growth to nominal interest rates. Had we estimated the same models 5, 10, or 15 years ago on different data samples, would we have found very different values for the coefficients? Standard stability tests suggest a reasonably high level of stability. In Germany, for example, the coefficient μ has remained very close to 1.0549 since 1984. Before that, it was in a range of 1.0149 to 1.0831.

8.5   The Term Structure of Interest Rates and the Perceived Rate of Nominal Growth

In the cross-country analysis that we have just presented, the bond yields taken into consideration are not perfectly homogeneous with respect to the maturity of the corresponding bond indices. Most of these indices have a 10-year constant maturity. But some of them have a shorter maturity, as some countries (e.g., Spain, Italy, South Korea) have started later than others to issue 10-year bonds. In these latter countries, the value of μ tends to be relatively low, while the average relative estimation error tends to be relatively high. This observation suggests that the link between the perceived rate of nominal growth and nominal interest rates is stronger at the long end than at the short end of the yield curve.

A thorough analysis of the German yield curve confirms this intuition, as shown in table 8.3. There is a very clear pattern whereby as maturity decreases, so does the ratio μ of the corresponding yield to the perceived rate of nominal growth. This is a consequence of the fact that the yield curve has been positively sloped most of the

TABLE 8.3
German Yield Curve

	λ	$1 + \lambda$	$\mu = 1/(1 + \lambda)$	e (%)
1-year	0.2024	1.2024	0.8317	28.79
2-year	0.0930	1.0930	0.9149	21.46
3-year	0.0429	1.0429	0.9588	18.16
4-year	0.0123	1.0123	0.9879	16.20
5-year	−0.0089	0.9911	1.0090	14.87
6-year	−0.0245	0.9755	1.0251	13.90
7-year	−0.0367	0.9633	1.0381	13.15
8-year	−0.0462	0.9538	1.0485	15.56
9-year	−0.0542	0.9458	1.0573	12.07
10-year	−0.0605	0.9395	1.0644	11.69
20-year	−0.1343	0.8657	1.1551	13.99
30-year	−0.1519	0.8481	1.1792	8.67

time. But simultaneously the average relative estimation error increases. This reflects the impact of monetary policy, which—under normal circumstances—is greater at the short end than at the long end of the curve.

8.6 Nominal Interest Rates at the End of the German Hyperinflation

Another very striking illustration of the relation between nominal interest rates and the perceived rate of nominal growth is provided by the German hyperinflation of 1919 to 1923. Bresciani-Turoni reports that when inflation peaked in November 1923, the call money rate on the Berlin Stock Exchange was as high as 30 percent a day for nonindexed loans.[7] Unfortunately, Bresciani-Turoni does not say on which day of November inflation peaked.

Be that as it may, a daily rate of 30 percent is equivalent to an annual continuous rate of 9,583 percent, since

$$\ln 1.30 = 0.262364 \tag{8.24}$$

and

$$0.262364 \times 365.25 = 95.828 \tag{8.25}$$

TABLE 8.4

Case of the German Hyperinflation

Annual log rates (%)	September 1923	October 1923	November 6 or 7, 1923	Source
Call money	1,572	1,781	na	Homer and Sylla
Call money	na	na	9,583	Bresciani-Turoni
z (dollar rate)	2,339 to 7,270	5,492 to 13,295	11,495	Bresciani-Turoni
z (import prices)	2,488 to 7,640	3,682 to 14,395	9,606	Bresciani-Turoni
z (dom. prices)	2,617 to 6,078	3,705 to 15,020	9,959	Bresciani-Turoni
χ (dollar rate)	448 to 1,174	923 to 1,980	1,744	Bresciani-Turoni
χ (import prices)	472 to 1,226	657 to 2,122	1,493	Bresciani-Turoni
χ (dom. prices)	492 to 1,007	660 to 2,202	1,540	Bresciani-Turoni

Table 8.4 compares the values of the call money rate, of the perceived rate of inflation, and of the rate of memory decay toward the end of the German hyperinflation.

According to Homer and Sylla, in September and October 1923, here again it is not clear when exactly, the interest on call money reached the annual rates of 1,606 percent and 1,825 percent, that is, respectively, 4.30 percent and 4.88 percent in terms of daily continuous rates.[8] Due to compounding, such daily rates are equivalent to annual continuous rates of 1,572 percent and 1,781 percent, respectively (or money lent multiplied by 6.7 and 54.2 million, respectively, in a year).

Given the difficulty of measuring prices accurately during hyperinflation and the necessity to use high-frequency data when prices are rising very fast, these astronomical rates of interest—1,572 percent in September, 1,781 percent in October, and 9,583 percent in November 1923—are surprisingly close to the perceived rate of inflation, which can be computed by applying the HRL formulation to the price data collected by Bresciani-Turoni.

The weekly data reproduced by Bresciani-Turoni suggest that inflation peaked around November 6 or 7, 1923. Bresciani-Turoni uses three different variables to measure the depreciation of the German Mark: the exchange rate to the dollar, that is, the price of gold in effect; an index of import prices; and finally an index of domestic prices. The corresponding perceived rates of inflation are, respectively, at annual continuous rates, 11,495 percent (November 7), 9,606 percent and 9,959 percent (November 6). At the risk of indulging in "one-point econometrics," these three figures are very close to the peak value in the call money rate: 30 percent per day or 9,583 percent at an annual continuous rate.

On the same date, the call money rate is definitely much closer to the perceived rates of inflation than to the corresponding rates of memory decay, that is, respectively, 1,744 percent, 1,493 percent, and 1,540 percent.

For the months of September and October, Homer and Sylla are not accurate enough as regards dates to lead us to firm conclusions. In September, according to Bresciani-Turoni, depending on the dates and the indices, the perceived rates of inflation fluctuated between 2,339 percent and 7,640 percent, while the rates of memory decay were located somewhere between 447 percent and 1,225 percent. The call money rate of 1,572 percent quoted by Homer and Sylla would then be between the maximum value of the psychological rate of interest and the minimum value of the perceived rate of inflation. The October data show a different configuration whereby the call money rate of 1,781 percent would be systematically much below the perceived rate of inflation, but between the minimum (656 percent) and maximum (1,980 percent) values of the psychological rates of interest.

8.7   The Curse of Obliging Data

Why did Allais fail to see the link between nominal interest rates and the perceived rate of nominal growth? Simply put, he did not see it because he was not looking for it. What he was trying to establish was a link between nominal interest rates and the rate of memory decay. He had, so to say, "framed" his research. Generally speaking, as shown in chapters 4 to 6, the HRL formulation only gives an auxiliary role to the perceived rate of nominal growth. Its key variables are the coefficient of psychological expansion and the rate of memory decay.

The second reason for Allais's failure to see the link between nominal interest rates and the perceived rate of nominal growth is that with the data he had selected to test his theory, British data from the nineteenth century, he encountered the curse of obliging data. Since these data were compatible with the postulate of psychological symmetry, he did not have to look for some alternative theory, as he would have if the British data had not been so obliging.

TABLE 8.5
Yield on British Consols: Comparison of Regressions on χ and z for $Z_0 = 120$ Percent

$Z_0 = 120\%$	Regression on χ	Regression on z
R-SQ	99.15%	76.95%
e	0.30%	1.57%
c_1	0.5178	0.8233
T-stat (c_1)	106.9416	18.0890

Even if he had, out of curiosity, compared a regression on the rate of memory decay with a regression on the perceived rate of nominal growth, he would have been confronted with misleading results in the case of British Consols. For $Z_0 = 120$ percent, he would have obtained table 8.5.

With the regression on the perceived rate of nominal growth, the adjustment is clearly of lower quality.

Even if Allais had searched for the value of Z_0 optimizing the regression on the perceived rate of nominal growth, namely, a much more plausible 78 percent (equivalent to $z_0 = 5.96$ percent), he would have been at pains to substitute the perceived rate of nominal growth for the rate of memory decay as the anchor for nominal interest rates, as shown in table 8.6.

Allais would only have been able to note a narrowing of the difference between the two regressions in terms of R-SQ, average absolute estimation errors, and T-stats. Whether he would have judged the value of the initialization parameter—78 percent instead of 120 percent (that is, $z_0 = 5.96$ percent instead of 12.44 percent)—to be more plausible with respect to economic conditions in 1815 will remain an open

TABLE 8.6
Yield on British Consols: Comparison of Regressions on χ and z for $Z_0 = 78$ Percent

$Z_0 = 78\%$	Regression on χ	Regression on z
R-SQ	98.79%	83.46%
e	0.36%	1.33%
c_1	0.5381	1.0953
T-stat (c_1)	89.5157	22.2384

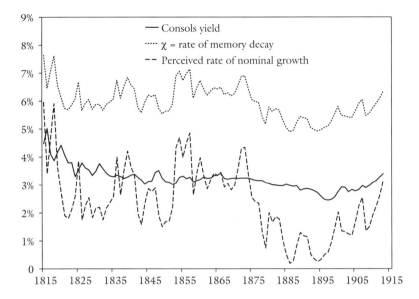

Figure 8.2 Yield on British Consols and the HRL formulation.

question. Without the benefit of having conducted a similar compara-tive analysis on other data, he would probably not have fully appreciated the fact of finding yet another coefficient close to 1 ($c_1 = 1.0953$).

An inspection of the data shows that the rejection of the perceived rate of nominal growth in the case of Bristish Consols is caused by 22 observations out of 98, that is, the years 1878 to 1900 (see figure 8.2). From 1815 to 1878, the perceived rate of nominal growth is indeed very close to the yield on British Consols, in any case much closer than the rate of memory decay. But from 1878 to 1900 the yield on Bristish Consols stopped tracking the perceived rate of nominal growth.

Can any theory explain the correlation generally observed between nominal interest rates and the perceived rate of nominal growth (or inflation)?

8.8 Nominal Interest Rates and the Perceived Rate of Nominal Growth: Theoretical Foundations

Contrary to Allais's postulate of psychological symmetry, the rate i at which we discount the future is certainly not identical to the rate χ at which we forget the past:

$$i \neq \chi \tag{8.26}$$

The 18 cases we have studied suggest that the rate which we use to discount the future is identical to the perceived rate of nominal growth.

$$i = z \quad \text{with} \quad z = \chi Z \tag{8.27}$$

That economic agents used to a high rate of nominal growth—say, 10 percent—would discount the future at a higher rate than agents used to a lower rate of growth—say, 5 percent—seems psychologically plausible, even though it seems "less logical" than Allais's postulate of psychological symmetry. In an economy that is perceived to grow fast, a given quantity of future goods seems closer at hand than in an economy that grows at a slower rate. For example, starting from 1 and growing at 5 percent a year, the value 1.4071 is reached in 7 years (84 months). At 10 percent annual growth, the same future value is reached after only 43 months. In an economy growing fast, the time needed (or given) to hit a certain target is shorter than in a slow-growth economy. Therefore, one would expect economic agents used to rapid nominal growth to be more impatient than agents used to slow nominal growth: in the extreme, they would somehow wish to abolish time. To be impatient is equivalent to giving little present value to future goods; it is equivalent to using a high discount rate.

Since $i = z = \chi Z$, depending on whether Z is smaller or bigger than 1, the psychological rate of interest can be lower or higher than the rate of memory decay:

- For $Z < 1, i < \chi$, economic agents discount the future at a lower rate than they forget the past: they have a long memory, they are patient, and the duration of their patience is longer than that of their memory ($\frac{1}{i} > \frac{1}{\chi}$).
- For $Z > 1, i > \chi$, economic agents discount the future at a higher rate than they forget the past: they have a short memory, they are impatient, and the duration of their patience is shorter than that of their memory ($\frac{1}{i} < \frac{1}{\chi}$).
- For $Z = 1, i = \chi$, the psychological rate of interest is equal to the rate of memory decay.

In light of this analysis, the value $Z = 1$ would play a particular role in drawing a line between two fundamentally different psychological states. For $\alpha = \beta = 1$ and $\chi_0 = 4.80$ percent a year, $Z = 1$ implies $z = \chi = 8.92$ percent a year (or a 9.33 percent annual decimal rate). When nominal growth speeds up (or when asset prices rise), not only does the duration of memory shrink, but also agents become more and more impatient: in the extreme, they want the future to happen "right now." In other words, irrational exuberance may be defined as a combination of short memory and high impatience, starting whenever the perceived rate of nominal growth (or the perceived return) exceeds 8.92 percent.

Seeking to explain the link observed in 18 different countries between nominal interest rates j and the perceived rate of nominal growth z, we have submitted that rapid nominal growth is likely to foster impatience in the form of high discount rates. Interestingly, this psychological explanation seems compatible with a totally different theoretical proposition: the golden rule of accumulation, according to which the rate of profit on capital should be equal to the growth rate of national income.

This golden rule answers the following question: which is the optimal level of savings and therefore of investment and of capital in a growing economy? In other words, which level of capital maximizes per capita consumption through time? If investment/saving is too low, opportunities to raise future living standards are forgone. On the contrary, if investment/saving is too high, it is current consumption that is forgone. The equality of the rate of profit with the rate of growth ensures that the level of capital is optimal, in the sense that it maximizes consumption for both present and future generations. In 1947, Allais had shown that the rate of interest should be equal to zero in a stationary state. In the early 1960s, several economists, including Allais, independently generalized this result by showing that the nominal rate of interest rate should be equal to the growth rate of national income in a dynamic state.[9]

The golden rule expresses a condition for growth to be balanced through time. Its value is normative. Its potential ability to explain observed phenomena is conditioned by the resolution of two difficulties:

- First, the establishment of a link between the aggregate rate of profit and the respective yields offered by various financial instruments (deposits, bonds, equities,...).
- Second, the specification of the process whereby economic agents are led to believe ex ante that a certain assumed rate of growth in nominal income is a reasonable "expectation."

The rate of profit considered in the theory of capital should be interpreted as being a weighted-average cost of capital. Depending on the risks associated with the way capital is raised, some dispersion around this average should be expected: funds representing debt should earn less than those representing equity. In other words, it is only the weighted average of all available prospective yields that should be close to the assumed rate of growth in nominal income: deposit rates should be lower; prospective equity returns should be higher; bond yields should be somewhere between these two extremes, probably rather close to the assumed rate of nominal growth.

In any case, the main issue is the second one: since the future is uncertain, which is the assumed rate of nominal growth that economic agents effectively use to price their financial assets and liabilities? The observations presented in this chapter suggest that it is the perceived rate of nominal growth. Of particular significance is the fact that the coefficients μ that we have empirically estimated are on average very close to 1, an order of magnitude consistent with the golden rule of accumulation.

8.9   Nominal Interest Rates and the Psychological Rate of Interest: Additional Questions and Insights

The results presented in the previous sections of this chapter raise questions, but also provide insights, which we must now discuss. The first two of them (negative liquidity premium, negative nominal interest rates) are specific to the reformulation presented in this essay. The other four (real interest rates, interest rates and the demand for money, Gibson's paradox, a comparison between the psychological rate of interest and Wicksell's natural rate of interest) also apply to Allais's initial formulation and are therefore based on his own comments.

8.9.1   *Negative Liquidity Premium*

In relationship 8.1, we have assumed the existence of a positive liquidity premium, which implied $\lambda > 0$. From relationship 8.19, there follows

$$\lambda = \frac{1}{\mu} - 1 \qquad (8.28)$$

Yet, we have encountered situations where $\mu > 1$, which implies $\lambda < 0$ and therefore a negative liquidity premium. Is there a contradiction between this empirical implication and our initial assumption? Not necessarily.

As we wrote the relationship

$$i_j = j + l_j \qquad (8.29)$$

we assumed that all the other factors (e.g., custodian fee, management fee, tax, etc.) potentially contributing to the difference between the pure rate of interest and the yield on long-term government bonds could be neglected. The fact that, in some cases, we have found μ to be marginally higher than 1 (for example, 1.01 in France, 1.05 in Germany, 1.02 in the United States, 1.08 in Canada) can be interpreted as proving that our assumption was too strong. If our assumption is not valid, our adjustment leads to overestimating μ and therefore underestimating λ. If all relevant factors were properly taken into account, the liquidity premium might still be positive.

8.9.2   *Negative Nominal Interest Rates*

Since $z = \chi Z$, with χ being always positive, z is negative whenever Z is itself negative. If the psychological rate of interest i is equal to the perceived rate of nominal growth z, then—under this reformulation—a negative psychological rate of interest becomes conceivable. And negative nominal interest rates become, by the same token, a mathematical possibility.

Both experience and theory suggest to disregard the possibility of negative nominal interest rates. Admittedly, since the outbreak of the financial crisis in 2007, there have been a few instances of very short-term government debt auctioned or briefly traded at negative nominal yield. But these examples are too isolated to invalidate the general observation that through time and space nominal interest rates have always been positive. Economic theorists have provided various rationalizations for this fact. Allais, for example, has demonstrated that while there is no reason preventing real interest rates from being negative in a barter economy, there are reasons, mainly institutional, forcing nominal interest rates to be positive in a monetary economy.

The mathematical possibility of negative nominal interest rates looks like a weak point of the reformulated theory of the psychological rate of interest. Its practical importance may, however, be very limited. In Japan, after many years of very low nominal growth, the perceived rate of nominal growth still remains positive (1.14 percent as of March 30, 2014). Despite the very sharp contraction in nominal activity posted during the US Great Depression, the perceived rate of nominal growth fell only marginally and briefly below zero (-0.49 percent in 1932, -0.69 percent in 1933). The behavior of the perceived rate of nominal growth in such extreme circumstances illustrates its low and falling elasticity with respect to actual rates of growth as it nears zero.

8.9.3   Real Interest Rates

According to the theory of the psychological rate of interest, as reformulated in this book, nominal interest rates are linked to the perceived rate of nominal growth z, which is in turn a function of the sequence of past rates of nominal growth. Thus, this theory does not break down nominal interest rates into real interest rates, on one hand, and an inflation risk premium, on the other. Therefore, neither does it have to make specific assumptions about the normal level of "real interest rates," nor does it have to deal with the potential variability of real interest rates as economic conditions change. Such parsimony is an advantage.

The reasons for directly explaining nominal interest rates by nominal growth are the following:

- If one has to pay a certain interest for borrowed money out of current income, what matters is how fast nominal income grows, or falls, regardless of the split between prices and volumes. A borrower's creditworthiness is as much affected by a 10 percent fall in units sold, prices being unchanged, as by a 10 percent fall in prices, units sold being constant. In both cases, nominal revenues fall by 10 percent, denting the ability to service debt out of current income.

- Economists have conjectured very early that profit "expectations" are the key driver of the demand for loanable funds.[10] In that sense, the rate of interest springs from the rate of profit. And the rate of profit is a function of nominal profits, which in turn depend on total nominal spending, regardless of the split between prices and volumes.

- From the lender's point of view, lending capital at a rate independent of the real growth rate of the economy (i.e., on the basis of inflation alone, implicitly assuming a constant real rate of interest) would be tantamount to forgoing a legitimate claim on the productivity gains that investment generates: for a given rate of inflation of, say, 2 percent, the economy is definitely doing better if it grows at 3 percent instead of 0, and the suppliers of capital should be compensated accordingly.

- In periods of rapid technological change, it is notoriously difficult to measure volumes and prices correctly, as shown by the controversy about the "hedonic adjustment" used by national accountants in the United States.

8.9.4 *Interest Rates and the Demand for Money Function*

At first glance and surprisingly, the HRL formulation of the demand for money does not contain any reference to interest rates, since we have

$$M_D = \phi_0 \Psi(Z) D \qquad (8.30)$$

The theory of the psychological rate of interest reveals, however, that the HRL formulation of the demand for money contains an implicit reference to the psychological rate of interest and therefore to nominal interest rates.

From the relationship

$$i = z = \chi Z = \frac{\chi_0}{\Psi(Z)} Z \qquad (8.31)$$

we get indeed

$$\Psi(Z) = \frac{\chi_0}{z} Z = \frac{\chi_0}{i} Z \qquad (8.32)$$

Substituting this expression for $\Psi(Z)$ in relation 8.30, we obtain

$$M_D = \phi_0 \frac{\chi_0}{z} ZD = \phi_0 \frac{\chi_0}{i} ZD \qquad (8.33)$$

Since $z = \chi Z$, where χ is always positive, z and Z always have the same sign. Therefore, the ratio Z/z is always positive. The perceived rate of nominal growth z can be equal to 0, only if the coefficient of psychological expansion Z is equal to 0. In this case, we have

$$\frac{Z}{z} = \frac{2}{\chi_0} \qquad \text{and} \qquad M_D = \phi_0 D \qquad (8.34)$$

which shows that relationship 8.33 is defined even when $z = 0$. This relationship indicates that for a given level of nominal spending D, the demand for money is inversely proportional to the psychological rate of interest. It also indicates that even if the psychological rate of interest were to fall to zero, the demand for money would not rise to infinity. According to this analysis, there cannot be such a thing as a liquidity trap.

Furthermore, we have seen that the following relationship holds between the psychological rate of interest $i = z$ and nominal interest rates

$$j = \mu z + \epsilon \qquad (8.35)$$

where ϵ represents the residual of the (j, z) adjustment. We can write

$$z = \frac{j - \epsilon}{\mu} \qquad (8.36)$$

and

$$M_D = \phi_0 \frac{\chi_0 \mu Z}{j - \epsilon} D \qquad (8.37)$$

Relationship 8.37 shows that, up to the terms μ and ϵ, the demand for money is inversely proportional to nominal interest rates. Since $j - \epsilon = j^*$, we can finally write

$$M_D = \phi_0 \frac{\chi_0 \mu Z}{j^*} D \qquad (8.38)$$

In other words, the demand for money is inversely proportional to the equilibrium value of nominal interest rates. As this equilibrium value is much less volatile than nominal interest rates, it could explain why the elasticity of the demand for money with respect to nominal interest rates is often found to be surprisingly low.

8.9.5   Gibson's Paradox

The correlation between the perceived rate of nominal growth and nominal interest rates helps to elucidate what Keynes called Gibson's paradox. According to the monetary theory of interest rates, it is the scarcity or abundance of money that explains the high or low level of interest rates. Gibson, however, observed the opposite in the longer term: nominal interest rates tend to rise whenever the quantity of money in circulation has increased.[11] Already in the eighteenth century, economists debated the impact of an increased money supply on the level of interest rates. Cantillon and Turgot, for example, were arguing that interest rates were not determined by the supply of money, but by the balance between the demand for and the supply of loanable funds. This debate continues to the present day in connection with "quantitative easing."

To show how his work sheds light on this issue, Allais introduces a distinction between two types of interest rate theories:

- The primary theories that deal with the transient effects of an increase in the money supply.
- The secondary theories that analyze the permanent effects.

To illustrate this distinction, Allais borrows an example from physics. If one throws a stone into a swimming pool, the first observable effect will be a fall in the water level at the point of impact, followed by the propagation of a circular wave around it. But once the surface of the water is still again, the permanent effect will be an elevation of the water level determined by the volume of the stone.

Combining Allais's theory of monetary dynamics with his theory of the psychological rate of interest, as reformulated in this chapter, one can explain Gibson's paradox in the simplest way. To the extent that the expansion in the money supply is achieved through open market operations, it brings about a fall in the interest rates on the securities bought by the central banks. But according to the fundamental equation of monetary dynamics, provided the increase in the money supply is large enough to offset the deflationary impact of a potentially negative initial imbalance between effective and desired money balances, it causes nominal spending to increase. This increase is even more pronounced if the initial gap between effective and desired balances is positive, that is, inflationary.

Provided the increase x_n in nominal spending exceeds the dynamic equilibrium rate z_{n-1}, it does in turn raise the perceived rate of nominal growth z_n. Since nominal interest rates are anchored on the perceived rate of nominal growth, the end result of an increase in the money supply is to raise the level of interest rates.

A change in the perceived rate of nominal growth might affect the market for loanable funds through different channels:

- It may impact the "expected" return on capital employed and hence the demand for loanable funds.
- On the supply side, it may alter the appetite for fixed-income securities: being a hedge against a fall in nominal income, these securities do not benefit from a rise in nominal income (credit risk aside).
- Finally, it may trigger policy responses on the part of central banks.

8.9.6   *The Psychological Rate of Interest and Wicksell's Natural Rate of Interest*

Allais observed that from an analytical point of view, the psychological rate of interest is akin to Wicksell's natural rate of interest, in the sense that a misalignment of market rates with respect to the psychological rate of interest triggers the kind of cumulative—inflationary or deflationary—adjustment described by Wicksell, when market rates are below or above the natural rate of interest. There is, however, a significant difference between Allais's psychological rate of interest and Wicksell's natural rate of interest: while the former can be estimated, the second cannot, thus limiting its potential for empirical applications.

The observations presented in this chapter suggest that the behavior of bond investors is in aggregate to a large extent driven by the rate of nominal growth they have got used to over time, that is, the one they invariably perceive to be "the new normal". Undoubtedly, the bond vigilantes are keen to rationalize their decisions by presenting the perceived rate of nominal growth as an "expected" rate of nominal growth. However, the words they use probably fail to correctly describe their thought process, notably the fact that their "core expectations" are in fact rooted in their memory.

Be that as it may, the correlation between nominal interest rates and the perceived rate of nominal growth is a clear indication that Allais's

HRL formulation can be used to explain economic and financial behavior beyond the field of monetary dynamics. As bond market participants have now experienced for some years a rather subdued level of nominal growth, the perceived rate of nominal growth on which they anchor nominal interest rates is low. And since the perceived rate of nominal growth is low, it is also rather inelastic. In other words, should nominal growth accelerate unexpectedly, bondholders are likely to respond, at least initially, rather slowly to such an outcome.

8.9.7   The Perceived Rate of Nominal Growth, Nominal Interest Rates, and the Valuation of Equities

The anchoring of long-term nominal interest rates on the perceived rate of nominal growth has some important implications for the consistency of the assumptions one makes when assessing the valuation of equities by means of one form or another of the dividend discount model (DDM). In its canonical form, this model has it that the price P of a share is a function of three variables: its current dividend d_0, the expected long-term growth rate g^* of this dividend, and r the discount rate, with $r > g^*$:

$$P(d_0, r, g^*) = \frac{d_0}{r - g^*} \qquad (8.39)$$

As for the discount rate r, it is equal to the current bond yield on long-term risk-free bonds augmented by the (ex-ante) equity risk-premium π:

$$r = j + \pi \qquad (8.40)$$

From relationships 8.39 and 8.40, it follows that the price of a share is ultimately a function of four variables:

$$P(d_0, j, \pi, g^*) = \frac{d_0}{\pi + j - g^*} \qquad (8.41)$$

Of these four variables, two are directly observable (the current dividend and long-term risk-free rate), one is set by investors themselves (the ex-ante equity risk premium) and one is meant to be an expected variable (the expected long-term dividend growth rate). For a particular company or even sector of the equity market, it is quite conceivable that the expected dividend growth rate be substantially higher or lower than expected nominal GDP growth.

But, at an asset class level, such a discrepancy becomes much harder to devise. Instead, it seems appropriate to assume that the long-term growth rate of aggregate dividends should track quite closely the long-term growth rate of nominal GDP (leaving aside the potential contribution of profits made in foreign countries). Now, we know from the analysis presented in this chapter that long-term nominal interest rates are anchored on the perceived rate of nominal growth, which means

$$j \approx g \tag{8.42}$$

Therefore, if an investment strategist is willing to make consistent assumptions, he or she has the choice between two options: either to introduce an expected long-term risk-free rate j^* in his DDM and to align it with the expected long-term growth rate in dividend g^*, or to align the latter with the current long-term risk-free rate j, which implies $g^* = g$. Whichever way he or she chooses to be consistent, the outcome will be

$$j^* - g^* \approx j - g \approx 0 \tag{8.43}$$

and

$$P = \frac{d_0}{\pi} \tag{8.44}$$

from which it follows that the ex-ante equity risk premium is nothing but the dividend yield dy, since

$$\pi = \frac{d_0}{P} = dy \tag{8.45}$$

To put it differently, the HRL formulation implies the paradoxical conclusion that nominal interest rates and dividend growth expectations are irrelevant with respect to the valuation of equities as an asset class. To the extent that nominal interest rates are almost never at the equilibrium value suggested by the HRL formulation but instead oscillate around it, this conclusion is probably somewhat too extreme: second-order risks and opportunities arise for equity investors from nominal interest rates being too low or too high with respect to perceived nominal growth. But, on the other hand, the behavior of Japanese equities since 1989 is a compelling reminder of Gibson's observation that low and falling nominal interest rates do not always benefit equity investors.

PART FOUR

The HRL Formulation and Financial Instability

CHAPTER NINE

Perceived Returns and the Modeling of Financial Behavior

ARGUABLY, ALLAIS did not have financial markets in mind when he conceived the HRL formulation of the demand for money. But following a path pointed out by Allais himself, chapter 8 of this book has confirmed, with the example of nominal interest rates, that the HRL formulation is relevant beyond the field of monetary dynamics. Financial market practitioners will probably not be surprised by this extension, for Allais's psychological assumptions are indeed very general and describe behavior they can observe on trading floors, in investment and risk committees, or during pitches to clients, at least from time to time.

Therefore, it is natural to test further the assumption that if Allais's insights are valid in their original field, they should be useful in other areas where "expectations" matter, that is, first and foremost in financial markets. All one needs to do in this respect, at least as a first step, is to apply the HRL algorithm to sequences of daily, weekly, monthly returns in order to compute perceived returns on specific securities or assets classes and then test whether these perceived returns can be used as explanatory variables in modeling investors' behavior, be it in terms of flows of money or of portfolio structure, including indebtedness.

Needless to say, the number of relationships liable to be investigated is almost infinite. Therefore, in this chapter, we will limit our investigation to a few examples that are particularly relevant with respect to the dynamics of financial instability. Our purpose is not to prove that the HRL formulation could explain buying or holding behavior with respect to any kind of financial instruments; it is rather to suggest that the HRL formulation is an assumption worth considering whenever one is trying to model financial behavior. Hence, this chapter will be mercifully brief. We will start by providing some empirical evidence of a positive feedback from past equity returns into the demand for equities. As this demand exhibits a nonlinear pattern that is similar to the one found by Allais in his HRL formulation of the supply of money, we will compare our findings with those of Allais. Finally, we will briefly discuss the policy implications of positive feedback.

9.1   Some Evidence of Positive Feedback from Past Returns to the Demand for Risky Assets

From the point of view of policymaking, one of the most pressing questions is whether there is any evidence of a cumulative process whereby rising prices would foster an increase in risk appetite, that is, a willingness, on the part of market participants, to hold increasingly large positions of risky assets. The theory of efficient markets holds that this cannot happen for it would be irrational on the part of investors to ignore the fundamental determinants of asset prices. Many academics and practitioners are not so sure, echoing, so to say, Cantillon and the analysis that we have already quoted in chapter 1, p. 3. According to Cantillon, who was a very shrewd speculator, there is little doubt that rising prices feed back into higher and higher "expected" returns, which in turn feed back into an increasing demand for credit.[1] In their analysis of the rises in US stock and house prices during the last two decades, Akerlof and Shiller expound very much the same argument:[2]

> If people tend to buy in reaction to stock price increases or sell in reaction to price decreases, then their reaction to past price changes has the potential to feed back into more price changes in the same direction. ... A vicious circle can develop, causing a continuation of the cycle, at least for a while. ... Most economists don't like these stories of psychological feedback. They consider it offensive to their core concept of human rationality. And they are dismissive for another reason: there are no standard ways to quantify the psychology of people. ... It appears that people had acquired a strong intuitive feeling that home prices can everywhere only go up. ... As home prices rose faster and faster, they reinforced the folk wisdom about increasing prices.

There has been a debate about the role played by margin debt—the credit provided by brokers to their clients to purchase stocks—in the inflation of the IT bubble in the 1990s. Some, like PIMCO's Paul McCulley, have argued that the inflation of this bubble might have been prevented had the Federal Reserve Board decided to raise the margin requirement (i.e., the required equity ratio) instead of leaving it unchanged at 25 percent of the market value of the stocks bought on credit, even when the rise in stock prices accelerated.

9.1.1 Definition of Variables

To see whether the HRL formulation can shed some light on this debate, let us first define the potentially relevant data. Let us assume that outstanding margin debt O_{MD} should be considered not in absolute, but in relative terms. Let us further assume that the ratio of margin debt to broad money supply O_{MD}/M_3 correctly measures margin debt in relative terms. Since January 1973, the starting point of the available time series, it has fluctuated between a minimum of 0.37 percent in December 1974 and a maximum of 4.45 percent in March 2000.[3] This is the ratio we will try to explain by past equity returns.

The measurement of equity returns is easier said than done, since—from 1995 onward—there has been a growing divergence between the S&P 500 index's path and the much steeper course followed by the NASDAQ index. Rather than arbitrarily select one of these two stock market indices, let us consider both simultaneously, leaving the data to decide whether one of them can be neglected.

Let us finally assume that the interest on margin debt ff is correctly approximated by the federal funds rate, and let us take it into account by computing the perceived *excess* return on both the S&P 500 and the NASDAQ indices:

$$Z_{SP} = \int_{-\infty}^{t} [x_{SP}(\tau) - ff(\tau)]e^{-\int_{\tau}^{t} \chi_{SP}(u)du}\, d\tau \qquad (9.1)$$

$$z_{SP} = \chi_{SP} Z_{SP} \qquad (9.2)$$

$$Z_{N} = \int_{-\infty}^{t} [x_{N}(\tau) - ff(\tau)]e^{-\int_{\tau}^{t} \chi_{N}(u)du}\, d\tau \qquad (9.3)$$

$$z_{N} = \chi_{N} Z_{N} \qquad (9.4)$$

TABLE 9.1
Present Value of Excess Returns and Perceived Excess Returns

	S&P 500	NASDAQ
Initialization parameter (Jan. 1973) (%)	36.44	36.44
Minimum value of Z	−59.02 (Aug. 1982)	−63.76 (Sept. 74)
Maximum value of Z	75.45 (Jul. 1999)	152.27 (Feb. 2000)
Minimum value of z	−2.20	−2.34
Maximum value of z	5.66	20.41

where x_{SP} and x_N are the returns of, respectively, the S&P 500 and the NASDAQ indices. Table 9.1 shows some selected values of the present value of excess returns and of the perceived excess returns. Note that the initialization parameter is computed from series of equity returns and federal funds rate that start well before January 1973. Hence, it cannot be used to "over fit" the data and should be considered as absolutely neutral.

9.1.2   Visual Investigation of the Relationship Between Relative Margin Debt and the Present Value of Excess Equity Returns

Having thus defined O_{MD}/M_3, Z_{SP}, and Z_N, we can now draw up two scatterplots to visualize the relationships between O_{MD}/M_3 on the vertical axis and on the horizontal axis, respectively, Z_{SP} and Z_N (figures 9.1 and 9.2). Both scatterplots suggest the existence of a nonlinear relationship between relative margin debt and the present value of past excess equity returns: the left ends of the scatterplots tend to be convex, while the remaining observations tend to exhibit an almost linear relationship. This pattern is more visible in the NASDAQ than in the S&P 500. What the data in our sample do not allow us to confirm is a concave relationship toward the right end of the scatterplots for high values of the present value of excess equity returns. Failing such empirical confirmation, we can only conjecture that the observed relationships are overall nonlinear.

9.1.3   Adjustment of Sample Data Through Linear Regression

If the minimum and maximum values of the ratio $P = O_{MD}/M_3$ were close, respectively, to 0 and 1, we could—through linear

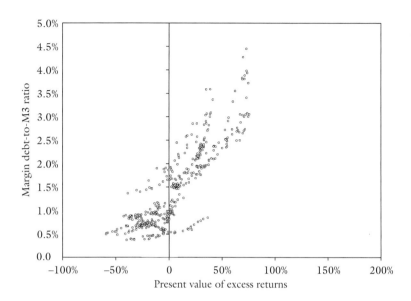

Figure 9.1 S&P 500 and margin debt.

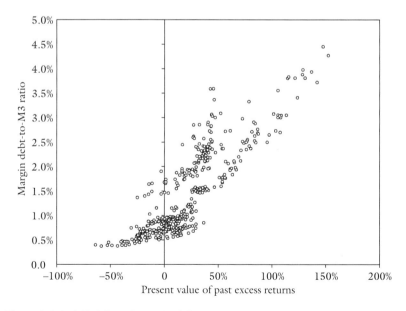

Figure 9.2 NASDAQ and margin debt.

regression—directly seek to fit the data with a function having the form

$$Y(Z_N, Z_{SP}) = \frac{e^{c_2 Z_{SP} + c_1 Z_N + c_0}}{1 + e^{c_2 Z_{SP} + c_1 Z_N + c_0}} \qquad 0 < Y < 1 \qquad (9.5)$$

for a simple transformation yields the following equivalent form:

$$Y = \frac{e^{c_2 Z_{SP} + c_1 Z_N + c_0}}{1 + e^{c_2 Z_{SP} + c_1 Z_N + c_0}} \Leftrightarrow \frac{Y}{1 - Y} = e^{c_2 Z_{SP} + c_1 Z_N + c_0} \qquad (9.6a)$$

$$\Leftrightarrow \ln \frac{Y}{1 - Y} = c_2 Z_{SP} + c_1 Z_N + c_0 \qquad (9.6b)$$

But in our sample data the ratio P is distributed between 0.37 percent and 4.45 percent. Hence, we must first compute a rescaled ratio P' by stating that the position of P' between 0 and 1 is proportional to the position of P between its unknown minimum and maximum values, respectively, $P_m < 0.37$ percent and $P_M > 4.45$ percent, that is,

$$\frac{P' - 0}{1 - 0} = \frac{1}{P_M - P_m}(P - P_m) \qquad (9.7)$$

P_m and P_M are unknown parameters, the values of which will be determined by optimizing the following linear regression:

$$\ln \frac{P'^*}{1 - P'^*} = c_2 Z_{SP} + c_1 Z_N + c_0 + \epsilon \qquad \text{with} \qquad 0 < P'^* < 1 \qquad (9.8)$$

Over our sample of 364 monthly observations beginning in January 1973 and ending in April 2003, we have found the optimal adjustment (R-SQ $=$ 87.72 percent) for $P_m = 0$ and $P_M = 5.60$ percent (see table 9.2).

TABLE 9.2
Bivariate Linear Regression of Relative Margin Debt on the Present Value of Past Returns

	Value	T-stat
c_0	−1.6629	84.48
c_1	1.3921	18.05
c_2	0.7277	7.63

TABLE 9.3
Univariate Linear Regression of Relative Margin
Debt on the Present Value of Past Returns

	Value	T-stat
c_0	−1.7464	99.19
c_1	1.9046	46.65

These results suggest that the present value of the excess returns on the S&P 500 plays a secondary role. A univariate regression on the present value of the excess returns on the NASDAQ yields indeed the results shown in table 9.3 but with a slightly lower R-SQ (85.74 percent).

In contrast, if, instead of using the present value of past excess returns as explanatory variable, we use the present value of past absolute returns, then the quality of the adjustment diminishes significantly. In other words, these data suggest that the risk-free rate of interest exerts some influence on the demand for risky assets. Based on these data, it remains an open issue whether the variable Z is better to use than the variable z.

From relationships 9.7 and 9.8 and using the bivariate regression, we get for the estimate of P (figure 9.3)

$$P^* = (P_M - P_m)\frac{e^{c_2 Z_{SP} + c_1 Z_N + c_0}}{1 + e^{c_2 Z_{SP} + c_1 Z_N + c_0}} + P_m \qquad (9.9)$$

Most importantly, Granger causality tests clearly indicate that the causality runs from the present value of excess equity returns to relative margin debt.

The null hypothesis that the present value of past excess returns does not cause margin debt can be rejected with almost certainty, while the opposite cannot be confidently rejected, as shown in table 9.4.

9.1.4 Additional Tests

In chapter 8, we saw how dangerous it can be to draw conclusions from one single set of obliging data. Bearing in mind that one counter-example is enough to prove a theory wrong, we would nevertheless like to show that the analysis we have just presented is compatible with at

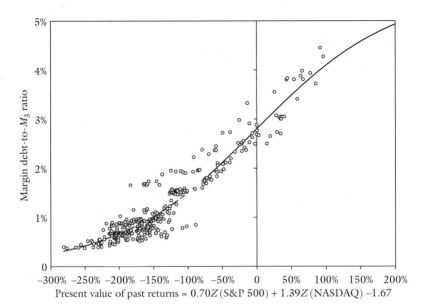

Figure 9.3 Margin debt and past equity returns: a nonlinear relationship.

least two other data sets. Admittedly these two examples still belong to US financial history, but the past they belong to—the 1920s and 1930s—is much more distant than the IT bubble.

The two aspects of financial behavior we want to explain in those years are margin debt,[4] once again, and bank debits at NYC banks,[5] that is, the nominal value of transactions cleared through banks. This time, we have a direct measure of the cost of borrowing funds to purchase stocks.[6] This is potentially important because the spread between the rate on brokers' loans and the discount rate of the Federal Reserve

TABLE 9.4
Granger Causality Tests on Relative Margin Debt
and the Present Value of Past Equity Returns

Observations: 443	F-stat	P
Z_N does not Granger cause P	38.7715	0.0000
P does not Granger cause Z_N	0.7774	0.4602
Z_{SP} does not Granger cause P	14.3006	0.0000
P does not Granger cause Z_{SP}	0.9489	0.3879

Board widened from virtually 0 in late 1923 to 380 basis points in May 1929, when the former reached almost 9 percent a year. As for equity returns, we have used the Cowles Commission index up until 1928 and the S&P 500 thereafter.

By applying the statistical analysis described above to these data from the Great Depression, we reach very similar conclusions, that is, the existence of a positive feedback from the present value of past equity returns to the demand for equities. However, there are three major differences between these two additional examples and margin debt between 1973 and 2003:

- The present value of past returns now leads the demand for equities by one month.
- The consideration of excess returns does not yield better adjustments than the mere consideration of absolute returns.
- While the adjustment of bank debits is remarkably stable (figure 9.4), it seems necessary to distinguish two regimes as regards the adjustment of margin debt (figure 9.5): one for the ascending phase and another for the descending phase.

In light of these three examples, we submit that there is some evidence of a feedback loop between rising prices and an increasing

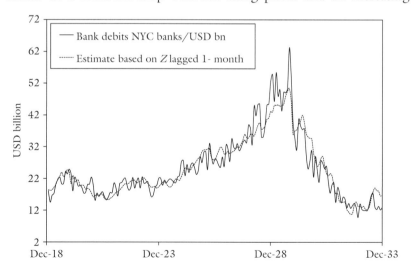

Figure 9.4 Bank debits in New York City and the present value of past equity returns.

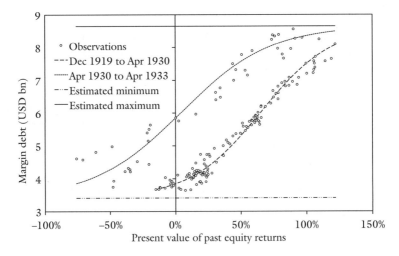

Figure 9.5 Margin debt and the present value of equity returns.

propensity to buy stock on margin or to trade stocks ("overtrading"). Or, to put it differently, there is some evidence that risk appetite tends to increase with respect to past returns, which suggests that financial markets participants may not always be quite rational. To this extent, the availability of credit has an impact on asset prices in the real world, too, and not just in Smith's experimental asset markets. Cantillon was right.

The HRL formulation sheds a somewhat provocative light on "liquidity," this notion or buzzword that financial market participants so frequently use without ever defining it precisely. When traders or investors make the case for adding risk to their portfolios by observing that there is "just too much liquidity chasing too few assets," thereby implicitly assuming that the causality runs from "liquidity" to asset prices, they actually allude to the transactions velocity of money in financial markets, which has the dimension of a flow, as opposed to the outstanding quantity of money, be this stock measured in absolute terms or as a share of the market portfolio. Whether this crucial distinction between stocks and flows is always present in their minds is doubtful.[7] Were it present, they would probably not make statements to the effect that "people have no choice but to put their money somewhere," for money does not disappear when it is invested in equities, bonds, real estate, or any other financial assets: it only changes hands, more or less frequently. While it is true that the stock of money in a given economy cannot vanish (barring outright bank failures, deleveraging on the part of the banks' customers, or capital outflows), the transactions velocity of money is essentially variable: bank debits in New York rose sharply in 1928 and 1929 and fell precipitously in 1930 (see figure 9.4), three years during which the US money supply was essentially stagnant (see table 6.1). The HRL formulation provides two important insights about the transactions velocity of money in financial markets ("liquidity" in market parlance). First, inverting the direction of the causality invoked by conventional wisdom, it suggests that "liquidity" is driven by the perceived rate of asset price inflation, that is, by past movements in asset prices. At the very least, the HRL formulation proposes that there is some interdependence between "liquidity" and price movements. Second, the HRL formulation submits that, as a bubble inflates, the perceived rate of asset price inflation becomes increasingly elastic with respect to actual price movements. In other words, the factor that drives velocity up, thereby creating an illusion of "liquidity surfeit," becomes increasingly prone to instability. By construction, this is bound to happen when cash balances are *relatively* scarce with respect to the market value of total assets.

9.2   The Supply of Money and the Demand for Risky Assets

On one hand, the function

$$\gamma(Z) = 1 - a' + a' \frac{1 + b'}{1 + b'e^{-a'Z}} \qquad (9.10)$$

that we have encountered in the HRL formulation of the endogenous supply of money (see chapter 4) provides us with a template to model the demand for risky assets. One reason for creating money through bank credit is indeed to bid for risky assets: people who borrow money from banks exchange it not only for goods and services but also for assets. To that extent, the supply of money and the demand for risky assets are two sides of the same coin. They both express "expectations."

This money supply function is a bounded, nonlinear, monotonic function increasing from $1 - a'$ to $1 + a'b'$. Transposed to risky assets, it describes a demand that increases with respect to the present value of past returns. The parameter a' sets the level of its lower bound and contributes, alongside b', to setting the distance between the lower and upper bounds. The higher the value of a', the lower the lower bound and the greater the distance to the upper one.

As we have seen in chapter 5 in the context of the HRL formulation of monetary dynamics, Allais's empirical work indicates the following ranges for parameters a', b', and α'.

$$0.8 \leq b' \leq 1.2 \tag{9.11}$$

$$1/3 \leq a' \leq 2/3 \tag{9.12}$$

$$\alpha' a' = 1 \tag{9.13}$$

$$3/2 \leq \alpha' \leq 3 \tag{9.14}$$

On the other hand, through linear regression, we have just estimated the coefficients c_0, c_1, and in one case c_2 of functions that have the following analytical form:

$$\Upsilon(Z_1, Z_2) = \frac{e^{c_2 Z_2 + c_1 Z_1 + c_0}}{1 + e^{c_2 Z_2 + c_1 Z_1 + c_0}} \tag{9.15}$$

At first glance, the analytical forms of the functions $\Upsilon(Z_1, Z_2)$ and $\gamma(Z)$ are different from each other. Yet, these two functions have the same graphic shape. Therefore, it is natural to establish an equivalence between these two different analytical expressions.

Let us first observe that the variables that we have adjusted through linear regression on the function $\Upsilon(Z_1, Z_2)$ had previously been rescaled from 0 to 1. For the lower limit of $\gamma(Z)$ to be equal to 0, we need to have $a' = 1$, which implies

$$\gamma(Z) = \frac{1 + b'}{1 + b' e^{-\alpha' Z}} \tag{9.16}$$

Let us now turn to the function $\Upsilon(Z)$:

$$\Upsilon(Z) = \frac{e^{c_1 Z + c_0}}{1 + e^{c_1 Z + c_0}} \Leftrightarrow \Upsilon(Z) = \frac{1}{1 + e^{-c_0} e^{-c_1 Z}} \tag{9.17a}$$

$$\Leftrightarrow (1 + e^{-c_0}) \Upsilon(Z) = \frac{1 + e^{-c_0}}{1 + e^{-c_0} e^{-c_1 Z}} \tag{9.17b}$$

By having $c_1 = \alpha'$ and $e^{-c_0} = b'$, we immediately get

$$(1 + b') \Upsilon(Z) = \frac{1 + b'}{1 + b' e^{-\alpha' Z}} = \gamma(Z) \tag{9.18}$$

$$(1 + b') \Upsilon(Z) = \gamma(Z) \quad \text{with} \quad \alpha' = c_1 \quad \text{and} \quad b' = e^{-c_0} \tag{9.19}$$

In light of these equivalences and by analogy with table 4.5, parameters c_0 and c_1 are easy to interpret:

- The lower the value of c_0 (i.e., the higher the value of b'), the more elevated the upper bound of the demand for risky assets.
- The higher the value of c_1 (i.e., the higher the value of α'), the faster the transition from a risk-off to a risk-on mode.

The elasticity of the demand for risky assets with respect to the present value of past returns is

$$e(\Upsilon(Z); Z) = \frac{\alpha' b' Z e^{-\alpha' Z}}{1 + b' e^{-\alpha' Z}} \tag{9.20}$$

With respect to the return x, the elasticity of the demand for risky assets is, according to relationships 4.65, 4.71, and 9.20

$$e(\Upsilon(Z(x)); x) = \frac{\alpha' b' Z e^{-\alpha' Z}}{1 + b' e^{-\alpha' Z}} \frac{(1 - e^{-pk})(1 + b e^{\alpha Z})}{1 + b e^{\alpha Z} + \alpha b Z e^{\alpha Z}} \tag{9.21}$$

From there it follows that the elasticity of the demand for risky assets with respect to the perceived return has the following limits:

$$\lim_{Z \to -\infty} e(\Upsilon(Z(x)); x) = \frac{\alpha' p \chi_0 Z}{1 + b} \tag{9.22a}$$

$$\lim_{Z \to +\infty} e(\Upsilon(Z(x)); x) = 0 \tag{9.22b}$$

The values reported in table 9.5 suggest that when positive feedback dynamics are present in financial markets, the behavior of market participants with respect to the present value of past returns is one of unstable ($\alpha' > 1$) bullishness ($b' > 1$).

TABLE 9.5
Estimated Values of Parameters of the Demand for Risky Assets Function

	c_2	$c_1 = \alpha'$	c_0	$b' = e^{-c_0}$	R-SQ (%)
Margin debt (1973–2003)	0.7277	1.3921	−1.6629	5.2746	87.72
Margin debt (1973–2003)		1.9046	−1.7464	5.7339	85.74
Bank debits (1919–1933)		1.9366	−1.9497	7.0266	87.80
Margin debt (1919–1930)		3.6782	−2.4053	11.0818	93.25
Margin debt (1930–1933)		2.9268	−0.1380	1.1480	86.83

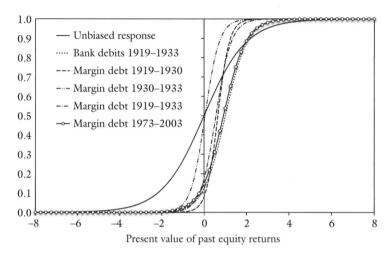

Figure 9.6 Empirical demand curves for risky assets.

Except for the model explaining margin debt between 1919 and 1930, the values we have found for α' are within the 1.5-to-3 range indicated by Allais in another context (in the case of the bivariate model explaining margin debt between 1973 and 2003, it is the sum $c_1 + c_2 = 2.1198$ that falls in the 1.5-to-3 range): this is quite remarkable. In contrast, the values we have found for b' are well in excess of the upper limit of the range indicated by Allais, that is, 1.2. Figure 9.6 illustrates how similar the estimated demand curves are.

Overall, this analysis suggests that while the default parameters $\alpha = b = 1$ and $\chi_0 = 0.40$ percent per month are valid to compute perceived returns, a theory of the demand for risky assets should assume that investors' responsiveness (or "excitability") with respect to perceived returns, their α', is higher than 2 and possibly close to 3. This is important, for the higher the value of α', the greater the potential for financial instability. A theory of the demand for risky assets should also assume that investors' propensity to being bullish, their b', can be very high.[8] The most important insight may be that research aiming at developing "market-specific schemes of expectations formation," as suggested by Blaug, should focus on estimating parameters α' and b' on a case-by-case basis, and on seeking to understand their variability over time and across markets, rather than on fiddling with parameters α, b, and χ_0.

9.3   Policy Implications

If further research confirms the existence of periods during which non-linear feedback dynamics dominate financial behavior, should policy-makers care, and if yes, what should they do?

9.3.1   *Benign Neglect Is Not an Option*

That the investors' response to past movement in prices is bounded could be interpreted as an invitation to benign neglect. The upper bound of investors' nonlinear response ensures that a bubble cannot inflate forever. In other words, unfettered market forces ensure that—sooner or later—the pendulum swings back to fundamentals, even though, as we have seen, there is some uncertainty as regards the level of the upper bound of this nonlinear response.

This argument would be acceptable if bubbles in asset prices did not leave behind them weakened lenders and borrowers. The evidence presented in this chapter supports the view that credit and money are very much endogenous to the private sector as they spring from the "expectations" held by borrowers and lenders. When these "expectations" happen to be wrong-footed, as they are bound to be, both the lenders and the borrowers have to deleverage. If this deleveraging is disorderly or not properly accommodated by monetary and fiscal policy, it can morph into outright debt deflation. Therefore, dealing with "irrational" feedback dynamics should be on the agenda of policymakers. Then the question is, How?

9.3.2   *Policy Rates Are Inappropriate*

The analysis presented in this chapter suggests that interest rates are not appropriate tools for preventing the inflation of asset bubbles. First, irrational as it may seem, there is no solid evidence that interest rates really matter in this context: the explanatory power of the perceived *excess* return is not always higher than that of the perceived *absolute* return. Second, even if interest rates did matter, Central Banks would need to raise them either very early on or to a very high level to materially influence the perceived excess return. Almost certainly, such actions would cause serious collateral damage to other sectors of the economy.

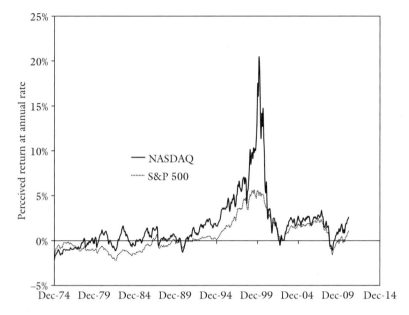

Figure 9.7   Perceived excess returns over the policy rate.

Figure 9.7 illustrates this challenge vividly with the 1990's information technology bubble. To prevent an early rise in the perceived excess
return from a level close to zero, the Federal Reserve should have kept
the difference between its policy rate and future equity returns as close
to zero as possible. Once positive feedback has set in, for its cumulative
dynamics to be reversed, the policy rate would need to be higher than
future equity returns. Any delay in trying to regain control of the situation would make this upward-moving target more and more out of
reach. Even if there existed a constituency supporting such a monetary
framework, it would be impossible to implement and it would entail
unacceptable risks. On this at least, Alan Greenspan was right:[9]

> It was far from obvious that bubbles, even if identified early, could be
> preempted short of the Central Bank inducing a substantial contrac-
> tion in economic activity, the very outcome we should be seeking to
> avoid . . . nothing short of a sharp increase in short-term rates that en-
> genders a significant economic retrenchment is sufficient to check a
> nascent bubble. The notion that a well-timed incremental tightening

could have been calibrated to prevent the late 1990's bubble is almost surely an illusion.

9.3.3   Regulation Is the Only Option

If interest rates are not appropriate tools for preventing the inflation of asset bubbles, we are left with the regulation of credit and taxation. Of course, there will always be a kind of arms race between regulators and regulated as well as between taxmen and taxpayers. Had the Federal Reserve raised the margin requirement, other sources of credit might well have accommodated the demand for credit to purchase stocks. Nothing prevents the proceeds of a mortgage refinancing or of a home equity loan to fund stock purchases. Failing a comprehensive, alert, and well-designed regulation of credit, aiming at containing the overall growth of bank and nonbank credit, isolated measures are bound to be circumvented. But if regulators declare a permanent unilateral cease-fire, it is hard to see how instability could not be pervasive.

Be that as it may, the existence of feedback dynamics in asset markets supports the view that the current paradigm of inflation targeting in goods and services markets is in fact a license to inflate bubbles. And this is even truer if policymakers overlook the role played by the perceived risk of loss.

CHAPTER TEN

Downside Potential Under Risk: The Allais Paradox and Its Conflicting Interpretations

IN THE PRECEDING CHAPTERS, we have seen that the HRL formulation can be used to model how people form return "expectations" under uncertainty. Were it not for its approximate semantics, the next question would be, And what about risk "expectations" under uncertainty? Bearing in mind Knight's critical distinction between risk and uncertainty, the more rigorously formulated question we want to address now is the following: can we use the HRL formulation to model how financial market participants form "expectations" of the dispersion of returns under uncertainty?

Investing in long-term financial assets can indeed be analyzed as a repetitive game in which investors hope to earn some excess return over time, provided they have enough financial staying power (capital) to survive intermediate shocks. By shocks, we mean truly catastrophic outcomes, either in absolute terms or relative to certain thresholds (e.g., benchmark returns, cost of liabilities, etc.). By intermediate shocks, we mean shocks that can happen at any time after the initial investment is made, that is, even before enough excess return has been accumulated to absorb them. A valuable insight should be to understand how market participants assess the frequency and magnitude of such adverse shocks and behave in response to this assessment.

Yet, albeit too frequent to be ignored, such disasters are rare enough to complicate statistical analysis, if not to make it impossible. Therefore, "even an infinitely-lived investor [using some form or another of Bayesian learning] will remain uncertain about the exact probability."[1] And so, it seems to be an interesting proposal to define the perceived risk of loss as the present value of past negative returns, computed according to the HRL formulation, and to consider it as a possible way to model how people assess downside potential under uncertainty. The preceding chapters have already made the general case for using the HRL formulation to account for learning processes under uncertainty. As regards the case for segregating losses, be they defined in absolute or relative terms, it is warranted by insights borrowed from the theory of choice under risk, notably by the well-known Allais paradox and the conflicting interpretations and theories it has inspired.

As we shall see in chapter 11, the perceived risk of loss is an attempt to introduce time into the theory of risky choices and in the Allais paradox. Time, this perennial complicating factor, is indeed totally absent from this field. Time is not needed to discover and estimate the potential outcomes and their respective probabilities, since they are given to the decision makers. There is no element whatsoever of intertemporal choice, since all the prospects under consideration are assumed to be either present ones or identically dated future ones. Finally, mathematical expectation, a concept playing an important role in the analysis of risky choices, is computed under the implicit but odd assumption that all outcomes can be considered simultaneously, even if only one of them will happen.

However, even in the world of risk, the simple, hypothetical, timeless world in which decision makers are assumed to have a perfect knowledge of the outcomes $(x_1, \ldots, x_i, \ldots, x_n)$ and probabilities $(p_1, \ldots, p_i, \ldots, p_n)$ defining a prospect P, economic analysis still struggles to identify and to quantify the factors that explain empirical choices among risky prospects, or between risky and sure ones. If, as suggested by the Saint Petersburg paradox, it is necessary to distinguish the psychological value from the monetary value of an outcome, what is the shape of the cardinal utility function and how can we test its compatibility with empirical data? If, as suggested by the Allais paradox, the expected utility theory fails to explain many empirical choices among risky prospects, which alternative theory best explains these "anomalies"? Is it prospect theory?

Therefore, it seems appropriate to dedicate this chapter to a brief overview of expected utility theory (section 10.1), followed by a presentation of the Allais paradox and a discussion of prospect theory (section 10.2), which has become its conventional interpretation. This preliminary step will facilitate the introduction of the perceived risk of loss and the assessment of its relevance, in chapter 11.

10.1 Expected Utility Theory: An Overview

10.1.1 The Saint Petersburg Paradox

In the beginning, there was a consensus that the psychological value of a risky prospect $(x_1, \ldots, x_i, \ldots, x_n; p_1, \ldots, p_i, \ldots, p_n)$ is given by its mathematical expectation

$$V(P) = E(P) = \sum_{i=1}^{n} x_i \, p_i \qquad (10.1)$$

with $\sum_{i=1}^{n} p_i = 1$ and x_i positive or negative.

Yet, this definition of the value of a risky prospect was quickly shown to be incompatible with some empirical observations. Imagine, for example, a game of chance, such as tossing a coin, in which if it comes up tails, the player wins nothing but the right to take another chance; when at the nth toss the coin finally comes up heads, the player wins 2^n ducats.[2] The resulting risky prospect is

$$P = \left(2, 2^2, \ldots, 2^n; \frac{1}{2}, \frac{1}{2^2}, \ldots, \frac{1}{2^n} \right) \qquad (10.2)$$

and its mathematical expectation is

$$E(P) = \sum_{i=1}^{n} \frac{2^i}{2^i} = n \qquad (10.3)$$

Therefore, this prospect should have an infinite value when n increases to infinity. Very early on, it had been observed that people deemed to be rational, people who pursue consistent goals with compatible means, were unwilling to pay more than 20 ducats (about 2,900 current USD) for participating in such a game. This paradox, known as the Saint Petersburg paradox, was resolved by Daniel Bernoulli in 1738.[3]

10.1.2 Bernoulli's Resolution of the Saint Petersburg Paradox: Cardinal Utility

Bernoulli's solution rests upon psychological introspection. He starts by asserting that "all men cannot use the same rule to evaluate the gamble." Why? Because "there is no doubt that a gain of one thousand ducats is more significant to a pauper than to a rich man though both gain the same amount." From this premise, Bernoulli infers, first, that "the determination of the value of an item must not be based on its price, but rather on the utility it yields"; second, that "the utility is dependent on the particular circumstances of the person making the estimate"; and third, that "no valid measurement of the value of a risk [a prospect] can be obtained without consideration being given to its utility."

Bernoulli then proceeds to conjecture that "it is highly probable that any increase in wealth ... will always result in an increase in utility which is inversely proportionate to the quantity of goods already possessed." With C being the player's capital (or endowment), dC its variation (positive or negative), c_1 a positive constant, and B Bernoulli's index of psychological value (or cardinal utility function), this conjecture takes the mathematical form

$$dB = c_1 \frac{dC}{C} \qquad (10.4)$$

from which we get

$$B(C) = c_1 \ln C + c_2 \qquad (10.5)$$

Please note that, at least at this stage, there is no need to know the values taken by c_1 and c_2. This is true because irrespective of its functional form, cardinal utility is always defined up to a linear transformation, since

$$[u(A) > u(B) \Leftrightarrow A \succ B] \Leftrightarrow [c_1 u(A) + c_2 > c_1 u(B) + c_2 \Leftrightarrow A \succ B] \qquad (10.6)$$

For the sake of simplicity, Bernoulli's index can be expressed as

$$B(C) = \ln C \qquad (10.7)$$

without any loss of information.

Contrary to Kahneman's interpretation, Bernoulli's formulation of cardinal utility does not depend on final wealth, but on changes in wealth with respect to the player's initial capital, as we have[4]

$$B(C) = B(C_0 + dC_0) = \ln(C_0 + dC_0) = \ln C_0 + \ln(1 + dC_0/C_0) \qquad (10.8)$$

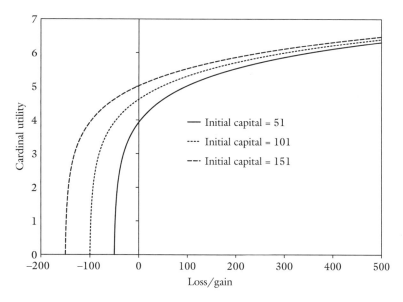

Figure 10.1 Bernoullian cardinal utility.

Once the player's initial capital is given, and of course it is not the same for all players, cardinal utility—as defined by Bernoulli—only depends on *relative changes* in wealth. And as long as a loss is not large enough to wipe out the whole capital $(dC_0 > -C_0)$, one can assign cardinal utility to losses, albeit one can question the steepness of the cardinal utility curve for losses $(dC_0 < 0)$ (see figure 10.1).

With these remarks in mind, we can write

$$B(C + V) = \sum_{i=1}^{n} p_i \ln (C + x_i) \qquad (10.9)$$

and

$$B(C + V) = \ln C + \sum_{i=1}^{n} p_i \ln(1 + x_i/C) \qquad (10.10)$$

10.1.3   *Expected Utility Theory*

Relationship 10.10 defines the expected utility of the risky prospect P under the assumption that cardinal utility is a loglinear function. The most general formulation of the expected utility of a risky prospect is

$$u(C + V) = \sum_{i=1}^{n} p_i u(x_i) \qquad (10.11)$$

According to expected utility theory, a prospect P_1 is preferable to a prospect P_2 if and only if it has higher expected utility.

$$P_1 \succ P_2 \Leftrightarrow u(P_1) > u(P_2) \qquad (10.12)$$

Expected utility theory rules out any empirical situation in which a prospect P_1 would have lower expected utility than a prospect P_2 and yet be preferred to P_2. In other words, it deems $u(P_1) < u(P_2)$ and $P_1 \succ P_2$ to be incompatible.

Bernoulli's resolution of the Saint Petersburg paradox rests on the fact that the expected utility of the gamble, unlike its mathematical expectation, does not rise to infinity. Why? Because Bernoulli substitutes $\ln x_i$ for x_i in relationship 10.1:

$$E(P) = \sum_{i=1}^{n} p_i x_i \rightarrow B(P) = \sum_{i=1}^{n} p_i \ln x_i \qquad (10.13)$$

Since $\ln x_i = i \ln 2$, it follows that the difference between two consecutive terms in relationship 10.13

$$p_i \ln x_i - p_{i-1} \ln x_{i-1} = \frac{(2 - i) \ln 2}{2^i} \qquad (10.14)$$

is negative as soon as $i > 2$ and tends toward 0 when i tends toward infinity. In other words, it is the concavity of Bernoulli's cardinal utility function that ensures the convergence of expected utility and resolves the Saint Petersburg paradox.

10.1.4   Doubts and Conjectures About Cardinal Utility

To summarize, Bernoulli's analysis asserted the existence of a psychological phenomenon called cardinal utility. It further suggested that cardinal utility functions must be concave for gains, but refrained from stating that the logarithmic function is the one and only possible cardinal utility function. Moreover, Bernoulli did not even outline a method to estimate cardinal utility empirically. He thus left the field open, first, to doubts, if not disbeliefs, about the possibility to do so; second, to a preference, among economists, for analytical methods based on ordinal utility; third, to theoretical conjectures, among advocates of cardinal utility, about the shape of the function representing it.[5]

The steepness of Bernoulli's cardinal utility curve for losses is indeed not the only thing that can be challenged. The fact that cardinal utility never stops increasing, in other words, the absence of a satiety effect, contradicts our intuition as well as our experience. If such a satiety effect did not exist, no wealthy men or women would ever have endowed foundations with large parts of their wealth. It is this kind of consideration which led Allais, openly inspired by Weber-Fechner's law expressing the psycho-physiological sensation of light as a function of luminous stimulus, to conjecture in 1943 that—for positive values of its argument at least—cardinal utility should have a logistic shape and have, as a result, an upper horizontal asymptote (see figure 10.2).[6]

Last but not least, even when cardinal utility remains to be specified as a function, it is always possible to assume that it is locally linear (see figure 10.3 and relationship 10.15). This simplifying assumption makes it possible to analyze risky prospects without referring to an explicit

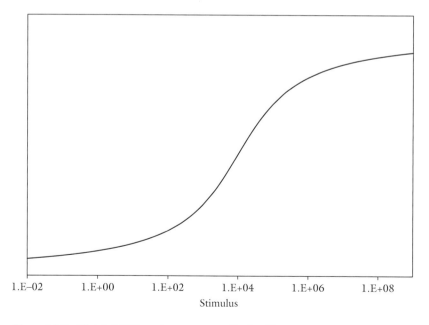

Figure 10.2 Allais's 1943 conjecture on cardinal utility.

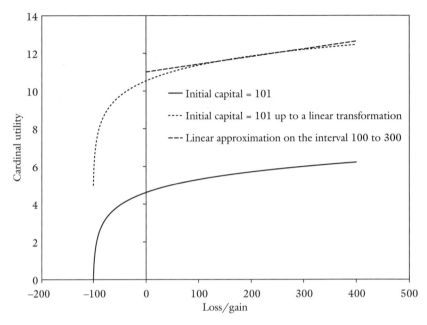

Figure 10.3 Cardinal utility functions defined up to a linear transformation and local linearity.

cardinal utility function, provided the monetary values of their constituent outcomes are of the same order of magnitude.

$$u(x_i) \approx c_1 x_i + c_2 \tag{10.15}$$

Since cardinal utility is always defined up to a linear transformation, this linear approximation is equivalent to

$$u(x_i) = x_i \qquad \text{with} \qquad u(0) = 0 \tag{10.16}$$

Such an approximation will be helpful in the analysis of many of the choice problems we are now going to consider.

10.2   The Allais Paradox and Its Conflicting Interpretations

In May 1952, Allais invited 23 prominent economists and mathematicians in Paris to discuss the theory of decision-making under risk, in light of the results of experiments he had conducted.[7] Ahead of this 1952 colloquium, Allais had designed a questionnaire, an abridged version of which one can freely download from the Internet, which comprised two groups of questions.[8] The first group (questions 1 to 5) was made of 22 simple questions in which respondents were asked to make choices between risky prospects. The second group (questions 6 to 10) consisted of 38 questions, which demanded greater introspection on the part of respondents, as they were asked to evaluate, first, psychologically equivalent gains (as in questions 631 to 634 and 651 to 654 reproduced in table 10.7, p. 225) and, second, the sure outcome they deemed equivalent to a prospect $(p; x)$, in which p is constant and x varies (and conversely). Allais gathered answers to the first 22 questions from 101 respondents, 52 of whom further answered the 38 questions from the second group. As 55 of these 101 respondents were Allais's students at the Ecole des Mines, he decided to ignore the answers given by 40 of them. Out of the remaining 61 respondents, he randomly selected 16. It happened that 2 of them—B. de Finetti and E. Malinvaud—were among the 23 participants to the Paris colloquium.

Out of the many questions designed by Allais, two have become famous for having brought to light what is now called the Allais paradox.[9] These two questions presented respondents with two pairs of risky prospects, respectively, A and B, and C and D, and asked them which prospect they preferred; question 35: A or B? and question 36: C or D? The respective prospects are described in table 10.1 in terms of 1952 French francs.[10] The gains are assumed to be important relative to the decision makers' initial capital. While an overwhelming majority of respondents preferred D over C, it appeared that about 53 percent of them simultaneously preferred A over B. This observation is now known as the Allais paradox.

TABLE 10.1

Questions 35 and 36 of the 1952 Questionnaire

Question	35		36	
Prospect	*A*	*B*	*C*	*D*
Probability		1%	89%	90%
Gain		0	0	0
Probability	100%	89%	11%	
Gain	100,000,000	100,000,000	100,000,000	
Probability		10%		10%
Gain		500,000,000		500,000,000

Let us see why Allais's experiment reveals a paradox and why this paradox violates the independence axiom, which holds that outcomes should be valued independently of one another. According to expected utility theory, the utilities of prospects A, B, C, and D are defined by[11]

$$u(A) = 100\% u(100) \tag{10.17a}$$
$$u(B) = 1\% u(0) + 89\% u(100) + 10\% u(500) \tag{10.17b}$$
$$u(C) = 89\% u(0) + 11\% u(100) \tag{10.17c}$$
$$u(D) = 90\% u(0) + 10\% u(500) \tag{10.17d}$$

The answers given to Allais's questionnaire revealed that a majority of respondents (53 percent) preferred A over B, which implies that A must have a higher utility than B.

$$A \succ B \Leftrightarrow u(A) > u(B) \tag{10.18}$$

By virtue of the independence axiom, if we add the same prospect

$$89\% u(0) - 89\% u(100) \tag{10.19}$$

to both terms of inequality 10.18, that should leave it unchanged.

$$u(A) > u(B) \tag{10.20}$$
$$\Leftrightarrow u(A) + 89\% u(0) - 89\% u(100) > u(B) + 89\% u(0) - 89\% u(100)$$

Now, if we substitute relationships 10.17a and 10.17b for $u(A)$ and $u(B)$ in 10.20 and rearrange the terms, we get

$$u(A) > u(B) \tag{10.21}$$
$$\Leftrightarrow \quad 100\% u(100) + 89\% u(0) - 89\% u(100)$$
$$> \quad 1\% u(0) + 89\% u(100) + 10\% u(500) + 89\% u(0) - 89\% u(100)$$

and, after simplifying,

$$u(A) > u(B) \Leftrightarrow 89\% u(0) + 11\% u(100) > 90\% u(0) + 10\% u(500) \tag{10.22}$$

in which we recognize $u(C)$ and $u(D)$.

Hence, by virtue of the independence axiom, the preference $A \succ B$ implies the preference $C \succ D$:

$$u(A) > u(B) \Leftrightarrow u(C) > u(D) \Leftrightarrow C \succ D \tag{10.23}$$

Yet, the preferences observed in Allais's experiment are $A \succ B$ *and* $D \succ C$, which—taken together—are incompatible with the independence axiom. That prominent economists, supposedly very rational people, could prefer D to C *and* A to B is the empirical observation known as the Allais paradox.[12]

10.2.1 Prospect Theory

As an empirical observation that economic agents violate the predictions of expected utility theory, the Allais paradox is hardly controversial. Preceding or following Allais's two most prominent experimental emulators, Daniel Kahneman and Amos Tversky, many researchers have not only confirmed the initial observation made by Allais, but also collected many additional ones. In contrast, how to interpret the Allais paradox has been and probably remains a challenge.

The prospect theory proposed by Kahneman and Tversky in 1979 purports to unseat expected utility theory and has become the standard interpretation of the Allais paradox.[13] According to prospect theory, choices are determined by the value V of prospects, an index in which decision weights w_i are substituted for probabilities and the value of prospects $v(x_i)$ for their cardinal utility $u(x_i)$.

$$u(P) = \sum_{i=1}^{n} p_i u(x_i) \rightarrow V(P) = \sum_{i=1}^{n} w_i v(x_i) \qquad \text{with} \qquad \sum_{i=1}^{n} w_i \neq 1$$
$$(10.24)$$

The intuition underpinning prospect theory is rather simple. Since the mathematical expectation of a distribution of outcomes does not always explain people's choices among risky prospects, it must be that people weigh these outcomes with something else than their probabilities, which Kahneman and Tversky propose to call decision weights and which reflect the impact of the probability p_i on the overall value of the prospect:

$$w_i = \pi(p_i) \qquad (10.25)$$

These decision weights express the fact that "people underweight outcomes that are merely probable in comparison with outcomes that are obtained with certainty," the so-called "certainty effect." In other words, "decision weights are generally lower than the corresponding probabilities, except in the range of low probabilities" (i.e., below

20 percent); they "are not probabilities" and "should not be interpreted as measures of degree or belief"; they "measure the impact of events on the desirability of prospects, and not merely the perceived likelihood of these events."

Therefore, people are risk-averse in choices involving sure gains: they don't gamble, if they can lock in a sure gain. As the proverb goes, a bird in the hand is worth two in the bush. Symmetrically, people are risk-seeking in choices involving sure losses: they do gamble, if gambling gives them a chance to spare themselves a sure loss. Among evils choose the least, as another proverb goes.

As for the value function, its arguments are gains and losses (allegedly as opposed to final states of wealth), and it is S-shaped: it is convex for losses, concave for gains, and falls more steeply for losses than it rises for gains.[14] Kahneman and Tversky did outline the S shape of their value function in their 1979 paper, but they did it without specifying its analytical form, apart from assuming

$$v(0) = 0 \qquad (10.26)$$

What they did at this stage was merely to give a stylized presentation of empirical observations made in the context of risky choices, leaving the actual scaling of their value function to further research. While recognizing that the "actual scaling is considerably more complicated than in utility theory, because of the introduction of decision weights," they did not suggest any methodology liable to disentangle this complexity. This being said, "if prospect theory had a flag, this image [the tilted S] would be drawn on it."[15]

Interestingly, it is through the hypermyopic lens of variance (or standard deviation) that Kahneman and Tversky deal with the potential influence of the dispersion of outcomes on observed choices.[16] On one hand, they observe that people prefer a sure gain of 3,000 (outcome B in P_3, table 10.4), which has nil variance, to an 80 percent chance of winning 4,000 and a 20 percent chance of winning nothing (outcome A in P_3), which has higher mathematical expectation (3,200 versus 3,000), but also higher variance (1,600 versus 0). This, they say, shows that people do not like dispersion as measured by variance. On the other hand, they note that people do not prefer a sure loss of 3,000 (outcome B in P_3', table 10.5), which also has nil variance, to an 80 percent chance of losing 4,000 and a 20 percent chance of losing nothing (outcome A in P_3'), even though B has not only higher mathematical expectation ($-3{,}000$ versus $-3{,}200$) but also lower standard deviation than A (0 versus $1{,}600$). From these two observations, which reveal that sure gains and losses generate opposite responses and that variance seems to matter for the former but not for the latter, they infer that variance (i.e., implicitly dispersion at large) is irrelevant to risky choices.[17]

10.2.2 *Prospect Theory: A Critique*

Unfortunately for prospect theory, it is quite easy and much more parsimonious to explain observed choices by means of moments of order higher than 2. The lth order moment of a distribution $(x_1, \ldots, x_i, \ldots, x_n; p_1, \ldots, p_i, \ldots, p_n)$ is

$$\mu_l = \sum_{i=1}^{n} p_i(x_i - \bar{x})^l \tag{10.27}$$

in which $\bar{x}$ is its mathematical expectation.

Thus, variance is the second-order moment of a distribution. The higher the order of a moment, the greater the weight given to large deviations from the mathematical expectation. By construction, even-order moments ($l = 2, 4, 6, 8, \ldots$) are always positive. They measure dispersion around the mathematical expectation, irrespective of the sign of the deviations. They are useful to describe distributions that are symmetric with respect to their mathematical expectations, but cannot deal with asymmetric distributions.

In contrast, odd-order moments ($l = 3, 5, 7, 9, \ldots$) can be positive, if positive deviations dominate negative ones, or negative in the opposite case, thus indicating whether a distribution is skewed to the right or to the left of its mathematical expectation. In other words, odd-order moments indicate whether there is an up- or downside with respect to a well-defined reference point: the mathematical expectation of the distribution.

Moments play an important role in probability theory and statistics. However, for the sake of comparability with mathematical expectation or between prospects in the present context, we will refer to the lth root of the corresponding lth-order moment as such roots have the same dimension as the mathematical expectation. Figure 10.4 plots the mathematical expectation, the square root of the variance (i.e., the standard deviation) and the cubic root of the third-order moment of the

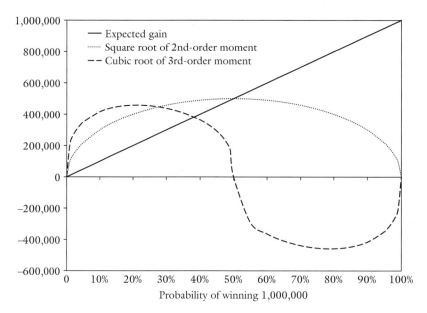

Figure 10.4 Distribution parameters of a constant-gain, variable-probability prospect.

following risky prospect: probability p of winning 1,000,000 and $1 - p$ of winning nothing, for p varying from 0 to 1.

Having fixed the gain at 1,000,000 allows us to isolate the effect of p on the distribution's mathematical expectation as well as on its second- and third-order moments. While the mathematical expectation rises linearly with respect to p, the standard deviation curve is concave and symmetric with respect to $p = 50$ percent, while the skewness curve is asymmetric, positive, and concave for $p < 50$ percent and negative and convex for $p > 50$ percent. Figure 10.5 shows the result of the same exercise when a loss is considered.

In figures 10.4 and 10.5, the mathematical expectation is $E_p(P) = \pm 10^6 p$, while the lth-order moment has the following analytic form:

$$\mu_{l,p}(P) = \left[p(1-p)^l + (1-p)(-p)^l \right] (\pm 10^6)^l \qquad (10.28)$$

The consideration of the third-order moment (or of its cubic root) suffices to explain most of the risky choices discussed by prospect theory. The four pairs of risky choices considered by Kahneman and Tversky in their so-called fourfold pattern (see table 10.2) involve a sure gain (or loss) and a risky prospect, the mathematical expectation

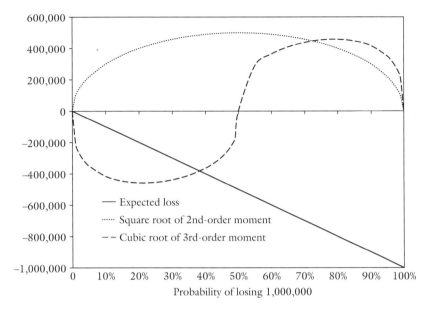

Figure 10.5 Distribution parameters of a constant-loss, variable-probability prospect.

of which is equal to the corresponding sure outcome, the risk consisting of either a high or a low probability gain or loss. In other words, the fourfold pattern is meant to highlight choices made at the left and right extremities of figures 10.4 and 10.5. It is presented as "the most distinctive implication of prospect theory."[18]

Kahneman and Tversky observe two types of choices:

- $B_1 \succ A_1$ and $B_4 \succ A_4$, in which risk aversion dominates, respectively, high-probability gains and low-probability losses.

TABLE 10.2
Prospect Theory's Fourfold Pattern[19]

	A_1	B_1	A_2	B_2	A_3	B_3	A_4	B_4
Probability	95%	100%	95%	100%	5%	100%	5%	100%
Gain/Loss	10,000	9,500	−10,000	−9,500	10,000	500	−10,000	−500
Probability	5%	0%	5%	0%	95%	0%	95%	0%
Gain/Loss	0	0	0	0	0	0	0	0
$\bar{x}$	9,500	9,500	−9,500	−9,500	500	500	−500	−500
$\sqrt[2]{\mu_2}$	2,179.5	0	2,179.5	0	2,179.5	0	2,179.5	0
$\sqrt[3]{\mu_3}$	−3,946.6	0	3,946.6	0	3,946.6	0	−3,946.6	0

- $A_2 \succ B_2$ and $A_3 \succ B_3$, in which risk-appetite dominates, respectively, high-probability losses and low-probability gains.

In all four problems, people actually seem to follow a unique and simple decision rule: they favor the outcome with the larger third-order moment, be it positive or nil, and they reject the outcome with the lower third-order moment, be it negative or nil. In other words, when confronted with two outcomes having the same mathematical expectations, one of them having nil variance, people opt for the one offering the larger upside (or smaller downside), which does not seem insane at all, to say the least.[20] Please note that we have indeed

$$\sqrt[3]{\mu_3(B_1)} > \sqrt[3]{\mu_3(A_1)} \qquad \text{and} \qquad \sqrt[3]{\mu_3(B_4)} > \sqrt[3]{\mu_3(A_4)} \quad (10.29)$$

as well as

$$\sqrt[3]{\mu_3(A_2)} > \sqrt[3]{\mu_3(B_2)} \qquad \text{and} \qquad \sqrt[3]{\mu_3(A_3)} > \sqrt[3]{\mu_3(B_3)} \quad (10.30)$$

Like it or not, the very problems considered by Kahneman and Tversky in their seminal work (see problems P_1 and P_2 in table 10.3; problems P_3, P_4, P_7, and P_8 in table 10.4; and problems P'_3, P'_4, P'_7 and P'_8 in table 10.5) allow to further generalize the claim that the dispersion of outcomes contributes to explaining choices among risky prospects. Contrary to the problems listed in table 10.2, these ten new problems involve choices between pairs of outcomes that have slightly

TABLE 10.3
Problems P_1 and P_2

Problem	1		2	
Outcome	A	B	C	D
Probability	33%	100%	33%	34%
Gain	2,500	2,400	2,500	2,400
Probability	66%		67%	66%
Gain	2,400		0	0
Probability	1%			
Gain	0			
Choice	18%	82%	83%	17%
$\bar{x}$	2,409	2,400	825	816
$\sqrt[2]{\mu_2}$	246.62	0	1,175.53	1,136.90
$\sqrt[3]{\mu_3}$	−518.70	0	1,055.11	997.55
$\sqrt[5]{\mu_5}$	−959.04	0	1,325.71	1,258.08

TABLE 10.4
Problems P_3, P_4, P_7, and P_8: Prospective Gains[22]

Problem	P_3		P_4		P_7		P_8	
Outcome	A	B	C	D	A	B	C	D
Probability	80%	100%	20%	25%	45%	90%	0.10%	0.20%
Gain	4,000	3,000	4,000	3,000	6,000	3,000	6,000	3,000
Probability	20%		80%	75%	55%	10%	99.90%	99.80%
Gain	0		0	0	0	0	0	0
Choice	20%	80%	65%	35%	14%	86%	73%	27%
$\bar{x}$	3,200	3,000	800	750	2,700	2,700	6	6
$\sqrt[2]{\mu_2}$	1,600.0	0	1,600.0	1,299.0	2,985.0	900.0	189.6	134.0
$\sqrt[3]{\mu_3}$	−1,831.5	0	1,831.5	1,362.8	1,748.5	−1,248.0	599.4	377.2

different mathematical expectations. In eight cases out of ten, it suffices to consider the algebraic sum of the mathematical expectation and of the third-order moment to predict observed choices.[21]

In P_1, for example, A has a slightly higher mathematical expectation than B (2,409 versus 2,400), but it has much greater downside (−518.70 versus 0). Despite its lower mathematical expectation, B is preferred to A by 82 percent of the respondents because

$$E(B) + \sqrt[3]{\mu_3(B)} > E(A) + \sqrt[3]{\mu_3(A)} \Rightarrow B \succ A \qquad (10.31)$$

The case for B becomes even more compelling when the fifth-order moment is considered.

In P_2, C has a marginally higher mathematical expectation than D (825 versus 816), but also a slightly higher standard deviation

TABLE 10.5
Problems P'_3, P'_4, P'_7, and P'_8: Prospective Losses

Problem	P'_3		P'_4		P'_7		P'_8	
Outcome	A	B	C	D	A	B	C	D
Probability	80%	100%	20%	25%	45%	90%	0.10%	0.20%
Loss	−4,000	−3,000	−4,000	−3,000	−6,000	−3,000	−6,000	−3,000
Probability	20%		80%	75%	55%	10%	99.90%	99.80%
Loss	0		0	0	0	0	0	0
Choice	92%	8%	42%	58%	92%	8%	30%	70%
$\bar{x}$	−3,200	−3,000	−800	−750	−2,700	−2,700	−6	−6
$\sqrt[2]{\mu_2}$	1,600.0	0	1,600.0	1,299.0	2,985.0	900.0	189.6	134.0
$\sqrt[3]{\mu_3}$	1,831.5	0	−1,831.5	−1,362.8	−1,748.5	1,248.0	−599.4	−377.2

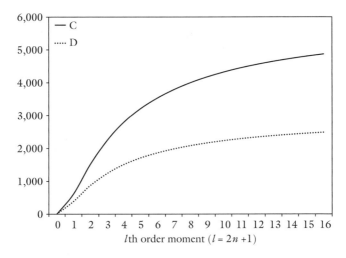

Figure 10.6 Comparison of the moments of two risky prospects.

(1,175.53 versus 1,136.90). As noted by Kahneman and Tversky about another similar problem, whether a 9 advantage in terms of mathematical expectation is enough to overcome a 38.63 increase in standard deviation is open for debate. However, the risk associated with C is perceived to be a "good" risk by 83 percent of the respondents, since it involves more upside than in D (1,055.11 versus 997.55). As in P_1, we have

$$E(C) + \sqrt[3]{\mu_3(C)} > E(D) + \sqrt[3]{\mu_3(D)} \Rightarrow C \succ D \qquad (10.32)$$

The same logic seems to be at work in problems P_3, P_4, and P_8 and their mirror problems P_3', P_4', and P_8', in which we systematically observe that

$$E(X) + \sqrt[3]{\mu_3(X)} > E(Y) + \sqrt[3]{\mu_3(Y)} \Rightarrow X \succ Y \qquad (10.33)$$

Figure 10.6 provides a graphic comparison of outcomes C and D in problem P_8. For each outcome, the plotted line represents $E(X) + \sqrt[2l+1]{\mu_{2l+1}(X)}$ as a function of l.

At first glance, the choices made in problems P_7 (and P_7') seem to contradict the logic that we have just expounded, since B is preferred to A by 86 percent of the respondents (and, respectively, A to B in P_7' by 92 percent of them) even though we have

$$E(B) + \sqrt[3]{\mu_3(B)} < E(A) + \sqrt[3]{\mu_3(A)} \qquad (10.34)$$

However, of all the problems discussed by Kahnman and Tversky in their seminal work, P_7 and P_7' are the only ones in which the choice to be made is between two risky prospects that have very different standard deviations (900 for B versus 2,984.96 for A), as B offers near certainty by means of a 90 percent chance of a 3,000 gain. Far from contradicting the view that dispersion matters, problems P_7 and P_7' rather suggest that all moments, odd as well as even, are potentially relevant, if the dispersion of the distribution under assessment warrants it.[23]

Neglecting the role of the dispersion of outcomes in decision-making leads to interpretations, which can be provocative but not quite convincing. Rabin and Thaler, for example, consider a 50-50 gamble of losing \$10 or gaining \$11.[24] They assert that if someone, call him Johnny, turns down such a gamble, he should be expected to turn down gambles in which there is a 50 percent chance of losing \$100 and a 50 percent chance of gaining Y, however large Y may be. Why? According to expected utility theory, Johnny has revealed to us that "his marginal utility for wealth must diminish incredibly rapidly." Within the expected utility framework, Johnny's rejection of the 50-50 gamble of losing \$10 or gaining \$11 implies indeed

$$\frac{1}{2}u(-10) + \frac{1}{2}u(11) < 0 \Leftrightarrow u(-10) < -u(11) \qquad (10.35)$$

In other words, Johnny's utility function is concave even for very small gains, and therefore a fortiori for larger ones. From there follows the prediction that Johnny will reject a 50-50 gamble of losing \$100 or gaining \$2.5 billion, or even more. This obviously absurd conclusion leads Rabin and Thaler to dismiss expected utility as an ex-hypothesis.

While we are inclined to agree with Rabin and Thaler that the expected utility theory has some serious shortcomings, the reasoning that leads them to this conclusion is questionable. How do Rabin and Thaler know that the utility function's assumed curvature is the only factor that can explain the rejection of the 50-50 gamble of losing \$10 or gaining \$11? More or less explicitly, they assume that other factors can be neglected, but they don't prove it rigorously. Actually, there may be another way, a much simpler one for that matter, to look at the problem. A 50-50 gamble of losing 100 or gaining Y has $(Y - 100)/2$ as mathematical expectation. All its odd-order moments are nil since if l is an odd integer,

$$\frac{1}{2}\left(\Upsilon - \frac{\Upsilon - 100}{2}\right)^{l} + \frac{1}{2}\left(-100 - \frac{\Upsilon - 100}{2}\right)^{l} = 0 \qquad (10.36)$$

Its standard deviation and the lth roots of the respective lth-order moments, where l is an even integer, are all equal to $(\Upsilon + 100)/2$. In other words, the mathematical expectation and the standard deviation are all that Johnny needs to know about the distribution of the gamble presented to him. Unless Johnny is totally insane, he should quickly figure out that he is actually looking at symmetric distributions, the *relative* dispersion of which decreases with respect to Υ, since the mathematical expectation–standard deviation ratio is

$$\rho = \frac{\Upsilon - 100}{\Upsilon + 100} \qquad (10.37)$$

Table 10.6 displays the values of ρ with respect to Υ, using Rabin and Thaler's numerical assumptions, and probably speaks for itself. Isn't it high time prospect theory's neglect of dispersion became an ex-mistake?

The manner in which prospect theory purports to establish that "losses loom larger than gains," one of its key tenets, provides another example of questionable interpretation of empirical observations. Kahneman and Tversky derive their proposition from the twofold observation that "most people find symmetric bets of the form $(x; 0.5; -x; 0.5)$ distinctly unattractive" and that "the aversiveness of symmetric fair bets generally increases with the size of the stake." Within the framework of prospect theory, the first observation can be formulated as

$$\pi(0.5)v(x) + \pi(0.5)v(-x) < 0 \qquad (10.38)$$

TABLE 10.6
Relationship Between the Gain and the Relative Dispersion of Outcomes in a 50-50 Gamble

	A	B	C	D	E	F
Υ	110	221	2,000	20,242	1,100,000	2,500,000,000
Math. exp.	5	60.50	950	10,071	549,950	1,249,999,950
Std. dev.	105	160.50	1,050	10,171	550,050	1,250,000,050
ρ	0.0476	0.3769	0.9048	0.9902	0.9998	1.0000

which implies

$$v(-x) < -v(x) \tag{10.39}$$

and

$$|v(-x)| > |v(x)| \tag{10.40}$$

and means that a loss of a given size is felt more intensively than a gain of the same size.

As for the second observation, and with $0 \le y \le x$, we can write it as

$$\pi(0.5)v(x) + \pi(0.5)v(-x) < \pi(0.5)v(y) + \pi(0.5)v(-y) \tag{10.41}$$

which implies

$$v(-x) - v(-y) < -[v(x) - v(y)] \tag{10.42}$$

and

$$|v(-x) - v(-y)| > |v(x) - v(y)| \tag{10.43}$$

and means that v is decreasing more, when the loss deepens from $-y$ to $-x$, than it is increasing when the gain rises from y to x.

Once again, under the assumption that the value function is locally linear in x, it is rather straightforward to explain this observation in terms of dispersion. The mathematical expectation of a fair bet is nil. All its odd-order moments are nil, too, confirming that a symmetric bet has neither an upside nor a downside with respect to its mathematical expectation. Finally, the standard deviation and all the lth roots of the respective even-order moments are equal to x. In other words, in such symmetric bets, the mathematical expectation–standard deviation ratio is always equal to zero. Why would someone be attracted by a series of gambles entailing an increasing dispersion of outcomes in exchange for a constantly nil mathematical expectation? We do believe that "losses loom larger than gains," but very much doubt that prospect theory establishes this principle rigorously, for it arbitrarily reduces a two-dimensional problem to a one-dimensional question, thus failing to disentangle the utility of sure outcomes from the choice between risky prospects.

Misinterpreted as it may be, the above example inadvertently sheds light on another methodological issue, which is whether we should rely on observations made in the context of risky choices to estimate any value (or cardinal utility) function.

Let us imagine a bet of the form $(x, 0.4; y, 0.1; -y, 0.1; -x, 0.4)$. We are now confronted with four potential outcomes $(x, y, -y, -x)$, but the gamble remains a symmetric one. Therefore, most people would find it unattractive, which would lead us to write

$$\pi(0.4)v(x) + \pi(0.1)v(y) + \pi(0.4)v(-x) + \pi(0.1)v(-y) < 0 \tag{10.44}$$

Could we extract any quantitative information about the value function from this four-variable single inequality? Obviously not, even if we knew the weighting coefficients for sure. The two-outcome symmetric bets considered by Kahneman and Tversky create an illusion of measurability where there is none, because of risk. They reveal an ordinal utility, but nothing more.

10.2.3   Allais's Interpretation of His Paradox

In light of the problems discussed in the previous paragraphs, be they problems imagined by Allais in 1952 or by other scholars later, it should not come as a surprise that ever since 1952 Allais has made the dispersion of risky outcomes the cornerstone of his paradox's own interpretation.

The behavioral economics and finance literature almost never fails to refer to the seminal role of the Allais paradox and to the 1953 Econometrica paper in which it was presented. But it almost always seems to ignore Allais's other works in this field. Furthermore, out of this seminal paper's 43 pages, only 3 are in English; the other 40 are in French. Bearing this in mind, it is not surprising that Allais's paradox is often perceived to be an intriguing "little" experiment.

Yet, Allais's 1953 paper is just the tip of a huge iceberg. It is itself an abridged version of a long report, which Allais had prepared in French ahead of the May 1952 Paris colloquium, a paper that reads very much like a research program and had to wait until 1979 to be published in English.[25] Besides reporting empirical anomalies and criticizing the axioms and postulates of what he took the risk to call "the

American School," Allais enunciated some very important conjectures in this paper:

- "The concept of psychological value (cardinal utility) $\gamma = \bar{s}(x)$ can be defined operationally by considering either psychologically equivalent variations Δx of x, or minimum perceptible thresholds (à la Weber-Fechner)."
- "Any theory of risk must necessarily take account of . . . the distinction between monetary and psychological values . . . the consideration of the mathematical expectation of psychological values . . . the consideration of the dispersion (i.e. the second-order moment) and, generally, of the overall shape of the probability distribution of psychological values."
- "The link between psychological and monetary values and the influence of the shape of the distribution of psychological values are inextricably interwoven, and no experiment concerning choice among uncertain (read risky) prospects can be relied on to determine psychological value (cardinal utility)."
- "The psychological value (cardinal utility) can be determined only by introspective observation of either psychologically equivalent increments or minimum perceptible thresholds" in a context from which risk must be absent.

Interestingly, when Allais refers to variance in his seminal work, it is always under the explicit assumption that the distribution under consideration is a Laplace-Gauss distribution, a symmetric distribution the variance of which is sufficient to describe its dispersion. Interestingly, too, he refers to variance as being a second-order moment, clearly suggesting that higher-order moments do exist and that variance is not apt to characterize asymmetric or fat-tailed distributions. Finally, always in the same text and to further drive home his view that the dispersion of outcomes defines risk, Allais states that the cardinal utility of a distribution is a function of its probability density function.

Allais summarized this research program by a very general formulation specifying the relationship of the psychological value $\bar{s}$ of a risky prospect P to its component γ

$$\bar{s}(P) = h[\overline{\Psi}(\gamma)] \tag{10.45}$$

where h is a certain function of the probability density $\overline{\Psi}$ of the psychological values γ. Thus, what remained to be done in parallel was

- On one hand, to measure cardinal utility.
- On the other hand, to specify the analytical formulation of the function h.

The subject matter of this book is Allais's theory of "expectations" under uncertainty. It is not his theory of choice under risk per se. If this chapter, dedicated as it is to laying the foundations of a new concept, the perceived risk of loss, touches upon the latter theory, then it is because of the critical role it gives to the dispersion of potential outcomes and, among them, to losses in particular. Therefore, this book is not the right place to discuss at great length whether Allais has completed the research program that he had set for himself in his 1952 paper. Enough will be said by outlining the solutions that he has proposed, first, to measure the cardinal utility of sure outcomes, be they gains or losses, and, second, to measure the cardinal utility of a risky prospect.

10.2.4   Allais's Invariant Cardinal Utility Function

In his 1952 (1979) and 1953 papers, Allais did not provide any estimation of cardinal utility (absolute satisfaction in his terminology, denoted $\overline{s}$), but he outlined a road map indicating how to do so.

First, he specified the condition that any experiment in this field should meet in order to collect workable empirical observations: "no experiment concerning choice among uncertain (read risky again) prospects can be relied on to determine psychological value." Why? Because "the link between psychological and monetary values and the influence of the shape of the distribution of the psychological values are inextricably interwoven." If so, what is to be done to measure the cardinal utility of a quantity x (of dollars, for example)? As in 1943, Allais answers that "the concept of psychological value (cardinal utility) can be defined operationally by considering minimum perceptible thresholds" (à la Weber and Fechner) in a risk-free context. However, he adds to this a new trail also to be followed in a risk-free context: the consideration of psychologically equivalent variations Δx of x. His conviction is indeed that anyone can answer, without hesitation, questions like this one: What is the gain X which, compared to $10,000, would generate the same increase in your satisfaction as a gain of $10,000 compared to $1,000? In other words, which is the value X such that

$$\bar{s}\,(U_0 + X) - \bar{s}\,(U_0 + 10{,}000) = \bar{s}\,(U_0 + 10{,}000) - \bar{s}\,(U_0 + 1{,}000)$$
$$(10.46)$$

where U_0 denotes the respondent's psychological capital (the capital he or she used to own)?[26]

The experimental quantification of psychologically equivalent increments is the bedrock of Allais's research on cardinal utility. It has enabled him to determine, up to a linear transformation, a cardinal preference function such that for two increments of utility that are deemed equivalent, the variation $\Delta\bar{s}$ has the same value.[28] However, in his 1952 and 1953 papers, Allais did not explain how to exploit the data, which he had collected by means of his 1952 questionnaire (see, for example, Finetti's answers in table 10.7). To a certain extent, this explanation came just 25 years later, but was not published in English before 1979.[29]

Unfortunately, Allais does not walk his reader through a numerical example to illustrate how the identification of psychologically equivalent intervals allows him to construct a respondent's empirical cardinal preference curve. He is content with referring to the theoretical and highly abstract analysis that he had exposed in 1943.[30]

My attempt to follow Allais along this path has stumbled over the following difficulty: how to assign consistent arbitrary values to the endpoints defining psychologically equivalent intervals? Finetti, for

TABLE 10.7

Identification of Psychologically Equivalent Intervals: Finetti's Answers[27]

Question	Psychological equivalent intervals (thousands 2012 USD)
651	$(U_0^*, U_0^* + 254) \approx (U_0^* + 254, U_0^* + \underline{1{,}141})$
652	$(U_0^*, U_0^* + 634) \approx (U_0^* + 634, U_0^* + \underline{1{,}775})$
653	$(U_0^*, U_0^* + 1{,}268) \approx (U_0^* + 1{,}268, U_0^* + \underline{6{,}339})$
654	$(U_0^*, U_0^* + 2{,}536) \approx (U_0^* + 2{,}536, U_0^* + \underline{20{,}285})$
631	$(U_0^* + 6{,}339, U_0^* + \underline{11{,}410}) \approx (U_0^* + 12{,}679, U_0^* + 25{,}356)$
632	$(U_0^* + 2{,}536, U_0^* + \underline{5{,}071}) \approx (U_0^* + 5{,}071, U_0^* + 10{,}142)$
633	$(U_0^* + 2{,}079, U_0^* + \underline{2{,}536}) \approx (U_0^* + 20{,}285, U_0^* + 25{,}356)$
634	$(U_0^* + \underline{205}, U_0^* + 254) \approx (U_0^* + 2{,}028, U_0^* + 2{,}536)$

example, stated that compared to a gain of 10 million of 1952 FFR (i.e., about 254,000 2012 USD), a gain of 45 million (i.e., about 1,141,000 dollars) would give him the same increase in satisfaction as a gain of 10 million compared to no gain at all (see question 651 in table 10.7). In other words,

$$\bar{s}\,(U_0 + 45) - \bar{s}\,(U_0 + 10) = \bar{s}\,(U_0 + 10) - \bar{s}\,(U_0) \qquad (10.47)$$

If, for example, we set $\bar{s}\,(U_0) = 0$, as is natural, and $\bar{s}\,(U_0 + 10) = 2$, it immediately follows from Finetti's answer to question 651 that

$$\bar{s}\,(U_0 + 45) = 2\bar{s}\,(U_0 + 10) = 4 \qquad (10.48)$$

Finetti's answer to question 652 implies that

$$\bar{s}\,(U_0 + 70) = 2\bar{s}\,(U_0 + 25) \qquad (10.49)$$

Now, to continue constructing Finetti's empirical cardinal utility curve, we need to assign a logical value to $\bar{s}\,(U_0 + 25)$. Since cardinal utility is assumed to be a monotonic increasing function, this value must logically fall somewhere between $\bar{s}\,(U_0 + 10)$ and $\bar{s}\,(U_0 + 45)$, that is, between 2 and 4. Is there a logical way to narrow this interval further based, for example, on the assumed properties of the derivatives of cardinal utility or of its integral?[31] If it exists, I must confess that I have not been able to find it, the lack of time being one reason among others.

As a mathematician, Allais is sometimes hard to follow because his virtuosity and ingenuity happen to make him somewhat too elliptic for the layman. But in my experience at least, his mathematical rigor is always beyond reproach. Therefore, I am inclined to accept his claim that by means of psychologically equivalent intervals, "the concept of a cardinal preference index is an operational one."

Having said this, the next steps of Allais's inquiry are easier to follow. When he plotted on a lin-log graph, the eight points representing the answers of each of the respondents, he saw that each set of points is approximately aligned along parallel straight lines.[32] Figure 10.7 provides a stylized representation of this observation, which suggested the following formulation to Allais

$$\bar{s}_i\,(U_0^i + X) = m\ln\,(U_0^i + X) + k_i \qquad (10.50)$$

where i denotes the respondent i.

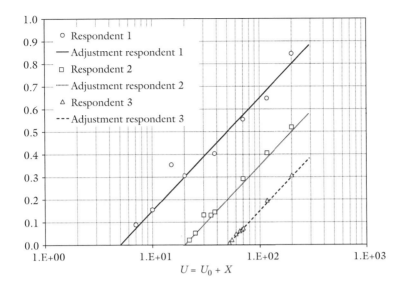

Figure 10.7   Representation of observed cardinal utility on a lin-log graph.

Nothing prevents us from setting $\overline{s}_i(U_0^i) = 0$, which implies $k_i = -m \ln U_0^i$. With this convention, relationship 10.50 becomes

$$\overline{s}_i(U_0^i + X) = m[(\ln(U_0^i + X) - \ln(U_0^i)]\qquad(10.51)$$

and

$$\overline{s}_i(U_0^i) = m \ln\left(1 + \frac{X}{U_0^i}\right)\qquad(10.52)$$

For scaling purposes on a five-moduli lin-log paper,[33] Allais decided to assign a one-unit change in satisfaction to a two-moduli change in the relative gain, that is,

$$m \times 2 \ln 10 = 1 \Leftrightarrow m = 0.2171\qquad(10.53)$$

Up to the parameter U_0^i, which defines the size of *relative* gains, this relationship is invariant: it is identical for all respondents (see figure 10.8). Hence, we can write

$$\overline{s}(U_0) = m \ln\left(1 + \frac{X}{U_0}\right)\qquad(10.54)$$

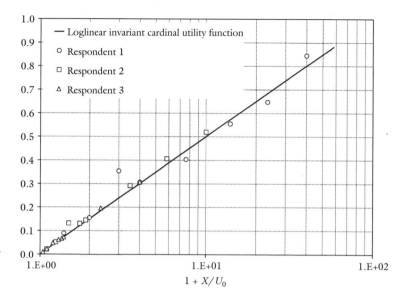

Figure 10.8 Empirical invariant cardinal utility: rescaled observations.

As for the parameter U_0, it can easily be estimated as follows. To a given value $\bar{s}(U) = \bar{s}(U_0 + X)$ correspond indeed both the effective U (or X) revealed by the respondent's answer to a given question and a theoretical U^* derived from the relationship

$$\bar{s}(U) = m \ln \frac{U^*}{U_0} \tag{10.55}$$

that is,

$$U^* = U_0 e^{\bar{s}(U)/m} \tag{10.56}$$

Allais defines the estimate U_0^* of U_0 as the value of U_0 that minimizes the sum S of the squared differences $(U - U^*)^2$

$$S = \sum_{i=1}^{8} (U_i - U_i^*)^2 \tag{10.57}$$

According to this estimation procedure, Finetti's psychological capital was 17 million 1952 FFR (i.e., about 431,000 2012 USD). The possibility of estimating an individual's psychological capital by means of questions on gains psychologically equivalent to her is far-reaching.

Whether this possibility is an impediment to the development of cardinal utility theory or a chance for it probably belongs more to the realm of politics than to pure economics.

In a paper presented in Venice in 1984, Allais extended his analysis to the very large gains he had previously decided to leave aside.[34] For relative gains larger than 10^4, respondents to the 1952 questionnaire either had been unable to identify psychologically equivalent intervals or had deemed all gains equivalents. In the meantime, by means of a new questionnaire designed in 1975, some new data had been collected. However, the loglinear model did not fit very well the small relative gains $(1 < 1 + X/U_0 < 10)$. To fit all available observations with one single formulation, Allais used the generating function

$$X = f(A) = A(2 + A/U_0) \qquad (10.58)$$

corresponding to the condition

$$\bar{s}(U_0 + X) = 2\bar{s}(U_0 + A) \qquad (10.59)$$

The knowledge of the generating function f determines the cardinal utility function $\bar{s}$, since

$$\bar{s}\left[f\left(\frac{A}{U_0}\right)\right] = 2\bar{s}\left(\frac{A}{U_0}\right) \qquad (10.60)$$

The cardinal utility function estimated by Allais with this method has the overall logistic shape he had conjectured in 1943; it has a horizontal asymptote for relative gains larger than 10^4 (see figure 10.9). It also exhibits a small hump for relative gains between 1 and 10 (see figure 10.10).[35]

Finally, in a paper presented in Budapest in 1988, Allais extended his estimation of cardinal utility to losses $(0 \leq 1 + X/U_0 \leq 1)$. Using the same generating function, he inferred the cardinal utility of relative losses from the knowledge of its value for relative gains.[36] Courtesy of Kluwer Academic Publishing, appendix F displays the values taken by Allais's invariant cardinal utility function, which is also plotted in figure 10.10.

The rising dotted lines in figure 10.10 show that, over a very large domain, two straight lines adjust Allais's invariant cardinal utility function with a high degree of accuracy. Table 10.8 displays the parameters of these two straight lines. The adjustment for gains confirms

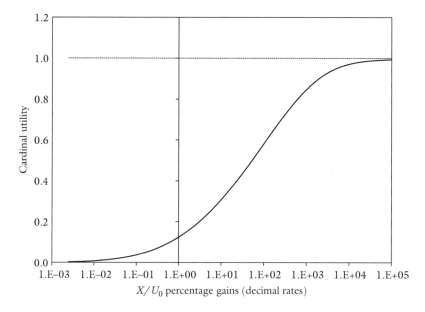

Figure 10.9　Allais's invariant cardinal utility function for gains.

Bernoulli's intuition over a very large domain (up to 10^3). The straight line for losses has a steeper slope (0.4022) than for gains (0.1260): in other words, according to Allais's invariant cardinal utility function, losses loom on average and over a wide domain about 3.2 times larger than gains. Needless to say, this is an important hypothesis to bear in mind in any analysis of the dynamics of financial instability.

As shown in table 10.9, Allais's cardinal utility function and Kahneman and Tversky's value function are easy to differentiate. What the two functions share is rather limited, namely, concavity for gains,

TABLE 10.8
Approximation of Allais's Invariant Cardinal Utility Function with Two
Straight Lines

	Losses	Gains	Gains
Domain	$0 \leq 1 + X/U_0 \leq 1$	$1 \leq 1 + X/U_0 \leq 10^3$	$10 \leq 1 + X/U_0 \leq 10^3$
Slope	0.4022	0.1260	0.1253
R-SQ	96.02%	99.54%	99.91%
Standard error	0.0064	0.0005	0.0002

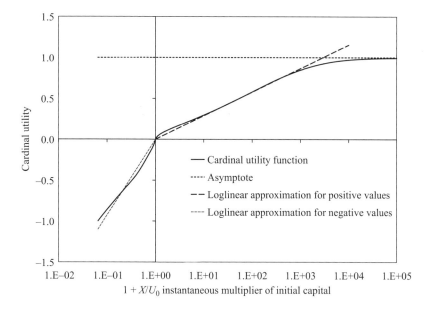

Figure 10.10 Allais's invariant cardinal utility function.

asymmetry between losses and gains, and the assignment of a nil utility (or value) to a nil gain.

10.2.5   The Nonlinearity of Indices $B_{1/2}$ and B_{200}

With Allais's cardinal utility function now at hand, we can revisit the interpretation of Allais's paradox by looking at another experiment, presented by Allais in his 1952 questionnaire, the result of which he considered to be the most compelling argument for taking the

TABLE 10.9
Comparison Between Kahneman and Tversky's Value Function and Allais's Cardinal Utility Function

	Value function	Cardinal utility function
Argument	Absolute gains and losses	Relative gains and losses
Satiety effect for large gains	No	Yes
Convexity for losses	Yes	No, or very moderate
Falsifiability	No, for lack of numerical values	Yes

TABLE 10.10

Prospects Corresponding to Indices $B_{1/2}$ (Questions 90 to 98) and B_{200} (Questions 70 to 78)

Prospect	$P_1(1/2;X)$	$P_2(p;200)$
Nature	Constant probability/variable gain	Variable probability/constant gain
Probability	50%	$25\% \leq p \leq 99.9\%$
Gain[38]	$10^2 \leq X \leq 10^9$	2×10^6
Probability	50%	$1 - p$
Gain	0	0

dispersion of outcomes into account when it comes to assessing the psychological value of a risky prospect.[37] Table 10.10 describes the risky prospects considered in this problem. Respondents were asked to assign monetary values X' to P_1 and X'' to P_2 as X and p increased from the lower to the higher limit of their respective ranges. What is, for example, the sure gain X' deemed equivalent to a 50 percent chance of gaining 1 million, 10 million, 100 million, etc.? Or, what is the sure gain equivalent to a 25 percent, 50 percent, 90 percent chance of gaining 200 million? Since prospect P_1 consists of a constant probability of a variable gain, while prospect P_2 offers a variable probability of a constant gain, comparing answers given in both cases will shed light on the influence of the preference for certainty.

Before proceeding further, we observe that, according to expected utility theory, the utilities of prospects P_1 and P_2 are linear, respectively, in X and p. We have indeed

$$B(P_1) = \frac{1}{2} B(U_0 + X) + \frac{1}{2} B(U_0) \qquad (10.61)$$

and

$$B(P_2) = p B(U_0 + 200) + (1 - p) B(U_0) \qquad (10.62)$$

Since $B(U_0) = 0$, these two relationships are actually equivalent to

$$B(P_1) = \frac{1}{2} B(U_0 + X) \qquad (10.63)$$

and

$$B(P_2) = p B(U_0 + 200) \qquad (10.64)$$

According to expected utility theory, the respective certain equivalents of these two prospects should be aligned on two straight lines, since the expected utilities of P_1 and P_2 are linear, respectively, in X and p. However, *none* of the 17 respondents gave answers that were compatible with the predictions of expected utility theory. In these two problems, expected utility theory was not violated by a small majority (53 percent) of rational subjects, as in the Allais paradox, but *unanimously* challenged by them.

For the sake of illustration, let us analyze some of the answers collected by Allais. Finetti, for example, deemed a 50 percent chance of gaining 1,000 million to be equivalent to a sure gain of 200 million. With U_0^* being Finetti's psychological capital, this statement means that

$$B_{1/2}(U_0^* + 200) = \frac{1}{2} B(U_0^* + 1{,}000) \qquad (10.65)$$

where $B_{1/2}$ denotes the utility assigned by the respondent to the risky prospect $(50\%, 1{,}000; 50\%, 0)$.

Now, from Allais's research on cardinal utility, we know that

$$B(U_0^* + X) = m\ln\left(1 + \frac{X}{U_0^*}\right) \qquad (10.66)$$

with $m = 0.2171$ for all subjects and $U_0^* = 17$ in Finetti's case. Hence, we can write

$$B_{1/2}(217) = \frac{1}{2} B(1{,}017)$$

$$\Leftrightarrow \quad B_{1/2}(217) = 0.5 \times 0.2171 \times \ln\left(1 + \frac{1{,}000}{17}\right)$$

$$\Leftrightarrow \quad B_{1/2}(217) = 0.4442$$

In other words, 0.4442 is the cardinal utility (or psychological value) implicitly assigned by Finetti to the risky prospect $(50\%, 1{,}000; 50\%, 0)$. Which is now the sure gain X^* to which corresponds a cardinal utility of 0.4442? It is such that

$$B(U_0^* + X^*) = 0.2171\ln\left(1 + \frac{X^*}{U_0^*}\right) = 0.4442$$

$$\Leftrightarrow \quad X^* = U_0^*(e^{0.4442/0.2171} - 1)$$

$$\Leftrightarrow \quad X^* = 114.48$$

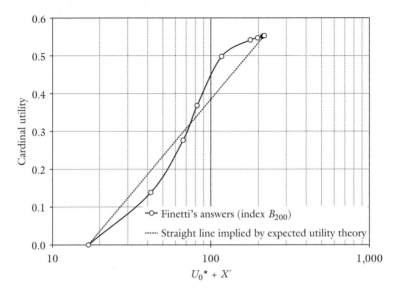

Figure 10.11   Finetti's answers to questions 71 to 78.

To sum it up, the sure gain (200) actually deemed equivalent by Finetti to a 50 percent chance of gaining 1,000 is larger than the theoretical sure gain (114.48) corresponding to the utility implied by his answer. In other words, Finetti valued positively the fact of taking a chance; he was risk-seeking. Interestingly, while Finetti's answers to questions 90 to 98 all lay to the *right*[39] of the theoretical straight line implied by expected utility theory, some other respondents' answers all lay to its left, which suggests that the population surveyed by Allais was not homogeneous as regards risk-taking.

Figure 10.11 shows Finetti's answers to questions 71 to 78: they are even more interesting, for they show that the same respondent can be risk-seeking in certain circumstances and risk-averse in others. Finetti deemed a 90 percent chance of gaining 200 million to be equivalent to a sure gain of 100 million, which means that

$$B_{200}\,(U_0^* + 100) = 0.90\,B\,(U_0^* + 200) \qquad (10.67)$$

and finally

$$B_{200}(117) = 0.4977 \qquad (10.68)$$

where B_{200} denotes the utility assigned by the respondent to the prospect $(p; 200)$.

To this utility, corresponds a theoretical absolute gain X^* such that

$$B(U_0^* + X^*) = 0.2171 \ln\left(1 + \frac{X^*}{U_0^*}\right) = 0.4977$$

$$\Leftrightarrow \quad X^* = 151.2 \tag{10.69}$$

In this case, the sure gain (100) deemed equivalent to a 90 percent chance of winning 200 is smaller than the theoretical sure gain (151.2) implied by Finetti's answer. In this situation, Finetti exhibited risk aversion. Finetti's seeming versatility is easy to rationalize as soon as one considers the distribution of prospects P_1 and P_2. The lth-order moments of P_1 and P_2 are

$$\mu_l(P_1) = \frac{1}{2}\left[\frac{1}{2}B(U_0 + X)\right]^l + \frac{1}{2}\left[-\frac{1}{2}B(U_0 + X)\right]^l \tag{10.70}$$

and

$$\mu_l(P_2) = [p(1-p)^l + (1-p)(-p)^l]\left[B(U_0 + 200)\right]^l \tag{10.71}$$

From these two relationships, we can infer that the dispersion of the risky prospect P_1 is constant and symmetric, while the dispersion of prospect P_2 is variable and asymmetric.

If l is an odd integer, $\mu_l(P_1) = 0$: the dispersion is symmetric. If l is an even integer, $\mu_l(P_1) = \left[\frac{B(U_0+X)}{2}\right]^l$, which implies that the dispersion–mathematical average ratio is constant:

$$\frac{\sqrt[l]{\mu_l(P_2)}}{\frac{B(U_0+X)}{2}} = 1 \tag{10.72}$$

As for the dispersion of P_2, it is shown up to a scaling factor in figure 10.4: to the left of the 50 percent probability threshold, the third-order moment is positive and points to a "good" risk; to the right, it is negative and points to a "bad" risk. It is quite noteworthy that Finetti, like all other respondents, tends to be risk-seeking where the third-order moment is positive and risk-averse where it is negative: he switches from a risk-seeking to a risk-averse mode somewhere between $p = 0.5$ and $p = 0.66$, that is, close to the point (0.50) where the third-order moment becomes negative. The main observation from this crucial part of Allais's 1952 questionnaire is twofold: first, *for all respondents*, the indices B, $B_{1/2}$, and B_{200} differ substantially; second, contrary to expected utility theory, neither $B_{1/2}$ nor B_{200} is linear in the mathematical expectations of the respective risky prospect. In other words, the dispersion of outcomes does matter.

10.2.6   *The Utility of a Risky Prospect*

Furthermore, the indices $B_{1/2}$ and B_{200} provide us with a remarkable and very intuitive heuristic to grasp the meaning of the analytic formulation given by Allais for the value of a risky prospect. Let us look again at figure 10.11, which plots the index B_{200}. Its shape is approximately that of a tilted and rising S. Overall, the psychological value of the risky prospect ($p; 200$) increases, albeit nonlinearly, with respect to the sure equivalent $U_0^* + X^*$, which in turn increases linearly with respect to the probability p. At the risk of stating the obvious, the mathematical expectation of this risky prospect ($p; 200$) does also increase linearly with respect to p (see figure 10.4). As for the deviations from the expected utility linear model, we have seen with figure 10.11 that a psychological value higher (respectively, lower) than the one implied by expected utility theory is associated with a positive (respectively, negative) third-order moment. As shown in figure 10.4, when plotted as a function of p, the third-order moment has approximately the shape of a horizontal S turned upside down. It does not take a rocket scientist to figure out that the weighted sum of an ascending straight line (representing mathematical expectation) and a horizontal S (representing the third-order moment) will produce a tilted and rising S, the exact shape of which will depend on the weights given to each component.

As for the index $B_{1/2}$, its shape is approximately that of a tilted, rising and asymmetric arc, which can be either concave or convex, depending on whether the subject is risk-averse or risk-seeking. From relationship 10.70, we know that the odd-order moments of the prospect $\left(\frac{1}{2}; X\right)$ are all nil and that its even-order moments have the following analytic expression:

$$\mu_l(P_1) = \left[\frac{B(U_0 + X)}{2}\right]^l \tag{10.73}$$

Therefore, the curve representing its variance (and all higher-order even moments) is not a straight line, but is convex. Once again, it does not take a rocket scientist to figure out that the weighted sum of an ascending straight line and a convex arc will produce a shape similar to that of index $B_{1/2}$.

From these two examples, it is rather intuitive to infer that the psychological value of a risky prospect must somehow be a function of its mathematical expectation and of its even- and odd-order moments.

For the sake of brevity, we refer the reader to Allais's proof that the psychological value $\bar{s}\,(U_0 + V)$ of a risky prospect $(p_1, p_2, \ldots, p_n; \bar{s}(x_1), \bar{s}(x_2), \ldots, \bar{s}(x_n))$ is indeed such that

$$\bar{s}\,(U_0 + V) = \bar{\bar{s}} + R(\mu_1, \ldots, \mu_l, \ldots, \mu_{2n+1}) \qquad (10.74)$$

where $\bar{\bar{s}}$ is its mathematical expectation and R, which measures the psychological value of risk, is a linear combination of its moments $\mu_l = \sum_{i=1}^{n} p_i (\bar{s}_i - \bar{\bar{s}})^l$.[40] So much for Allais's "little experiment."

10.2.7   *The Equity Risk Premium Puzzle: A Conjecture*

By way of a conclusion to this long chapter, it is time to formulate a conjecture pertaining to the (ex post) equity premium puzzle. Equities are known to be riskier investments than Treasury bills: their daily, weekly, monthly returns fluctuate indeed much more than the returns on Treasury bills. Fairness suggests that in the fullness of time equity returns should be higher than Treasury bill returns, in order to compensate equity investors for the discomfort caused by the greater short-run variability of the returns they earn. In other words, the return differential between equities and Treasury bills should be positive. But how large should this ex post equity risk premium be? The puzzle springs from the observation, first made by Mehra and Prescott, that the empirical (or historical) ex post equity risk premium has been much more elevated than what standard equilibrium models imply.[41]

These models tend to share two features. Firstly, as noted by Benartzi and Thaler, two advocates of prospect theory, these models are content with taking returns into account, thereby neglecting their cardinal utility.[42] Secondly, these models assume risk to be properly defined and measured by the variance and covariance of returns, thereby neglecting higher-order moments: overlooked by Mehra and Prescott, this point is in any case considered as irrelevant by prospect theory, as we have seen in section 10.2.1. Allais's invariant cardinal utility function and the relationship that he has established between the cardinal utility of a risky prospect and its moments suggest nevertheless that there may exist an alternative and parsimonious way to solve the equity risk premium puzzle. Table 10.11 displays the parameters that characterize

TABLE 10.11
Dispersion of Returns and Respective Utilities on 3-month UST-bills, 20-year UST-bonds, and S&P 500

	Holding Period	UST-bill return (%)	Utility	UST-bond return (%)	Utility	S&P 500 return (%)	Utility
Average	1-month	0.29	0.0024	0.44	0.0007	0.80	-0.0011
	1-year	3.44	0.0166	5.33	0.0143	9.60	0.0119
	2-year	6.87	0.0264	10.67	0.0280	19.21	0.0334
	3-year	10.43	0.0348	16.60	0.0427	28.17	0.0500
	4-year	13.75	0.0414	21.33	0.0501	38.41	0.0692
	5-year	17.78	0.0493	26.66	0.0632	47.06	0.0911
Square-root of 2nd-order moment	1-month	0.25	0.0020	2.24	0.0148	5.54	0.0323
	1-year	2.94	0.0114	8.53	0.0344	19.43	0.0806
	2-year	5.75	0.0169	11.65	0.0386	26.28	0.0934
	3-year	8.41	0.0209	13.60	0.0370	32.23	0.1075
	4-year	11.07	0.0248	18.58	0.0444	33.33	0.0842
	5-year	13.44	0.0268	20.49	0.0341	30.97	0.0445
Cubic-root of 3rd-order moment	1-month	0.25	0.0016	1.96	-0.0141	-4.77	-0.0387
	1-year	2.85	0.0067	7.93	-0.0327	-19.22	-0.0976
	2-year	5.39	0.0081	9.49	-0.0379	-29.45	-0.1323
	3-year	7.92	0.0092	9.30	-0.0371	-37.88	-0.1632
	4-year	10.00	0.0061	17.86	-0.0476	-27.92	-0.1181
	5-year	11.53	0.0075	20.12	0.0173	12.57	-0.0295
4th-root of 4th-order moment	1-month	0.36	0.0027	3.68	0.0219	10.17	0.0540
	1-year	4.06	0.0138	12.04	0.0472	27.72	0.1256
	2-year	7.75	0.0204	15.40	0.0520	42.43	0.1756
	3-year	11.35	0.0256	16.83	0.0503	54.30	0.2147
	4-year	14.48	0.0300	27.00	0.0666	44.43	0.1547
	5-year	17.07	0.0323	27.59	0.0435	36.25	0.0520

the distribution of the returns and respective utilities on 3-month US Treasury-bills, 20-year US Treasury bonds, and the S&P 500 over non-overlapping holding periods of 1 month, 1, 2, 3, 4, and 5 years, from 1926 to 2013.[43]

Even if one leaves cardinal utility aside for a second, the first interesting observation is that the third-order moment of equity returns has been negative, even over long holding periods (up to four years), which indicates that downside risk has dominated upside risk. In other words, the risk associated with equities tends to be a bad risk, a risk that investors should therefore dislike. In contrast, the third-order moment of Treasury bill and Treasury bond returns has been positive for all holding periods.

Now, the consideration of cardinal utility—as estimated by Allais—further accentuates the contrast between the respective risk-reward profiles of equities, bills, and bonds. Surprising as it may seem, if not to the average man in the street at least to investment professionals, the mean utility of monthly equity returns has been negative, too. Two factors explain this observation: the most important one is the asymmetrical shape of Allais's cardinal utility function and its concavity for gains; then comes the negative skewness of monthly equity returns that we have discussed above. Let us bear in mind the rule of thumb according to which a 1 percent loss costs in terms of utility 3.2 times as much as the approximately loglinear benefit brought about by a 1 percent gain. Owning equities only generates a positive mean utility over longer holding periods. But, the third-order moment of the utility of equity returns has been negative, too, irrespective of the length of the holding period. Interestingly, the same holds true for 20-year US Treasury bonds up to 4 years. If Allais is right in saying that the cardinal utility of a risky prospect is a function not only of its mean, but also of its moments, the negative skewness of the utility of equity returns may be lying at the heart of the equity risk premium puzzle.

Formulating arbitrage relationships between equities, bonds, and bills that are consistent with Allais's definition of the cardinal utility of a risky prospect, testing whether these relationships can explain the ex post equity risk premium, are topics that this book, as it goes to press, leaves to future research.

CHAPTER ELEVEN

Downside Potential Under Uncertainty: The Perceived Risk of Loss

FROM OUR DISCUSSION of the Allais paradox and cardinal utility in chapter 10, there are two insights to take away: first, the dispersion of outcomes matters; second, losses loom larger than gains. While the second insight is independent of any consideration of time, the first one is closely connected with the flow of time.

As a matter of fact, if—even in the universe of risk—the distribution of potential outcomes matters alongside their mathematical expectation, it is precisely because insightful individuals understand that the latter is a concept that implicitly assumes that all potential outcomes happen at once in given and fixed proportions, while—given enough time in the real world—each of these outcomes will materialize with a known frequency, but in an unknown sequence.[1]

If the distribution of outcomes and the psychological asymmetry between gains and losses are two highly relevant considerations in the seemingly timeless universe of risk, it seems natural to expect that they must be even more pertinent in a world of uncertainty, a world in which neither the potential outcomes nor their respective frequencies are "given" ex ante to market participants, but must be guessed from experience in the fullness of time.[2] Market participants know indeed that the volatility of asset returns is volatile (heteroskedasticity); that large price movements, be they negative or positive, tend to cluster; and that the distributions of returns can be locally quite skewed. In short, they know that they have to deal with uncertainty much more than with risk.

In this uncertain world where outcomes are subject to the law of memory decay suggested by the HRL formulation, any sequence of returns in which losses become, for whichever reason, less and less frequent should increase the market participants' propensity to take risk, thus ultimately begetting instability.

Looking back at table 10.1, it is rather straightforward to translate the choices that it presents into the basic portfolio choices facing investors: outcome A is the risk-free asset, while outcomes B, C, and D represent risky assets. The insight from question 35 is that if investors have the possibility to secure a certain gain and if they simultaneously assign an even low probability to the worst-case scenario for high-return/high-risk assets, they will opt for security. They will be risk-averse. To put it differently, a low risk-free rate may not be a sufficient condition to foster risk appetite and ignite a bubble. The worst-case scenario must also be perceived to be as benign as possible. The insight from question 36 is that if the worst-case scenarios for two risky assets are perceived to be of the same order of magnitude, investors will prefer the asset with the larger upside. They will be risk-seeking. If the worst-case scenario for the assets with the largest upside (equities) is perceived to fall to a level not materially different from the worst-case scenario for the assets with a smaller upside (bonds), then the case for equities becomes compelling and investors will strongly prefer them to bonds. As in question 35, the downside risk matters again, but this time as an incentive to take risks.

These empirical findings and the conjectures they inspire underpin the construction of the perceived risk of loss, that is, the present value of past losses, computed according to the HRL formulation (section 11.1). Whether the perceived risk of loss explains the pricing of some financial assets and plays a role in the inception of financial bubbles will be discussed in the next two sections (respectively, sections 11.2 and 11.3). One of the strong claims made by the HRL formulation and throughout this book is that collective human psychology is on average constant through time and space. Section 11.4 discusses whether institutional or demographic factors might justify to qualify this claim. Finally, section 11.5 introduces the perceived risk of loss in the discussion of moral hazard.

11.1   Combining the Allais Paradox with the HRL Formulation: The Perceived Risk of Loss

While the perceived return is computed using the daily, weekly, or monthly returns of a given financial asset or asset class, the perceived risk of loss is derived from the subset of negative returns, the positive returns being replaced by zeros. To benefit from the rising elasticity of the HRL formulation with respect to outcomes of increasing magnitudes, one just needs to use the absolute values of the negative returns as inputs. For example, the following sequence of returns

$$S = (\ldots, -5.5\%, -3.6\%, +4\%, -1.3\%, +2.5\%, +0.3\%, \ldots)$$

becomes the following sequence of losses:

$$S^- = (\ldots, 5.5\%, 3.6\%, 0\%, 1.3\%, 0\%, 0\%, \ldots)$$

It goes without saying that one can also compute the perceived chance of gain by applying the HRL formulation to the subset of positive returns

$$S^+ = (\ldots, 0\%, 0\%, 4\%, 0\%, 2.5\%, 0.3\%, \ldots)$$

as well as perceived volatility, by considering the following sequence, which only consists of the absolute values of returns:

$$S^* = (\ldots, 5.5\%, 3.6\%, 4\%, 1.3\%, 2.5\%, 0.3\%, \ldots)$$

The HRL formulation implies that two factors determine the level of the perceived risk of loss:

- The frequency of individual losses.
- The size of individual losses.

A sequence of returns containing many back-to-back large losses will generate a higher perceived risk of loss than a sequence containing few, distant, small losses. An important point to bear in mind is that when the perceived risk of loss is low, it is also inelastic: in other words, it takes big and frequent losses to raise a low perceived risk of loss. At the other end, if the risk of loss is high, it is also elastic; the mere absence of large losses is enough to bring it down. This probably explains why financial markets seem to be so prone to forget crises so quickly.[3] When a sequence of frequent and large losses comes to an end, the perceived risk of loss is very elastic and therefore falls back very quickly.

As we are used to thinking in terms of annualized rates of return and annualized volatility, it is convenient to express the perceived risk of loss as an annual rate, too. There is a minor time-scaling issue here. If, for example, we work with monthly returns and if, as Allais did, the rate of memory decay is expressed as a monthly rate, then the HRL algorithm will yield a perceived risk of loss also expressed as a monthly rate. By which factor should we multiply this monthly perceived risk of loss to annualize it? One simple way to answer this question is to compute the perceived risk of loss over subsets of data having different frequencies (monthly losses, bimonthly losses, quarterly losses) and find out through linear regression the value of the time exponent that best fits the data. The few examples on which we have conducted this analysis suggest that the exponent is typically between 0.6 and 0.7 and in any case higher than 0.5. This being said, the possibility always exists to eschew this annualization issue by expressing all other variables, such as the perceived return or the risk-free rate of return, at the same rate as the perceived risk of loss, irrespective of the data frequency.

For the sake of a sanity check, it might be useful to give some numerical indications on the average and extreme values taken by the perceived return, the perceived risk of loss, the perceived chance of gain, and the perceived volatility for a few asset markets. Table 11.1 shows two series of numbers: first, monthly log rates; then, between parentheses, their annualized decimal equivalents (for a time exponent equal to 0.65). As regards the perceived risk of loss, we show its absolute value.

11.2   Is the Perceived Risk of Loss Relevant?

Now, is the perceived risk of loss a useful theoretical concept? If that is the case, the perceived risk of loss should help to explain, at least partially, the degree of risk aversion expressed in the pricing of various financial instruments. For example, does the perceived risk of loss bear any relationship to corporate spreads or implied volatility? It would make sense to observe a widening of credit spreads when the perceived

TABLE 11.1
Perceived Parameters for Different Asset Markets

	Low	Average	High
S&P 500/1857 to 2010			
Perceived return	−0.23%(−2.71%)	0.31%(3.83%)	1.45%(19.02%)
Perceived risk of loss	0.55%(2.75%)	1.29%(6.25%)	6.33%(27.27%)
Perceived chance of gain	0.78%(3.99%)	1.62%(8.54%)	4.83%(27.27%)
Perceived volatility	1.57%(8.19%)	2.88%(15.79%)	13.06%(92.82%)
NASDAQ/1971 to 2010			
Perceived return	−0.03%(−0.31%)	0.68%(8.70%)	3.30%(48.58%)
Perceived risk of loss	0.87%(4.29%)	1.97%(9.34%)	6.03%(26.16%)
Perceived chance of gain	0.96%(4.93%)	2.61%(14.11%)	5.99%(35.19%)
Perceived volatility	2.89%(15.64%)	4.85%(28.13%)	13.54%(97.53%)
NIKKEI 225/1955 to 2010			
Perceived return	−0.13%(−1.50%)	0.66%(8.46%)	2.11%(28.75%)
Perceived risk of loss	0.75%(3.72%)	1.66%(7.97%)	3.27%(15.18%)
Perceived chance of gain	1.33%(6.90%)	2.18%(11.63%)	4.06%(22.64%)
Perceived volatility	1.86%(9.83%)	3.78%(21.07%)	7.38%(44.92%)
US House Prices/1969 to 2010			
Perceived return	0.16%(1.94%)	0.46%(5.71%)	0.74%(9.26%)
Perceived risk of loss	0.27%(1.36%)	0.38%(1.90%)	0.59%(2.91%)
Perceived chance of gain	0.27%(1.39%)	0.41%(2.09%)	0.59%(3.01%)
Perceived volatility	0.85%(4.37%)	1.24%(6.45%)	1.59%(8.33%)

risk of loss on equities increases, as falling equity prices imply higher risk for bond holders. Similarly, the demand for downside risk hedging through put options should increase, and therefore implied volatility should rise, when the perceived risk of loss moves up.

Let us start with the relative spread $S_{BAA/AAA}$ between Moody's BAA and AAA corporate bond yields, on one hand, and the perceived risk of loss PRL_{SP500} on the S&P 500 on the other hand.[4] We have looked at the relationship between these two variables on 7,862 daily observations from January 2, 1980, to February 17, 2011. If, in the relationship $S_{BAA/AAA} = c_1 PRL_{SP500} + c_2$, we allow the constant c_2 to be different from 0, we find a R-SQ of 55.19 percent (versus 50.37 percent for perceived volatility and 42.03 percent for the perceived chance of gain). If the constant c_2 is forced to 0, the R-SQ falls to 51.38 percent. Finally, by setting the value of the time exponent at 0.706 to annualize the daily perceived risk of loss, we find $c_1 = 1.000758 \approx 1$ with a very high degree of statistical significance (figure 11.1). Furthermore, pairwise Granger causality tests conclude without any ambiguity that

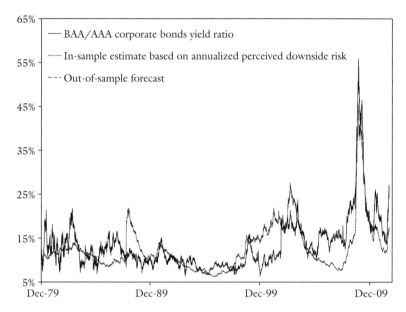

Figure 11.1 United States: corporate bond yields ratio and the perceived risk of loss on equities.

the causality runs from the perceived risk of loss to corporate spreads, and not the other way around. Parsimonious as it may be, this model is one indication that the perceived risk of loss is a relevant theoretical concept.

Let us now turn to implied volatility as measured by the Chicago Board Options Exchange Market Volatility Index (VIX) and see whether we can explain it with our perceived volatility, chance of gain, and risk of loss on the 6,403 observations between January 2, 1986, and March 3, 2009. Two major bear markets—the first one from 2000 to 2003, the second one from 2007 to 2009—have occurred during this period. As the VIX is an average of the implied volatility on both calls and puts, the results are more ambiguous than with corporate spreads. Reassuring is the high correlation between the VIX and perceived volatility (R-SQ of 60.20 percent with $b = 0$, 67.15 percent with $b \neq 0$). The correlation between the VIX and the perceived risk of loss is lower (respectively, 43.64 percent and 54.51 percent) than with perceived volatility, but higher than with the perceived chance of gain (respectively, 42.30 percent and 43.79 percent). If both the perceived chance of gain and the perceived risk of loss are used as explanatory

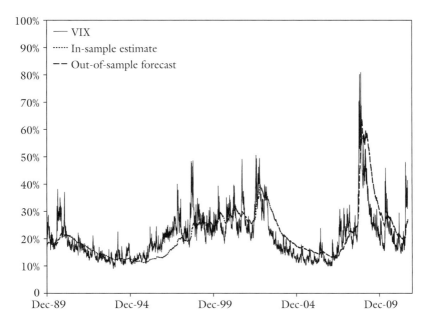

Figure 11.2 S&P 500: implied volatility, estimate based on the S&P 500 perceived upside and downside volatilities.

variables, the latter is given a greater weight than the former, even though their order of magnitude is very much the same (if the constant is not forced to 0, the coefficient of the perceived chance of gain even becomes negative) (figure 11.2). If anything, all this suggests that implied volatility is correlated with the perceived risk of loss more than with the perceived chance of gain. However, the results of Granger causality tests are very ambiguous.

Based on these two models, we can probably agree to give the perceived risk of loss the benefit of the doubt until further econometric research provides additional evidence or counter evidence.

11.3   The Perceived Risk of Loss and Incipient Bubbles

To stay clear of the annualization issue mentioned in section 11.1, as all data used in this section have a monthly frequency, all derived variables are expressed at monthly rates.

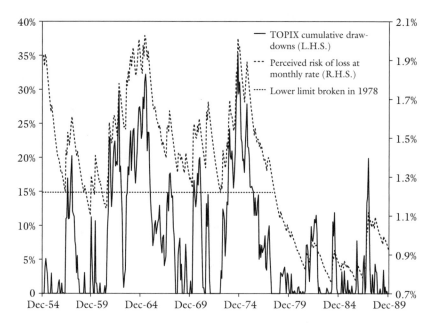

Figure 11.3 Cumulative drawdowns on the Tokyo Stock Exchange Price Index (TOPIX) and the perceived risk of loss in the Japanese equity market.

The solid line in figure 11.3 shows the absolute value of cumulative drawdowns in Japanese equities from 1954 to 1989. The dotted line represents the corresponding perceived risk of loss, expressed at a monthly rate. The remarkable fact on this chart is the fall in the perceived risk of loss to unprecedented levels from September 1978 onward, 4 years before the Japanese equity market switched to a bubble mode.

In figure 11.4, we stay in Japan, we keep the perceived risk of loss, but we overlay the perceived return on Japanese equities with the solid line and the risk-free rate of return with the dashed line. What can we see? In Japan, in late 1984, when the pace of the rise in equity prices definitely accelerated, the perceived risk of loss had been falling below the perceived rate of return, which in turn was higher than the yield on Japanese Government Bonds (JGBs).

The same pattern appeared in the United States 10 years later. But let us start with a very long view of the perceived risk of loss going back to the 1860s (figure 11.5). A log scale is needed to highlight the magnitude of its relative change. This very long view shows how exceptionally low the perceived risk of loss was in the mid-1990s, with

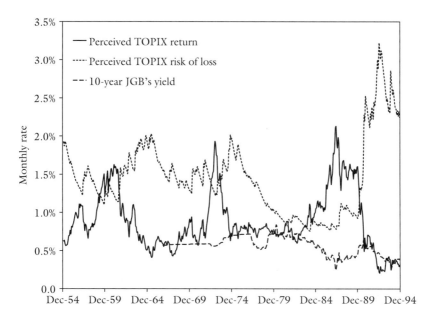

Figure 11.4 Perceived return and risk of loss in the Japanese bubble.

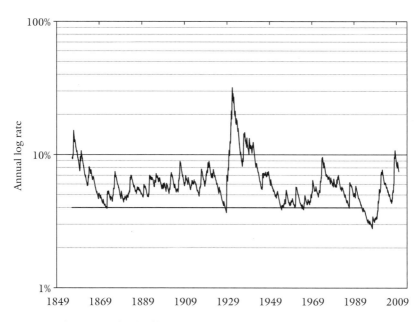

Figure 11.5 Perceived risk of loss on US equities, Cowles Commission Stock Index chained with S&P 500 after 1928.

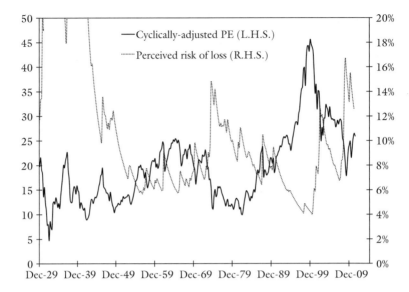

Figure 11.6 S&P 500: Cyclically adjusted PE and perceived risk of loss.

the decisive break happening in March 1993, two years before the US equity bubble started in earnest.

The solid line in figure 11.6 is the S&P 500 cyclically adjusted Price Earnings Ratio (PER). From the mid-1990s onward, it rose to levels never experienced before. It may not be an accident that the inflation of the biggest equity bubble in US history (the equity market between 1995 and 2000) was preceded by and coincided with a period during which the perceived risk of loss—the dotted line—fell to levels never experienced before, too.

As in Japan, the fall in the perceived risk of loss in the United States was caused by a long period without any serious setbacks in equity prices: 84 months without a cumulative drawdown of 10 percent or more from 1990 to 1997 (figure 11.7).

As in Japan, the relative positions of the perceived equity return and of the risk-free rate of interest are worth noticing (figure 11.8). The perceived return on the S&P 500 rose above the level of the federal funds rate in 1985. But until 1991, this gap was relatively modest. It widened in the following years to narrow only marginally in 1994. By then, the perceived return on the S&P 500 had exceeded the federal funds rate for almost 10 years in a row.

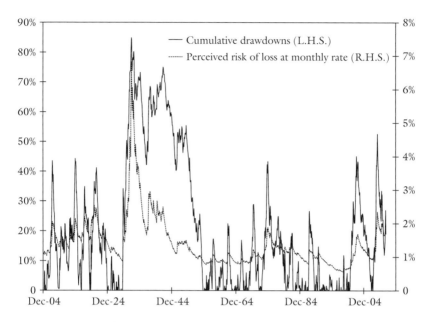

Figure 11.7 S&P 500: cumulative drawdowns and perceived risk of loss.

It is remarkable that the fall of the perceived risk of loss to unprecedented levels is hard to explain in terms of fundamentals, at least in terms of what Minsky would call the assuredness of cash flows, which is measured in figure 11.9 as the perceived risk of cash flow contraction—or, in other words, the present value of past contractions in EBITDA.

US house prices after 1997 provide another example of the perceived risk of loss falling into uncharted territory in a context of very low risk-free rates.[5] The movement accelerated in 2002 as, for the first time since 1969, the perceived return on homes exceeded mortgage rates and the risk-free rate of return fell below the perceived risk of loss.

Three examples may not be enough to build a theory of financial bubbles. On the other hand, we don't have a so many examples of major bubbles. With this caveat in mind, falls in the perceived risk of loss seem to play an important role in the inflation of financial bubbles. When losses become not only less and less frequent but also smaller and smaller, as has been the case in the United States after the 1987 crash until 1994, or in Japan between 1974 and 1984, agents are most likely to become increasingly confident that buying equities is a one-way bet. As a consequence, they tend to increase not only their equity

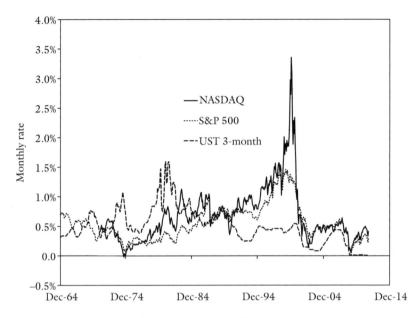

Figure 11.8 S&P 500 and NASDAQ perceived returns.

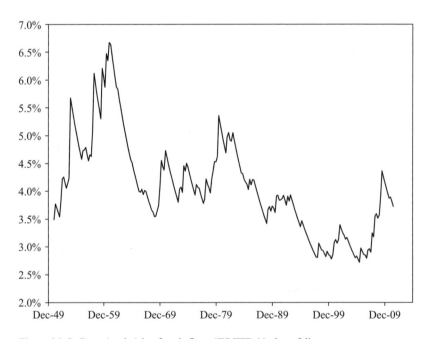

Figure 11.9 Perceived risk of cash flow (EBITDA) shortfall.

exposure but also their leverage, paying little attention to valuation. But in doing so, they plant the seeds of future instability. As forecasted by Minsky, "Stability begets instability."

To sum it up, the recipe to blow a bubble seems to be the following:

- First, you need a few years of robust perceived return—close to 10 percent a year—reflecting sound fundamentals.
- Second, you need a positive and widening spread between the perceived return and the risk-free rate of return.
- Third, you need a fall in the perceived risk of loss.

When these conditions are met, the rise in prices ends up being perceived as a one-way bet. Catastrophic losses are forgotten, and with them, risk awareness and caution.

11.4 Stability of Allais's Three Fundamental Psychological Parameters

In previous developments, we have dealt with five key parameters:

- Three of them—χ_0, α, and b—determine the present value of past returns (and perceived rates of return).
- The other two—α' and b'—determine how investors' demand for risky assets responds in a nonlinear way to the present value of past returns.

The empirical tests presented in this book tend to confirm two of Allais's critical claims:

- First, the parameters χ_0, α, and b are constant ($\chi_0 = 4.8$ percent per annum, $\alpha = b = 1$).
- Second, the parameters α' and b' are variable within a range.

It is quite a remarkable fact that Allais's HRL formulation yields good adjustments of empirical data outside its original field, without any change in the values of the three parameters χ_0, α, and b. Not only are our own adjustments good, but also we have been unable to improve them by changing any of the value of the parameters. In addition, we have seen that in most cases the causality runs in the right direction, that is, from the estimated "expectations" of economic agents to their observed behavior. Claiming that χ_0, α, and b are constant is quite a strong proposition since it is tantamount to holding that collective human psychology is constant through time and space, as far as learning from experience and forgetting the past are concerned.

Yet, we have also observed that some of the correlations presented in this book have broken down in the years 2002 to 2004, as is the case with margin debt. If these correlations still held, either investors' demand for risky assets should be lower than what we observe or, despite two almost back-to-back major equity bear markets in less than a decade, perceived returns should be higher than estimated under the assumptions $\chi_0 = 4.80$ percent and $\alpha = b = 1$. Which is the more plausible of these two explanations? To which extent could institutional or demographic changes explain this empirical finding? To answer these questions, let us first review the meanings of these three parameters.

While χ_0, the rate of memory decay in a stationary state, only impacts the rate of memory decay $\chi(Z)$, α and b intervene in both $\Psi(Z)$ and $\chi(Z)$, since the latter is, up to the constant multiplier χ_0, equal to the inverse of $\Psi(Z)$, the relative desired balances function:

$$\Psi(Z) = \frac{1+b}{1+be^{\alpha Z}} \Rightarrow \Psi'(Z) = -\frac{(1+b)\alpha be^{\alpha Z}}{(1+be^{\alpha Z})^2} \qquad (11.1)$$

$$\chi(Z) = \frac{\chi_0}{\Psi(Z)} = \chi_0 \frac{1+be^{\alpha Z}}{1+b} \Rightarrow \chi'(Z) = \frac{\chi_0 \alpha be^{\alpha Z}}{1+b} \qquad (11.2)$$

Therefore, one can discuss the stability of α and b from either point of view, relative desired balances or the rate of memory decay. It is Allais's focus on relative desired balances that led him to posit both the asymptotic postulate ($\alpha = 1$, see p. 85) and the postulate of psychological symmetry ($b = 1$, see p. 86). Our focus being primarily the rate of memory decay, we have to clarify the meaning of these two postulates in terms of forgetting:

- By setting the steepness of the asymptotic limit of the elasticity of relative desired balances with respect to the present value of past rates of nominal growth, α determines how fast relative desired balances reach their upper or lower bounds (see p. 87); by the same token, by setting the slope of the asymptotic limit of the elasticity of the rate of memory decay with respect to the present value of past rates of nominal growth (or returns), α determines how fast the rate of memory decay is increasing with respect to the present value of past rates of nominal growth (or returns).[6]

- As for the parameter b, it reflects the psychological posture of holders of money balances (bullish for $b < 1$, neutral for $b = 1$, bearish for $b > 1$, see table 4.5, p. 89), but it also determines whether economic agents forget good or bad news more or less easily (for $Z < 0$, the lower the value of b, the higher the rate of memory decay; conversely, for $Z > 0$, the lower the value of b, the lower the rate of memory decay).

From 4.57b, we have

$$\lim_{Z \to +\infty} e(\chi(Z); Z) = \alpha Z \tag{11.3}$$

which is equivalent to

$$\lim_{Z \to +\infty} \frac{d\chi}{\chi} = \alpha(x - z)\, dt \tag{11.4}$$

By setting $\alpha = 1$, the asymptotic postulate implies that the limit elasticity of the rate of memory decay with respect to the present value of past returns is equal to the latter. This proposition is in turn equivalent to assuming that the rate of increase in the rate of memory decay tends toward the forecasting error $x - z$. In other words, the asymptotic postulate sets a limit to the increase in economic agents' forgetting when they are confronted with an "unexpected" outcome in a context of increasing returns.

While the postulate of psychological symmetry has clear implications in terms of desired relative balances, its meaning in terms of rate of memory decay is less straightforward, since—unlike $\Psi'(Z) - \chi'(Z)$ is not an even function. However, to $b = 1$, which expresses a lack of bias in terms of relative desired balances, corresponds what can be deemed to be a neutral rate of memory decay. If $b > 1$, the rate of memory decay is lower than the neutral rate for $Z < 0$, and higher for $Z > 0$: this propensity to forget negative returns more slowly and positive returns more quickly than normal expresses a bearish bias. Conversely, to $b < 1$ corresponds a bullish bias.[7]

To sum it up, the three fundamental psychological assumptions that we need to challenge are the following:

- In a context of increasing returns ($Z \to +\infty$), the rate of increase in the rate of memory decay is equal to the forecasting error $x - z$, since $\alpha = 1$.
- All other parameters being equal, there exists a neutral rate of memory decay defined by $b = 1$.
- Last but not least, in a steady state ($Z = 0$), economic agents forget the past at a constant rate $\chi_0 = 4.80$ percent per annum.

From an empirical point of view, it is to be stressed that not all correlations have collapsed. The important relationship between the perceived rates of nominal growth and nominal interest rates has continued to hold. The HRL formulation of the demand for money and the fundamental equation of monetary dynamics jointly provide a good adjustment of global, Japanese, and European rates of nominal growth. The correlations between the perceived risk of loss, on one hand, and implied volatility or corporate spreads, on the other, have been stable. Whether future research will provide fresh examples of stable or unstable relationships remains to be seen.

One should also bear in mind that we have only presented univariate models using either the perceived return or the perceived risk of loss as explanatory variables. Bivariate models combining these two variables may (or may not) yield more-stable relationships. Here again, future research will be useful.

In any case, the divergence between estimated and observed behavior that has arisen in a few instances may be a valuable indication that some new factors, transient or permanent, could be disturbing the "normal" functioning of some segments of financial markets. Identifying these potential disruptive factors and assessing their sustainability may be more fruitful than the mere rejection of the three structural psychological assumptions $\chi_0 = 4.80\%$, $\alpha = 1$, and $b = 1$ on the grounds of a few cases of unstable relationships.

One could, for example, contend that the investment world is replete with agency problems that are implicitly absent from Allais's formulation of the demand for money. In Allais's world, the decisions to dispose of or to accumulate money balances are made by their holders. In contrast, an increasing share of total financial assets is managed not by their owners, but by agents—money managers—whose performance is almost always measured in relative terms, against benchmarks. For these agents, who compete against one another for market shares, missing a rally is a bigger business risk than being caught in a bear market. For these money managers, it is not rational to have the symmetric psychological posture implied by $b = 1$. For these agents, the rational posture is to forget returns asymmetrically: faster than their principals for negative returns, more slowly for positive returns. Such a bullish bias would imply $b < 1$. Similarly, for these agents, it is rational to respond as quickly as possible to "unexpected" positive returns, which would imply $\alpha > 1$. If Kindleberger is right in observing that "there is nothing so disturbing to one's well-being and judgment as to see a friend get rich," money managers may share such bullish biases with a few principal investors. Having $\alpha > 1$ and $b < 1$ would raise the perceived equity returns in recent years and thereby contribute to close the gap between the estimated and the observed behavior of investors. This being said, leaving α and b unchanged, the same biases could be expressed by having $\alpha' > 1$ and $b' > 1$, as suggested by the observations presented in chapter 9.[8]

Let us now discuss the stability of the rate of memory decay in a stationary state. Based on data from the first half of the twentieth century, Allais's empirical tests of the HRL formulation suggest that $\chi_0 = 0.40$ percent per month. To which extent can we consider this value as independent of the period studied? To which extent can it be influenced by demographic structures?

In a stationary state, since $Zt = 0$, the collective rate of memory decay remains, by definition, constant

$$\chi = \chi_0 \frac{1 + be^{\alpha Z}}{1 + b} = \chi_0 \frac{1 + b}{1 + b} = \chi_0 \qquad (11.5)$$

and the HRL formulation becomes equivalent to a standard exponential average, the average length of which is easy to compute, using the following relationship:

$$\delta(\chi_0) = \frac{\int_0^{+\infty} te^{-\chi_0 t}\, dt}{\int_0^{+\infty} e^{-\chi_0 t}\, dt} = \frac{\frac{1}{\chi_0^2}}{\frac{1}{\chi_0}} = \frac{1}{\chi_0} \qquad (11.6)$$

Therefore, a monthly rate of memory decay equal to 0.40 percent means that the average length of collective memory in a stationary state is equal to 250 months (or 20.83 years). Since

$$\int_0^{\frac{1}{\chi_0}} e^{-\chi_0 t}\, dt = \frac{1}{\chi_0}\left(1 - \frac{1}{e}\right) \qquad (11.7)$$

TABLE 11.2

Length of Memory and Rate of Memory Decay by Population Group

Group	1	2	3	4	5	6	7	8
Average length of memory*	60	120	180	240	300	360	420	480
Rate of memory decay[†]	1.67%	0.83%	0.56%	0.42%	0.33%	0.28%	0.24%	0.21%

* In months.
[†] At monthly rate.

it also means that, in a stationary state, the aggregate relative weight of data that are less than 250 months old is

$$1 - \frac{1}{e} = 63.21\% \qquad (11.8)$$

Now, the population able to remember the past is not homogeneous. Because older people have lived longer, they must have a longer memory than younger people. In other words, their rate of memory decay must be smaller than that of the younger generations.[9] This observation suggests to divide the population into groups defined by the average length of their memory (or by the equivalent rate of memory decay), as shown for example, in table 11.2.

The aggregate decay factor can be interpreted as being the weighted average of the decay factors of the respective age groups.

As for the weighting coefficients w_i, they should reflect the age structure in the countries that Allais studied. We have not sought to access this information directly. Neither can this age structure be estimated through linear regression, as this method assigns negative weights to some groups and systematically gives a dominant weight to group 4, the group closest to 0.40 percent (or 250 months).

Over time, populations age or rejuvenate. By randomly generating some artificial age structures, one can assess the sensitivity of the collective rate of memory decay with respect to aging or rejuvenation. For any set of randomly generated w_i with $\sum w_i = 1$, one just needs to compute the series of

$$k_t = \sum_{i=1}^{8} w_i e^{-\chi_0^i t} \qquad \text{for} \qquad t = 0, -1, -2, -3, -4, \ldots \qquad (11.9)$$

TABLE 11.3

Collective Rate of Memory Decay and Length of Collective
Memory for Two Different Populations

Simulation (%)	Old population	Young population
w_8	41.00%	9.51%
w_7	15.89	2.85
w_6	1.90	1.45
w_5	14.74	0.23
w_4	2.94	4.05
w_3	12.04	17.45
w_2	1.06	31.91
w_1	10.41	32.55
Collective rate of memory decay (%)	0.31	0.64
Length of collective memory	318.57	155.56

The collective rate of memory decay that best fits k_t is

$$\chi_0^* = \frac{1}{\sum k_t} \tag{11.10}$$

Such numerical simulations show that only very skewed age structures can cause the collective rate of memory decay to deviate substantially from 0.40 percent (as shown in table 11.3). In most cases, the
collective rate of memory remains very close to 0.40 percent.

This table also shows that, relative to $\chi_0 = 0.40$ percent, the shortening of memory caused by a young or rejuvenating population is larger
than the lengthening caused by an old or aging one. In short, juvenility
begets instability. If a sector of the economy turns out to be predom-
inantly populated by young people, the ruling "expectations" in this
sector are likely to be the expression of a very short memory of the past.
This is even more true if this sector is not in a stationary state.

All in all, of course one cannot rule out that institutional and demographic changes could make Allais's three fundamental psychological
parameters unstable over time or across countries. However, the case
for having

$$\alpha > 1 \qquad b < 1 \qquad \chi_0 > 0.40\% \text{ per month} \tag{11.11}$$

does not seem to be particularly strong.

TABLE 11.4
Impact of Changes in HRL Structural Psychological Parameters

Monthly log rate	$\alpha = b = 1, \chi_0 = 0.40\%$	$\alpha = 6, b = 0.1, \chi_0 = 1.60\%$
Average	0.41%	0.44%
Standard deviation	0.30	0.56
Minimum	−0.21	−1.69
Maximum	1.45	2.81

While such changes would have little impact on the average perceived return, they would have a larger one on its volatility and extreme values, as shown in table 11.4 for the S&P 500.

The same holds true for the perceived risk of loss. If warranted, these changes would make the collective rate of memory decay χ and "expectations" more unstable.

11.5   The Perceived Risk of Loss and Moral Hazard

It remains to be tested whether, to express a supposedly fresh bullish bias on the part of market participants, the mere resetting of the three structural parameters χ_0, α, and b is enough to entirely close the gap between observed risk appetite and perceived returns (by raising the latter during the last 10 years or so). Preliminary inspection of the data suggests, however, that it cannot be the case and that something else needs to be considered to explain the conundrum of "resilient bullish behavior" in a context of "diminished return expectations." This something else does not seem to be the perceived risk of loss either, for while it has subsided since its 2003 and 2009 peaks, it remains elevated and seems too high to be compatible with observed risk appetite. The fact is that market participants behave as if they had more or less forgotten two back-to-back deep bear markets.

To explain this conundrum, one has no choice but to look for factors distinct from past price movements. One has to conclude that, past price movements notwithstanding, investors expect little downside risk or have little to fear from it. How can this be? The history of equity market fluctuations cannot be isolated from the policy responses they have triggered. Several times during the last 20 to 30 years, policymakers have been confronted with falling asset values and the risk of recession or even debt deflation. In such circumstances, policymakers—especially in the United States—have repeatedly asserted their willingness to do "whatever it takes" to prevent the worst-case scenario from materializing. And they have delivered, be it through monetary policy, fiscal policy, or a combination of both. Therefore, it may well be the case that market participants now trust that downside risk is, so to say, limited by decree. This knowledge may lead them to take more risks than they would otherwise. Hence, moral hazard—defined as the propensity to take more "insured" risk—would be the reason for the conundrum that we observe.

To the extent that it takes potential policy responses into account, moral hazard seems to fit with the rational expectations framework. If market participants know that policymakers will intervene whenever markets are in need of a bailout, it is indeed rational on their part to have a resilient and high risk appetite. What is nevertheless the true nature of this "expectation"? How have market participants learned that policymakers are not only willing to do, but also are doing "whatever it takes" to limit the downside risk? Wasn't there a learning process leading to this core belief, and wasn't it based on experience acquired over time? Indeed, it was. Moral hazard is a backward-looking "expectation," may be even the mother of all adaptive "expectations."

Now, if moral hazard is a backward-looking "expectation," can the HRL formulation quantify it? And what should we measure: policymakers' words or their deeds? European policymakers' inability to tame the European sovereign debt crisis with mere statements of intentions, until the announcement of outright monetary transactions (OMT) by the European Central Bank's President suggests that deeds matter more than words. Had it not echoed back to markets similar statements and moves made previously by other Central Bankers, like Alan Greenspan in October 1987, would Mario Draghi's announcement have been that credible? Was it really a case of successful expectations management within a rational expectations framework? Or was it just another case of learning through time and experience? Monetary policy and fiscal policy are the two primary tools that policymakers can use "to put their money where there mouth is." The willingness to expand both the monetary base in real terms and the public debt relative to tax revenues reveals policymakers' preference. As shown in figure 11.10, the HRL formulation can be used to compute the perceived rate of growth in these two variables:

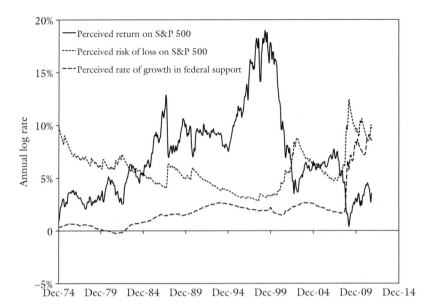

Figure 11.10 The mother of all expectations.

- The real monetary base.
- The public debt–tax revenues ratio.

This analysis suggests not only that moral hazard has never been so high since 2008, but also that it is rising. Whether this adaptive "expectation" resists the test of time will ultimately depend on sovereign solvency and the credibility of central banks, in the EMU and elsewhere. Be that as it may, the point to stress is that the conundrum of "resilient bullish behavior" in a context of "diminished return expectations" does not contradict the HRL formulation, since it can be explained within this very framework.

Should policymakers have as an objective to inflate a bubble in a given risky asset, they should, according to the perceived risk of loss framework, not only cut the risk-free rate of return, but also ensure, by deeds or by credible commitments to act, that the size and the frequency of the losses incurred on this risky asset remain of the same order of magnitude as the losses incurred on other less risky assets. They do not even need a "good story" à la Kindleberger. Conversely, policymakers keen to avoid fostering moral hazard should tolerate if not welcome some occasional losses to cheer other investors up, thus following Voltaire's recommendation to behead a general from time to time so as to "encourager les autres"—encourage others.

To the long-term, long-only investor, the HRL formulation offers a framework to steer investments. To maximize realized returns, such an investor should look for situations where the risk-free rate is low or falling, the perceived return robust and rising, the perceived risk of loss low and falling. To minimize downside risk, such an investor should eschew situations in which the risk-free rate is rising, the perceived return exuberant, and the perceived risk of loss can only increase from a low level. Finally, he or she should be ready to provide liquidity to other market participants once the perceived risk of loss has risen to elevated levels. In short, he or she should be attracted by situations in which risk-taking is not perceived to have paid-off and be very wary of positively sloped *perceived* market lines (i.e., the line displayed on a scatterplot in which the perceived risk of loss is on the horizontal axis and the perceived return on the vertical one).

CHAPTER TWELVE

Conclusion

THIS BOOK being nothing but an invitation to add Allais's HRL formulation to the tool kit of any scholar, economist or not, interested in "expectations" formation, it seems appropriate to conclude our inquiry by summarizing in a comparative way and with the rational expectations terminology what makes Allais's contribution original, important, and modern.

To start with, many of the rational expectations theorists' criticisms of standard adaptive expectations do not apply to the HRL formulation. Allais's algorithm is not a constant-gain one; it is a time-varying algorithm. As a consequence, the sum of the weights on the lagged variable is not restricted to 1. The distributions of its one-period-ahead forecasting errors do not exhibit any pattern liable to be arbitraged away by astute market participants; in the general case where the observed variable's distribution is leptokurtotic, so, too, is the distribution of the forecasting errors.

This being said, in Allais's formulation, "expectations" are not endogenous to the model, since there is no such thing in it as "the" model purporting to explain and forecast the variable of interest with other, theoretically relevant variables. While this restriction may look at first glance as a serious breach of rationality and orthodoxy, one can nevertheless find it admissible given the natural interdependence between economic variables and the resulting complexity of their relationships. Theorists have long recognized that, confronted with such complexity, economic agents may have no choice but to indulge in or to fall back on bounded rationality, rational inattention, and other forms of rationality fatigue. The HRL formulation contends that, in an uncertain world, "expectations" are rooted in what people remember of their own experience, according to a well-specified and stable law of forgetting.

From a purely mathematical point of view, the HRL formulation and rational learning have some important features in common. Like recursive ordinary least square (OLS) regression, the HRL formulation belongs to the realm of Bayesian inference. In both algorithms, the gain is time-varying. In both algorithms, the recursion needs to be initialized in a subjective way.

For all their mathematical commonalities, the HRL formulation and rational learning differ substantially. Contrary to recursive OLS learning, which relies on linear regression, the HRL formulation is a nonlinear filter. Contrary to recursive OLS learning, it does not assume linear relationships in the economy or in the minds of economic agents. Contrary to recursive OLS learning, the HRL formulation does not weigh all past observations equally. The magnitude of the relative changes observed per unit of physical time and the flow of time itself have a direct impact on the weights given to past observations. This also distinguishes the HRL formulation from the 1990s adaptive expectations, namely, recursive OLS linear regression with forgetting.

Last but not least, the HRL algorithm is a parsimonious one: it leaves little to be cut by Occam's razor. A slide rule is enough to implement it. The parsimony of the HRL formulation makes it easy to test its compatibility with empirical observations: data permitting, it is an easy-to-falsify proposition.

Parsimony, nonlinearity and time variability of the gain, unequal weighting of past observations according to a well-specified and stable law of forgetting, absence of patterns in forecasting errors—these are the features that make Allais's HRL formulation worth the consideration of economists wishing to explore or to revisit the unsettled and important question of "expectations" formation.

Between the REH and the HRL formulation, there is another more subtle, more fundamental difference that appears clearly in the light of Pribram's and Phelps' taxonomies of economic theories. Both authors observe that the methods of economic analysis and the conflicts between economic theories are nothing but the reflection of the conflicts and methods present in other intellectual disciplines, first and foremost in philosophy, the matrix of all sciences. To describe these methods and conflicts, the two authors do not use the same vocabulary, but the issues they address are similar and the distinctions they establish have very much the same meaning. Pribram opposes the essentialistic to the hypothetical school.[1] According to the essentialistic school the

> [human] mind has been endowed with the capacity of adjusting its concepts exactly to the real order of outside phenomena ... the human intellect is able to achieve "full insight" into the nature and essence of things and events with the aid of concepts regarded as eternally valid or at least absolutely valid under certain historical conditions ... In polar opposition to the essentialistic patterns of thought stands the "hypothetical" pattern, the adherents of which are inclined to question the real existence of any concepts outside the mind or at least the faculty of the intellect to grasp such concepts.

The hypothetical school believes indeed that

> all abstract notions are freely formed by the mind in accordance with rules which are likely to differ from those underlying the course of actual events. These methods imply that any attempts to arrive at an understanding of such events must start from assumptions which can be considered the more useful and reliable the better they assist the student in establishing causal relationships between the phenomena under observation and enable him to devise a consistent body of doctrine.

As for Phelps, he distinguishes two main schools: the classic and the modern ones.[2] To the classic school he attributes the idea that there exists an absolute truth the objective knowledge of which is possible. To the modern one he attributes the death of "objective" truth and the rule of subjectivism. From this, we can conclude that Pribram's essentialistic school and Phelps's classic school can be considered as almost equivalent. And the same holds true for their hypothetical and modern schools. If there is a significant difference between Pribram and Phelps in this respect, it lies in the fact that Phelps sees the conflict between the classic and the modern school as the twentieth century's hallmark, while Pribram traces the secular struggle between the essentialistic and the hypothetical schools back to the classical Greek philosophers. Be that as it may, the two authors consider that the achievements of the hypothetical/modern school dwarf those of the essentialistic/classic one.

Given these definitions, to which school, respectively, belong the REH and the HRL formulation? Considering the REH's claim that economic agents all use the same "true" model of the economy, Phelps places it without any ambiguity in his classic school.[3] Therefore, it seems logical to think that had Pribram had the opportunity to assess the REH, he would have classified it within his essentialistic school, in company with scholastic economics, the physiocrats, the Ricardian socialists, the German cameralists, and the Marxists, to name but a few.

As for the HRL formulation, the author of this book firmly believes that it belongs to the hypothetical school. Hopefully, the reader has been presented enough material—both theoretical and empirical—to reach the same conclusion on her or his own. Such a conclusion is clearly consistent with Allais's conception and practice of science:[4]

Science relies on models, and any scientific model is made of three steps:

- A set of explicit assumptions
- All the logical consequences, nothing but the logical consequences, derived from these assumptions
- The confrontation of these consequences with empirical data

Of these three steps, only the first and the third ones matter to the economist. The second one, which is purely logical and mathematical, that is, tautological, is only interesting from a mathematical point of view ... The model and the theory which it expresses should be accepted, at least provisionally [i.e., until the discovery of fresh incompatible data], or rejected, depending on whether its assumptions and consequences are compatible or not with empirical data ... As regards science, the notion of "truth" is all but relative. There only exist models that are more or less compatible with empirical data ... Whichever its empirical verifications might be, the best one can hope to say about a theory is that everything happens as if its assumptions actually matched the true nature of phenomena.

As for mathematics, they are and they can be nothing but a tool ... for a theory to be scientifically valuable, it is not enough that it rests upon some rigorous axiomatisation. In the development of science, that is, in the construct of theories and models, it is creative intuition that plays the critical role. It is by means of intuition, itself based on experience, that hypotheses are selected.

The HRL formulation is almost as old as the REH. That it has been ignored by the REH advocates was to be expected. More surprising is the fact that it has been ignored, too, by the many academics, policymakers, and practitioners who have always questioned the most extreme claims made by the REH. Had Allais called his theory of psychological time and memory decay a general theory of "expectations" under uncertainty, he may have better shown that a credible alternative to the REH has existed ever since this hypothesis has been formulated. What a cruel irony that economists have failed for so long to make the best competitive use of all existing theoretical resources!

Strictly speaking, Allais's theory of economic and financial behavior is not one of expectations-driven behavior. It is instead a theory of behavior driven by habits. Nevertheless, its field of application is broad, because that of expectations proper is narrow. As highlighted by the high priests of rational expectations, the REH does not hold under uncertainty, and it is rational to form adaptive expectations in the presence of interdependent economic variables, between which feedback loops develop.

As a matter of fact, Allais's HRL formulation is much more sophisticated, much more rational, so to say, than the standard adaptive expectations model tolerated by the REH advocates when economic variables are interdependent. In Allais's model, economic agents do learn from their mistakes, seemingly faster than economists. They do so not only by adjusting their "expectations" for a fraction of the "forecasting error" they have just made, but also by instantaneously and continuously increasing or decreasing their rate of memory decay.

Furthermore, the variability of the rate of memory decay is endogenous both to economic agents and to the environment they are responding to. It is endogenous to economic agents' psychology because there is substantial evidence that the three psychological parameters α, b, and χ_0 that shape their response to new information, be it rates of nominal growth or rates of returns, are constant through time and space. And once these three parameters are set, the rate of memory decay responds mechanistically to the sequence of rates of growth (or returns) experienced by economic agents. In Allais's model, "expectations" are endogenous to human psychology and to the paths followed by the economic variables of interest. If anything, this seems preferable to expectations being endogenous to "the" model, as demanded by the REH—if only because it is much more feasible and economical than estimating "the" REH-compliant model.

It is precisely because the rate of memory decay is context-dependent that the forecasting errors generated by the HRL formulation do not exhibit any exploitable pattern. Allais's formulation suggests that versatile as human psychology may be in aggregate, it can nevertheless be modeled and predicted, because its fundamental mechanisms are constant through time and space: we respond in a nonlinear way to what we perceive to be "normal," based on what we remember; the duration of our memory is variable. If such psychological stability does exist, it is possible to substitute psychology for normative rationality as the foundation of economics.

Whether our human pride likes it or not, Allais's economic agents are "excitable animals." In the extreme, that is, under hyperinflation or in a very powerful bull market, they end up having a very short memory and being very impatient. The shortening of memory during a bull market impacts both the return and the risk of loss they perceive to be "normal." This book insists on the perceived risk of loss being a major source of financial instability, for the absence of large and persistent drawdowns in securities' prices triggers an increase in risk appetite. According to this framework, a policy aiming at dampening downside volatility in asset prices is bound to foster moral hazard and an ever-larger need for backstopping financial markets with taxpayers' money.

Hopefully, this book will be appreciated as an invitation to "think outside the box," for this is nothing but its limited ambition. Its usefulness should be measured by its ability to inspire deeper and broader research on financial instability. In the meantime, academics, policymakers, and corporate leaders could at least, as a precaution, question the nature of what they call their expectations or other agents' expectations. This might spare us a few tragic mistakes.

How to Compute Z_n and z_n

A.1 Variable (Time Series of Any Frequency)

$W_n > 0$

A.1.1 Parameters

$$\alpha \;=\; b = 1$$

$Z_0 \;=\;$ initialization parameter (or initial prior), negative, positive, or nil

$\chi_0 \;=\;$ 0.40% per month (or 1.20% per quarter, or 4.80% per year)

$p \;=\;$ time-scaling factor ensuring that $\overline{x_n}$ is expressed at same periodic rate as χ_0

If χ_0 is observed as a monthly rate, $p = 0.0329, 0.2300, 1, 3,$ or 12 if W_n is observed, respectively, at a daily, weekly, monthly, quarterly, or annual frequency.

A.2 Step 1: Rate of Change at Monthly Log (or Continuous) Rate

$$\overline{x_n} = \frac{1}{p} \ln \frac{W_n}{W_{n-1}} = \frac{\ln W_n - \ln W_{n-1}}{p}$$

A.3   Step 2: Forecasting Error at Monthly Log (or Continuous) Rate

$$k'_n = \overline{x_n} - \frac{\chi_0 Z_{n-1}}{\Psi^*_{n-1}} = \overline{x_n} - \chi_{n-1} Z_{n-1} = \overline{x_n} - z_{n-1}$$

A.4   Step 3: Carried-Forward Rate of Memory Decay at Monthly Log (or Continuous) Rate

$$k_n = \frac{\chi_0}{\Psi^*_{n-1}} \left[1 + \alpha Z_{n-1} \left(1 - \frac{\Psi^*_{n-1}}{1+b} \right) \right]$$

$$= \chi_{n-1} \left[1 + \alpha Z_{n-1} \left(1 - \frac{\Psi^*_{n-1}}{1+b} \right) \right]$$

$$k_n = \chi_{n-1} + Z_{n-1} \chi'_{n-1}$$

A.5   Step 4: Coefficient of Psychological Expansion (Dimensionless Number)

$$Z_n = Z_{n-1} + \frac{k'_n}{k_n}(1 - e^{-pk_n})$$

A.6   Step 5: Relative Desired Balances (Dimensionless Number)

$$\Psi^*_{n-1} = \frac{1+b}{1 + be^{\alpha Z_{n-1}}}$$

A.7   Step 6: Rate of Memory Decay at Monthly Log (or Continuous) Rate

$$\chi_n = \chi_0 \frac{1 + be^{\alpha Z_n}}{1+b} = \frac{\chi_0}{\Psi^*_n}$$

A.8   Step 7: Perceived Rate of Change at Monthly Log (or Continuous) Rate

$$z_n = \chi_n Z_n$$

A.9   Step 8: Perceived Rate of Change at Monthly Decimal (or Discrete) Rate

$$g_n = e^{z_n} - 1$$

Nominal Interest Rates and the Perceived Rate of Nominal Growth

TABLE B.1
Relationship Between Perceived Nominal Growth and Long-Term Nominal Interest Rates

31/12/2006	Beg	Z_0 (%)	z_0 (%)	min i (%)	max i (%)	Lag	DF	R-SQ (%)	e (%)	μ	P (%)
Australia	30/06/1969	89.06	7.35	4.95	15.76	6	149	78.36	15.97	0.95	0.02
Canada	30/06/1962	48.00	3.01	4.00	16.92	5	178	73.04	16.61	1.08	0.00
France	31/03/1965	75.00	5.61	3.08	16.18	0	167	88.27	13.33	1.01	18.37
Germany	30/06/1960	66.00	4.65	3.04	10.53	0	186	77.03	12.43	1.05	0.00
Italy	31/03/1961	70.00	5.06	2.89	19.34	3	183	83.04	20.51	0.81	0.00
Japan	31/12/1974	135.09	15.76	0.53	9.82	0	128	87.08	25.83	0.63	0.00
N. Zealand	30/09/1987	128.00	14.12	5.16	15.09	0	77	89.54	9.15	1.01	43.06
S. Africa	30/06/1961	60.00	4.06	4.69	17.32	5	182	83.02	15.50	0.96	0.01
S. Korea	30/09/1973	134.66	15.66	3.35	29.87	0	135	80.92	23.49	0.77	0.00
Spain	30/06/1978	122.31	12.91	3.13	16.41	0	115	66.57	29.31	0.80	0.00
Sweden	31/12/1980	115.00	11.48	3.01	12.86	0	104	79.45	19.58	0.99	82.94
Switzerland	31/12/1970	68.00	4.85	1.92	7.07	2	144	69.94	15.86	0.83	0.00
UK	31/03/1957	84.51	6.75	4.10	16.48	0	199	74.63	18.66	0.95	0.03
USA	31/12/1958	52.21	3.36	3.30	14.76	0	192	77.95	16.19	1.02	11.55
Argentina	29/02/1980	219.61	52.65	2.07	724.72	0	324	76.28	68.14	0.71	0.00
Brazil	31/01/1980	168.96	26.02	11.82	718.87	0	325	80.66	50.16	1.05	7.08
Chile	31/01/1977	260.89	91.32	1.68	90.80	0	361	77.15	43.04	0.88	0.00
Mexico	31/01/1978	147.43	18.99	5.09	139.96	0	375	76.61	37.69	0.97	13.70

Proofs

C.1   Muth's Critique of Exponential Average

Except for many typos in the subscripts of the relationships written by Muth, his line of reasoning is rather easy to follow. To present Muth's reasoning with notations consistent with those used in this book, we shall use the equivalences displayed in table C.1.

Muth's starting point is the exponential average y of a variable x.

$$y_{n-1} = y_{n-2} + k(x_{n-1} - y_{n-2}) \Leftrightarrow$$

$$y_{n-1} = k \sum_{i=1}^{\infty} (1-k)^{i-1} x_{n-i} \qquad 0 \le k \le 1 \tag{C.1}$$

Muth assumes the variable x to be a linear combination of independent normally distributed random shocks

$$x_n = \epsilon_n + \sum_{i=1}^{\infty} w_i \epsilon_{n-i} \qquad \text{with} \qquad E(\epsilon_n) = 0 \tag{C.2}$$

Since $E(\epsilon_n) = 0$, the conditional mathematical expectation of x_n is

$$E(x_n/\epsilon_{n-1}, \epsilon_{n-2}, \dots) = \sum_{i=1}^{\infty} w_i \epsilon_{n-i} \tag{C.3}$$

This is the expectation of x_n given $\epsilon_{n-1}, \epsilon_{n-2}, \dots$ In other words, the only information lacking to give the value of x_n is the latest shock ϵ_n.

TABLE C.1
Notation Equivalence Table

	Muth	Here
Exponential average	y_t^e	y_{n-1}
Variables to be forecasted/smoothed	y_{t-1}	x_{n-1}
Parameter of the exponential average	β	k

Now, from the above, we can independently write the exponential average of x at $n - 1$ as

$$y_{n-1} = \sum_{j=1}^{\infty} v_j x_{n-j} \tag{C.4}$$

and we can use y_{n-1} as a forecast of x_n.

The natural question surveyed by Muth is the following: which assumptions do we need to make as regards the w_i for y_{n-1} to be equal to $E(x_n/\epsilon_{n-1}, \epsilon_{n-2}, \ldots)$? To answer this question, Muth first expresses $E(x_n/\epsilon_{n-1}, \epsilon_{n-2}, \ldots)$ as a linear combination of $x_{n-1}, x_{n-2}, \ldots$, by using the following generalization of relationship C.2:

$$x_{n-j} = \epsilon_{n-j} + \sum_{i=1}^{\infty} w_i \epsilon_{n-j-i} \tag{C.5}$$

Substituting relationship C.5 for x_{n-j} in C.4, we get

$$y_{n-1} = \sum_{j=1}^{\infty} v_j \left(\epsilon_{n-j} + \sum_{i=1}^{\infty} w_i \epsilon_{n-j-i} \right) \tag{C.6}$$

and after rearranging the terms, we have

$$y_{n-1} = v_1 \epsilon_{n-1} + \sum_{i=2}^{\infty} \left(v_i + \sum_{j=1}^{i+1} v_j w_{i-j} \right) \epsilon_{n-i} \tag{C.7}$$

By comparing relationships C.3 and C.7, one can immediately express the w_i in terms of the v_i, since

$$w_1 = v_1 \tag{C.8}$$

and

$$w_i = v_i + \sum_{j=1}^{i-1} v_j w_{i-j} \qquad \text{for} \qquad i = 2,3,4,\ldots \qquad \text{(C.9)}$$

We can now use the assumption that the v_j are the coefficients of an exponential average, that is,

$$v_j = k(1-k)^{j-1} \qquad \text{for} \qquad j = 2,3,4,\ldots \qquad \text{(C.10)}$$

Hence, for y_{n-1} to be equal to $E(x_n/\epsilon_{n-1}, \epsilon_{n-2}, \ldots)$, we must have

$$w_i = k(1-k)^{i-1} + k \sum_{j=1}^{i-1} (1-k)^{j-1} w_{i-j} \qquad \text{(C.11)}$$

From there, it follows, by recurrence, that $w_1 = w_2 = \cdots = k$. Hence, x_n can be written as follows:

$$x_n = \epsilon_n + k \sum_{i=1}^{\infty} \epsilon_{n-i} \qquad \text{(C.12)}$$

In other words, for an exponential average to be an optimal forecast, the process that is to be predicted must be the sum of two components:

- The latest random shock ϵ_n, which has a weight of unity.
- The sum of all previous shocks $\sum_{i=1}^{\infty} \epsilon_{n-i}$, which has a constant weight k, with $0 \le k \le 1$.

This second component represents the permanent effect of all previous shocks: it is the anchor of the process that is to be predicted. The parameter k sets the weight of the "noise" relative to this permanent component: the lower the value of k, the higher the impact of the noise. Overall, this means that the process to be predicted has to show some degree of stability, that is, some degree of autocorrelation.

Muth generalized his demonstration beyond a one-period-ahead forecast by showing that it holds for any forecast span. He further demonstrated that the use of using exponential averages remains appropriate if the permanent and transitory components in each period are independent rather than perfectly correlated.

C.2   Exponential Smoothing as a Linear Regression on a Constant

The function

$$f(a) = \sum_{i=0}^{n-1} (1 - k)^i (x_{n-i} - a)^2 \qquad (C.13)$$

is minimized when $f'(a) = 0$

$$f'(a) = -2 \sum_{i=0}^{n-1} (1 - k)^i (x_{n-i} - a) = 0 \qquad 0 < k < 1 \qquad (C.14)$$

and is equivalent to

$$(x_n - a) + (1 - k)(x_{n-1} - a) + \cdots + (1 - k)^{n-1}(x_1 - a) = 0 \quad (C.15)$$

$$\begin{aligned} x_n + (1 - k)x_{n-1} + \cdots + (1 - k)^{n-1} x_1 \\ = a[1 + (1 - k) + \cdots + (1 - k)^n] \end{aligned} \qquad (C.16)$$

$$a = \frac{x_n + (1 - k)x_{n-1} + (1 - k)^2 x_{n-2} + \cdots + (1 - k)^{n-1} x_1}{1 + (1 - k) + (1 - k^2) + \cdots + (1 - k)^n} \qquad (C.17)$$

$$a = \frac{k}{1 - (1 - k)^n} \sum_{j=0}^{n-1} (1 - k)^j x_{n-j} \qquad (C.18)$$

Hence

$$\lim_{n \to +\infty} a = k \sum_{i=0}^{n-1} (1 - k)^i x_{n-i} = y_n \qquad (C.19)$$

C.3   Malinvaud's Rational Expectations Example

Let us first define the variables considered as "relevant" by this model (see table C.2). Let us proceed further by defining the relationships considered "relevant." The model first assumes that the price level p_n depends on both expected prices p_n^e and excess demand d_n:

$$p_n = p_n^e + \alpha d_n \qquad \alpha > 0 \qquad (C.20)$$

TABLE C.2
Variables in Malinvaud's Model

$m_n = \ln M_n$	money supply
$p_n = \ln P_n$	price level
p_n^e	expected value of p_n
$y_n = \ln Y_n$	volume of output
d_n	excess demand/liquidity measured in terms of real money balances
μ	demand for real money balances
$\bar{y}$	volume of output when $d_n = 0$

It further assumes that the volume of output y deviates from its normal level $\bar{y}$ commensurately with excess demand.

$$y_n = \bar{y} + \beta d_n \qquad (C.21)$$

As for the excess demand d_n, it is measured by the gap between real balances M_n/P_n and a demand for money μ that is assumed to be constant in real terms.

$$d_n = m_n - p_n - \mu = \ln \frac{M_n}{P_n} - \mu \qquad (C.22)$$

Under the REH, to be model-consistent, the expected value p_n^e of the price level p_n at n is conditional on the information I available at $n - 1$:

$$p_n^e = \varphi(I_{n-1}) \qquad (C.23)$$

Let us then search for the analytical expression of the expected price level. By substituting relationship C.22 for d_n in relationship C.20, we obtain

$$p_n = \frac{1}{1+\alpha} p_n^e + \frac{\alpha}{1+\alpha} m_n - \frac{\alpha}{1+\alpha} \mu \qquad (C.24)$$

After we write

$$\gamma = \frac{\alpha}{1+\alpha} \qquad (C.25)$$

relationship C.24 becomes

$$p_n = (1-\gamma) p_n^e + \gamma m_n - \gamma \mu \qquad (C.26)$$

Let us now assume that the growth rate in the money supply $d \ln M$ is exogenous and equal to the sum of a constant term g and a random term ϵ_n with zero mean, so that

$$m_n = m_{n-1} + g + \epsilon_n \qquad \text{(C.27)}$$

Since $E(\epsilon) = 0$, and both m_{n-1} and g are known when expectations are formed, the expected money supply is

$$m_n^e = E(m_n / I_{n-1}) = m_{n-1} + g \qquad \text{(C.28)}$$

and relationship C.27 can be written as

$$m_n = m_n^e + \epsilon_n \qquad \text{(C.29)}$$

By substituting relationship C.29 for m_n in relationship C.26, we obtain

$$p_n = (1 - \gamma) p_n^e + \gamma m_n^e - \gamma \mu + \gamma \epsilon_n \qquad \text{(C.30)}$$

from which we can compute the expected price level

$$p_n^e = E(p_n / I_{n-1}) = (1 - \gamma) p_n^e + \gamma m_n^e - \gamma \mu \qquad \text{(C.31)}$$

since $E(p_n^e) = p_n^e$, $E(m_n^e) = m_n^e$, μ is constant, and $E(\epsilon_n) = 0$.

After we rearrange the terms and simplify for γ, relationship C.31 can be written as

$$p_n^e = m_n^e - \mu \qquad \text{(C.32)}$$

In other words, the expected price level is equal to the difference between the expected money supply and the demand for money. By substituting relationship C.29 for m_n^e in relationship C.30, we have

$$p_n = m_n^e - \mu + \gamma \epsilon_n \qquad \text{(C.33)}$$

From there and relationship C.22, it follows that the expected value of excess demand is zero

$$d_n^e = m_n^e - p_n^e - \mu \Rightarrow d_n^e = m_n^e - (m_n^e - \mu) - \mu = 0 \qquad \text{(C.34)}$$

and since $d_n^e = 0$, the expected volume of output is equal to its normal value

$$y_n^e = \overline{y} + \beta d_n^e = \overline{y} \qquad \text{(C.35)}$$

Finally, excess demand and the volume of output can be formulated in terms of the unexpected change in the money supply. Substituting relationships C.29 and C.33 for, respectively, m_n and p_n in relationship C.22, we get

$$d_n = (1 - \gamma)\epsilon_n \tag{C.36}$$

and

$$y_n = \overline{y} + \beta(1 - \gamma)\epsilon_n \tag{C.37}$$

In other words, if this model expresses "the relevant theory," then

- Neither the expected price level p_n^e, nor the expected output level y_n^e depends on the parameter α or β.
- The expected money supply m_n^e has no impact on d_n and y_n: money is neutral.
- It only impacts the price level p_n and price expectations p_n^e.

C.4   Rational Expectations and Nonlinear Forms

As we have seen with the example borrowed from Malinvaud, a REH model implies at some point to compute the mathematical expectation of a variable that has a random component. In this case, the logarithm of money supply m_n was the sum of m_{n-1}, of a constant term g, and of a random term ϵ_n having zero mean, so that—according to the REH—the expected money supply was equal to its mathematical expectation:

$$m_n = m_{n-1} + g + \epsilon_n \Rightarrow m_n^e = m_{n-1} + g \tag{C.38}$$

In mathematical terms, this relationship says that the money supply is a linear function of a random variable. Therefore, it is itself a random variable of the general form:

$$f(X) = c_1 X + c_0 \tag{C.39}$$

with

$$X = \epsilon \quad c_1 = 1 \quad \text{and} \quad c_0 = m_{n-1} + g \tag{C.40}$$

We know that:[1]

$$f(X) = c_1 X + c_0 \Rightarrow E(f(X)) = c_1 E(X) + c_0 \tag{C.41}$$

In other words, the mathematical expectation of a linear function of a random variable is equal to the value taken by this function when its argument is equal to the mathematical expectation of this random variable.

$$E(f(X)) = f(E(X)) \tag{C.42}$$

This is mathematically convenient, for the mathematical expectation of such a random linear function has analytical tractability. Things are getting more complex with nonlinear functions of a random variable, for the mathematical expectation of such functions is not equal to the value they take for the mathematical expectation of the random variable. In general, by application of Taylor series expansion about the mathematical expectation $E(X)$ of a random variable X, a function of a random variable can be expressed as

$$f(X) = f(E(X)) + f^{(1)}(E(X))[X - E(X)]$$
$$+ \frac{f^{(2)}(E(X))}{2!}[X - E(X)]^2$$
$$+ \cdots + \frac{f^{(n)}(E(X))}{n!}[X - E(X)]^n + \cdots \tag{C.43}$$

where $Y = f(X)$ is assumed to be a nonlinear function of the random variable X. From there, since $E(X)$ is a constant, it follows that we have

$$E(f(X)) = E(f(E(X))) + f^{(1)}(E(X))E(X - E(X))$$
$$+ \frac{f^{(2)}(E(X))}{2!}E((X - E(X))^2)$$
$$+ \cdots + \frac{f^{(n)}(E(X))}{n!}E((X - E(X))^n) + \cdots \tag{C.44}$$

and

$$E(f(X)) = f(E(X))$$
$$+ \frac{f^{(2)}(E(X))}{2!}E((X - E(X))^2)$$
$$+ \cdots + \frac{f^{(n)}(E(X))}{n!}E((X - E(X))^n) + \cdots \tag{C.45}$$

that is,

$$E(f(X)) \approx f(E(X)) + \frac{f^{(2)}(E(X))}{2!}\{E(X^2) - [E(X)]^2\} \quad \text{(C.46)}$$

By comparing relationships C.42 and C.46, one can see that the mathematical expectation of a nonlinear function of a random variable is not equal to the value taken by this function when its argument is equal to the mathematical expectation of the random variable.

For example, for $f(X) = e^{\alpha X}$, we get

$$E(e^{\alpha X}) \approx e^{\alpha(E(X))} + \frac{\alpha^2 e^{\alpha E(X)}}{2}\{E(X^2) - [E(X)]^2\} \quad \text{(C.47)}$$

C.5 Recursive OLS Linear Regression

C.5.1 Definition of the Vectors and Matrix

Y_{n-1} $(n-1; 1)$ vector containing $n-1$ observations of the dependent variable

X_{n-1} $(n-1; m)$ matrix containing $n-1$ observations of the m independent variables (including the constant, if any)

β_{n-1} $(m; 1)$ vector containing m regression parameters

E_{n-1} $(n-1; 1)$ vector containing $n-1$ residuals (assumed to be normally distributed)

$$Y_{n-1} = \begin{pmatrix} y_1 \\ y_2 \\ \cdot \\ \cdot \\ \cdot \\ \cdot \\ \cdot \\ y_{n-1} \end{pmatrix} \qquad X_{n-1} = \begin{pmatrix} x_{11} & x_{21} & \cdots & x_{(m-1)1} & 1 \\ x_{12} & x_{22} & \cdots & x_{(m-1)2} & 1 \\ \cdot & \cdot & & \cdot & \cdot \\ \cdot & \cdot & & \cdot & \cdot \\ \cdot & \cdot & \cdots & \cdot & \cdot \\ \cdot & \cdot & & \cdot & \cdot \\ \cdot & \cdot & \cdots & \cdot & \cdot \\ x_{1(n-1)} & x_{2(n-1)} & \cdots & x_{(m-1)(n-1)} & 1 \end{pmatrix}$$

$$\text{(C.48)}$$

$$\beta_{n-1} = \begin{pmatrix} c_{1(n-1)} \\ c_{2(n-1)} \\ \cdot \\ \cdot \\ \cdot \\ \cdot \\ \cdot \\ c_{m(n-1)} \end{pmatrix} \qquad E_{n-1} = \begin{pmatrix} \epsilon_{1(n-1)} \\ \epsilon_{2(n-1)} \\ \cdot \\ \cdot \\ \cdot \\ \cdot \\ \cdot \\ \epsilon_{m(n-1)} \end{pmatrix} \qquad (C.49)$$

C.5.2   Linear Regression

With these notations, the linear regression model is

$$\Upsilon_{n-1} = X_{n-1}\beta_{n-1} + E_{n-1} \qquad (C.50)$$

and the problem is to find the vector β_{n-1} that minimizes the sum of the squared residuals

$$S_{n-1} = E_{n-1}^T E_{n-1} = \sum_{i=1}^{n-1} \epsilon_i^2 \qquad (C.51)$$

with

$$E_{n-1} = \Upsilon_{n-1} - X_{n-1}\beta_{n-1} \qquad (C.52)$$

From relationship C.52, we get

$$E_{n-1}^T = (\Upsilon_{n-1} - X_{n-1}\beta_{n-1})^T = \Upsilon_{n-1}^T - \beta_{n-1}^T X_{n-1}^T \qquad (C.53)$$

and therefore

$$S_{n-1} = E_{n-1}^T E_{n-1} = (\Upsilon_{n-1}^T - \beta_{n-1}^T X_{n-1}^T)(\Upsilon_{n-1} - X_{n-1}\beta_{n-1}) \quad (C.54)$$

$$S_{n-1} = \Upsilon_{n-1}^T \Upsilon_{n-1} - \Upsilon_{n-1}^T X_{n-1}\beta_{n-1}$$
$$- \beta_{n-1}^T X_{n-1}^T \Upsilon_{n-1} + \beta_{n-1}^T X_{n-1}^T X_{n-1}\beta_{n-1} \qquad (C.55)$$

Given that $\Upsilon_{n-1}^T X_{n-1}\beta_{n-1} = (\beta_{n-1}^T X_{n-1}^T \Upsilon_{n-1})^T$ and $\beta_{n-1}^T X_{n-1}^T \Upsilon_{n-1}$ is a scalar, it follows that

$$\Upsilon_{n-1}^T X_{n-1}\beta_{n-1} = \beta_{n-1}^T X_{n-1}^T \Upsilon_{n-1} \qquad (C.56)$$

and

$$S_{n-1} = \Upsilon_{n-1}^T \Upsilon_{n-1} - 2\beta_{n-1}^T X_{n-1}^T \Upsilon_{n-1} + \beta_{n-1}^T X_{n-1}^T X_{n-1}\beta_{n-1} \quad \text{(C.57)}$$

and S_{n-1} is minimized when its derivative with respect to β_{n-1} is equal to zero.

The derivative of the first term is

$$\frac{\partial \Upsilon_{n-1}^T \Upsilon_{n-1}}{\partial \beta_{n-1}} = 0 \quad \text{(C.58)}$$

The derivative of the second term is

$$\frac{\partial \beta_{n-1}^T X_{n-1}^T \Upsilon_{n-1}}{\partial \beta_{n-1}} = \frac{\partial \beta_{n-1}^T (X_{n-1}^T \Upsilon_{n-1})}{\partial \beta_{n-1}} = X_{n-1}^T \Upsilon_{n-1} \quad \text{(C.59)}$$

The derivative of the third term is

$$\frac{\partial \beta_{n-1}^T X_{n-1}^T X_{n-1}\beta_{n-1}}{\partial \beta_{n-1}} = \frac{\partial \beta_{n-1}^T (X_{n-1}^T X_{n-1})\beta_{n-1}}{\partial \beta_{n-1}}$$

$$= [X_{n-1}^T X_{n-1} + (X_{n-1}^T X_{n-1})^T]\beta_{n-1}$$

$$\text{(C.60)}$$

which is equivalent to

$$\frac{\partial \beta_{n-1}^T X_{n-1}^T X_{n-1}\beta_{n-1}}{\partial \beta_{n-1}} = 2X_{n-1}^T X_{n-1}\beta_{n-1} \quad \text{(C.61)}$$

Hence

$$\frac{\partial S_{n-1}}{\partial \beta_{n-1}} = 0 \Leftrightarrow -2X_{n-1}^T \Upsilon_{n-1} + 2X_{n-1}^T X_{n-1}\beta_{n-1} = 0$$

$$\Leftrightarrow X_{n-1}^T X_{n-1}\beta_{n-1} = X_{n-1}^T \Upsilon_{n-1}$$

$$\Leftrightarrow \beta_{n-1} = (X_{n-1}^T X_{n-1})^{-1} X_{n-1}^T \Upsilon_{n-1} \quad \text{(C.62)}$$

Hence, the well-known solution of the linear regression problem is

$$\beta_{n-1} = (X_{n-1}^T X_{n-1})^{-1} X_{n-1}^T \Upsilon_{n-1} \quad \text{(C.63)}$$

C.5.3   Recursive Linear Regression

From relationship C.63, we have

$$\beta_n = (X_n^T X_n)^{-1} X_n^T Y_n \tag{C.64}$$

Our aim is to establish a relationship between β_n and β_{n-1}. As

$$X_n^T X_n = X_{n-1}^T X_{n-1} + x_n^T x_n \tag{C.65}$$

and

$$X_n^T Y_n = X_{n-1}^T Y_{n-1} + x_n^T y_n \tag{C.66}$$

with

$$x_n = \begin{pmatrix} x_{1n}, & x_{2n}, & \ldots & x_{(m-1)n} & 1 \end{pmatrix} \tag{C.67}$$

we can write relationship C.64 as

$$\beta_n = (X_{n-1}^T X_{n-1} + x_n^T x_n)^{-1} (X_{n-1}^T Y_{n-1} + x_n^T y_n) \tag{C.68}$$

According to the matrix inversion lemma

$$(X_{n-1}^T X_{n-1} + x_n^T x_n)^{-1} = (X_{n-1}^T X_{n-1})^{-1}$$
$$- \frac{(X_{n-1}^T X_{n-1})^{-1} x_n^T x_n (X_{n-1}^T X_{n-1})^{-1}}{1 + x_n (X_{n-1}^T X_{n-1})^{-1} x_n^T} \tag{C.69}$$

Hence we can write relationship C.68 as follows:

$$\beta_n = \left[(X_{n-1}^T X_{n-1})^{-1} - \frac{(X_{n-1}^T X_{n-1})^{-1} x_n^T x_n (X_{n-1}^T X_{n-1})^{-1}}{1 + x_n (X_{n-1}^T X_{n-1})^{-1} x_n^T} \right]$$
$$\times (X_{n-1}^T Y_{n-1} + x_n^T y_n) \tag{C.70}$$

From there, we get

$$\beta_n = (X_{n-1}^T X_{n-1})^{-1} X_{n-1}^T Y_{n-1} + (X_{n-1}^T X_{n-1})^{-1} x_n^T y_n$$
$$- \frac{(X_{n-1}^T X_{n-1})^{-1} x_n^T x_n (X_{n-1}^T X_{n-1})^{-1} X_{n-1}^T Y_{n-1}}{1 + x_n (X_{n-1}^T X_{n-1})^{-1} x_n^T}$$
$$- \frac{(X_{n-1}^T X_{n-1})^{-1} x_n^T x_n (X_{n-1}^T X_{n-1})^{-1} x_n^T y_n}{1 + x_n (X_{n-1}^T X_{n-1})^{-1} x_n^T} \tag{C.71}$$

$$\beta_n = \beta_{n-1} + (X_{n-1}^T X_{n-1})^{-1} x_n^T y_n$$

$$- \frac{(X_{n-1}^T X_{n-1})^{-1} x_n^T x_n (X_{n-1}^T X_{n-1})^{-1} X_{n-1}^T \Upsilon_{n-1}}{1 + x_n (X_{n-1}^T X_{n-1})^{-1} x_n^T}$$

$$- \frac{(X_{n-1}^T X_{n-1})^{-1} x_n^T x_n (X_{n-1}^T X_{n-1})^{-1} x_n^T y_n}{1 + x_n (X_{n-1}^T X_{n-1})^{-1} x_n^T} \qquad (C.72)$$

By factoring the terms $(X_{n-1}^T X_{n-1})^{-1} x_n^T$, $1 + x_n (X_{n-1}^T X_{n-1})^{-1} x_n^T$, and y_n in three right-hand terms of this relationship and with

$$K_n = \frac{(X_{n-1}^T X_{n-1})^{-1} x_n^T}{1 + x_n (X_{n-1}^T X_{n-1})^{-1} x_n^T} \qquad (C.73)$$

we get

$$\beta_n = \beta_{n-1} + K_n [y_n + y_n x_n (X_{n-1}^T X_{n-1})^{-1} x_n^T$$

$$- x_n (X_{n-1}^T X_{n-1})^{-1} X_{n-1}^T \Upsilon_{n-1} - x_n (X_{n-1}^T X_{n-1})^{-1} x_n^T y_n]$$

$$= \beta_{n-1} + K_n \{ y_n - x_n \beta_{n-1} + y_n [x_n (X_{n-1}^T X_{n-1})^{-1} x_n^T$$

$$- x_n (X_{n-1}^T X_{n-1})^{-1} x_n^T] \} \qquad (C.74)$$

Hence, we finally get

$$\beta_n = \beta_{n-1} + K_n (y_n - x_n \beta_{n-1}) \qquad (C.75)$$

with

$$K_n = \frac{(X_{n-1}^T X_{n-1})^{-1} x_n^T}{1 + x_n (X_{n-1}^T X_{n-1})^{-1} x_n^T} \qquad (C.76)$$

C.6   Linear Regression with Forgetting

To prove that the coefficients of a linear regression with forgetting depend on the exponential averages, variance, and covariance of the variables of interest, we will consider the simple case of a univariate regression between a dependent variable Υ and an independent variable X. In this case, the problem is to find the coefficients c_1 and c_0 minimizing the sum of the squared residuals

$$\sum_{i=1}^{n} \epsilon_i^2 = \sum_{i=1}^{n} (y_i - c_1 x_i - c_0)^2 \qquad (C.77)$$

The well-known solution of this problem is

$$c_1 = \frac{\text{cov}(X, Y)}{\text{var}(X)} \tag{C.78}$$

$$c_0 = E(Y) - c_1 E(X) \tag{C.79}$$

Let us now consider the case of a univariate linear regression with a forgetting coefficient k such that $0 < k < 1$. The problem is now to minimize the exponentially weighted sum of the squared residuals

$$L_k(c_1, c_0) = \sum_{i=0}^{n} (1-k)^i \epsilon_{n-i}^2 = \sum_{i=0}^{n} (1-k)^i (y_{n-i} - c_1 x_{n-i} - c_0)^2 \tag{C.80}$$

which is equivalent to solving the following system of two equations for c_1 and c_0:

$$\frac{\partial L_k(c_1, c_0)}{\partial c_1} = 0 \quad \Leftrightarrow \quad c_1 \sum_{i=0}^{n} (1-k)^i x_{n-i}^2 + c_0 \sum_{i=0}^{n} (1-k)^i x_{n-i}$$

$$= \sum_{i=0}^{n} (1-k)^i x_{n-i} y_{n-i} \tag{C.81a}$$

$$\frac{\partial L_k(c_1, c_0)}{\partial c_0} = 0 \quad \Leftrightarrow \quad c_1 \sum_{i=0}^{n} (1-k)^i x_{n-i} + c_0 \sum_{i=0}^{n} (1-k)^i$$

$$= \sum_{i=0}^{n} (1-k)^i y_{n-i} \tag{C.81b}$$

Since

$$\lim_{n \to +\infty} \sum_{i=0}^{n} (1-k)^i = \lim_{n \to +\infty} \frac{1 - (1-k)^{n+1}}{1 - (1-k)} = \frac{1}{k} \tag{C.82}$$

from relationship C.81b, we get

$$c_1 \sum_{i=0}^{n} (1-k)^i x_{n-i} + \frac{c_0}{k} = \sum_{i=0}^{n} (1-k)^i y_{n-i}$$

$$\Leftrightarrow \quad c_0 = k \sum_{i=0}^{n} (1-k)^i y_{n-i} - c_1 k \sum_{i=0}^{n} (1-k)^i x_{n-i}$$

$$\Leftrightarrow \quad c_0 = E_k(Y) - c_1 E_k(X) \tag{C.83}$$

where, according to relationship 1.4, $E_k(Y)$ and $E_k(X)$ are the exponential averages of Y and X.

Multiplying relationship C.81b by k and substituting

$$k \sum_{i=0}^{n} (1-k)^i y_{n-i} - c_1 k \sum_{i=0}^{n} (1-k)^i x_{n-i} \tag{C.84}$$

for c_0, we get

$$c_1 k \sum_{i=0}^{n} (1-k)^i x_{n-i}^2 + c_0 k \sum_{i=0}^{n} (1-k)^i x_{n-i} = k \sum_{i=0}^{n} (1-k)^i x_{n-i} y_{n-i}$$

$$\Leftrightarrow \cdots + \left[k \sum_{i=0}^{n} (1-k)^i y_{n-i} - c_1 k \sum_{i=0}^{n} (1-k)^i x_{n-i} \right] k \sum_{i=0}^{n} (1-k)^i x_{n-i} = \cdots$$

$$\Leftrightarrow c_1 \left\{ k \sum_{i=0}^{n} (1-k)^i x_{n-i}^2 - \left[k \sum_{i=0}^{n} (1-k)^i x_{n-i} \right]^2 \right\}$$

$$= \cdots - \left[k \sum_{i=0}^{n} (1-k)^i x_{n-i} \right] \times \left(k \sum_{i=0}^{n} (1-k)^i y_{n-i} \right)$$

$$\Leftrightarrow c_1 = \frac{k \sum_{i=0}^{n} (1-k)^i x_{n-i} y_{n-i} - [k \sum_{i=0}^{n} (1-k)^i x_{n-i}][k \sum_{i=0}^{n} (1-k)^i y_{n-i}]}{k \sum_{i=0}^{n} (1-k)^i x_{n-i}^2 - [k \sum_{i=0}^{n} (1-k)^i x_{n-i}]^2}$$

$$\Leftrightarrow c_1 = \frac{E_k(XY) - E_k(X) E_k(Y)}{E_k(X^2) - [E_k(X)]^2} = \frac{\mathrm{cov}_k(X_n, Y_n)}{\mathrm{var}_k(X_n)} \tag{C.85}$$

We see that all we have done by introducing forgetting in linear regression is to substitute exponential averages, variance, and covariance, that is, adaptive expectations, for arithmetic averages, variance, and covariance in the formulation of the coefficients c_0 and c_1. This analysis can easily be extended to a multivariate regression. Of course, another alternative is to apply forgetting not to the residuals but to the variables themselves, which leads to formulate the loss function as

$$L_k(c_1, c_0) = \sum_{i=0}^{n} [(\sqrt{1-k})^i y_{n-i} - (\sqrt{1-k})^i c_1 x_{n-i} - (\sqrt{1-k})^i c_0]^2$$

$$\tag{C.86}$$

This would leave our conclusion unchanged: the coefficients found by recursive OLS linear regression with forgetting are functions of exponentially smoothed quantities, that is, adaptive expectations.

C.7   Discrete Formulation of Z

In discrete time, the time scale is divided into elementary periods of equal duration p, so that we have

$$d\tau = du = p \qquad (C.87)$$

By convention, let us define this elementary period as being the time unit

$$p = 1 \qquad (C.88)$$

By application of the mean-value theorem between two consecutive points i and $i - 1$, we have:[2]

$$\int_{i-1}^{i} x(\tau)\, d\tau = x(\zeta)(i - i + 1) = \overline{x_i} \qquad \text{with} \qquad x_{i-1} \neq \overline{x_i} \neq x_i$$
$$(C.89)$$

and

$$\overline{x_i} = \frac{\ln D_i - \ln D_{i-1}}{p} = \ln \frac{D_i}{D_{i-1}} \qquad (C.90)$$

where $\overline{x_i}$ is the average rate of growth prevailing between $i - 1$ and i.

Similarly, between two consecutive points $j - 1$ and j, we can write

$$\int_{j-1}^{j} \chi(u)\, du = \chi(\xi)(j - j + 1) = \overline{\chi_j} \qquad \text{with} \qquad \chi_{j-1} \neq \overline{\chi_j} \neq \chi_j$$
$$(C.91)$$

where $\overline{\chi_j}$ is the average rate of memory decay prevailing between $j - 1$ and j.

The decay factor between two consecutive points $j - 1$ and j is defined by the following relationship:

$$e^{-\int_{j-1}^{j} \chi(u)\, du} = e^{-\overline{\chi_j}} \qquad (C.92)$$

The last point on the discrete time scale is defined by

$$t = n \qquad (C.93)$$

The decay factor applied to the last observed growth rate $\overline{x_n}$ is

$$e^{-\int_{n}^{n} \chi(u)\, du} = e^0 = 1 \qquad (C.94)$$

Hence, we can write

$$Z_n = \overline{x_n} + \sum_{i=-\infty}^{n-1} \overline{x_i} e^{-\sum_{j=i+1}^{n} \overline{\chi_j}} = \overline{x_n} + \overline{x_{n-1}} e^{-\overline{\chi_n}} + \overline{x_{n-2}} e^{-(\overline{\chi_n} + \overline{\chi_{n-1}})} + \cdots$$

$$(C.95)$$

Since the elementary period is assumed to be small, we have

$$\overline{\chi_j} \approx 0 \Rightarrow e^{-\overline{\chi_j}} \approx \frac{1}{1 + \overline{\chi_j}} \qquad (C.96)$$

and

$$Z_n = \overline{x_n} + \frac{\overline{x_{n-1}}}{1 + \overline{\chi_n}} + \frac{\overline{x_{n-2}}}{(1 + \overline{\chi_n})(1 + \overline{\chi_{n-1}})} + \cdots \qquad (C.97)$$

In this formula, Z clearly appears as the present value of a series of observations discounted by a series of time-varying rates of memory decay.

This discrete formulation is also helpful to establish an equivalence with the differential expression of Z.

From relationship C.97, we have

$$Z_{n-1} = \overline{x_{n-1}} + \frac{\overline{x_{n-2}}}{1 + \overline{\chi_{n-1}}} + \frac{\overline{x_{n-3}}}{(1 + \overline{\chi_{n-1}})(1 + \overline{\chi_{n-2}})} + \cdots \qquad (C.98)$$

Therefore

$$Z_n = \overline{x_n} + \frac{Z_{n-1}}{1 + \overline{\chi_n}} \qquad (C.99)$$

Since $\overline{\chi_j} \approx 0$, we have

$$\frac{1}{1 + \overline{\chi_j}} = 1 - \overline{\chi_j} \qquad (C.100)$$

and

$$Z_n = \overline{x_n} + (1 - \overline{\chi_n})Z_{n-1} \Leftrightarrow Z_n - Z_{n-1} = \overline{x_n} - \overline{\chi_n} Z_{n-1} \qquad (C.101)$$

and

$$\frac{dZ}{dt} = x(t) - \chi(t)Z(t) \qquad (C.102)$$

C.8   Formulation of $\Psi(Z)$ by Integration of its Derivative

Relationship

$$\frac{1}{\Psi}\frac{d\Psi}{dt} = -\alpha\left(1 - \frac{\Psi}{1+b}\right)\frac{dZ}{dt} \qquad (C.103)$$

is equivalent to

$$\frac{d\Psi}{dZ} = -\alpha\left(1 - \frac{\Psi}{1+b}\right)\Psi \qquad (C.104)$$

Since the first derivative of $f(x) = e^{\alpha x}$ is $f'(x) = \alpha e^{\alpha x}$, the ratio $f'(x)/f(x)$ is constant and equal to α. More generally, for the ratio $f'(x)/f(x)$ to be equal to a constant, $f(x)$ must have an exponential form. For example, if $f(x) = k/e^{\alpha x}$

$$f'(x) = \frac{-\alpha k e^{\alpha x}}{(e^{\alpha x})^2} = -\alpha f(x) \qquad (C.105)$$

and with $y = f(x)$

$$\frac{dy}{dx} = -\alpha y \qquad (C.106)$$

Let us then assume that $\Psi(Z)$ has the following form

$$\Psi(Z) = \frac{k}{p + qe^{\alpha Z}} \qquad (C.107)$$

and let us observe that the first derivative of Ψ can be expressed as a function of Ψ

$$\frac{d\Psi}{dZ} = \frac{-\alpha k q e^{\alpha Z}}{(p + qe^{\alpha Z})^2} = -\alpha\frac{qe^{\alpha Z}}{p + qe^{\alpha Z}}\frac{k}{p + qe^{\alpha Z}} = -\alpha\frac{qe^{\alpha Z}}{p + qe^{\alpha Z}}\Psi(Z) \qquad (C.108)$$

The term $qe^{\alpha Z}$ can also be written as a function of Ψ

$$\Psi(Z) = \frac{k}{p + qe^{\alpha Z}} \Leftrightarrow p + qe^{\alpha Z} = \frac{k}{\Psi(Z)} \Leftrightarrow qe^{\alpha Z} = \frac{k}{\Psi(Z)} - p \qquad (C.109)$$

Hence, we can write

$$\frac{qe^{\alpha Z}}{p + qe^{\alpha Z}} = \frac{\frac{k}{\Psi(Z)} - p}{\frac{k}{\Psi(Z)}} = 1 - \frac{p\Psi(Z)}{k} \qquad (C.110)$$

and substitute for this term in C.108, which gives

$$\frac{d\Psi}{dZ} = -\alpha \left[1 - \frac{p\Psi(Z)}{k} \right] \Psi(Z) \qquad (C.111)$$

For relationship C.111 to be equivalent to C.104, we need to have

$$1 - \frac{p\Psi(Z)}{k} = 1 - \frac{\Psi(Z)}{1+b} \Rightarrow p = 1 \qquad \text{and} \qquad k = 1 + b \quad (C.112)$$

with $p = 1$ and $k = 1 + b$, C.107 becomes

$$\Psi(Z) = \frac{1+b}{1+qe^{\alpha Z}} \qquad (C.113)$$

By definition of Ψ, we know that we must have $\Psi(0) = 1$:

$$\Psi(0) = \frac{1+b}{1+q} = 1 \Rightarrow q = b \qquad (C.114)$$

Finally, we get

$$\Psi(Z) = \frac{1+b}{1+be^{\alpha Z}} \qquad (C.115)$$

C.9   Differential Expression of Z

The differential expression $\frac{dZ}{dt}$ of $Z(t) = \int_{-\infty}^{t} x(\tau) e^{-\int_{\tau}^{t} x(u) du} d\tau$ is obtained by applying Leibniz's rule of differentiation under the integral sign.

Let

$$F(y) = \int_{a(y)}^{b(y)} f(x, y) \, dx \qquad (C.116)$$

Then, according to Leibniz's rule,

$$\frac{dF}{dy} = \frac{\partial}{\partial y} \int_{a(y)}^{b(y)} f(x, y) \, dx$$

$$= \int_{a(y)}^{b(y)} \frac{\partial f}{\partial y} \, dx + f(b(y), y) \frac{db}{dy} - f(a(y), y) \frac{da}{dy} \qquad (C.117)$$

Now, $Z(t)$ can be written

$$Z(t) = \int_{-\infty}^{t} x(\tau)e^{-\int_{\tau}^{t} \chi(u)du}d\tau = \int_{-\infty}^{t} f(\tau,t)d\tau = \int_{a(t)}^{b(t)} f(\tau,t)\,d\tau$$

(C.118)

with

$$f(\tau,t) = x(\tau)e^{-\int_{\tau}^{t} \chi(u)du}$$

(C.119)

Hence,

$$\frac{dZ}{dt} = \int_{a(t)}^{b(t)} \frac{\partial f}{\partial t}d\tau + \frac{db}{dt}\Big[f[b(t),t]\Big] - \frac{da}{dt}\Big[f[a(t),t]\Big]$$

(C.120)

with

$$a(t) = -\infty \Rightarrow \frac{da}{dt} = 0$$

(C.121)

$$b(t) = t \Rightarrow \frac{db}{dt} = 1$$

(C.122)

$$\frac{\partial f}{\partial t} = -\chi(t)x(\tau)e^{-\int_{\tau}^{t} \chi(u)du}$$

(C.123)

and

$$f[b(t),t] = f(t,t) = x(t)e^{-\int_{t}^{t} \chi(u)du} = x(t)e^{0} = x(t)$$

(C.124)

Substituting C.121, C.122, C.123, and C.124 in C.120, we obtain

$$\frac{dZ}{dt} = -\chi(t)\int_{-\infty}^{t} x(\tau)e^{-\int_{\tau}^{t} \chi(u)du}d\tau + 1x(t) = x(t) - \chi(t)Z(t)$$

(C.125)

$$\frac{dZ}{dt} = x(t) - \chi(t)Z(t)$$

(C.126)

C.10   Dynamic Equilibrium and Definition of *z*

From 4.33 and proof C.9, we have

$$\frac{dZ}{dt} = x - \chi Z$$

(C.127)

In a dynamic equilibrium process, Z is by definition constant. For Z to be constant, one must have $\frac{dZ}{dt} = 0$, which implies $x = \chi Z$.

$$\frac{dZ}{dt} = 0 \Rightarrow x = \chi Z \tag{C.128}$$

In a dynamic equilibrium process, the product χZ plays a role equivalent to that of Cagan's expectation coefficient (or expected inflation) E in the relationship $dE/dt = \beta\,(C - E)$ (see table 4.2, p. 80). Its first derivative is indeed

$$\frac{d(\chi Z)}{dt} = \chi \frac{dZ}{dt} + Z \frac{d\chi}{dt} = \chi(x - \chi Z) + Z \frac{d\chi}{dt} \tag{C.129}$$

In a dynamic equilibrium process, since we have

$$\frac{dZ}{dt} = 0 \Rightarrow \frac{d\chi}{dt} = 0 \tag{C.130}$$

it follows that

$$\frac{d(\chi Z)}{dt} = \chi(x - \chi Z) \tag{C.131}$$

Let us define z as

$$z = \chi Z \tag{C.132}$$

Then

$$\frac{dz}{dt} = \chi(x - z) \tag{C.133}$$

where z is the dynamic equilibrium rate. If $x = z$, $dz/dt = 0$ and z remains constant. If $x \neq z$, according to C.129

$$\frac{dz}{dt} = \chi(x - z) + z \frac{dx}{dt}$$

C.11 Discretization and Computation of Z

To compute Z_n, one would need to know $\Psi(Z_n)$. However, as Z_n is not known yet, $\Psi(Z_n)$ is not known either. Since we know the form of the derivative of $\Psi(Z_n)$, using limited development, we can nevertheless estimate $\Psi^*(Z_n)$ as a function of $\Psi^*(Z_{n-1})$ and Z_{n-1}. By doing so, we shall take into consideration the variation of Ψ on the interval $[t_{n-1}, t_n]$ of duration p.

From 4.33 and proof C.9, we have

$$\frac{dZ}{dt} = x - \frac{\chi_0 Z}{\Psi^*(Z)} \Leftrightarrow \frac{dZ}{dt} + \frac{\chi_0 Z}{\Psi^*(Z)} = x \qquad \text{(C.134)}$$

By applying a first-order limited development

$$f(x) \approx f(x_0) + (x - x_0) f'(x_0) \qquad \text{(C.135)}$$

to $\Psi^*(Z_n)$, we get

$$\Psi^*(Z_n) \approx \Psi^*(Z_{n-1}) + (Z_n - Z_{n-1}) \frac{d\Psi^*}{dZ}(Z_{n-1}) \qquad \text{(C.136)}$$

From 4.31, we have

$$\frac{d\Psi^*}{dZ}(Z_{n-1}) = -\alpha \left[1 - \frac{\Psi^*(Z_{n-1})}{1 + b} \right] \Psi^*(Z_{n-1}) \qquad \text{(C.137)}$$

By substituting C.137 in C.136, we obtain

$$\Psi^*(Z_n) = \Psi^*(Z_{n-1}) - \alpha(Z_n - Z_{n-1})\Psi^*(Z_{n-1}) \left[1 - \frac{\Psi^*(Z_{n-1})}{1 + b} \right] \qquad \text{(C.138)}$$

Let us write $y(t) = Z(t) - Z(n - 1)$ as in C.139 from which we get

$$y(t) = Z(t) - Z_{n-1} \Leftrightarrow Z(t) = y(t) + Z_{n-1} \Rightarrow \frac{dy}{dt} = \frac{dZ}{dt} \qquad \text{(C.139)}$$

since Z_{n-1} is constant on $[t_{n-1}, t_n]$. Also

$$\Psi^*(Z_{n-1}) = \Psi^*_{n-1} \qquad \text{(C.140)}$$

With these notations, from C.136, we get

$$\Psi^*(Z_n) = \Psi^*_{n-1} + y \frac{d\Psi^*}{dZ}(Z_{n-1}) \qquad \text{(C.141)}$$

Substituting C.139, C.140, and C.141 in C.134, we get

$$\frac{dy}{dt} + \frac{\chi_0}{\Psi^*_{n-1} + y \frac{d\Psi^*}{dZ}(Z_{n-1})}(y + Z_{n-1}) = x_n \qquad \text{(C.142)}$$

Now, once again, using a first-order limited development *and ne-glecting second-order terms* (like terms in y^2 since $y \simeq 0$), we can write

$$\frac{\chi_0}{\Psi^*_{n-1} + y \frac{d\Psi^*}{dZ}(Z_{n-1})} \approx \frac{\chi_0}{\Psi^*_{n-1}} \left[1 - y \frac{1}{\Psi^*_{n-1}} \frac{d\Psi^*}{dZ}(Z_{n-1}) \right] \quad \text{(C.143)}$$

To demonstrate C.143, we have

$$f(y) = \frac{\chi_0}{\Psi^*_{n-1} + y \frac{d\Psi^*}{dZ}(Z_{n-1})} \quad \text{(C.144)}$$

which implies

$$f(0) = \frac{\chi_0}{\Psi^*_{n-1}} \quad \text{(C.145)}$$

Further, we have

$$f(y) = \frac{\chi_0}{u(y)} \quad \text{(C.146)}$$

which implies

$$f'(y) = \frac{-\chi_0 u'(y)}{u^2(y)} \quad \text{(C.147)}$$

with

$$u(y) = \Psi^*_{n-1} + y \frac{d\Psi^*}{dZ}(Z_{n-1}) \quad \text{(C.148a)}$$

$$u'(y) = \frac{d\Psi^*}{dZ}(Z_{n-1}) \quad \text{(C.148b)}$$

and

$$u^2(y) = \left[\Psi^*_{n-1} + y \frac{d\Psi^*}{dZ}(Z_{n-1}) \right]^2 \quad \text{(C.149)}$$

Then relationship C.147 can be written as

$$f'(y) = \frac{-\chi_0 \frac{d\Psi^*}{dZ}(Z_{n-1})}{\left[\Psi^*_{n-1} + y \frac{d\Psi^*}{dZ}(Z_{n-1}) \right]^2} \quad \text{(C.150)}$$

or, more simply,

$$f'(0) = \frac{-\chi_0 \frac{d\Psi^*}{dZ}(Z_{n-1})}{(\Psi^*_{n-1})^2} \quad \text{(C.151)}$$

Using C.145 and C.151 to express C.144 as a first-order limited development, we get

$$f(y) = f(0) + yf'(0) = \frac{\chi_0}{\Psi_{n-1}^*} + y \left[\frac{-\chi_0 \frac{d\Psi^*}{dZ}(Z_{n-1})}{(\Psi_{n-1}^*)^2} \right] \quad \text{(C.152a)}$$

$$= \frac{\chi_0}{\Psi_{n-1}^*} \left[1 - y \frac{1}{\Psi_{n-1}^*} \frac{d\Psi^*}{dZ}(Z_{n-1}) \right] \quad \text{(C.152b)}$$

where Z_{n-1} is a given constant.

Substituting relationship C.152b in relationship C.142, we obtain

$$\frac{dy}{dt} + \frac{\chi_0}{\Psi_{n-1}^*} \left[1 - y \frac{1}{\Psi_{n-1}^*} \frac{d\Psi^*}{dZ}(Z_{n-1}) \right] (y + Z_{n-1}) = x_n \quad \text{(C.153)}$$

where all the terms in y are now on the same line. From relationship 4.31, we have

$$\frac{d\Psi^*}{dZ}(Z_{n-1}) = -\alpha \left[1 - \frac{\Psi^*(Z_{n-1})}{1+b} \right] \Psi^*(Z_{n-1})$$

$$\text{with} \qquad \Psi_{n-1}^* = \Psi^*(Z_{n-1}) \quad \text{(C.154)}$$

Hence, the term $1 - y \frac{1}{\Psi_{n-1}^*} \frac{d\Psi^*}{dZ}(Z_{n-1})$ in relationship C.153 can be written as

$$1 - y\frac{1}{\Psi_{n-1}^*} \frac{d\Psi^*}{dZ}(Z_{n-1}) = 1 - y\frac{1}{\Psi_{n-1}^*} \left\{ -\alpha \left[1 - \frac{\Psi^*(Z_{n-1})}{1+b} \right] \Psi^*(Z_{n-1}) \right\}$$

$$= 1 + \alpha y \left[1 - \frac{\Psi^*(Z_{n-1})}{1+b} \right] \quad \text{(C.155)}$$

which allows relationship C.153 to become successively

$$\frac{dy}{dt} + \frac{\chi_0}{\Psi_{n-1}^*} \left[1 + \alpha y \left(1 - \frac{\Psi_{n-1}^*}{1+b} \right) \right] (y + Z_{n-1}) = x_n \quad \text{(C.156)}$$

$$\frac{dy}{dt} + \frac{\chi_0}{\Psi_{n-1}^*} \left[(y + Z_{n-1}) + \alpha(y + Z_{n-1})y \left(1 - \frac{\Psi_{n-1}^*}{1+b} \right) \right] = x_n$$

$$\text{(C.157)}$$

$$\frac{dy}{dt} + \frac{\chi_0}{\Psi^*_{n-1}}\left[y + Z_{n-1} + \alpha y^2\left(1 - \frac{\Psi^*_{n-1}}{1+b}\right) + \alpha y Z_{n-1}\left(1 - \frac{\Psi^*_{n-1}}{1+b}\right)\right]$$
$$= x_n \tag{C.158}$$

and since y^2 terms can be neglected, successively again,

$$\frac{dy}{dt} + \frac{\chi_0}{\Psi^*_{n-1}}\left[y + Z_{n-1} + \alpha y Z_{n-1}\left(1 - \frac{\Psi^*_{n-1}}{1+b}\right)\right] = x_n \tag{C.159}$$

$$\frac{dy}{dt} + \frac{\chi_0}{\Psi^*_{n-1}}\left\{y\left[1 + \alpha Z_{n-1}\left(1 - \frac{\Psi^*_{n-1}}{1+b}\right)\right] + Z_{n-1}\right\} = x_n \tag{C.160}$$

$$\frac{dy}{dt} + y\left\{\frac{\chi_0}{\Psi^*_{n-1}}\left[1 + \alpha Z_{n-1}\left(1 - \frac{\Psi^*_{n-1}}{1+b}\right)\right]\right\} + \frac{\chi_0}{\Psi^*_{n-1}}Z_{n-1} = x_n \tag{C.161}$$

$$\frac{dy}{dt} + y\left\{\frac{\chi_0}{\Psi^*_{n-1}}\left[1 + \alpha Z_{n-1}\left(1 - \frac{\Psi^*_{n-1}}{1+b}\right)\right]\right\} = x_n - \frac{\chi_0}{\Psi^*_{n-1}}Z_{n-1} \tag{C.162}$$

which is a first-order linear equation in y, the solution of which is well known.

Let us have

$$k_n = \frac{\chi_0}{\Psi^*_{n-1}}\left[1 + \alpha Z_{n-1}\left(1 - \frac{\Psi^*_{n-1}}{1+b}\right)\right] \tag{C.163}$$

$$k'_n = \overline{x_n} - \frac{\chi_0}{\Psi^*_{n-1}}Z_{n-1} \tag{C.164}$$

which are both constant on the integration interval, with

$$\overline{x_n} = \frac{1}{p}\ln\frac{D_n}{D_{n-1}} \tag{C.165}$$

Then relationship C.162 can be written as

$$\frac{dy}{dt} + k_n y = k'_n \quad \text{with} \quad y(t) = Z(t) - Z_{n-1} \tag{C.166}$$

By having

$$v'(t) = \frac{dy}{dt} \qquad v(t) = y \qquad a(t) = -k_n \qquad b(t) = k'_n \qquad (C.167)$$

$$t_0 = t_{n-1} \qquad t = t_n \qquad t_n - t_{n-1} = p \qquad (C.168)$$

the general solution of relationship C.166 is

$$v(t) = \left(x_0 + \frac{b}{a} \right) e^{a(t - t_0)} - \frac{b}{a} \qquad (C.169)$$

or, in this specific case,

$$y(t) = \left[y(0) - \frac{k'_n}{k_n} \right] e^{-pk_n} + \frac{k'_n}{k_n} \qquad (C.170)$$

with

$$y(t) = Z(t) - Z_{n-1} \qquad \text{and} \qquad y(0) = 0 \qquad (C.171)$$

$$Z(t) - Z_{n-1} = -\frac{k'_n}{k_n} e^{-pk_n} + \frac{k'_n}{k_n} \qquad (C.172)$$

from which, for $t = n$, we get

$$Z_n = Z_{n-1} + \frac{k'_n}{k_n}(1 - e^{-pk_n}) \qquad (C.173)$$

$$x_n = \frac{1}{p} \ln \frac{D_n}{D_{n-1}} = \frac{\ln D_n - \ln D_{n-1}}{p} \qquad (C.174)$$

$$k'_n = \overline{x_n} - \frac{\chi_0 Z_{n-1}}{\Psi^*_{n-1}} \qquad (C.175)$$

$$k_n = \frac{\chi_0}{\Psi^*_{n-1}} \left[1 + \alpha Z_{n-1} \left(1 - \frac{\Psi^*_{n-1}}{1 + b} \right) \right] \qquad (C.176)$$

$$Z_n = Z_{n-1} + \frac{k'_n}{k_n}(1 - e^{-pk_n}) \qquad (C.177)$$

$$\Psi^*_{n-1} = \frac{1 + b}{1 + be^{\alpha Z_{n-1}}} \qquad (C.178)$$

C.12   Asymptotic Postulate $\alpha = 1$

By definition, we have

$$M_D = \phi_0^* \Psi(Z) D \qquad (C.179)$$

From C.179, by differentiation, we get

$$\frac{1}{M_D}\frac{dM_D}{dt} = \frac{1}{D}\frac{dD}{dt} + \frac{1}{\Psi(Z)}\frac{d\Psi(Z)}{dt} \tag{C.180}$$

which is equivalent to

$$\frac{1}{M_D}\frac{dM_D}{dt} = x + \frac{1}{\Psi(Z)}\frac{d\Psi(Z)}{dt} \tag{C.181}$$

Since

$$\frac{dZ}{dt} = x - \chi Z = x - z \Leftrightarrow x = z + \frac{dZ}{dt} \tag{C.182}$$

relationship C.181 is equivalent to

$$\frac{1}{M_D}\frac{dM_D}{dt} = z + \frac{dZ}{dt} + \frac{1}{\Psi(Z)}\frac{d\Psi(Z)}{dt} \tag{C.183a}$$

or $\quad \frac{1}{M_D}\frac{dM_D}{dt} = z + \frac{dZ}{dt} + \frac{1}{\Psi(Z)}\frac{d\Psi(Z)}{dZ}\frac{dZ}{dt} \tag{C.183b}$

$$\frac{1}{M_D}\frac{dM_D}{dt} = z + \frac{dZ}{dt}\left[1 + \frac{\Psi'(Z)}{\Psi(Z)}\right] \tag{C.183c}$$

From our studies of elasticities (see relationship 4.56a), we know that

$$\lim_{Z \to +\infty}\frac{\Psi'(Z)}{\Psi(Z)} = \lim_{Z \to +\infty}\frac{-\alpha b e^{\alpha Z}}{1 + b e^{\alpha Z}} = -\alpha \tag{C.184}$$

Hence, when $Z \to +\infty$, as is the case toward the end of a hyperinflation, from relationship C.183c, we have

$$\frac{1}{M_D}\frac{dM_D}{dt} \to z + (1 - \alpha)\frac{dZ}{dt} \tag{C.185}$$

Since $M_D \approx M$ and (according to 4.78) $z \to x$ when $Z \to +\infty$, we can also write

$$\frac{1}{M}\frac{dM}{dt} \to x + (1 - \alpha)\frac{dZ}{dt} \tag{C.186}$$

in which the term $(1 - \alpha)dZ/dt$ as in C.186 represents the relative change in relative desired balances.

Under hyperinflationary circumstances, since changes in relative desired balances become negligible, it seems natural to postulate that the rate of inflation x tends toward the rate of increase in the money supply

$$x \to \frac{1}{M} \frac{dM}{dt} \qquad \text{(C.187)}$$

For this to be verified, we must have

$$\alpha = 1 \qquad \text{(C.188)}$$

C.13   Vernon Smith's Model of Momentum Traders and Adaptive Expectations

As we have seen in table 4.2, Cagan considers an exponential average E of past inflation rates C, the elasticity of expected inflation with respect to current inflation being β.

$$C = \frac{d \ln P}{dt} \qquad \text{(C.189)}$$

$$\frac{dE}{dt} = \beta\,(C - E) \qquad \text{with} \qquad 0 < \beta < 1 \qquad \text{(C.190)}$$

Smith defines the expectations of momentum traders as

$$\frac{d\zeta_1}{dt} = c_1 \left[q_1\, p^{-1}(t)\, \frac{dp(t)}{dt} - \zeta_1 \right] \qquad \text{(C.191)}$$

where q_1 is the weight given to momentum traders (as opposed to q_2 which is the weight given to rational investors). Supposedly, $q_1 + q_2 = 1$ and $0 < c_1 < 1$, but Smith fails to clarify these two assumptions.

Let us have

$$\frac{1}{p(t)} \frac{dp(t)}{dt} = C \qquad \text{(C.192a)}$$

$$c_1 = \beta \qquad \text{(C.192b)}$$

$$\zeta_1 = q_1\, E \qquad \text{(C.192c)}$$

and substitute these new notations in C.191

$$\frac{d\zeta_1}{dt} = c_1 \left[q_1\, p^{-1}(t) \frac{dp(t)}{dt} - \zeta_1 \right] \tag{C.193}$$

$$\Leftrightarrow \frac{d(q_1 E)}{dt} = \beta(q_1 C - q_1 E) \tag{C.194}$$

$$\Leftrightarrow q_1 \frac{dE}{dt} = q_1[\beta(C - E)] \tag{C.195}$$

$$\frac{dE}{dt} = \beta(C - E) \tag{C.196}$$

which is nothing but Cagan's formulation.

Instead of computing the exponential average of a fraction q_1 of relative price changes, Smith could as well compute the exponential average of these relative price changes and give it a weight equal to q_1. It is quite surprising that Smith also fails to report the numerical values taken by c_1 in his numerical simulations. He only observes that "large values of c_1 can lead to unstable oscillations," which is not surprising since large values of c_1 are equivalent to very elastic expectations or to a very short memory. Smith writes as if he wanted to advocate "adaptive expectations" without mentioning these two words.

As for Smith's formulation of total investor sentiment (or preference function), it bears a close resemblance to Allais's Ψ function, since

$$\tanh x = \frac{e^x - e^{-x}}{e^x + e^{-x}} = \frac{e^{2x} - 1}{e^{2x} + 1} \tag{C.197}$$

For $\alpha = b = 1$, we have

$$\Psi(Z) = 1 - \tanh\frac{Z}{2} \Leftrightarrow \tanh\frac{Z}{2} = 1 - \Psi(Z) \tag{C.198}$$

Smith's total investor sentiment function is

$$k(\zeta) = \frac{1}{2}[1 + \tanh(\zeta_1 + \zeta_2)] \tag{C.199}$$

where ζ_2 measures the price deviation from fundamental value.

For $\zeta_2 = 0$ and $\zeta_1 = \frac{Z}{2}$, we have

$$k\left(\frac{Z}{2}\right) = \frac{1}{2}\left(1 + \tanh\frac{Z}{2}\right) = \frac{1}{2}[2 - \Psi(Z)] \tag{C.200}$$

$$k\left(\frac{Z}{2}\right) = 1 - \frac{\Psi(Z)}{2} \tag{C.201}$$

While Allais's Ψ is a bounded nonlinear function decreasing between 2 and 0, Smith's k is a bounded nonlinear function increasing between 0 and 1, which allows Smith to interpret it as a cumulative frequency distribution.

C.14   The HRL Formulation of Monetary Dynamics

On one hand, from the fundamental equation of monetary dynamics, we have

$$x = \frac{1}{D}\frac{dD}{dt} = V\frac{M - M_D}{M} + \frac{1}{M}\frac{dM}{dt} \qquad (C.202)$$

with

$$D = MV \qquad \text{and} \qquad T = \frac{1}{V} \qquad (C.203)$$

where M and M_D are two functions of Z.

On the other hand, according to the HRL formulation, we have

$$\frac{dZ}{dt} = x - \chi Z \qquad (C.204)$$

Relationships C.202 and C.204 form a system of two equations in which two functions, $x(Z)$ and $Z(x)$, mutually depend on each other. To study the behavior of this system over time, we have to find a way of reducing the two relationships C.202 and C.203 to a single one.

C.14.1   *The General Model of Monetary Dynamics*

The differential expression of the Newcomb-Fisher equation of exchanges is

$$D = MV \Rightarrow \frac{1}{D}\frac{dD}{dt} = \frac{1}{V}\frac{dV}{dt} + \frac{1}{M}\frac{dM}{dt} \qquad (C.205)$$

From relationship C.202, we have

$$\frac{1}{D}\frac{dD}{dt} = V\frac{M - M_D}{M} + \frac{1}{M}\frac{dM}{dt} \qquad (C.206)$$

By comparing relationships C.205 and C.202, and by eliminating the term $\frac{1}{M}\frac{dM}{dt}$, we get

$$\frac{1}{V}\frac{dV}{dt} = V\frac{M - M_D}{M} \Leftrightarrow \frac{1}{V}\frac{1}{V}\frac{dV}{dt} = 1 - \frac{M_D}{M} \qquad \text{with} \qquad \frac{1}{V} = T \tag{C.207}$$

Therefore, a simplified form of the fundamental equation of monetary dynamics is

$$T\frac{1}{V}\frac{dV}{dt} = 1 - \frac{M_D}{M} \qquad \text{with} \qquad V = \frac{D}{M} \tag{C.208}$$

The demand for money M_D is given by

$$M_D = \phi_0^* D\Psi(Z) \tag{C.209}$$

and the response time T by

$$T = T_0^*\Psi(Z) \tag{C.210}$$

with the differential expression of the coefficient of the psychological expansion being

$$\frac{dZ}{dt} = x - \chi(Z)Z \tag{C.211}$$

The rate of growth in aggregate nominal spending is

$$x = \frac{1}{D}\frac{dD}{dt} \tag{C.212}$$

As for the supply of money, it is given by

$$M = q\,B\gamma(Z) \qquad \text{with} \qquad B = B_0 e^{\rho t} \tag{C.213}$$

which means that the base-money multiplier is a function $\gamma(Z)$, while the monetary base is assumed to grow at a constant rate ρ.

Once again, the rate of memory decay is given by

$$\chi(Z) = \frac{\chi_0^*}{\Psi(Z)} \tag{C.214}$$

while the response time is

$$T = T_0^*\Psi(Z) \tag{C.215}$$

Let us adopt the following general notation convention. For any function G of $Z(t)$

$$Z = Z(t) \qquad G(t) = G(Z) \tag{C.216}$$

$$Z_0 = Z(t=0) \qquad G_0 = G(t=0) \qquad G_0 = G(Z_0) \tag{C.217}$$

Note that G_0 should be carefully distinguished from

$$G_0^* = G(Z=0) \tag{C.218}$$

Let us also define

$$K(Z) = \frac{-\Psi'(Z)}{\Psi(Z)} \tag{C.219}$$

with

$$\Psi(Z) = \frac{1+b}{1+be^{\alpha Z}} \qquad \Psi'(Z) = \frac{-\alpha b(1+b)e^{\alpha Z}}{(1+be^{\alpha Z})^2} \qquad \text{and} \qquad \alpha = b = 1 \tag{C.220}$$

and in the same vein

$$K'(Z) = \frac{\gamma'(Z)}{\gamma(Z)} \tag{C.221}$$

with

$$\gamma(Z) = 1 - a' + a'\frac{1+b'}{1+b'e^{-\alpha'Z}} \qquad \gamma'(Z) = \frac{\alpha'a'b'(1+b')e^{-\alpha'Z}}{(1+b'e^{-\alpha'Z})^2} \tag{C.222}$$

From relationship C.222 follows

$$\gamma'(0) = \frac{\alpha'a'b'}{1+b'} \tag{C.223}$$

For $b' = 1$, we have

$$\gamma'(0) = \frac{\alpha'a'}{2} \tag{C.224}$$

For the money supply and the demand for money functions to behave symmetrically when $Z = 0$, we need to have

$$\gamma'(0) = -\Psi'(0) = \frac{1}{2} \Rightarrow \alpha'a' = 1 \tag{C.225}$$

Tests of the HRL formulation of the money supply suggest the following ranges for the parameters of the money supply function:

$$\alpha' a' = 1 \qquad 0.8 \le b' \le 1.2 \qquad \frac{1}{3} \le a' \le \frac{2}{3} \qquad \frac{3}{2} \le \alpha' \le 3$$

$$(C.226)$$

Finally, the money supply function and its derivative take the following remarkable values:

$$\gamma(0) = 1 \qquad 1 - a' \le \gamma(Z) \le 1 + a'b' \tag{C.227}$$

$$\gamma'(0) = \frac{b'}{1 + b'} \qquad \lim_{Z \to \pm\infty} \gamma'(Z) = 0 \tag{C.228}$$

C.14.2 Structure of Dynamic Equilibrium Processes

C.14.2.1 CONDITIONS FOR DYNAMIC EQUILIBRIUM[3] The first condition is that the supply of and the demand for money be and remain equal, which implies that the coefficient of psychological expansion must be constant:

$$M_{De}(t) = M_e(t) \qquad Z(t) = Z_e \tag{C.229}$$

The second condition is that nominal spending must grow at a constant rate x_e

$$x = \frac{1}{D} \frac{dD}{dt} \Rightarrow x_e = \frac{1}{D_e} \frac{dD_e}{dt} \tag{C.230}$$

which, according to relationship C.211, must, in turn, be equal to the dynamic equilbrium rate z_e:

$$x_{e_{\cdot}} = \frac{\chi_0^* Z_e}{\Psi(Z_e)} = z_e \tag{C.231}$$

C.14.2.2 IMPLICATIONS OF DYNAMIC EQUILIBRIUM Relationships C.209 and C.213 give us the equilbrium values of the supply and of the demand for money

$$M_{De}(t) = \phi_0^* D_e(t)\Psi(Z_e) \tag{C.232a}$$

$$M_e(t) = qB_0 e^{\rho t}\gamma(Z_e) \tag{C.232b}$$

By differentiating relationship C.232a, we get

$$\frac{dM_{De}}{dt} = \phi_0^* \Psi(Z_e) \frac{D_e}{dt} \Leftrightarrow \frac{dM_{De}(t)}{dt} = \frac{M_{De}(t)}{D_e(t)} \frac{D_e}{dt}$$

$$\Leftrightarrow \frac{1}{M_{De}(t)} \frac{dM_{De}(t)}{dt} = \frac{1}{D_e(t)} \frac{dD_e(t)}{dt} \quad (C.233)$$

By differentiating relationship C.232b, we get

$$\frac{dM_e(t)}{dt} = qB_0 \rho e^{\rho t} \gamma(Z_e) = \rho M_e(t) \Leftrightarrow \frac{1}{M_e(t)} \frac{dM_e(t)}{dt} = \rho \quad (C.234)$$

Since $M_{De}(t) = M_e(t)$, we have

$$\frac{1}{M_{De}(t)} \frac{dM_{De}(t)}{dt} = \frac{1}{M_e(t)} \frac{dM_e(t)}{dt} \quad (C.235)$$

From relationships C.231, C.232a, and C.232b, we see that the rates of growth in nominal spending, in the demand for money, and in the supply of money are all equal to the rate of growth in the monetary base

$$\frac{1}{M_e} \frac{dM_e}{dt} = \frac{1}{M_{De}} \frac{dM_{De}}{dt} = \frac{1}{D_e} \frac{dD_e}{dt} = \rho \quad (C.236)$$

which also implies, from relationships C.231 and C.236, that the dynamic equilibrium rate is equal to the rate of growth in the monetary base

$$\rho = \frac{\chi_0^* Z_e}{\Psi(Z_e)} = z_e \quad (C.237)$$

Relationship C.232a implies furthermore that the velocity of money is constant in dynamic equilibrium, since

$$\frac{1}{V_e} \frac{dV_e}{dt} = \frac{1}{D_e} \frac{dD_e}{dt} - \frac{1}{M_e} \frac{dM_e}{dt} = 0 \quad (C.238)$$

$$V(t) = V_e \quad (C.239)$$

In a dynamic equilibrium process, relationship C.214 is equivalent to

$$\chi_e = \chi(Z_e) = \frac{\chi_0^*}{\Psi(Z_e)} \quad (C.240)$$

while relationship C.215 is equivalent to

$$T_e = T_0^* \Psi(Z_e) \tag{C.241}$$

with

$$V_e T_e = 1 \tag{C.242}$$

Relationships C.241 and C.242 imply

$$V_e = \frac{1}{T_0^* \Psi(Z_e)} = \frac{V_0^*}{\Psi(Z_e)} \tag{C.243}$$

while relationships C.241, C.242, and C.243 imply

$$V_0^* T_0^* = 1 \tag{C.244}$$

From relationships C.229 and C.232a we get

$$V_e = \frac{D_e}{M_e} = \frac{D_e}{M_{De}} = \frac{D_e}{\phi_0^* D_e \Psi(Z_e)} = \frac{1}{\phi_0^* \Psi(Z_e)} \tag{C.245}$$

and from relationships C.243 and C.245

$$V_e = \frac{1}{T_0^* \Psi(Z_e)} = \frac{1}{\phi_0^* \Psi(Z_e)} \tag{C.246}$$

Finally, by comparing C.243 and C.245, we have

$$\phi_0^* = T_0^* \tag{C.247}$$

Allais estimates that in a stationary state, the response time and the transactions velocity of money take the following values:

$$T_0^* = 0.75 \text{ month} = \frac{1}{16} \text{ year} \qquad V_0^* = \frac{1}{T_0^*} = 16 \text{ per year} \tag{C.248}$$

C.14.3   *Differential Equations in $V(t)$ and $Z(t)$ of the General Model of Monetary Dynamics*

Let us start from the simplified expression of the fundamental equation of monetary dynamics (C.208)

$$T \frac{1}{V} \frac{dV}{dt} = 1 - \frac{M_D}{M} \tag{C.249}$$

Using relationships C.215, C.241, and C.242, the left term of relationship C.249 can be written as

$$T \frac{1}{V} \frac{dV}{dt} = T_0^* \Psi(Z) \frac{1}{V} \frac{dV}{dt} = \frac{T_e}{\Psi(Z_e)} \Psi(Z) \frac{1}{V} \frac{dV}{dt} = \frac{1}{V_e} \frac{\Psi(Z)}{\Psi(Z_e)} \frac{1}{V} \frac{dV}{dt}$$

$$\text{(C.250)}$$

Using relationships C.209, C.247, C.244, and C.243, the right term of relationship C.249 can be written as

$$1 - \frac{M_D}{M} = 1 - \frac{\phi_0^* D \Psi(Z)}{M} = 1 - \phi_0^* V \Psi(Z) = 1 - T_0^* V \Psi(Z)$$

$$= 1 - \frac{V}{V_0^*} \Psi(Z) = 1 - \frac{V}{V_e} \frac{\Psi(Z)}{\Psi(Z_e)}$$

$$\text{(C.251)}$$

Hence, the fundamental equation of monetary dynamics (relationship C.249) is equivalent to

$$\frac{\Psi(Z)}{V_e \Psi(Z_e)} \frac{1}{V} \frac{dV}{dt} = 1 - \frac{V}{V_e} \frac{\Psi(Z)}{\Psi(Z_e)} \qquad \text{with} \qquad V_e \Psi(Z_e) = V_0^*$$

$$\text{(C.252)}$$

Let us now turn to the second equation in our system, namely, the differential expression of Z. By inserting the term

$$-\frac{1}{M} \frac{dM}{dt} + \frac{1}{M} \frac{dM}{dt} \qquad \text{(C.253)}$$

in relationship C.211, we get

$$\frac{dZ}{dt} = \frac{1}{D} \frac{dD}{dt} - \frac{1}{M} \frac{dM}{dt} - \frac{\chi_0^* Z}{\Psi(Z)} + \frac{1}{M} \frac{dM}{dt} \qquad \text{(C.254)}$$

The second term $\frac{1}{M} \frac{dM}{dt}$ can be transformed as follows into a term in Z. From relationship C.213, we have indeed a relationship between M and Z.

$$M(t) = q B_0 e^{\rho t} \gamma(Z(t)) \qquad \text{(C.255)}$$

Since

$$\frac{d\gamma(Z(t))}{dt} = \frac{d\gamma}{dZ} \frac{dZ}{dt} = \gamma'(Z) \frac{dZ}{dt} \qquad \text{(C.256)}$$

we can write

$$\frac{dM}{dt} = qB_0 e^{\rho t} \left[\rho \gamma(Z) + \gamma'(Z) \frac{dZ}{dt} \right] \qquad \text{(C.257)}$$

By dividing the left member of relationship C.257 by M and the right one by its equivalent $qB_0 e^{\rho t} \gamma(Z(t))$, we get

$$\frac{1}{M} \frac{dM}{dt} = \frac{qB_0 e^{\rho t} [\rho \gamma(Z) + \gamma'(Z) \frac{dZ}{dt}]}{qB_0 e^{\rho t} \gamma(Z(t))} = \rho + \frac{\gamma'(Z)}{\gamma(Z)} \frac{dZ}{dt} \qquad \text{(C.258)}$$

Since $\frac{1}{V} \frac{dV}{dt} = \frac{1}{D} \frac{dD}{dt} - \frac{1}{M} \frac{dM}{dt}$ (relationship C.205), by using relationship C.258, relationship C.254 becomes

$$\frac{dZ}{dt} = \frac{1}{V} \frac{dV}{dt} - \frac{\chi_0^* Z}{\Psi(Z)} + \rho + \frac{\gamma'(Z)}{\gamma(Z)} \frac{dZ}{dt} \qquad \text{(C.259)}$$

which is equivalent to

$$\left[1 - \frac{\gamma'(Z)}{\gamma(Z)} \right] \frac{dZ}{dt} = \frac{1}{V} \frac{dV}{dt} - \frac{\chi_0^* Z}{\Psi(Z)} + \rho \qquad \text{(C.260)}$$

From relationships C.215, C.243, and C.246 we have the following equivalences:

$$T = T_0^* \Psi(Z) \Leftrightarrow T_0^* = \frac{1}{V_e \Psi(Z_e)} \Leftrightarrow T = \frac{1}{V_e} \frac{\Psi(Z)}{\Psi(Z_e)} \qquad \text{(C.261)}$$

Multiplying both members of relationship C.260 by T, we get

$$T \left[1 - \frac{\gamma'(Z)}{\gamma(Z)} \right] \frac{dZ}{dt} = T \frac{1}{V} \frac{dV}{dt} - T \frac{\chi_0^* Z}{\Psi(Z)} + T\rho \qquad \text{(C.262)}$$

and after substituting for T according to relationship C.261,

$$\left[1 - \frac{\gamma'(Z)}{\gamma(Z)} \right] \frac{1}{V_e} \frac{\Psi(Z)}{\Psi(Z_e)} \frac{dZ}{dt}$$
$$= \frac{1}{V_e} \frac{\Psi(Z)}{\Psi(Z_e)} \frac{1}{V} \frac{dV}{dt} - \frac{1}{V_e} \frac{\Psi(Z)}{\Psi(Z_e)} \frac{\chi_0^* Z}{\Psi(Z)} + \frac{1}{V_e} \frac{\Psi(Z)}{\Psi(Z_e)} \rho \qquad \text{(C.263)}$$

We have thus established two equivalences:

- The first one, pertaining to the fundamental equation of monetary dynamics, is between relationships C.208 and C.252:

$$T \frac{1}{V} \frac{dV}{dt} = 1 - \frac{M_D}{M} \Leftrightarrow \frac{\Psi(Z)}{V_e \Psi(Z_e)} \frac{1}{V} \frac{dV}{dt} = 1 - \frac{V}{V_e} \frac{\Psi(Z)}{\Psi(Z_e)}$$
$$\text{(C.264)}$$

- The second one, concerning the HRL formulation, is between relationships C.211 and C.263:

$$\frac{dZ}{dt} = \frac{1}{D}\frac{dD}{dt} - \frac{1}{M}\frac{dM}{dt} - \frac{\chi_0^* Z}{\Psi(Z)} + \frac{1}{M}\frac{dM}{dt} \tag{C.265}$$

$$\Leftrightarrow \left[1 - \frac{\gamma'(Z)}{\gamma(Z)}\right]\frac{1}{V_e}\frac{\Psi(Z)}{\Psi(Z_e)}\frac{dZ}{dt} = \frac{1}{V_e}\frac{\Psi(Z)}{\Psi(Z_e)}\left[\frac{1}{V}\frac{dV}{dt} - \frac{\chi_0^* Z}{\Psi(Z)} + \rho\right]$$

Since relationships C.252 (or C.264) and C.263 (or C.265) both contain the term $\frac{\Psi(Z)}{V_e\Psi(Z_e)}\frac{1}{V}\frac{dV}{dt}$, we are on our way to reducing our two initial equations into a single one.

C.14.4 Endogenous Fluctuations Around a Dynamic Equilibrium Process

To put relationships C.252 and C.263 in a linear form, let us first define the following functions $f(t)$ and $g(t)$:

$$\frac{V(t)}{V_e} = 1 + f(t) \qquad Z(t) = Z_e + g(t) \tag{C.266}$$

where $f(t)$ and $g(t)$ are first-order quantities. *We shall neglect second-order terms.*[4]

From relationship C.252, and relationships 1 and 4 in note 4, we have the following equivalences:

$$\frac{\Psi(Z)}{V_e\Psi(Z_e)}\frac{1}{V}\frac{dV}{dt} = 1 - \frac{V}{V_e}\frac{\Psi(Z)}{\Psi(Z_e)}$$

$$\Leftrightarrow \frac{1}{V_e}[1 - K_e g(t)]\frac{df(t)}{dt} = 1 - [1 + f(t)][1 - K_e g(t)] \tag{C.267}$$

$$\Leftrightarrow \frac{1}{V_e}\frac{df(t)}{dt} - \frac{K_e}{V_e}g(t)\frac{df(t)}{dt}$$
$$= 1 - [1 - K_e g(t) + f(t) - K_e f(t)g(t)]$$

Since the product of two first-order quantities is of second order, we have $g(t)\frac{df(t)}{dt} \approx 0$ and $f(t)g(t) \approx 0$, and relationship C.267 can be written as

$$\frac{1}{V_e}\frac{df(t)}{dt} = K_e g(t) - f(t) \tag{C.268}$$

from which we have

$$g(t) = \frac{1}{K_e}\left[\frac{1}{V_e}\frac{df(t)}{dt} + f(t)\right] \tag{C.269}$$

Let us now turn to relationship C.263. After eliminating the V_e term in both members, we get

$$\left[1 - \frac{\gamma'(Z)}{\gamma(Z)}\right]\frac{\Psi(Z)}{\Psi(Z_e)}\frac{dZ}{dt} = \frac{\Psi(Z)}{\Psi(Z_e)}\frac{1}{V}\frac{dV}{dt} - \frac{\chi_0^* Z}{\Psi(Z_e)} + \rho\frac{\Psi(Z)}{\Psi(Z_e)} \tag{C.270}$$

Let us reformulate the right member. From relationship C.266, and relationships 4 and 6 in note 4, we have, respectively, $Z(t) = Z_e + g(t)$, $\frac{\Psi(Z)}{\Psi(Z_e)} \approx 1 - K_e g(t)$, and $\frac{1}{V}\frac{dV}{dt} \approx \frac{df(t)}{dt}$. Substituting these terms in the right member of relationship C.270, we obtain

$$\left[1 - \frac{\gamma'(Z)}{\gamma(Z)}\right]\frac{\Psi(Z)}{\Psi(Z_e)}\frac{dZ}{dt}$$
$$= [1 - K_e g(t)]\frac{df(t)}{dt} - \chi_e[Z_e + g(t)] + \rho[1 - K_e g(t)] \tag{C.271}$$

and

$$\left[1 - \frac{\gamma'(Z)}{\gamma(Z)}\right]\frac{\Psi(Z)}{\Psi(Z_e)}\frac{dZ}{dt}$$
$$= \frac{df(t)}{dt} - K_e g(t)\frac{df(t)}{dt} - \chi_e Z_e - \chi_e g(t) + \rho - \rho K_e g(t) \tag{C.272}$$

Since the quantity $g(t)\frac{df(t)}{dt}$ is a second-order quantity and $\chi_e Z_e = z_e = \rho \Leftrightarrow -\chi_e Z_e + \rho = 0$ (relationships C.237 and C.240), relationship C.272 becomes

$$\left[1 - \frac{\gamma'(Z)}{\gamma(Z)}\right]\frac{\Psi(Z)}{\Psi(Z_e)}\frac{dZ}{dt} = \frac{df(t)}{dt} - \chi_e g(t) - K_e \rho g(t) \tag{C.273}$$

or, after regrouping the terms in $g(t)$,

$$\left[1 - \frac{\gamma'(Z)}{\gamma(Z)}\right]\frac{\Psi(Z)}{\Psi(Z_e)}\frac{dZ}{dt} = \frac{df(t)}{dt} - (\chi_e + K_e \rho)g(t) \tag{C.274}$$

We can now turn to the left member of relationship C.274. From relationship C.266, we have

$$Z = Z_e + g(t) \Rightarrow \frac{dZ}{dt} = \frac{dg(t)}{dt} \tag{C.275}$$

Hence, by substitution, we get

$$\frac{\Psi(Z)}{\Psi(Z_e)}\frac{dZ}{dt} = [1 - K_e g(t)]\frac{dg(t)}{dt} = \frac{dg(t)}{dt} - K_e g(t)\frac{dg(t)}{dt} \quad \text{(C.276)}$$

Since $g(t)\frac{dg(t)}{dt}$ is a second-order quantity, relationship C.276 becomes

$$\frac{\Psi(Z)}{\Psi(Z_e)}\frac{dZ}{dt} = \frac{dg(t)}{dt} \quad \text{(C.277)}$$

and relationship C.274 becomes

$$\left[1 - \frac{\gamma'(Z)}{\gamma(Z)}\right]\frac{dg(t)}{dt} = \frac{df(t)}{dt} - (\chi_e + K_e\rho)g(t) \quad \text{(C.278)}$$

Since the terms in g^2 can be neglected, we have

$$\gamma(Z) = \gamma(Z_e) + g\gamma'(Z_e) \Rightarrow g\gamma(Z) = g\gamma(Z_e)$$

$$\gamma'(Z) = \gamma'(Z_e) + g\gamma''(Z_e) \Rightarrow g\gamma'(Z) = g\gamma'(Z_e)$$

$$\frac{g\gamma'(Z)}{g\gamma(Z)} = \frac{g\gamma'(Z_e)}{g\gamma(Z_e)} \Leftrightarrow \frac{\gamma'(Z)}{\gamma(Z)} = \frac{\gamma'(Z_e)}{\gamma(Z_e)} = K'_e \quad \text{(C.279)}$$

and finally

$$(1 - K'_e)\frac{dg(t)}{dt} = \frac{df(t)}{dt} - (\chi_e + K_e\rho)g(t) \quad \text{(C.280)}$$

with

$$K_e = \frac{-\Psi'_e}{\Psi_e} \qquad K'_e = \frac{\gamma'_e}{\gamma_e} \qquad \chi_e = \frac{\chi_0^*}{\Psi_e} \quad \text{(C.281)}$$

We have thus established two equivalences:

- The first one, concerning the fundamental equation of monetary dynamics, is between relationships C.208 and C.268:

$$T\frac{1}{V}\frac{dV}{dt} = 1 - \frac{M_D}{M} \Leftrightarrow \frac{1}{V_e}\frac{df(t)}{dt} = K_e g(t) - f(t) \quad \text{(C.282)}$$

- The second one, concerning the HRL formulation, is between relationships C.211 and C.280:

$$\frac{dZ}{dt} = \frac{1}{D}\frac{dD}{dt} - \frac{\chi_0^* Z}{\Psi(Z)} \Leftrightarrow (1 - K'_e)\frac{dg(t)}{dt} = \frac{df(t)}{dt} - (\chi_e + K_e\rho)g(t)$$

$$\text{(C.283)}$$

Relationship C.268 gives us the possibility to express

- $g(t)$ as a function of $f(t)$ and df/dt
- Then $dg(t)/dt$ as a function of df/dt and d^2f/dt^2

and to substitute both expressions in relationship C.280, so as to end up with a second-order differential equation in f (all the terms in g having been eliminated).

With relationship C.269, we have seen that

$$g(t) = \frac{1}{K_e}\left[\frac{1}{V_e}\frac{df(t)}{dt} + f(t)\right] \qquad (C.284)$$

and according to C.280

$$(1 - K_e')\frac{dg(t)}{dt} = \frac{df(t)}{dt} - (\chi_e + K_e\rho)g(t) \qquad (C.285)$$

By differentiating relationship C.284, we get

$$\frac{dg(t)}{dt} = \frac{1}{K_e}\left[\frac{1}{V_e}\frac{d^2f(t)}{d^2t} + \frac{df(t)}{dt}\right] \qquad (C.286)$$

By substituting relationships C.284 and C.286 for $g(t)$ and $dg(t)/dt$ in relationship C.285, we obtain

$$(1 - K_e')\frac{1}{K_e}\left[\frac{1}{V_e}\frac{d^2f(t)}{dt^2} + \frac{df(t)}{dt}\right]$$
$$= \frac{df(t)}{dt} - (\chi_e + K_e\rho)\frac{1}{K_e}\left[\frac{1}{V_e}\frac{df(t)}{dt} + f(t)\right] \qquad (C.287)$$

$$\frac{1 - K_e'}{K_e V_e}\frac{d^2f(t)}{dt^2} + \left(\frac{1 - K_e'}{K_e} - \frac{K_e}{K_e} + \frac{\chi_e + K_e\rho}{K_e V_e}\right)\frac{df(t)}{dt}$$
$$+ \frac{\chi_e + K_e\rho}{K_e}f(t) = 0 \qquad (C.288)$$

and finally, after simplifying for K_e,

$$\frac{1 - K_e'}{V_e}\frac{d^2f(t)}{dt^2} + \left(1 - K_e' - K_e + \frac{\chi_e + K_e\rho}{V_e}\right)\frac{df(t)}{dt}$$
$$+ (\chi_e + K_e\rho)f(t) = 0 \qquad (C.289)$$

Using the same relationships C.268 and C.280, but the other way round, one can easily demonstrate that the function $g(t)$ defined by relationship C.266 satisfies the same second-order linear differential equation as the function $f(t)$.

From relationship C.285, we have indeed

$$\frac{df(t)}{dt} = (1 - K'_e) \frac{dg(t)}{dt} + (\chi_e + K_e \rho) g(t) \tag{C.290}$$

By differentiating relationship C.290, we get

$$(1 - K'_e) \frac{d^2 g(t)}{dt^2} = \frac{d^2 f(t)}{dt^2} - (\chi_e + K_e \rho) \frac{dg(t)}{dt} \tag{C.291}$$

By differentiating equation C.268, we get

$$\frac{1}{V_e} \frac{d^2 f(t)}{dt^2} = K_e \frac{dg(t)}{dt} - \frac{df(t)}{dt} \tag{C.292}$$

From relationships C.290 and C.292

$$\frac{1}{V_e} \frac{d^2 f(t)}{dt^2} = K_e \frac{dg(t)}{dt} - (1 - K'_e) \frac{dg(t)}{dt} - (\chi_e + K_e \rho) g(t) \tag{C.293}$$

By differentiating relationship C.290, we obtain

$$\frac{d^2 f(t)}{dt^2} = (1 - K'_e) \frac{d^2 g(t)}{dt^2} + (\chi_e + K_e \rho) \frac{dg(t)}{dt} \tag{C.294}$$

From relationships C.293 and C.294, we finally get

$$\frac{1}{V_e} \left[(1 - K'_e) \frac{d^2 g(t)}{dt^2} + (\chi_e + K_e \rho) \frac{dg(t)}{dt} \right]$$
$$= K_e \frac{dg(t)}{dt} - (1 - K'_e) \frac{dg(t)}{dt} - (\chi_e + K_e \rho) g(t) \tag{C.295}$$

and

$$\frac{(1 - K'_e)}{V_e} \frac{d^2 g(t)}{dt^2} + \left(1 - K'_e - K_e + \frac{\chi_e + K_e \rho}{V_e} \right) \frac{dg(t)}{dt}$$
$$+ (\chi_e + K_e \rho) g(t) = 0 \tag{C.296}$$

C.14.5 *Endogenous Fluctuations–Discussion*

Relationship C.289 is a second-order linear differential equation

$$Af'' + Bf' + Cf = 0 \qquad\qquad (C.297)$$

the solution of which is well known

$$f = \lambda e^{s_1 t} + \mu e^{s_2 t} \qquad\qquad (C.298)$$

where λ and μ are two arbitrary constants and s_1 and s_2 are the two roots of the following equation in s:

$$As^2 + Bs + C = 0 \qquad\qquad (C.299)$$

namely,

$$s = \frac{-B \pm \sqrt{B^2 - 4AC}}{2A} \qquad\qquad (C.300)$$

The discriminant Δ of the equation in s is

$$\Delta = B^2 - 4AC \qquad\qquad (C.301)$$

C.14.5.1 REAL ROOTS If $\Delta > 0$, the two roots are real numbers.

The coefficient $A = (1 - K'_e)/V_e$ is always positive, since empirical observation shows that K'_e is always smaller than 1. Since we have, on one hand

$$C = \chi_e + K_e \rho \qquad \chi_e = \frac{\chi_0^*}{\Psi_e} \qquad \rho = \frac{\chi_0^* Z_e}{\Psi_e} \qquad (C.302)$$

which implies

$$C = \frac{\chi_0^*}{\Psi_e} + \frac{K_e \chi_0^* Z_e}{\Psi_e} = \frac{\chi_0^*}{\Psi_e}(1 + K_e Z_e) \qquad (C.303)$$

and, on the other hand, according to C.219

$$K_e = \frac{1}{1 + e^{-Z_e}} \qquad\qquad (C.304)$$

we get

$$1 + K_e Z_e = 1 + \frac{Z_e}{1 + e^{-Z_e}} > 0 \qquad\qquad (C.305)$$

From this, it follows that the ratio C/A, which is equal to the product $s_1 s_2$, is always positive.

$$s_1 s_2 = \frac{(-B)^2 - (B^2 - 4AC)}{4A^2} = \frac{C}{A} > 0 \tag{C.306}$$

Therefore, if the two roots are real numbers, they must have the same sign.

The roots s_1 and s_2 are both positive if $B < 0$ (for then $(-B + \sqrt{B^2 - 4AC})/2A > 0$) and both negative if $B > 0$ (for then $(-B - \sqrt{B^2 - 4AC})/2A < 0$).

C.14.5.2 COMPLEX ROOTS If $\Delta < 0$, the two roots are complex numbers. In this case, we have

$$s_1 = \frac{-B + \imath\sqrt{4AC - B^2}}{2A} = \sigma_1 + \imath\sigma_2 \tag{C.307}$$

and

$$f(t) = Pe^{\sigma_1 t} \cos \sigma_2(t - \tau) \tag{C.308}$$

where P and τ are two arbitrary constants.

Furthermore, we have

$$\sigma_1 = \frac{-B}{2A} \qquad \sigma_2 = \frac{\sqrt{4AC - B^2}}{2A} = \frac{2\pi}{\Theta} \tag{C.309}$$

which gives the following pseudo-period:

$$\Theta = \frac{4\pi A}{\sqrt{4AC - B^2}} \tag{C.310}$$

In both cases (s_1 and s_2), if $B > 0$, then $f(t)$ tends toward 0 and the equilibrium is stable:

$$B > 0 \Rightarrow \sigma_1 = -\frac{B}{2A} < 0 \Rightarrow e^{\sigma_1 t} \to 0 \tag{C.311}$$

If $B < 0$, then $f(t)$ does not tend toward 0 and the equilibrium is unstable. All in all, there exist four possible configurations as shown in table C.3.

TABLE C.3
Roots Type for Various Possible Cases

	$\Delta > 0$	$\Delta < 0$
$B > 0$	Aperiodic stability	Pseudo-periodic stability
$B < 0$	Aperiodic instability	Pseudo-periodic instability and limit cycle
	Real roots	Complex roots

C.14.5.3 EXISTENCE OF A LIMIT CYCLE: Z (AND V) CANNOT GROW BOUNDLESSLY If the equilibrium is unstable ($B < 0$), one can easily demonstrate that instability cannot last infinitely. From C.208, we have

$$T \frac{1}{V} \frac{dV}{dt} = 1 - \frac{M_D}{M} \qquad (C.312)$$

and from C.261 and C.262

$$[1 - K'(Z)]T \frac{dZ}{dt} = T \frac{1}{V} \frac{dV}{dt} - T_0^* \chi_0^* Z + \rho T_0^* \Psi(Z) \qquad (C.313)$$

By contradiction, one can demonstrate that V cannot increase endlessly. If this were the case, we would always have, according to C.312,

$$M_D < M \qquad \text{since} \qquad T \frac{1}{V} \frac{dV}{dt} > 0 \Leftrightarrow \frac{M_D}{M} < 1 \qquad (C.314)$$

that is, according to relationship C.209,

$$M_D = \phi_0^* D(t) \Psi(Z) < M \qquad (C.315)$$

or equivalently

$$\frac{D(t)}{M} < \frac{1}{\phi_0^* \Psi(Z)} \Rightarrow V(t) < \frac{1}{\phi_0^* \Psi(Z)} \qquad (C.316)$$

If V increased boundlessly, this inequality would hold only if Z could increase too infinity, too, since

$$\lim_{Z \to +\infty} \Psi(Z) = 0 \qquad (C.317)$$

And yet, from relationships C.312, C.313, and C.314, we have

$$[1 - K'(Z)]T\frac{dZ}{dt} = 1 - \phi_0^* V \Psi(Z) - T_0^* \chi_0^* Z + \rho T_0^* \Psi(Z) \quad \text{(C.318)}$$

which, according to C.317, is equivalent when $Z \to +\infty$ to

$$[1 - K'(Z)]T\frac{dZ}{dt} = 1 - T_0^* \chi_0^* Z \qquad \text{(C.318a)}$$

Therefore, Z (and V) cannot increase endlessly, for in this case the right member of relationship C.318 would end up being negative, while the left one would remain positive. Hence, if there is instability, there necessarily exists a limit cycle.

From this it follows, according to table C.3, that in order to have a limit cycle, the necessary and sufficient condition is

$$B < 0 \qquad \text{(C.319)}$$

namely,

$$1 - K_e - K_e' + \frac{\chi_e + K_e \rho}{V_e} < 0 \qquad \text{(C.320)}$$

The necessary and sufficient condition for the existence of a limit cycle is then that the sum $K_e + K_e'$ be large enough. In this case, one can consider that the order of magnitude of the limit cycle period Θ^* corresponds to the pseudo-period Θ defined by relationship C.310.

C.15   Computation of Endogenous Fluctuations

C.15.1   *Approximate Integration of the Differential Equation of Monetary Dynamics*

We observe that

$$\frac{1}{V}\frac{dV}{dt} = \frac{d\ln V}{dt} = \frac{\ln V_{n+1} - \ln V_n}{dt} = \frac{\ln V_{n+1} - \ln V_0^* - \ln V_n + \ln V_0^*}{dt}$$

$$= \frac{\ln \frac{V_{n+1}}{V_0^*} - \ln \frac{V_n}{V_0^*}}{dt} = \frac{d\ln(\frac{V}{V_0^*})}{dt} \qquad \text{(C.321)}$$

According to relationships C.215, C.244, C.247, and C.261, the two differrential equations of monetary dynamics, respectively, relationships C.249 and C.262, can be written as

$$T \frac{d \ln(\frac{V}{V_0^*})}{dt} = 1 - \frac{V}{V_0^*} \Psi(Z) \tag{C.322}$$

$$\left[1 - \frac{\gamma'(Z)}{\gamma(Z)} \right] T \frac{dZ}{dt} = T \frac{d \ln(\frac{V}{V_0^*})}{dt} - T_0^* \chi_0^* Z + \rho T_0^* \Psi(Z) \tag{C.323}$$

with

$$V_0^* = 16 \qquad T_0^* = \frac{1}{16} \tag{C.324}$$

Between t_n and t_{n+1}, a time interval of variable length, we have

$$T \frac{d \ln(\frac{V}{V_0^*})}{dt} = \ln \frac{V_{n+1}}{V_0^*} - \ln \frac{V_n}{V_0^*} \qquad \text{since} \qquad dt = T \tag{C.325}$$

and

$$T \frac{dZ}{dt} = Z_{n+1} - Z_n \qquad \text{again, since} \qquad dt = T \tag{C.326}$$

C.15.2 Recurrence Relationships

From relationships C.322, C.323, C.324, and C.326, we have

$$\ln \frac{V_{n+1}}{V_0^*} = \ln \frac{V_n}{V_0^*} + 1 - \frac{V_n \Psi(Z_n)}{V_0^*} \tag{C.327}$$

and

$$Z_{n+1} = Z_n + \frac{1 - \frac{V_n \Psi(Z_n)}{V_0^*} - T_0^* \chi_0^* Z_n + \rho T_0^* \Psi(Z_n)}{1 - \frac{\gamma'(Z_n)}{\gamma(Z_n)}} \tag{C.328}$$

By using these two relationships, it is possible to compute V_n/V_0^* and Z_n by recurrence, starting from the initial values V_1/V_0^* and Z_1.

C.15.3 Derivatives

From relationship C.325, we get

$$\frac{d \ln(\frac{V}{V_0^*})}{dt} = \frac{\ln(\frac{V_{n+1}}{V_0^*}) - \ln(\frac{V_n}{V_0^*})}{T_0^* \Psi(Z_n)} \tag{C.329}$$

and from relationship C.326

$$\frac{dZ}{dt} = \frac{Z_{n+1} - Z_n}{T_n} = \frac{Z_{n+1} - Z_n}{T_0^* \Psi(Z_n)} \tag{C.330}$$

C.15.4   Observation

Relationships C.327 and C.328 cannot be used if the two initial values are equal to the equilibrium values:

$$Z_1 = Z_e \qquad \frac{V_1}{V_0^*} = \frac{1}{\Psi(Z_e)} \tag{C.331}$$

C.15.5   Computation of Significant Quantities

Knowing Z_n and V_n, one can derive from them the following expressions:

$$T_n = T_0^* \Psi(Z_n) \qquad \chi_n = \frac{\chi_0}{\Psi(Z_n)} \tag{C.332}$$

$$t_n = \sum_1^n T_0^* \Psi(Z_n) \tag{C.333}$$

$$M_n = M_1 e^{\rho(t_n - t_1)} \frac{\gamma(Z_n)}{\gamma(Z_1)} \tag{C.334}$$

$$D_n = M_n V_n \tag{C.335}$$

$$\frac{M_{Dn}}{M_n} = \frac{V_n}{V_0^*} \Psi(Z_n) = \phi_0^* V_n \Psi(Z_n) \qquad \phi_0^* = \frac{1}{V_0^*} \tag{C.336}$$

The initial value M_1 of M is given, as are the initial values V_1 and Z_1 of V and Z.

From relationship C.336, we have $\frac{M_{D1}}{M_1} = \frac{V_1}{V_0^*} \Psi(Z_1)$. This ratio measures the initial monetary disequilibrium in the system.

$$\frac{V_1}{V_0^*} \Psi(Z_1) > 1 \Leftrightarrow M_{D1} > M_1 \Rightarrow \text{deflationary initial disequilibrium}$$

$$\tag{C.337}$$

$$\frac{V_1}{V_0^*} \Psi(Z_1) < 1 \Leftrightarrow M_{D1} < M_1 \Rightarrow \text{inflationary initial disequilibrium}$$

$$\tag{C.338}$$

C.15.6 Presence of an Exogenous Factor

Under the assumption that the generation of endogenous fluctuations is disturbed by an exogenous factor $X(t)$, one substitutes $x(t) + X(t)$ for $x(t)$ in the expression of the coefficient of psychological expansion $Z(t)$, which gives

$$Z(t) = \int_{-\infty}^{t} [x(\tau) + X(\tau)] e^{-\int_{\tau}^{t} \chi(u) du} d\tau \tag{C.339}$$

and

$$\frac{dZ}{dt} = \frac{1}{D}\frac{dD}{dt} + X(t) - \frac{\chi_0^*}{\Psi(Z)} Z \tag{C.340}$$

Relationship C.208 remains unchanged:

$$T \frac{1}{V}\frac{dV}{dt} = 1 - \frac{M_D}{M} \tag{C.341}$$

From relationship C.340, it follows that relationships C.254, C.259, C.260, and C.262, respectively, become

$$\frac{dZ}{dt} = \frac{1}{D}\frac{dD}{dt} + X(t) - \frac{1}{M}\frac{dM}{dt} - \frac{\chi_0^*}{\Psi(Z)} + \frac{1}{M}\frac{dM}{dt} \tag{C.342}$$

$$\frac{dZ}{dt} = \frac{1}{V}\frac{dV}{dt} - \frac{\chi_0^*}{\Psi(Z)} + \rho + \frac{\gamma'(Z)}{\gamma(Z)}\frac{dZ}{dt} + X(t) \tag{C.343}$$

$$\left[1 - \frac{\gamma'(Z)}{\gamma(Z)}\right]\frac{dZ}{dt} = \frac{1}{V}\frac{dV}{dt} - \frac{\chi_0^* Z}{\Psi(Z)} + \rho + X(t) \tag{C.344}$$

$$\left[1 - \frac{\gamma'(Z)}{\gamma(Z)}\right] T\frac{dZ}{dt} = T\frac{1}{V}\frac{dV}{dt} - T\frac{\chi_0^* Z}{\Psi(Z)} + T\rho + TX(t) \tag{C.345}$$

$$\left[1 - \frac{\gamma'(Z)}{\gamma(Z)}\right] T\frac{dZ}{dt} = T\frac{1}{V}\frac{dV}{dt} + T_0^*\Psi(Z)X(t) - T_0^*\chi_0^* Z + \rho T_0^*\Psi(Z) \tag{C.346}$$

with

$$T = T_0^*\Psi(Z) \tag{C.347}$$

Relationship C.327 remains unchanged:

$$\ln \frac{V_{n+1}}{V_0^*} = \ln \frac{V_n}{V_0^*} + 1 - \frac{V_n\Psi(Z_n)}{V_0^*} \tag{C.348}$$

Relationship C.328 becomes

$$Z_{n+1} = Z_n + \frac{1 - \frac{V_n \Psi(Z_n)}{V_0^*} - T_0^* \chi_0^* Z_n + \rho T_0^* \Psi(Z_n) + X_n T_0^* \Psi(Z_n)}{1 - \frac{\gamma'(Z_n)}{\gamma(Z_n)}}$$

(C.349)

with

$$X_n = X(t_n)$$

(C.350)

$$t_n = \sum_1^n T_0^* \Psi(Z_n)$$

(C.351)

In Allais's simulations, the exogenous factor is given the form

$$X(t) = r \cos\left(2\pi \frac{t}{\theta}\right)$$

(C.352)

with θ varying between 5 and 10 years and $r = 0.05$. A more "realistic" but still deterministic structure which does mimic a random walk perfectly is the following almost-periodic function

$$X(t) = \sum_{i=1}^{l} a_i \cos(2\pi f_i(t - t_i)) \qquad \text{with} \qquad a_i > 0 \quad \text{and} \quad f_i = \frac{1}{T_i}$$

(C.353)

where the f_i are irrational numbers.

Comparison Between the Kalman Filter and Allais's HRL Algorithm

	Kalman Filter	OLS Regression ($m = 1$)	Exponential Average ($m = 1$)	Allais' HRL ($m = 1$)
Observations $n = 0, 1, \ldots, N$	Υ_n ($m \times 1$) vector	y_n (1×1) vector	x_n (1×1) vector	$\bar{x}_n$ (1×1) vector
System state	Z_n^* ($K \times 1$) vector	$\beta_{n+1}^* = \beta_n^* (= \beta_0^* = \beta^*)$ ($K \times 1$) vector	y_n^* (1×1) vector	Z_n^* (1×1) vector
Disturbances	ϵ_n ($K \times 1$) vector	0	0	0
Measurement errors	η_n ($m \times 1$) vector	η_n (1×1) vector	η_n (1×1) vector	η_n (1×1) vector
Variance Covariance matrix	$\Omega = \begin{pmatrix} Q & S \\ S & R \end{pmatrix}$ $Q = \text{var}(\epsilon_n)$ $R = \text{var}(\eta_n)$ $S = \text{cov}(\epsilon_n, \eta_n)$	$\Omega = \begin{pmatrix} 0 & 0 \\ 0 & R \end{pmatrix}$ $Q = 0$ $R = \sigma^2$ $S = 0$		
Transition matrix	A_n ($K \times K$) matrix	Id ($K \times K$) matrix	$A_n = 1$	Id (1×1) vector $\chi_n = \chi_0 \dfrac{1 + b_t^\alpha Z_n^*}{1+b}$
Measurement matrix	C_n ($m \times K$) matrix	x_n ($1 \times K$) vector	$C_n = 1$	$z_n = \chi_n Z_n^*$
Signal	$C_n Z_n^*$	$x_n \beta^*$	y_n	
Transition equation	$Z_{n+1}^* = A_n Z_n^* + \epsilon_n$	$\beta_{n+1}^* = \beta_n^*$		
Measurement equation	$\Upsilon = C_n Z_n^* + \eta_n$	$y_n = x_n \beta^* + \eta_n$	$x_n = y_n + \eta_n$	$\bar{x}_n = z_n + \eta_n$

	Kalman Filter	OLS Regression ($m = 1$)	Exponential Average ($m = 1$)	Allais' HRL ($m = 1$)
Filtering problem	$Z_n = E(Z_n^* / \Upsilon_0, \Upsilon_1, \ldots, \Upsilon_n)$	$\beta_n = E(\beta_n^* / y_0, y_1, \ldots, y_n)$ $\beta_n = (X_n^T X_n)^{-1} X_n^T \Upsilon_n$		$Z_n = E(Z_n^* / \overline{x_0}, \overline{x_1}, \ldots, \overline{x_n})$
Squared filtering error	$\sum_{n,n} = \mathrm{var}(Z_n^* - Z_n)$	$\sum_{n,n} = \mathrm{var}(y_n - x_n\beta)$		
Gain	$S = 0 \Rightarrow$ $K_n = \sum_{n-1,n} C_n^T (C_n \sum_{n-1,n} C_n^T + R)^{-1}$	$S = 0 \Rightarrow$ $K_n = \frac{(X_{n-1}^T X_{n-1})^{-1} x_n^T}{1 + x_n(X_{n-1}^T X_{n-1})^{-1} x_n^T}$	$K_n = k$	$K_n = \frac{1 - e^{-pk_n}}{k_n}$ $k_n = x_{n-1} + \frac{x_0 {}^{\alpha b} Z_{n-1} e^{\alpha Z_{n-1}}}{1+b}$
Updating equation	$Z_n = Z_{n-1} + K_n(\Upsilon_n - C_n Z_{n-1})$	$S = 0 \Rightarrow$ $\beta_n = \beta_{n-1} + K_n(y_n - x_n\beta_{n-1})$	$y_n = y_{n-1} + k(x_n - y_{n-1})$	$Z_n = Z_{n-1} + K_n(\overline{x_n} - X_{n-1} Z_{n-1})$

A Note on the Theory of Intertemporal Choice

E.1   The Theory of Intertemporal Choice in a Nutshell

The theory of intertemporal choice is one of the basic topics in behavioral economics.[1] It presents itself as an alternative to the discounted utility model proposed by Samuelson in 1937.[2] The key assumptions made in Samuelson's model are that people discount future outcomes at a constant rate, which implies that all future outcomes are discounted at the same rate, irrespective of their distance in time. The theory of intertemporal choice is inspired by empirical observations, "anomalies," which are interpreted as being incompatible with the discounted utility model.[3] The purpose of this short note is to discuss whether Allais's HRL formulation and invariant cardinal utility function can help us to interpret these "anomalies" in a different light.

Enough will be said by focusing on three of them: hyperbolic discounting (proximate outcomes are discounted at higher rates than distant ones), which is the hallmark of the theory of intertemporal choice; the sign effect (gains are discounted more than losses); and the magnitude effect (small outcomes are discounted more than large ones).

The key empirical findings supporting the hyperbolic discounting hypothesis are twofold. First, observed preferences for smaller-sooner outcomes over larger-later rewards imply that people's discount rates are higher over shorter time horizons than over longer ones. Second, the discount factors observed over a series of increasing time horizons are much easier to fit with hyperbolic functions, in which discount rates

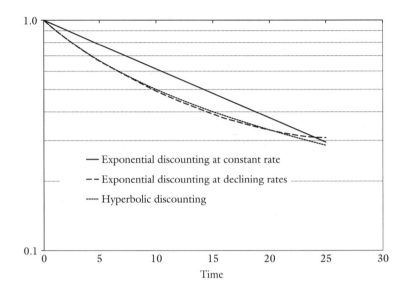

Figure E.1 Discount factor under different discounting models.

decline with respect to the horizon, than with exponential functions, in which the discount rate is assumed to be constant.[4]

All this is all the more puzzling as the discount rates estimated under the hyperbolic discounting hypothesis tend to be very high, if not astronomical, when compared with the nominal interest rates observed in capital markets.[5]

E.2   Intertemporal Choice and the HRL Formulation

That people may be using discount rates, which vary with the discounting horizon, is an easy-to-accept working assumption within the HRL formulation's framework. If people forget the past at a time-varying rate, why would they not discount the future in the same manner? It is actually quite easy to show that any sequence of declining one-period discount rates ($r_1 > r_2 > \cdots > r_n$) yields a sequence of declining exponential discount factors

$$df_p = e^{-\sum_i^p r_i} \tag{E.1}$$

that looks distinctively hyperbolic (see figure E.1 in which the vertical axis scale is a logarithmic one).

The proposition that such sequences of horizon-dependent discount rates should always be declining, and this always from an initial high (if not astronomical) level, is much harder to reconcile with the HRL formulation, unless all the subjects surveyed happen to have been conditioned by inflationary, if not hyperinflationary, personal experiences. According to the HRL formulation, nominal interest rates are indeed firmly anchored on perceived rates of nominal growth, which are in turn a function of past rates of nominal growth.[6] In other words, if the HRL formulation is valid, it suggests that the hyperbolic discounting hypothesis may be derived from unrecognized measurement errors. What could be the cause of these measurement errors? It could be the malignant neglect of cardinal utility.

E.3   Intertemporal Choice and Cardinal Utility

E.3.1   *Apparent Discount Rates Versus True Discount Rates: A Theoretical Approach*

As noted by Frederick, Loewenstein, and O'Donoghue (not to mention other scholars), "the standard approach to estimate discount rates assumes that the utility function is linear in the magnitude of the choice objects . . . . If, instead, the utility function for the good in question is concave, estimates of time preference will be biased upwards."[7] For the sake of clarity, in what follows, we shall call *apparent* the discount rates r directly observed in intertemporal choices between monetary values and *true* the discount rates r' derived from the intertemporal choices between different cardinal utilities.

If the cardinal utility function U is linear in X, apparent and true discount factors are the same, since

$$\frac{u(X_n)}{u(X_{n+\Delta n})} = \frac{c_1 X_n}{c_1 X_{n+\Delta n}} = \frac{X_n}{X_{n+\Delta n}} \tag{E.2}$$

with $\Delta n > 0$ and $X_{n+\Delta n} > X_n > 0$.

However, if the cardinal utility function is not linear in X, if, for example, it is equal to $\sqrt{X}$, a concave function among others,[8] then we will have

$$\frac{u(X_n)}{u(X_{n+\Delta n})} = \sqrt{\frac{X_n}{X_{n+\Delta n}}} > \frac{X_n}{X_{n+\Delta n}} \tag{E.3a}$$

$$\Leftrightarrow \frac{-\frac{1}{2}\ln\frac{X_n}{X_{n+\Delta n}}}{\Delta n} < \frac{-\ln\frac{X_n}{X_{n+\Delta n}}}{\Delta n} \tag{E.3b}$$

$$r'_{n,n+\Delta n} < r_{n+\Delta n} \tag{E.4}$$

The apparent discount rate r will overestimate the true discount rate r', and irrespective of the analytical form of the (concave) utility function, *this overestimation will increase as the discounting horizon Δn shrinks.*

E.3.2 *Apparent Discount Rates Versus True Discount Rates: Quantification of the Measurement Error According to Allais's Invariant Cardinal Utility Function*

Bearing this analysis in mind, let us now try to quantify this measurement error, under the assumption that Allais's invariant cardinal utility function is a valid formulation. The argument of this function is not the absolute gain (or loss) X, but a capital index defined by the ratio

$$\frac{U_0 + X}{U_0} = 1 + \frac{X}{U_0} \tag{E.5}$$

where U_0 is the subject's psychological capital (i.e., the capital she is used to own) and X/U_0 the relative gain (or loss). From this, we immediately see that failing some assumption about the subject's capital, there is nothing we can learn about her true discount rate. Let us consider Thaler's empirical finding that $15 today is equivalent to $20 in 1 month, $50 in 1 year, $100 in 10 years.[9] From this observation, Thaler deduces that the apparent discounting rates are 345 percent over 1 month, 120 percent over 1 year, and 19 percent over 10 years.[10] Let us now assume that the subject's capital is $50. Then the respective multipliers of the initial capital are 1.3, 1.4, 2.0, and 3.0, to which correspond, according to Allais's invariant cardinal utility function, the utilities 0.0688, 0.0799, 0.1242, and 0.1681. The respective true discount factors ($0.0799/0.0688$, $0.1242/0.0688$, and $0.1681/0.0688$) imply the following true discount rates: 179 percent, 59 percent and 9 percent. Of course, one can make any other assumption about the

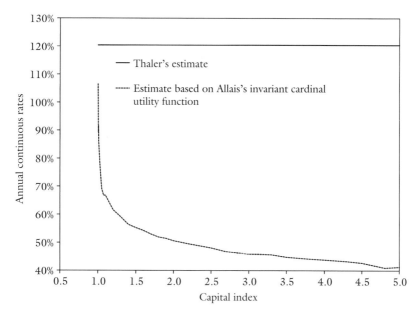

Figure E.2 A 1-year discount rate.

subject's capital and repeat this exercise as many times as wished. As a rule of thumb, and this irrespective of the discounting horizon, one can conclude that neglecting the cardinal utility function's curvature, as estimated by Allais, leads to overestimating true discount rates by a multiplier factor slightly larger than 2 (see figure E.2 in which the discount horizon is 1 year).

E.3.3   Small Relative Gains Are Discounted More Than Large Ones

Another important observation is that, irrespective of the discount horizon, the overestimation of true discount rates is larger in absolute terms for large relative gains than for smaller ones (figure E.2 looks very much the same over a 1-month as well as a 10-year discounting horizon). One of the anomalies noticed by behavioral economics is that apparent discount rates are higher for small gains than for large gains. As suggested by figure E.2, the same pattern is present in the true discount rates derived from Allais's invariant cardinal utility function for a given discount horizon. Please note that the hyperbolic dotted

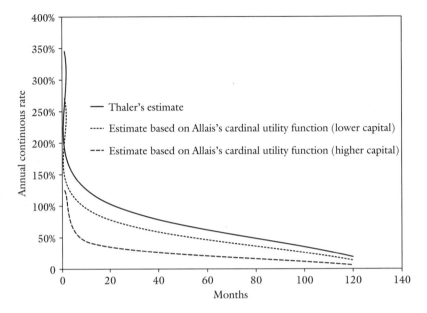

Figure E.3 The hyperbolic discounting hypothesis.

line displayed on figure E.2 is not the one on the basis of which the hyperbolic discounting assumption is formulated, since—in this graph—the horizontal axis refers not to time, but to the subject's capital index, and the values displayed are true as opposed to apparent discount rates.

E.3.4   Hyperbolic Discounting of Utility

Nevertheless, hyperbolic discounting seems to be applied to utility values, too. The three data points reported by Thaler are enough to sketch out a hyperbolic discounting pattern for true discount rates with respect to time[11] and to see, as well, how the level of true discount rates over short horizons is strongly dependent upon the assumption made about the subject's psychological capital (see figure E.3). In other words, there seems to be a strong connection between hyperbolic discounting and the discounting of small relative gains, as if it were one single phenomenon disguised in two different sets of clothes. It should be easy to assess the impact of small relative gains on both apparent and true discount rates by presenting subjects with intertemporal choices involving either small relative gains only, or large relative gains only, but no combination of both.

This being said, the seemingly special status of small relative gains begs the following question: is there anything special about the shape of Allais's invariant cardinal utility function in the region of small gains that might explain hyperbolic discounting?

E.3.5   *Shape of Allais's Cardinal Utility Function for Small Relative Gains*

A close look at the graph of Allais's invariant cardinal utility function reveals a small hump to the right of the point whose abscissa is 1, that is, in the region of small relative gains (see figure 10.10). To better appreciate the behavior of the cardinal utility function for small relative gains, one needs a magnifying glass. First, one must rebase both the function and its arguments from 100, using the point (1.0010, 0.0010) as the base point. Then one must draw a scatterplot of the two rebased series on a log-log graph and overlay a straight line of slope 1. Only then does it become obvious that Allais's cardinal utility function rises much faster than its argument when relative gains are positive but smaller than about 40 percent, the abscissa for which the slope of the tangent is approximately equal to 1 (see figure E.4). In this region, marginal utility

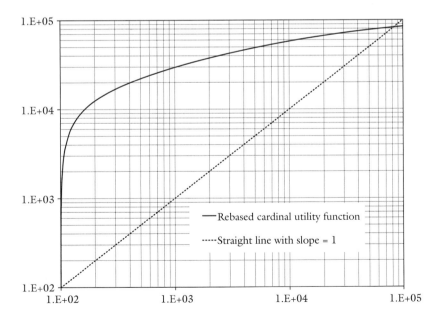

Figure E.4 Rebased cardinal utility function.

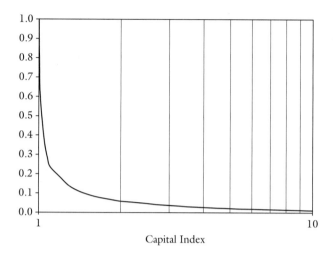

Figure E.5 Marginal utility.

(the first derivative of cardinal utility) diminishes very quickly from an initial level, which is equal to 1 (see table E.1). As a result and as shown by figure E.5, Allais's marginal utility curve has a hyperbolic shape.

As noted by Frederick et al. (2002), "diminishing marginal utility motivates a person to spread consumption over time." One can indeed afford to wait for the small increase in utility that comes with large relative gains, but cannot wait for the large increase in utility that comes with small relative gains. Put differently, the low marginal utility of large relative gains implies low true (and apparent) discount rates, while the high marginal utility of small relative gains implies high true (and apparent) discount rates. Since hyperbolic discounting is found in circumstances where people prefer smaller-sooner outcomes over larger-later rewards, it seems logical to infer that hyperbolic discounting could be nothing but a consequence of the hyperbolic shape of Allais's marginal utility curve.

In other words, the choice between smaller-sooner outcomes and larger-later rewards is not a mere intertemporal choice; it is also a choice between different utilities. It is a two-dimensional problem, the solution of which cannot be a single number. A thirsty man lost in the Australian outback will always prefer a glass of fresh water today over two glasses tomorrow, not because he is indulging in hyperbolic discounting, but because he is dying of thirst. And, at the same time,

TABLE E.1
Equivalence Table

$1 + X/U_0$	U	Marginal utility	$d \ln U$
1.0000	0.0000	0.9700	
1.0010	0.0010	1.0000	
1.0025	0.0023	0.8667	0.8329
1.0050	0.0043	0.8000	0.6257
1.0071	0.0057	0.6667	0.2819
1.0100	0.0075	0.6207	0.2744
1.0250	0.0150	0.5000	0.6931
1.0500	0.0240	0.3600	0.4700
1.0750	0.0311	0.2840	0.2592
1.1000	0.0370	0.2360	0.1737
1.2000	0.0552	0.1820	0.4000
1.3000	0.0688	0.1360	0.2202
1.4000	0.0799	0.1110	0.1496
1.5000	0.0894	0.0950	0.1123
1.6000	0.0977	0.0830	0.0888
1.7000	0.1052	0.0750	0.0740
1.8000	0.1121	0.0690	0.0635
1.9000	0.1184	0.0630	0.0547
2.0000	0.1242	0.0580	0.0478

he may well prefer two glasses in a year to one glass in a year minus a day, under the assumption that he will have survived until then.

To put it simply, failing some very high true discount rates, no intertemporal choice between small gains would ever be possible. Let us now investigate further the connection between the slope of the cardinal utility curve and true discount rates. The discount factor and the discount rate between two quantities Q_n and $Q_{n+\Delta n}$ are defined by the relationship

$$df_{n,n+\Delta n} = \frac{Q_n}{Q_{n,n+\Delta n}} = e^{-r_{n,n+\Delta n}\Delta n} \qquad \text{with} \qquad \Delta n > 0 \qquad (E.6)$$

which is equivalent to

$$r_{n,n+\Delta n} = \frac{1}{\Delta n}(\ln Q_{n+\Delta n} - \ln Q_n) \qquad (E.7)$$

This means that the discount rate derived from the temporal equivalence between Q_n and $Q_{n+\Delta n}$ is nothing but the average growth rate that has Q_n grown to $Q_{n+\Delta n}$ over the time span Δn.[12] Table E.1 displays the log rate of change between consecutive points of Allais's cardinal utility curve in the region of small gains.

E.3.6   Gains Are Discounted More Than Losses

Within Allais's cardinal utility framework, even if people discount gains and losses at the same true rate, it will seem that they discount gains more than losses. This apparent discounting asymmetry results not from the fact that Allais's cardinal utility function is steeper for losses than for gains, but from the possibility to approximate it by loglinear forms over a large domain.

Let us first consider a numerical example. Let us imagine a subject with a psychological capital of 1,000 and a true discount rate of 10 percent that she applies over a given one-period time horizon to gains as well as to losses. What will her apparent discount rates be for a gain and a loss of same size, say, 100?

Let us start with the gain. Since $U_0 = 1,000$ and $X = 100$, the subject's capital index is

$$\frac{U_0 + X}{U_0} = \frac{1,100}{100} = 1.10 \tag{E.8}$$

To this capital index of 1.10 corresponds, according to Allais, a utility of 0.0370. Discounted at the true rate of 10 percent over one period, this utility is equivalent to 0.0355, to which corresponds a capital index of 1.085, that is, a gain of 85. From this, it follows that the apparent discount rate applied to the gain of 100 over a one-period time horizon is

$$-\ln(85/100) = 16.25\% \tag{E.9}$$

As for the loss of 100, it implies a capital index of 0.90, to which corresponds a utility of -0.0792. Discounted at the true rate of 10 percent, this utility is equivalent to -0.0717, to which corresponds a capital index of 0.91, that is, a loss of 90. In other words, the apparent discount rate applied to the loss of 100 is

$$-\ln(-90/-100) = 10.54\% \tag{E.10}$$

Let us now follow a more formal approach. Over a large domain, Allais's invariant cardinal utility function can be approximated by two straight lines, one for losses, the other for gains. The asymmetric discounting of gains and losses is a consequence of this loglinear approximation. With

$$C = 1 + \frac{X}{U_0} \qquad \text{(E.11)}$$

being the subject's capital index, we have indeed

$$U(C) = U \approx a_1 \ln C \quad \text{if} \quad X > 0 \Leftrightarrow C > 1 \qquad \text{(E.12)}$$

and

$$U(C) = U \approx a_2 \ln C \quad \text{if} \quad X < 0 \Leftrightarrow C < 1 \qquad \text{(E.13)}$$

with $a_2 > a_1$.

Let us now consider $X_1 > 0$ and $X_2 = -X_1 < 0$. If the subject's true discount rate is $r' > 0$, the discounted value U'_1 of U_1 is such that

$$U'_1 = e^{-r'} U_1 \approx a_1 \ln C'_1 \qquad \text{(E.14)}$$

in which C'_1 is the capital corresponding to the discounted utility U'_1. To U'_1 corresponds a certain X'_1 defined by the following relationship:

$$X'_1 = (C_1^{e^{-r'}} - 1) U_0 \qquad \text{(E.15)}$$

Now, since $X_1 = (C_1 - 1) U_0$, the corresponding apparent discount rate is

$$r_1 = -\ln \frac{X'_1}{X_1} = -\ln \frac{C_1^{e^{-r'}} - 1}{C_1 - 1} \qquad \text{(E.16)}$$

Similarly, for $X_2 = -X_1 < 0$, we have $X'_2 = (C_2^{e^{-r'}} - 1) U_0$ and

$$r_2 = -\ln \frac{X'_2}{X_2} = -\ln \frac{C_2^{e^{-r'}} - 1}{-(C_1 - 1)} \qquad \text{(E.17)}$$

Let us now see why r_2 is necessarily smaller than r_1. Since $C_2 < 1 < C_1 \Leftrightarrow C_2^{e^{-r'}} - 1 < 0 < C_1^{e^{-r'}} - 1$, we just need to show that $|C_2^{e^{-r'}} - 1| > |C_1^{e^{-r'}} - 1|$. As $C_2^{e^{-r'}} = e^{e^{-r'} \ln C_2}$, we can write $C_2^{e^{-r'}} \approx 1 + e^{-r'} \ln C_2$ and $C_2^{e^{-r'}} - 1 \approx e^{-r'} \ln C_2$. Finally, we get

$$C_2^{e^{-r'}} - 1 < C_1^{e^{-r'}} - 1 \Leftrightarrow e^{-r'} \ln C_2 < e^{-r'} \ln C_1 \Leftrightarrow \ln C_2 < \ln C_1 \qquad \text{(E.18)}$$

and

$$\ln C_2 < \ln C_1 \Leftrightarrow |\ln C_2| > |\ln C_1| \Leftrightarrow r_2 < r_1 \qquad \text{(E.19)}$$

E.3.6.1   CONCLUSION This short note did not purport to provide a comprehensive assessment of the theory of intertemporal choice. But it shows that the empirical findings, which underpin the hyperbolic discounting hypothesis and other related generalizations, must absolutely be interpreted within a cardinal utility framework. Absent an explicit cardinal utility function to interpret those findings, the risk is high to enter into barren debates or to infer hasty conclusions. That Allais's cardinal utility function, a function clearly not estimated in reference to the theory of intertemporal choice, seems nevertheless able to explain some intertemporal anomalies is noteworthy and lends plausibility to Allais's estimation. Advances in the theory of intertemporal choice are subject to further research on cardinal utility functions in general and Allais's function in particular.

Allais's Cardinal Utility Function

TABLE F.1
Allais's Cardinal Utility Function

	Capital Multiplier (1a)	Cardinal Utility (2a)	Capital Multiplier (1b)	Cardinal Utility (2b)	Capital Multiplier (1c)	Cardinal Utility (2c)	Capital Multiplier (1d)	Cardinal Utility (2d)
1	0.065	−1.000	0.82	−0.1290	4.5	0.2103	300	0.7183
2	0.070	−0.975	0.83	−0.1230	4.8	0.2171	340	0.7332
3	0.080	−0.931	0.84	−0.1170	5.0	0.2214	350	0.7366
4	0.090	−0.894	0.85	−0.1110	5.2	0.2255	400	0.7521
5	0.100	−0.860	0.86	−0.1050	5.5	0.2313	450	0.7654
6	0.120	−0.803	0.87	−0.0984	6.0	0.2407	500	0.7771
7	0.140	−0.754	0.88	−0.0921	7.0	0.2572	600	0.7967
8	0.160	−0.712	0.89	−0.0857	8.0	0.2717	700	0.8126
9	0.180	−0.676	0.90	−0.0792	9.0	0.2847	800	0.8258
10	0.200	−0.645	0.91	−0.0725	9.5	0.2906	900	0.8370
11	0.220	−0.617	0.92	−0.0656	10.0	0.2963	1000	0.8467
12	0.240	−0.591	0.93	−0.0586	10.5	0.3018	1110	0.8551
13	0.260	−0.569	0.94	−0.0513	11	0.3070	1200	0.8636
14	0.280	−0.548	0.95	−0.0437	12	0.3169	1300	0.8692
15	0.300	−0.528	0.96	−0.0358	13	0.3260	1400	0.8752
16	0.320	−0.508	0.97	−0.0275	14	0.3345	1500	0.8806
17	0.340	−0.490	0.98	−0.0188	15	0.3425	1600	0.8855
18	0.360	−0.472	0.99	−0.0097	16	0.3500	1700	0.8900
19	0.380	−0.454	1.00	0.0000	17	0.3570	1800	0.8941
20	0.400	−0.437	1.0010	0.0010	18	0.3638	1900	0.8978
21	0.420	−0.418	1.0025	0.0023	19	0.3701	2000	0.9013
22	0.440	−0.401	1.0050	0.0043	20	0.3762	2300	0.9104
23	0.460	−0.384	1.0071	0.0057	23	0.3930	2500	0.9155
24	0.480	−0.367	1.0100	0.0075	25	0.4030	2700	0.9200
25	0.500	−0.350	1.0250	0.0150	30	0.4254	3000	0.9259
26	0.520	−0.334	1.0500	0.0240	35	0.4446	3500	0.9338
27	0.540	−0.318	1.0750	0.0311	40	0.4614	4000	0.9401
28	0.560	−0.302	1.10	0.0370	45	0.4763	4500	0.9452
29	0.580	−0.287	1.20	0.0552	50	0.4897	5000	0.9495
30	0.600	−0.272	1.30	0.0688	60	0.5131	6000	0.9561
31	0.620	−0.257	1.40	0.0799	70	0.5331	7000	0.9610
32	0.640	−0.243	1.50	0.0894	80	0.5504	8000	0.9649
33	0.660	−0.229	1.60	0.0977	90	0.5657	9000	0.9680
34	0.680	−0.216	1.70	0.1052	100	0.5794	10000	0.9705
35	0.700	−0.203	1.80	0.1121	110	0.5918	11000	0.9726
36	0.710	−0.196	1.90	0.1184	120	0.6030	12000	0.9744
37	0.720	−0.190	2.00	0.1242	130	0.6134	13000	0.9759
38	0.730	−0.184	2.20	0.1349	140	0.6229	15000	0.9784
39	0.740	−0.177	2.50	0.1488	150	0.6318	17000	0.9803
40	0.750	−0.171	2.70	0.1570	170	0.6478	20000	0.9825

TABLE F.1

Allais's Cardinal Utility Function (*Continued*)

	Capital Multiplier (1a)	Cardinal Utility (2a)	Capital Multiplier (1b)	Cardinal Utility (2b)	Capital Multiplier (1c)	Cardinal Utility (2c)	Capital Multiplier (1d)	Cardinal Utility (2d)
41	0.760	−0.165	3.00	0.1681	180	0.6550	25000	0.9850
42	0.770	−0.159	3.30	0.1781	190	0.6619	30000	0.9868
43	0.780	−0.153	3.50	0.1842	200	0.6684	40000	0.9890
44	0.790	−0.147	3.80	0.1927	230	0.6858	50000	0.9903
45	0.800	−0.141	4.00	0.1981	250	0.6961	60000	0.9912
46	0.810	−0.135	4.30	0.2056	270	0.7055	70000	0.9918
47							100000	0.9930

Source: Allais, M. (1991), *Cardinal utility: History, empirical findings and applications.* Theory and decision 31, Kluwer Academic, Dordrecht, pp. 99–140. Table 1, p. 133, and Table 7, p. 127, ©Kluwer Academic Publishers, with kind permission from Springer Science & Business Media B.V.

Notes

Introduction

1. Knight, F. (1921), *Risk, uncertainty and profit*, Beard Books, Washington, D.C., 2002, p. 19: "Uncertainty must be taken in a sense radically distinct from the familiar notion of Risk.... The term 'risk,' as loosely used in everyday speech and in economic discussions, really covers two things which, functionally at least, in their causal relations to economic organization are categorically different.... The essential fact is that 'risk' means in some cases a quantity susceptible of measurement, while at other times it is something distinctly not of this character; and there are far-reaching and crucial differences in the bearings of the phenomenon depending on which of the two is really present and operating.... It will appear that a measurable uncertainty, or 'risk' proper...is so far different from an unmeasurable one that it is not in effect an uncertainty at all. We shall accordingly restrict the term 'uncertainty' to cases of the non-quantitative type. It is 'true' uncertainty, and not risk..., which forms the basis of a valid theory of profit and accounts for the divergence between actual and theoretical competition."

2. Lucas, R. E., Jr. (1977), *Understanding business cycles*, in Brunner, K., and Meltzer, A. (eds.), *Stabilization of the domestic and international economy*, vol. 5, Carnegie-Rochester Series on Public Policy, North Holland Publishing Company, New York, pp. 7–29.

3. Phelps, E. S., and Frydman, R. (2013), *Rethinking expectations: The way forward for macroeconomics*, Princeton University Press, Princeton, NJ.

4. Volatility is indeed volatile.

5. Guesnerie, R. (2001 and 2005), *Assessing rational expectations* (1 and 2), MIT Press, Cambridge, MA.

6. Kindleberger, C. P. (1978), *Manias, panics and crashes (A history of financial crises)*, 4th ed., Wiley, New York, 2001.

7. In hedge finance, current cash flows cover debt servicing (capital and interest). In speculative finance, they only cover interest payments. In Ponzi finance, they cover neither interest nor principal payments.

8. As measured by a Fisher volume index eliminating currency fluctuations.

9. Caginalp, G., Porter, D., and Smith, V. L. (2000), *Overreactions, momentum, liquidity and price bubbles in laboratory and field asset markets*, The Journal of Psychology and Financial Markets, 2000, vol. 1, no. 1, pp. 24–48; Gjerstad, S., and Smith, V. L. (2009), *Monetary policy, credit extension, and housing bubbles: 2008 and 1929, critical review*, A Journal of Politics and Society, vol. 21, nos. 2–3.

10. Renshaw, E. (1988), *The crash of October 19 in retrospect*, The Market Chronicle, vol. 22, 1.

11. 1911–2010, 1988 laureate of the Prize in Economic Sciences in Memory of Alfred Nobel.

12. Fisher, I. (1896), *Appreciation and interest*, American Economic Association, Pickering & Chatto, London, 1996; Fisher, I. (1930), *The theory of interest*, Chap. 19, *Relation to money and prices*, Pickering & Chatto, London, 1996; Wicksell, K. (1898), *Interest and prices*, Chap. 8, *The natural rate of interest on capital and the rate of interest on loans*, Augustus M. Kelley, Fairfield, NJ, 1965; Knight, F. (1921), *Risk, uncertainty and profit*, Chap. 8, Beard Books, Washington, D.C., 2002; Hayek, F. (1936), *Economics and knowledge*, Presidential address delivered to the London Economic Club on November 10, 1936, Economica (1937), vol. 4, pp. 33–54. Keynes, J. M. (1936), *The general theory of employment, interest and money*, Chap. 12, *The state of long-term expectations*, Harcourt Brace Jovanovich, New York, 1964; Hicks, J. (1939), *Value and capital*, Oxford University Press (repr.) 2001; Friedman, M. (1968), *Factors affecting the level of interest rates*, in *Savings and Residential Financing: 1968 Conference Proceedings*, Jacobs, D. P. and Pratt, R. T., (eds.), The United States Saving and Loan League, Chicago, IL, p. 375.

13. Allais, M. (1966), *A restatement of the quantity theory of money*, American Economic Review, vol. 56, no. 5, December, pp. 1123–1157.

14. Fisher, I. (1932), *Booms and depressions*, Pickering & Chatto, London, 1996; Fisher, I. (1933), *The debt-deflation theory of great depressions*, Econometrica, vol. 1, issue 4, October, pp. 337–357; Minsky, H. P. (1975), *John Maynard Keynes*, Columbia University Press, New York; Minsky, H. P. (1982), *Can "it" happen again?* Sharpe, New York; Minsky, H. P. (1986a), *The financial instability hypothesis: Capitalist production and the behavior of the economy in financial crises: Theory, history and policy*, eds. C. Kindleberger and J-P. Laffargue, Cambridge University Press, New York; Minsky, H. P. (1991), *The financial instability hypothesis: A clarification* in *The risk of economic crisis*, ed. Martin Feldstein; Kindleberger, C. P. (1985), *Rational expectations and*

collective memory, in *Keynesianism vs monetarism and other essays in financial history,* Allen and Unwin, London.

15. See, for example, Sargent, T. J. (1999), *The conquest of American inflation,* Princeton University Press, Princeton, NJ.

16. See appendix D.

17. Cagan, P. (1956), *The monetary dynamics of hyper-inflation,* in Friedman, M. (ed.), *Studies in the quantity theory of money,* University of Chicago Press, Chicago.

18. Camerer, C. F., Loewenstein, G., and Rabin, M. (2004), *Advances in behavioral economics,* Princeton University Press, Princeton, NJ; Allais, M. (1953), *Le comportement de l'homme rationnel devant le risque: Critique des postulats et axiomes de l'école Américaine,* Econometrica, vol. 21, pp. 503–546; Allais, M. (1965), *Reformulation de la théorie quantitative de la monnaie,* Société d'études et de documentation économiques, industrielles et sociales (SEDEIS), Paris.

19. Cantillon, R. (1755), *Essai sur la nature du commerce en général,* Institut National d'Etudes Démographiques (INED), Paris, 1997.

20. Samuelson, P. A. (1982), *A chapter in the history of Ramsey's optimal feasible taxation and optimal public utility prices,* in *Economic essays in honour of Jorgen H. Gelting,* Andersen, S., Larsen, K., Norregard Rusmussen, P., and Vibe-Pedersen, J. (eds), Danish Economic Association, Copenhagen, pp. 164–165, note 3. Reprinted in the Collected Scientific Papers of P. A. Samuelson, vol. 5 (1986), MIT, Cambridge.

21. Keynes, J. M. (1936), *The general theory of employment, interest and money,* Chap. 12, *The state of long-term expectations,* Harcourt Brace Jovanovich, New York, 1964.

1. The Progressive Emergence of Expectations

1. Cantillon, R. (1755), *Essai sur la nature du commerce en général,* Institut National d'Etudes Démographiques, Paris, 1997, Part 1, Chap. 13.

2. Cantillon, *Essai sur la nature du commerce en général,* Part 2, Chap. 10.

3. In 1720, according to Cantillon, the market interest rate in London rose from 5 percent to 60 percent per annum.

4. Wicksell, K. (1898), *Interest and prices,* Chap. 8, *The natural rate of interest on capital and the rate of interest on loans,* Augustus M. Kelley, Fairfield, NJ, 1965.

5. The closeness of Wicksell's "gambling spirit" with Keynes's "animal spirits" is striking.

6. Wicksell, K. (1906), *Lectures on political economy,* vol. 2, Augustus M. Kelley, Fairfield, NJ, 1965.

7. And he adds the following: "Exactly the same effects would be visible with an unchanged, or even a higher, rate of interest, if meanwhile the expected profit on capital had considerably increased."

8. Hicks summarized this argument by saying it assumes the "elasticity of expectations" with respect to actual price changes to be equal to 1.

9. Knight, F. (1921), *Risk, uncertainty and profit*, Beard Books, Washington, D.C., 2002.

10. Keynes, J. M. (1936), *The general theory of employment, interest and money*, Chap. 12, *The state of long-term expectations*, Harcourt Brace Jovanovich, New York, 1964.

11. Much of his analysis of expectations was already present in Keynes, J. M. (1924), *A tract on monetary reform*, Prometheus Books, New York, 2000.

12. Schumpeter, J. (1939), *Business cycles*. Reprinted in 1989 by Porcupine Press, Philadelphia.

13. Haberler, G. (1937), *Prosperity and depression. A theoretical analysis of cyclical movements*, 2011, Transaction Publishers, New Brunswick, NJ.

14. Lundberg, E. (1937), *Studies in the theory of economic expansion*, Chap. 9, 1964, Augustus M. Kelley, Fairfield, NJ.

15. Hayek, F. (1936), *Economics and knowledge*, Presidential address delivered to the London Economic Club on November 10, 1936, Economica (1937), vol. 4, pp. 33-54.

16. Fisher, I. (1896), *Appreciation and interest*, American Economic Association, Pickering & Chatto, London, 1996.

17. Heterogeneity of forecasts, in modern parlance.

18. Fisher, I. (1930), *The theory of interest*, Chap. 19, *Relation to money and prices*, Pickering & Chatto, London, 1996.

19. Cagan, P. (1956), *The monetary dynamics of hyper-inflation*, in *Studies in the quantity theory of money*, ed. Milton Friedman, University of Chicago Press, Chicago.

20. Cagan approached the problem in terms of forecasting error and error correction coefficients, while Allais put the stress on the decay of human memory.

2. Rational Expectations Are Endogenous to and Abide by "the" Model

1. Muth, J. F. (1960), *Optimal properties of exponentially-weighted forecasts*, Journal of the American Statistical Association, vol. 55, no. 290, June, pp. 299–306.

2. Gourgieroux, C., and Monfort, A. (1995), *Séries temporelles et modèles dynamiques*, 2nd ed., Economica, Paris, pp. 106–110.

3. In chapter 3, we shall see that both Cagan and Allais empirically encountered and recognized the shortcomings of exponential smoothing in the early 1950s. It is this empirical encounter that led Allais to the HRL formulation.

4. Sargent, T. J., and Wallace, N. (1973), *Rational expectations and the dynamics of hyperinflation*, International Economic Review, vol. 14, no. 2, June.

5. Muth, J. F. (1961), *Rational expectations and the theory of price movements*, Econometrica, vol. 29, no. 3, July.

6. Lucas, R. E. (1972), *Expectations and the neutrality of money*, Journal of Economic Theory, vol. 4, pp. 103–124.

7. Lucas, R. E. (1976), *Econometric policy evaluation: A critique*, Carnegie-Rochester Conference Series on Public Policy, North Holland, New York, vol. 1, pp. 19–46.

8. Sargent, T. J., and Wallace, N. (1976), *Rational expectations and the theory of economic policy*, Journal of Monetary Economics, July, pp. 199–214.

9. Arrow, J. K. (1986), *Rationality of self and others in an economic system*, Journal of Business, vol. 59, no. 4, part 2, October, pp. 385–399, reprinted in *The New Palgrave: Utility and Probability*, Eatwell J., Milgate M., Newman P. (eds), Norton, New York.

10. Knight would have said *risky* instead of *uncertain*.

11. Malinvaud, E. (1991), *Voies de la recherche macroéconomique*, Points-Seuil, Paris, 1993, pp. 546–549.

12. Read *risk*.

13. Read *risk*.

14. Lucas, R., and Sargent, T. (1979), *After Keynesian macroeconomics*, The Federal Reserve Bank of Minneapolis, Quarterly Review 321, Spring.

15. Guesnerie, R. (2001), *Assessing rational expectations*, MIT Press, Cambridge, MA.

16. Modigliani, F. (1977), *The monetarist controversy, or should we foresake stabilization policy?* American Economic Review, vol. 67, no. 2, pp. 1–17, March.

17. Friedman, B. M. (1975), *Rational expectations are really adaptive after all*, unpublished paper, Harvard University, Cambridge, MA.

18. Lucas, R. (1975), *An equilibrium model of the business cycle*, Journal of Political Economy, vol. 83, no. 6, pp. 11–21.

19. Gowers, T. (ed.) (2008), *The Princeton companion to mathematics*, Princeton University Press, Princeton, NJ, p. 160.

20. In other words, $P(E) = \sum_i P(E|H_i) \times P(H_i)$ for all i.

21. Lindley, D. V. (1990), *Thomas Bayes* in *The New Palgrave: Utility and Probability*, Eatwell J., Milgate M., Newman P. (eds.), Norton, New York.

22. Parent, E., and Bernier, J. (2007), *Le raisonnement Bayésien: Modélisation et inférence*, Springer-Verlag, Paris.

23. Wonnacott, Thomas H., and Ronald, J. (1990), *Introductory statistics*, 5th ed., Wiley, New York.

24. Pastor, L., and Veronesi, P. (2009), *Learning in financial markets*, Annual Review of Financial Economics, vol. 1, pp. 361–381.

25. Sargent, T. J. (1999), *The Conquest of American inflation*, Princeton University Press, Princeton, NJ.

26. Another suggestion is to do rolling recursive OLS linear regression on an arbitrarily decided number of observations.

27. See, for example, Sargent, T. J. (1999), *The Conquest of American inflation*, Princeton University Press, Princeton, NJ.

28. www.nobelprize.org.

29. Kay, J. (2011), *The random shock that clinched a brave Nobel Prize*, Financial Times, October 18.

30. Gide, C., and Rist, C. (1944), *Histoire des doctrines économiques depuis les physiocrates jusqu'à nos jours*, Livre 6, Chap. 2, *Le conflit des théories des crises*, 6th ed., Dalloz, Paris, 2000.

31. Sargent, T., and Wallace, N. (1976), *Rational expectations and the theory of economic policy*, Studies in Monetary Economics, Federal Reserve Bank of Minneapolis, October 1976; Journal of Monetary Economics, July.

32. Phelps, E. (2009), *A fruitless clash of economic opposites*, Financial Times, November 3.

33. Arrow, J. K. (1986), *Rationality of self and others in an economic system*, Journal of Business, vol. 59, no. 4, part 2, October, pp. 385–399, reprinted in *The New Palgrave: Utility and Probability*, Eatwell J., Milgate M., Newman P. (eds.), Norton, New York.

34. Sargent, T. J., and Wallace, N. (1973), *Rational expectations and the dynamics of hyperinflation*, International Economic Review, vol. 14, no. 2, June.

35. Woodford, M. (1999), *Revolution and evolution in twentieth-century macroeconomics*, Princeton University Press, Princeton, NJ, note 51, p. 24.

36. Blaug, M. (1996), *Economic theory in retrospect*, 5th ed., Cambridge University Press, Cambridge, p. 685.

37. Screpanti, E., and Zamagni, S. (2005), *An outline of the history of economic thought*, Oxford University Press, Oxford.

38. Woodford, M. (2008), *Convergence in macroeconomics: Elements of the new synthesis*, prepared for the annual meeting of the American Economics Association.

39. The so-called Duhem-Quine problem.

40. Woodford, M. (2011), *What's wrong with economic models?* Institute for New Economic Thinking (INET), New York.

41. Lucas, R. (1995), *Monetary neutrality*, Nobel Prize lecture, December 7.

42. Bootle, R. (1997), *The death of inflation*, Nicholas Brealey, London. Quote used with kind permission of Roger Bootle.

43. Simon, H. A. (1997), *An empirically based microeconomics*, First lecture (Rationality in Decision Making), Raffaele Mattioli Foundation, Cambridge University Press, Cambridge.

Introduction to Part II

1. Allais, M. (2001), *Fondements de la dynamique monétaire*, Editions Clément Juglar, Paris.
2. Cagan, P. (1956), *The monetary dynamics of hyper-inflation*, in Friedman, M. (ed.), *Studies in the Quantity Theory of Money*, University of Chicago Press, Chicago.
3. Sargent, T. J., and Wallace, N. (1973), *Rational expectations and the dynamics of hyperinflation*, International Economic Review, vol. 14, no. 2.

3. Macrofoundations of Monetary Dynamics

1. Allais, M. (1954a), *Les fondements comptables de la macro-économique* , 2nd ed., Presses Universitaires de France, Paris, 1993.
2. In *Value and capital*, Hicks uses the same starting point, but—as far as I can judge—he did not exploit it as far as Allais did.
3. One simply needs to consider the government as an additional business selling services against taxes and to present the rest of the world as another additional business buying (importing) domestic goods and services or selling (exporting) foreign goods and services.
4. Blaug, M. (1996), *Economic theory in retrospect*, 5th ed., Cambridge University Press, Cambridge, Chap. 16, p. 646.
5. Blaug, M. (1996), *Economic theory in retrospect*, Chap. 16, p. 647.
6. Albeit arguably, fixed-term deposits are more likely to be precautionary balances than currency and demand deposits.
7. Blaug, M. (1996), *Economic theory in retrospect*, Chap. 5, pp. 54–55.
8. Gide, C., and Rist, C. (1944), *Histoire des doctrines économiques*, 6th ed., *Conflit des théories des crises*, Book 6, Chap. 2, Dalloz, Paris, 2000.
9. Allais, M. (1953b), *Illustration de la théorie des cycles économiques par un modèle monétaire non linéaire*. Extraits de la communication au Congrès Européen de la Société d'Econométrie, Innsbrück, 2/9/1953, Econometrica, January 1954, pp. 116–117.
10. Allais, M. (1954b), *Explication des cycles économiques par un modèle non linéaire à régulation retardée*. Communication au Congrès Européen de la Société d'Econométrie, Uppsala, 4/8/1954, Metroeconomica, vol. 8, fascicule I, pp. 4–83, April 1956.

11. In the Innsbruck paper, the two functions depend only on $x = \frac{1}{D}\frac{dD}{dt}$, the latest growth rate in nominal spending. In the two later papers, they depend on the exponentially smoothed sequence of growth rates.

12. This function was chosen for its simplicity and illustrative properties. It belongs to this book, not to Allais, but, needless to say, it is directly inspired by his later works.

4. Microfoundations of Monetary Dynamics

1. Allais, M. (1965), *Reformulation de la théorie quantitative de la monnaie*, Société d'études et de documentation économiques, industrielles et sociales (SEDEIS), Paris.

2. The two formulations become equivalent when the rate of inflation becomes dominant relative to the real rate of growth.

3. As in the Uppsala (1954) and Paris (1955) papers, Allais observes that this formulation is very close to Boltzmann's oblivion function and to Volterra's dampening function.

4. This recursive relationship makes it very easy to compute an exponential average.

5. Minsky, H. P. (1986b), *Stabilizing an unstable economy*, Yale University Press, New Haven, CT.

6. Quoted by the Financial Times, August 27 and 28, 2005.

7. In physical time.

8. In psychological time.

9. In physical time.

10. In psychological time.

11. Besides Einstein, there are many examples in literature and politics of implicit reference to psychological time. For example, Lenin is believed to have said, "Sometimes decades pass and nothing happens, and then sometimes weeks pass and decades happen."

12. The term Z is nothing but the numerator of relationship 4.2 under the assumption that r varies over time.

13. One of the fundamental principles of economic analysis is to present economic issues as optimization problems in which a certain quantity must be minimized or maximized. According to this principle, it seems logical to conjecture that relationship 4-31 (or 4-52) should be the solution of a certain optimization problem that, as it happened, Allais has not explicitly laid out. I wish I had been able to formulate this important problem before this book goes to press. Further research will hopefully close this gap.

14. For $E \approx 0$, $e^{-\alpha E - \gamma} \approx (1 - \alpha E)e^{-\gamma}$.

15. Allais, M. (2001), *Fondements de la dynamique monétaire*, pp. 82–84 and pp. 469–472.

16. If $\alpha = 0$ or $b = 0$, then $\Psi(Z) = 1$ and the HRL formulation becomes equivalent to an exponential average, where χ_0 remains the only parameter.

17. Caginalp, G., Porter, D., and Smith, V. L. (2000), *Overreactions, momentum, liquidity and price bubbles in laboratory and field asset markets*, The Journal of Psychology and Financial Markets, vol. 1, no. 1, pp. 24–48.

18. Prat, G., (1999), *Temps psychologique, oubli et intérêt chez Maurice Allais*, *Discussion Papers (REL—Recherches Economiques de Louvain)* 65(2) 1999022, Université catholique de Louvain, Institut de Recherches Economiques et Sociales (IRES), Louvain.

19. Portelli, G., Ruffier, F., Roubieu, F. and Franceschini, N. (2011), *Honeybees' speed depends on dorsal as well as lateral, ventral and frontal optic flows*, Plos ONE, May, vol. 6, Issue 5.

5. The Fundamental Equation of Monetary Dynamics

1. Allais, M. (1968), *L'équation fondamentale de la dynamique monétaire*, Monnaie et Développement, fascicule 1, Ecole Nationale Supérieure des Mines de Paris, pp. 75–86.

2. In the Anglo-Saxon literature, transactions are usually denoted by the letter T; however, as Allais uses the letter T to denote his response period, it seems appropriate to designate transactions with the letter Q to prevent any risk of confusion.

3. As opposed to the income velocity of money v, which is defined by the ratio $v = Y/M$, where Y represents national income.

4. Leaving aside, for the time being, nonbank credit.

5. Hicks, J. (1939), Value and capital Part III, *The foundations of dynamic economics*, Chap. 9, *The method of analysis*, reprinted in 2001 by Oxford University Press, Oxford.

6. He even states that a first-rate business should show flexibility in this regard.

7. Allais, M. (1968b), *La génération endogène des fluctuations conjoncturelles*, reprinted in *Fondements de la dynamique monétaire*, Editions Clément Juglar, Paris, 2001, pp. 969–1010.

8. Samuelson's oscillator has the same mathematical form, but its theoretical foundations, variables, and parameters are totally different.

9. Allais, M. (1982), *La génération exogène des fluctuations conjoncturelles*, Rapport d'activité scientifique du Centre d'Analyse Economique, CNRS, pp. 17–27, July.

10. Allais, M. (1983), *Fréquence, probabilité et hasard*, CNRS, Journal de la Société Statistique de Paris.

6. Joint Testing of the HRL Formulation of the Demand for Money and of the Fundamental Equation of Monetary Dynamics

1. Notes 10–13, pp. 1256, 1258, and 1259.

2. Friedman M., Jacobson Schwartz A., (1963), *A monetary history of the United States 1867-1960*, Princeton University Press, Princeton, NJ.

3. See, for example, Quantitative Micro Software, (2007) *EViews 6, User's guide*, Irvine, CA or the works of the Nobel laureates Software who 'formulated these techniques: Engle', Granger, Sims.

4. For example, the GARCH(1,1) specification

$$Y_t = X'_t + \epsilon_t \tag{1}$$

$$\sigma_t = \omega + \alpha \epsilon^2_{t-1} + \beta \sigma^2_{t-1} \tag{2}$$

is equivalent to exponentially weighted moving average (EWMA) variance measures defined by the recursion

$$\sigma^2_t = (1 - \lambda)\epsilon^2_t + \lambda \sigma^2_{t-1} \tag{3}$$

where $\omega = 0$, $\alpha = 1 - \lambda$, and $\beta = \lambda$.

7. Allais's HRL Formulation: Illustration of Its Dynamic Properties by an Example of Hyperinflation (Zimbabwe 2000-2008)

1. Allais, M. (1966), *A restatement of the quantity theory of money*, American Economic Review, vol. 56, no. 5, pp. 1123-1156, December.

2. Cagan, P. (1964), *Comment by Phillip Cagan*, in *Fondements de la dynamique monétaire*, Editions Clément Juglar, Paris, pp. 1057-1060; Cagan, P. (1969), *Allais' monetary theory, interpretation and comment*, Journal of Money, Credit and Banking, pp. 427-462, August; Darby, M. (1970), *Allais' restatement of the quantity theory: Comment*, American Economic Review, pp. 444-446, June; Scadding, J. L. (1972), *Allais' restatement of the quantity theory: Note*, American Economic Review, pp. 151-154, March.

3. Allais, M. (1969), *Growth and inflation, A reply to the observations of the discussants*, Journal of Money, Credit and Banking, pp. 427-462, August; Allais, M. (1970), *Allais' restatement of the quantity theory: Reply*, The American Economic Review, pp. 447-456, June; Allais, M. (1975), *The hereditary and relativistic formulation of the demand for money, circular reasoning or a real structural relation? A reply to Scadding's note*, American Economic Review,

pp. 454–464, June; Allais, M. (1986b), *The empirical approaches of the hereditary and relativistic theory of the demand for money: Results, interpretation, criticisms and rejoinders*, Economia della Scelte Pubbliche, Journal of Public Finance and Public Choice (Fondazione Luigi Einaudi), pp. 3–83.

4. Allais used an IBM 7094 computer.

5. Allais, M. (1972), *Forgetfulness and interest*, Journal of Money, Credit and Banking, pp. 40–73, see note 22, pp. 46–47, February.

6. J. P. P. Henri (or Henry) (1848–1907).

7. Case in which the constant is forced to zero, that is, when the average forecasting error is assumed to be equal to zero.

8. See section 2.12.

9. Kindleberger, C. (1985), *Keynesianism vs. monetarism and other essays in financial history*, Chap. 6, *Collective memory vs. rational expectations: Some historical puzzles in macro-economic behavior*, Allen & Unwin, London.

10. In his *Economics of inflation*, a book whose subject is the German hyperinflation, Bresciani-Turoni speaks most of the time of the depreciation of the mark. His original title in Italian is *Le vicende del Marco Tedesco*. The first sentence of Lionel Robbins's foreword to the English edition starts with the words "The depreciation of the mark."

11. Hanke, S. H., Krus, N., (2012), World hyperinflations, Cato Institute Working Paper no 8, August 15.

12. Shiller, R. J. (1999), *Irrational exuberance*, Princeton University Press, Princeton, NJ.

13. This is in sharp contrast with Andrei Shleifer's formulation where the reaction of positive feedback traders is supposed to be proportional to the latest price change. See Shleifer, A. (2000), *Inefficient markets (An introduction to behavioral finance)*, Oxford University Press, Oxford.

8. The HRL Formulation and Nominal Interest Rates

1. Allais, M. (1972), *Forgetfulness and Interest*, Journal of Money, Credit and Banking, February; Allais, M. (1974), *The psychological rate of interest*, Journal of Money, Credit and Banking, August.

2. During a conversation on April 25, 2002, Maurice Allais bluntly told the author of this book that his theory of the psychological rate of interest "did not work."

3. Allais, M. (1943), *A la recherche d'une discipline économique*, Clément Juglar, Paris, 1994, Allais, M. (1947), *Economie et intérêt*, Clément Juglar, Paris, 1998.

4. O'Donoghue, J., Goulding, L., and Allen, G. (2004), *Consumer price inflation since 1750*, Economic Trends, no. 604, pp. 38–46.

5. Polanyi, K. (1944), *The great transformation*, Gallimard, Paris, 1972.

6. Datastream time series: USGDP ... B.

7. Bresciani-Turoni, C. (1937), *The economics of inflation*, Augustus M. Kelley, New York.

8. Homer, S., and Sylla, R. (1996), *A history of interest rates*, 3rd ed., Rutgers University Press, New Brunswick, NJ.

9. Allais, M. (1960), *Influence du coefficient capitalistique sur le revenu réel par tête*, 32nd Congress of the International Statistical Institute, Tokyo, Document no 61, June; Allais, M. (1962), *The influence of the capital-output ratio on real national income*, Econometrica, October, vol. 30, pp. 700–728; Desrousseaux, J. (1961), *Expansion stable et taux d'intérêt optimal*, Annales des Mines, November, pp. 829–844; Phelps, E. S. (1961), *The golden rule of accumulation: A fable for growthmen*, The American Economic Review, vol. 51, September, pp. 638–643; Robinson, J. (1962), *A neoclassical theorem*, Review of Economic Studies, June, vol. 29, pp. 219–226; von Weizsäcker, C. (1962), *Wachstum, Zins und optimale Investisionsquote*, J. C. B Mohr (Paul Siebeck), Tübingen; and Swan, T. (1963), *Of golden ages and production functions*, in Berril, K. (ed.), *Economic development with special reference to East Asia*, St. Martin's, New York: we refer the reader to their work for a detailed demonstration of the golden rule of accumulation.

10. Cantillon, R. (1755), *Essai sur la nature du commerce en général*, INED, Paris, 1997; or Mill, J. S. (1848), *Principles of political economy*, Augustus M. Kelley, Fairfield, NJ, 1987.

11. Gibson, A. H., (1923), *The future course of high class investment values*, Banker's Magazine (London), 115, January, pp. 15–34.

9. Perceived Returns and the Modeling of Financial Behavior

1. Speculative or Ponzi finance to borrow Minsky's words.

2. Akerlof, G. A., and Shiller, R. J. (2009), *Animal spirits*, Princeton University Press, Princeton, NJ.

3. Datastream time series USCBDMGNA.

4. NBER Macro History database time series M14074: US loans on securities by member banks.

5. NBER Macro History database time series M12017a: Bank debits NYC USD bn.

6. NBER Macro History database time series M13003: NYSE 90-day time loan.

7. See for example the famous statement made by Chuck Prince, then Citigroup's CEO, in an interview to the Financial Times on July 9, 2007: "When the music stops, in terms of liquidity, things will be complicated. But as long as the music is playing, you've got to get up and dance. We're still dancing".

8. See table 4.5, page 89.

9. Greenspan, A. (2002), *Economic volatility*, Remarks at the Symposium sponsored by the Federal Reserve Bank of Kansas City, Jackson Hole, Wyoming, August 30, Federal Reserve Board, Washington, D.C.

10. Downside Potential Under Risk: The Allais Paradox and Its Conflicting Interpretations

1. Koulovatianos, C., and Wieland, V. (2011), *Asset pricing under rational learning about rare disasters*, Institute for Monetary and Financial Stability, Goethe-Universität, Frankfurt am Main, Working Papers Series no. 46.

2. As 1 ducat weighs about 0.11 troy ounce, assuming a gold price of USD 1,300, one ducat is worth about 143 current USD in early 2014.

3. Bernoulli, D. (1954), *Exposition of a new theory on the measurement of risk*, Econometrica, vol. 22, no. 1, pp. 26–36. Translated from Latin into English from Papers of the Imperial Academy of Science in Petersburg, vol. 6, 1738, pp. 175–192.

4. Kahneman, D. (2011), *Thinking, fast and slow*, Chap. 25, *Bernoulli's errors*, Farrar, Straus and Giroux, New York.

5. In many problems, ordinal utility suffices to find solutions.

6. Allais, M. (1943), *A la recherche d'une discipline économique*, Clement Juglar, no. 69, pp. 162–165.

7. J. K. Arrow, M. Boiteux, D. van Dantzig, B. de Finetti, M. Fréchet, M. Friedman, R. Frisch, R. Gibrat, G. Guilbaud, R. Hutter, W. Jaffé, H. Lavaill, J. Marschak, E. Malinvaud, P. Massé, G. Morlat, R. Roy, P. A. Samuelson, L. J. Savage, L. J. Shackle, J. Ville, and H. Wold.

8. Allais, M. (1953), *La psychologie de l'homme rationnel devant le risque: la théorie et l'expérience*, Journal de la Société Statistique de Paris, Book 94, pp. 47–73; http://archive.numdam.org/ARCHIVE/JSFS/JSFS 1953 94 /JSFS 1953_1953 94 47 0.pdf; in its full version, the questionnaire consisted of 400 questions.

9. Questions 35 and 36, the only two questions reproduced in Allais's ubiquitously quoted 1953 Econometrica article.

10. 100 million 1952 FFR is roughly equivalent to 2.536 million 2012 USD.

11. Using 1 million as unit.

12. Without referring to utility, it is possible to give a less rigorous but may be more intuitive explanation of the Allais paradox. Respondents should have preferred B to A and D to C, since B and D have higher mathematical expectation than, respectively, A and C. Yet, in choice 1, a majority of respondents preferred A to B, while in choice 2, a majority of the same respondents preferred D to C. The preference $D \succ C$ is consistent with the maximization of

mathematical expectation, since D is the prospect with the higher probability-weighted gain (500m versus 110m). In contrast, the preference $A \succ B$ contradicts the maximization of mathematical expectation, since A has lower mathematical expectation than B(100m versus 139m). In terms of mathematical expectation, the difference between A and C is the same as between B and D, namely, 89m = 89% × 100m. The empirical observation that A is preferred to B and C to D suggests that the outcome (100m; 89%), which is embedded in both A and B, is not taken into account independently from the other outcomes (x_i, p_i) present in these two prospects, contrary to the independence axiom. In other words, the outcome (100m; 89%) seems to be valued more in A, where there is no risk at all, than in B, which entails some risk.

13. Kahneman, D., and Tversky, A. (1979), *Prospect theory: An analysis of decision under risk*, Econometrica, vol. 47, no. 2, March.

14. It is not clear whether prospect theory considers gains and losses in absolute or relative terms, although the first hypothesis seems the most likely.

15. Kahneman, D. (2011), *Thinking, fast and slow*, Chap. 26, *Prospect theory*, Farrar, Straus and Giroux, New York.

16. See problems P_3 in table 10.4 and P_3' in table 10.5.

17. See Kahneman and Tversky, *Prospect theory: An analysis of decision under risk*, Econometrica, vol. 47, no. 2, March p. 269.

18. Kahneman, D., and Tversky, A. (1992), *Advances in prospect theory: Cumulative representation of uncertainty*, Journal of Risk and Uncertainty, vol. 5, pp. 297–323.

19. In the first two problems, the values of the gains and losses are close enough to ignore the potential impact of utility. This approach is more questionable in the last two problems, even though local linearity of cardinal utility may still be assumed.

20. The *possibility effect* alluded to by Kahneman and Tversky can seemingly be measured by odd-order moments.

21. In these two problems, the gains are so close to each other that the potential impact of utility can safely be ignored.

22. Here, too, the potential impact of utility can probably be ignored as the values of the gains are in a maximum ratio of 2 to 1. The same remark applies to table 10.5.

23. The *certainty effect* alluded to by Kahneman and Tversky can seemingly be measured by even-order moments.

24. Rabin, M., and Thaler, R. (2001), *Anomalies: Risk aversion*, The Journal of Economic Perspectives, vol. 15, no. 1, pp. 219–232.

25. Allais, M. (1979) [1952], *The foundations of a positive theory of choice involving risk and a criticism of the postulates and axioms of the American school*, in Allais, M., and Hagen, O., *Expected utility and the Allais paradox*, D. Reidel, Dordrecht, pp. 24–145.

26. Before we proceed further, let us observe that an empirical observation of the general type

$$\bar{s}(U_4) - \bar{s}(U_3) = \bar{s}(U_2) - \bar{s}(U_1) \tag{1}$$

implies that cardinal utility can only be determined up to a linear transformation. Let us assume that cardinal utility is actually a linear transformation f of $\bar{s}$, such that

$$f(U) = c_1 \bar{s}(U) + c_2 \tag{2}$$

Then if empirical observation reveals that relative to U_3, the gain U_4 provides the same increase in satisfaction as U_2 with respect to U_1, the only relationship we can write is

$$f(U_4) - f(U_3) = f(U_2) - f(U_1) \tag{3}$$

which is equivalent to

$$c_1 \bar{s}(U_4) + c_2 - c_1 \bar{s}(U_3) - c_2 = c_1 \bar{s}(U_2) + c_2 - c_1 \bar{s}(U_1) - c_2 \tag{4}$$

and finally to

$$\bar{s}(U_4) - \bar{s}(U_3) = \bar{s}(U_2) - s(U_1) \tag{5}$$

The information contained in c_1 and c_2 is lost.

27. The answers given by the subject (Finetti in this case) are underlined; in his questionnaire, Allais formulated his questions using round numbers of 1952 French francs, such as 10, 25, and 50 million. To facilitate a contemporary reader's introspection, these round numbers have been converted to 2012 USD and rounded to the nearest \$1,000, at the risk of some persistent oddity.

28. In contrast, Kahneman and Tversky (1979) only allude to minimum perceptible thresholds.

29. Allais, M. (1977), *The so-called Allais' paradox and rational decisions under uncertainty*, in Allais, M., and Hagen, O. (1979), *Expected utility hypotheses and the Allais paradox*.

30. Allais, M. (1943), *A la recherche d'une discipline économique*, paragraph nos. 68–69, pp. 156–177.

31. $d^2\bar{s}/dU^2 < 0$ and $d^3\bar{s}/dU^3 < 0$

32. In a lin-log graph, one plots the abscissa along a base-10 logarithmic scale and the ordinates along a linear scale.

33. Bear in mind that this analytical work was conducted some years before the advent of Excel, MATLAB, or Eviews as we know them today.

34. Allais, M. (1986a), *Determination of cardinal utility according to an intrinsic invariant model*, in *Recent developments in the foundations of utility and risk theory*, D. Reidel Publishing Company, Dordrecht, pp. 83–120.

35. Negligible as it may seem, this small hump provides some interesting insights as regards hyperbolic discounting (see appendix E on intertemporal choice).

36. Allais, M. (1991), *Cardinal utility: History, empirical findings and applications. Theory and decision 31*, Kluwer Academic, Dordrecht, pp. 99–140.

37. Questions 71 to 78 and 90 to 98.

38. 1952 French francs.

39. And not *below.*

40. Allais, M. (1977), *The so-called Allais' paradox and rational decisions under uncertainty*, in Allais and Hagen, (1979), *Expected utility hypotheses and the Allais paradox*, pp. 481–3, 550–52, 607–9.

41. Mehra, R., Prescott, E.C. (1985), *The equity premium: A puzzle*, Journal of Monetary Economics, 15, pp. 145–161.

42. Benartzi, S., Thaler, R. (1995), *Myopic loss aversion and the equity premium puzzle*, Quarterly Journal of Economics, vol. 110, no. 1, February, pp. 73–92.

43. Data source: Morningstar, (2014), *2014 Ibbotson Stocks, Bonds, Bills and Inflation (SSBI) Classic Yearbook*, Morningstar, Chicago, IL.

11. Downside Potential Under Uncertainty: The Perceived Risk of Loss

1. From a purely formal point of view, there is no difference at all between mathematical expectation and a cocktail recipe. But someone ordering a gin and tonic is not expecting to be served two full glasses of gin first, followed by five full glasses of tonic (or vice versa).

2. To take an extreme example, until Monday, October 19, 1987, close of business, nobody knew that the Dow Jones Index could fall by 22.6 percent in one trading session.

3. Marks, H. (2011), *How quickly they forget*, Letter to Oaktree's clients.

4. By relative spread, we mean the difference between the logarithms of BAA and AAA bond yields.

5. Median price of existing homes.

6. A simple way to visualize the role of α is to observe the behavior of the logarithm of the rate of memory decay when the present value of past returns tends toward infinity. From the definition of $\chi(Z)$, we have

$\lim_{Z \to +\infty} \ln \chi(Z) = \alpha Z + \ln \chi_0 + \ln b - \ln(1 + b)$, which is the equation of an asymptotic line having α for slope.

7. With

$$\chi_b(Z) = \chi_0 \frac{1 + be^{\alpha Z}}{1 + b} \tag{1}$$

and

$$\chi_1(Z) = \chi_0 \frac{1 + be^{\alpha Z}}{2} \tag{2}$$

we have indeed

$$\chi_b(Z) = \chi_1(Z) = \frac{\chi_0}{2}(e^{\alpha Z} - 1)(b - 1) \tag{3}$$

8. Keynes's famous analogy between financial markets and beauty contests could be given a quantitative content by assuming $\alpha > 1$ and $b < 1$, or $\alpha' > 1$ and $b' > 1$ or both!

9. This assumption concurs with recent research. See, for example, Malmendier, U., and Nagel, S. (2009), *Depression babies: Do macroeconomic experiences affect risk-taking?* and (2011), *Learning from inflation experience*, UC Berkeley and Stanford University, NBER and CPER. The two authors claim to have found that "individuals learn from data experienced over their life-times, rather than from all 'available' data." For example, "young individuals place more weight on recently experienced inflation than older individuals," or "individuals who have experienced low stock-market returns throughout their lives report lower willingness to take financial risk" and "recent return experiences have stronger effects, but experiences early in life still have significant influence, even several decades later."

12. Conclusion

1. Pribram, K. (1951), *Prolegomena to a history of economic reasoning*, The Quarterly Journal of Economics, vol. 65, no. 1, February.

2. Phelps, E. (1985), *Political economy: An introductory text*, Norton, New York.

3. Phelps, E. (1987), *Marchés spéculatifs et anticipations rationnelles*, Revue Française d'économie, vol. 2, no. 3.

4. Allais, M. (1989), *Autoportraits, ma philosophie de la méthode économique*, Montchrestien, Paris.

Appendix C Proofs

1. Rinne, H. (2003), *Taschenbuch der Statistik*, Harri Deutsch Verlag, Frankfurt am Main, pp. 213–217.

2. Bronstein, I. N., Semendjajew, K. A., Musiol, G., Mühlig, H., (2006), *Taschenbuch der Mathematik*, 6th ed., Verlag Harri Deutsch, Frankfurt am Main, p. 461.

3. The subscript e designates the equilibrium value of all the variables considered in this demonstration.

4. Neglecting second-order terms, we have, for example,

$$\lim_{g \to 0} \frac{\Psi(Z_e + g) - \Psi(Z_e)}{g} = \Psi'(Z_e) \Rightarrow \Psi(Z) = \Psi(Z_e + g) \approx \Psi(Z_e) + g\Psi'(Z_e) \tag{1}$$

$$\Psi(Z) \approx \Psi(Z_e) + g\Psi'(Z_e) \tag{2}$$

$$\frac{\Psi|(Z)}{\Psi(Z_e)} \approx \frac{\Psi(Z_e) + g\Psi'(Z_e)}{\Psi(Z_e)} \approx 1 + \frac{\Psi'(Z_e)}{\Psi(Z_e)} g \approx 1 - K_e g \tag{3}$$

$$\frac{\Psi(Z)}{\Psi(Z_e)} \approx 1 - K_e g \tag{4}$$

$$V(t) = V_e(1 + f(t)) \Rightarrow \ln V(t) = \ln V_e + \ln(1 + f(t)) \tag{5a}$$

$$\Rightarrow \frac{1}{V}\frac{dV}{dt} = \frac{d\ln V(t)}{dt} = \frac{d\ln(1 + f(t))}{dt} \approx \frac{df(t)}{dt} \tag{5b}$$

$$\frac{1}{V}\frac{dV}{dt} \approx \frac{df(t)}{dt} \tag{6}$$

Appendix E A Note on the Theory of Intertemporal Choice

1. Camerer, C., Loewenstein, G., and Rabin, M. (2004), *Advances in behavioral economics*, Princeton University Press, Princeton, NJ.

2. Samuelson, P. A. (1937), *A note on measurement of utility*, Review of Economic Studies, vol. 4, pp. 155–161.

3. Frederick, S., Loewenstein, G., and O'Donoghue, T. (2002), *Time discounting and time preference: A critical review*, Journal of Economic Literature, vol. 40, pp. 351–401, June.

4. Discount factors are the present value–future value ratios of outcomes deemed equivalent albeit distant in time.

5. See Table 6-1 in Frederick, S., Loewenstein, G., and O'Donoghue, T., *Time discounting and time preference.*

6. See chapter 8 of this book.

7. See Frederick, S., Loewenstein, G., and O'Donoghue, T., *Time discounting and time preference.*

8. A possibility alluded to by Daniel Bernoulli in 1738, quoting a contribution by Gabriel Cramer, dated 1728.

9. Thaler, R. (1981), *Some empirical evidence on dynamic inconsistency,* Economic Letters, vol. 8, pp. 201–207.

10. Please note that these rates are annual continuous (log) rates.

11. Smoothed by means of Excel's built-in function.

12. Relationship E.7 is identical to relationship 4.37, section 4.3, p. 76.

Bibliography

Akerlof, G. A., Shiller, R. J. (2009), *Animal spirits*, Princeton University Press, Princeton, NJ.

Allais, M. (1943), *A la recherche d'une discipline économique*, Clément Juglar, Paris, 1994.

——(1947), *Economie et intérêt*, Clément Juglar, Paris, 1998.

——(1953a), *Le comportement de l'homme rationnel devant le risque: Critique des postulats et axiomes de l'école Américaine*, Econometrica, vol. 21, pp. 503–546.

——(1953b), *Illustration de la théorie des cycles économiques par un modèle monétaire non linéaire*, Econometrica, January 1954, pp. 116–117.

——(1953c), *La psychologie de l'homme rationnel devant le risque: la théorie et l'expérience*, Journal de la Société Statistique de Paris, vol. 94, pp. 47–73.

——(1954a), *Les fondements comptables de la macro-économique*, 2nd ed., Presses Universitaires de France, Paris, 1993.

——(1954b), *Explication des cycles économiques par un modèle non linéaire à régulation retardée*, Communication au Congrès Européen de la Société d'Econométrie, Uppsala, 4/8/1954, Metroeconomica, vol. 8, April 1956, fascicule I, pp. 4–83.

——(1965), *Reformulation de la théorie quantitative de la monnaie*, Société d'études et de documentation économiques, industrielles et sociales (SEDEIS), Paris.

——(1966), *A restatement of the quantity theory of money*, American Economic Review, vol. 56, no. 5, pp. 1123–1156.

——(1968a), *L'équation fondamentale de la dynamique monétaire*, Monnaie et Développement, fascicule I, Ecole Nationale Supérieure des Mines de Paris, pp. 75–86.

——(1968b), *La génération endogène des fluctuations conjoncturelles*, reprint in *fondements de la dynamique monétaire* (2001), pp. 969–1010.

—(1969), *Growth and inflation, A reply to the observations of the discussants*, Journal of Money, Credit and Banking, vol. 1, no. 3, pp. 441–462.

—(1970), *Allais' restatement of the quantity theory: Reply*, The American Economic Review, vol. 60, no. 3, pp. 447–456.

—(1972), *Forgetfulness and interest*, Journal of Money, Credit and Banking, vol. 4, no. 1, pp. 40–73, note 22, pp. 46–47.

—(1974), *The psychological rate of interest*, Journal of Money, Credit and Banking, August, vol. 6, no. 3, pp. 285–331.

—(1975), *The hereditary and relativistic formulation of the demand for money, circular reasoning or a real structural relation? A reply to Scadding's note*, American Economic Review, vol. 65, no. 3, pp. 454–464.

—(1977), *The so-called Allais' paradox and rational decisions under uncertainty*, in Allais and Hagen, O. (1979), *Expected utility hypotheses and the Allais paradox*, D. Reidel Publishing Company, Dordrecht.

—(1979) [1952], *The foundations of a positive theory of choice involving risk and a criticism of the postulates and axioms of the American school*, in Allais, M., and Hagen, O. *Expected utility and the Allais paradox*, D. Reidel Publishing Company, Dordrecht, pp. 24–145.

—(1982), *La génération exogène des fluctuations conjoncturelles*, Rapport d'activité scientifique du Centre d'Analyse Economique, CNRS, July, pp. 17–27.

—(1983), *Fréquence, probabilité et hasard*, CNRS, Journal de la Société Statistique de Paris, vol. 124, no. 3, pp. 144–221.

—(1986a), *Determination of cardinal utility according to an intrinsic invariant model*, in *Recent developments in the foundations of utility and risk theory*, D. Reidel Publishing Company, Dordrecht, pp. 83–120.

—(1986b), *The empirical approaches of the hereditary and relativistic theory of the demand for money: Results, interpretation, criticisms and rejoinders*, Economia della Scelte Pubbliche, Journal of Public Finance and Public Choice (Fondazione Luigi Einaudi), vol. 4, no. 1, pp. 3–83.

—(1987), *The Allais paradox*, in *The new Palgrave*, Norton, New York.

—(1989), *Autoportraits, Ma philosophie de la méthode économique*, Montchrestien, Paris.

—(1991), *Cardinal utility: History, empirical findings and applications. Theory and decision 31*, Kluwer Academic, Dordrecht, pp. 99–140.

—(2001), *Fondements de la dynamique monétaire*, Editions Clément Juglar, Paris.

Arrow, J. K. (1986), *Rationality of self and others in an economic system*, Journal of Business, vol. 59, no. 4, part 2, October, pp. 385–399, reprinted in *The new Palgrave: Utility and probability*, Eatwell, J., Milgate, M., and Newman, P. (eds.), Norton, New York.

Benartzi, S., Thaler, R. (1995), *Myopic loss aversion and the equity premium puzzle*, Quarterly Journal of Economics, vol. 110, no. 1, February, pp. 73–92.

Bernoulli, D., 1954 (1738), *Exposition of a new theory on the measurement of risk*, Econometrica, vol. 22, no. 1, pp. 26–36. Translated from Latin into English from *Papers of the Imperial Academy of Science in Petersburg*, vol. 6, 1738, pp. 175–192.

Blaug, M. (1996), *Economic theory in retrospect*, 5th ed., Cambridge University Press, Cambridge, England, Chap. 16, p. 646.

Bootle, R. (1997), *The death of inflation*, Nicholas Brealey, London.

Bresciani-Turoni, C. (1937), *The economics of inflation*, Augustus M. Kelley, New York.

Bronstein, I. N., Semendjajew, K. A., Musiol, G., Mühlig, H., (2006), *Taschenbuch der Mathematik*, 6th ed., Verlag Harri Deutsch, Frankfurt am Main, p. 461.

Cagan, P. (1956), *The monetary dynamics of hyper-inflation*, in *Studies in the quantity theory of money*, ed. Milton Friedman, University of Chicago Press, Chicago.

—(1964), *Comment by Phillip Cagan in Fondements de la dynamique monétaire*, Editions Clément Juglar, Paris, pp. 1057–1060.

—(1969), *Allais' monetary theory, interpretation and comment*, Journal of Money, Credit and Banking, vol. 1, no. 3, pp. 427–432.

—(1987), *Hyperinflation*, in *The new Palgrave*, Norton, New York.

Caginalp, G., Porter, D., and Smith, V. L. (2000), *Overreactions, momentum, liquidity and price bubbles in laboratory and field markets*, The Journal of Psychology and Financial Markets, 2000, vol. 1, no. 1, pp. 24–48.

Camerer, C. F., Loewenstein, G., and Rabin, M. (2004), *Advances in behavioral economics*, Princeton University Press, Princeton, NJ.

Cantillon, R. (1755), *Essai sur la nature du commerce en général*, INED, Paris, 1997.

Darby, M. (1970), *Allais' restatement of the quantity theory: Comment*, American Economic Review, vol. 60, no. 3, pp. 444–446.

Fisher, I. (1896), *Appreciation and interest*, American Economic Association, Pickering & Chatto, London, 1996.

—(1930), *The theory of interest*, Chap. 19, *Relation to money and prices*, Pickering & Chatto, London, 1996.

—(1932), *Booms and depressions*, Pickering & Chatto, London, 1996.

—(1933), *The debt-deflation theory of great depressions*, Econometrica, vol. 1, issue 4, October, pp. 337–357.

Frederick, S., Loewenstein, G., and O'Donoghue, T. (2002), *Time discounting and time preference: A critical review*, Journal of Economic Literature, vol. 40, pp. 351–401.

Friedman, B. M. (1975), *Rational expectations are really adaptive after all*, unpublished paper, Harvard University, Cambridge, MA.

Friedman M., Jacobson Schwartz A., (1963), A monetary history of the United States 1867-1960, Princeton University Press, Princeton, NJ.

Friedman, M. (1968), *Factors affecting the level of interest rates*, in *Savings and residential financing: 1968 Conference Proceedings*, Jacobs, D. P., and Pratt, R. T., (eds.), The United States Saving and Loan League, Chicago, IL, p. 375.

Gide, C., and Rist, C. (1944), *Histoire des doctrines économiques*, 6th ed., Livre 6, Chap. 2, *Conflit des théories des crises*, Dalloz, Paris, 2000.

Gibson, A. H., (1923), *The Future Course of High Class Investment Values*, Banker's Magazine (London), 115, January, pp. 15-34.

Gjerstad, S., and Smith, V. L. (2009), *Monetary policy, credit extension, and housing bubbles: 2008 and 1929*, Critical Review, A Journal of Politics and Society, vol. 21, nos. 2-3.

Gourgieroux, C., and Monfort, A. (1995), *Séries temporelles et modèles dynamiques*, 2nd ed., Economica, Paris, pp. 106-110.

Gowers, T. (ed.) (2008), *The Princeton companion to mathematics*, Princeton University Press, Princeton, NJ, p. 160.

Greenspan, A. (2002), *Economic volatility*, Remarks at the Symposium sponsored by the Federal Reserve Bank of Kansas City, Jackson Hole, Wyoming, August 30, 2002, Federal Reserve Board, Washington, D.C.

Guesnerie, R. (2001, 2005), *Assessing rational expectations*, vols. 1 and 2, MIT Press, Cambridge, MA.

Haberler, G. (1937), *Prosperity and depression, A theoretical analysis of cyclical movements*, Harvard University Press, Transaction Publishers, New Brunswick, NJ, 2011.

Hanke, S. H., Krus, N., (2012), *World hyperinflations*, Cato Institute Working Paper no 8, August 15.

Hayek, F. (1936), *Economics and knowledge*, Presidential adress delivered to the London Economic Club on November 10, 1936, Economica (1937), vol. 4, pp. 33-54.

Hicks, J. (1939), *Value and Capital* Part III, *The foundations of dynamic economics*, Chap. 9, *The method of analysis*, reprinted in 2001 by Oxford University Press, Oxford.

Homer, S., and Sylla, R. (1996), *A history of interest rates*, 3rd ed., Rutgers University Press, New Brunswick, NJ.

Kahneman, D. (2011), *Thinking, fast and slow*, Farrar, Straus and Giroux, New York.

Kahneman, D., and Tversky, A. (1979), *Prospect theory: An analysis of decision under risk*, Econometrica, vol. 47, no. 2 (March), pp. 263-291.

—(1992), *Advances in prospect theory: cumulative representation of uncertainty.* Journal of Risk and Uncertainty, 5, pp. 297–323.

Kay, J. (2011), *The random shock that clinched a brave Nobel prize*, Financial Times, October 18.

Keynes, J. M. (1924), *Tract on monetary reform*, Prometheus Books, New York, 2000.

—(1936), *The general theory of employment, interest and money*, Chap 12, *The state of long-term expectations*, Harcourt Brace Jovanovich, New York, 1964.

Kindleberger, C. P. (1978), *Manias, panics and crashes (A history of financial crises)*, 4th ed., Wiley, 2001.

—(1985), *Rational expectations and collective memory*, in *Keynesianism vs monetarism and other essays in financial history*, Allen and Unwin, London.

Knight, F. (1921), *Risk, uncertainty and profit*, Beard Books, Washington, D.C., 2002.

Koulovatianos, C., and Wieland, V. (2011), *Asset pricing under rational learning about rare disasters*, Institute for Monetary and Financial Stability, Goethe-Universität, Frankfurt am Main, Working Papers Series no. 46.

Lindley, D. V. (1990), *Thomas Bayes* in *The new Palgrave: Utility and probability*, Eatwell, J., Milgate, M., and Newman, P. (eds), Norton, New York.

Lucas, R. E. (1972), *Expectations and the neutrality of money*, Journal of Economic Theory, vol. 4, pp. 103–124.

—(1975), *An equilibrium model of the business cycle*, Journal of Political Economy, vol. 83, no. 6, pp. 11–21.

—(1976), *Econometric policy evaluation: A critique*, Carnegie-Rochester Conference Series on Public Policy, vol. 1, pp. 19–46.

—(1977), *Understanding business cycles*, in Brunner, K., and Meltzer, A. (eds.), *Stabilization of the domestic and international economy*, vol. 5, Carnegie-Rochester Series on Public Policy, North Holland Publishing Company, New York, pp. 7–29.

—and Sargent, T. (1979), *After Keynesian macroeconomics*, The Federal Reserve Bank of Minneapolis, Quarterly Review 321, Spring.

Lucas, R. (1995), *Monetary neutrality*, Nobel Prize lecture, December 7.

Lundberg, E. (1937), *Studies in the theory of economic expansion*, Chap. 9, 1964, Augustus M. Kelley, Fairfield, NJ.

Malinvaud, E. (1991), *Voies de la recherche macroéconomique*, réédition Points-Seuil, Paris, 1993, pp. 546–549.

Malmendier, U., and Nagel, S. (2009), *Depression babies: Do macroeconomic experiences affect risk-taking?* and (2011), *Learning from inflation experience*, UC Berkeley and Stanford University, NBER and CPER.

Marks, H. (2011), *How quickly they forget*, Letter to Oaktree's clients.

Mehra, R., and Prescott, E.C. (1985), *The equity premium: A puzzle*, Journal of Monetary Economics, 15, pp. 145–161.

Mill, J. S. (1848), *Principles of political economy*, Augustus M. Kelley, Fairfield, NJ, 1987.

Minsky, H. P. (1980), *John Maynard Keynes*, Columbia University Press, New York, 1975.

—(1982), *Can "it" happen again?*, Sharpe, New York.

—(1986a), *The financial instability hypothesis: Capitalist production and the behavior of the economy*, in *Financial crises: Theory, history and policy*, eds. C. Kindleberger and J-P. Laffargue, Cambridge University Press, New York.

—(1986b), *Stabilizing an unstable economy*, Yale University Press, New Haven, CT.

—(1991), *The financial instability hypothesis: A clarification*, in *The risk of economic crisis*, ed. Martin Feldstein, National Bureau of Economic Research, The Chicago University Press, Chicago.

Modigliani, F. (1977), *The monetarist controversy, or should we forsake stabilization policy?* American Economic Review, vol. 67, no. 2, March, pp. 1–17.

Morningstar, (2014), *2014 Ibbotson Stocks, Bonds, Bills and Inflation (SSBI) Classic Yearbook*, Morningstar, Chicago, IL.

Muth, J. F. (1960), *Optimal properties of exponentially-weighted forecasts*, Journal of the American Statistical Association, vol. 55, no. 290, June, pp. 299–306.

—(1961), *Rational expectations and the theory of price movements*, Econometrica, vol. 29, no. 3, July.

O'Donoghue, J., Goulding, L., and Allen, G. (2004), *Consumer price inflation since 1750*, Economic Trends, no. 604, pp. 38–46.

Parent, E., and Bernier, J. (2007), *Le raisonnement Bayésien: Modélisation et inférence*, Springer-Verlag, Paris.

Pareto, V. (1896), *Cours d'économie politique*, Librairie Droz, Genève, 1964 (vol. 2, livre 2, chap. 4, *Les crises économiques*).

Pastor, L., and Veronesi, P. (2009), *Learning in financial markets*, Annual Review of Financial Economics, vol. 1, pp. 361–381.

Phelps, E. (1985), *Political economy: An introductory text*, Norton, New York, N.Y.

—(1987), *Marchés spéculatifs et anticipations rationnelles*, Revue Française d'Economie, vol. 2, no. 3.

—(2009), *A fruitless clash of economic opposites*, Financial Times, November 3.

—and Frydman, R. (2013), *Rethinking expectations: The way forward for macroeconomics*, Princeton University Press, Princeton, NJ.

Polanyi, K. (1944), *The great transformation*, Gallimard, Paris, 1972.

Portelli G., Ruffier F., Roubieu F., Franceschini N., (2011), *Honeybees' speed depends on dorsal as well as lateral, ventral and frontal optic flows*, Plos ONE, May, vol. 6, Issue 5.

Prat G. 1999, *Temps psychologique, oubli et intérêt chez Maurice Allais*, Discussion Papers (REL–Recherches Economiques de Louvain, 65(2)) 1999022, Université catholique de Louvain, Institut de Recherches Economiques et Sociales (IRES), Louvain.

Pribram, K. (1951), *Prolegomena to a history of economic reasoning*, The Quarterly Journal of Economics, vol. 65, no. 1, February.

Rabin, M., and Thaler, R. (2001), *Anomalies: Risk aversion*. The Journal of Economic Perspectives, vol. 15, no. 1, pp. 219–232.

Renshaw, E. (1988), *The crash of October 19 in retrospect*, The Market Chronicle, vol. 22.

Rinne, H. (2003), *Taschenbuch der Statistik*, Harri Deutsch Verlag, Frankfurt-am-Main, Germany, pp. 213–217.

Samuelson, P. A. (1937), *A note on measurement of utility*, Review of Economic Studies, vol. 4, pp. 155–161.

—(1983), *A chapter in the history of Ramsey's optimal feasible taxation and optimal public utility price*, in *Economic essays in honour of Jorgen Gelting*, pp. 164–165, note 3. See Introduction note 20.

Sargent, T. J. (1999), *The conquest of American inflation*, Princeton University Press, Princeton, N.J.

Sargent, T. J., and Wallace, N. (1973), *Rational expectations and the dynamics of hyperinflation*, International Economic Review, vol. 14, no. 2.

—(1976), *Rational expectations and the theory of economic policy*, Journal of Monetary Economics, July, pp. 199–214.

Scadding, J. L. (1972), *Allais' restatement of the quantity theory of money: Note*, American Economic Review, vol. 62, pp. 151–154.

Schumpeter, J. (1939), *Business cycles*, reprinted in 1989 by Porcupine Press, Philadelphia, PA.

Screpanti, E., and Zamagni, S. (2005), *An outline of the history of economic thought*, Oxford University Press, New York.

Shiller, R. J. (1999), *Irrational exuberance*, Princeton University Press, Princeton, N.J.

Shleifer, A. (2000), *Inefficient markets (An introduction to behavioral finance)*, Oxford University Press, New York.

Simon, H. A. (1997), *An empirically based microeconomics*, First lecture (Rationality in Decision making)–Raffaele Mattioli Foundation, Cambridge University Press, Cambridge, UK.

Thaler, R. (1981), *Some empirical evidence on dynamic inconsistency*, Economic Letters, vol. 8, pp. 201–207.

Wicksell, K. (1898), *Interest and prices*, Chap 8, *The natural rate of interest on capital and the rate of interest on loans*, Augustus M. Kelley, Fairfield, NJ, 1965.

—(1906), *Lectures on political economy*, vol. 2, Augustus M. Kelley, Fairfield, NJ., 1965.

Wonnacott, T. H., and Ronald, J. (1990), *Introductory statistics*, 5th ed., Wiley, New York.

Woodford, M. (1999), *Revolution and evolution in twentieth-century macroeconomics*, Princeton University Press, Princeton, NJ, note 51, p. 24.

—(2008), *Convergence in macroeconomics: Elements of the new synthesis*, prepared for the annual meeting of the American Economics Association.

—(2011), *What's wrong with economic models?* Columbia University Press, New York.

Index